岸本斉史

There are so many movie trilogies and series these days, like *The Matrix*, *The Lord of the Rings*, *Harry Potter*, etc. It gladdens me that my favorite film worlds continue to live on.

—*Masashi Kishimoto, 2004*

Author/artist Masashi Kishimoto was born in 1974 in rural Okayama Prefecture, Japan. After spending time in art college, he won the Hop Step Award for new manga artists with his manga **Karakuri** (Mechanism). Kishimoto decided to base his next story on traditional Japanese culture. His first version of **Naruto**, drawn in 1997, was a one-shot story about fox spirits; his final version, which debuted in **Weekly Shonen Jump** in 1999, quickly became the most popular ninja manga in Japan.

NARUTO VOL. 21
SHONEN JUMP Manga Edition

STORY AND ART BY MASASHI KISHIMOTO

Translation & English Adaptation/Naomi Kokubo, Eric-Jon Rössel Waugh
Touch-Up Art & Lettering/Sabrina Heep
Consultant/Mari Morimoto
Design/Yvonne Cai
Editor/Joel Enos

Printed in the U.S.A.

Published by VIZ Media, LLC
P.O. Box 77010
San Francisco, CA 94107

10 9 8 7
First printing, October 2007
Seventh printing, May 2019

VIZ MEDIA
viz.com

ratings.viz.com
RATED T TEEN

PARENTAL ADVISORY
NARUTO is rated T for Teen and is recommended for ages 13 and up. This volume contains realistic and fantasy violence.

SHONEN JUMP
shonenjump.com

[redacted]DITION

NARUTO

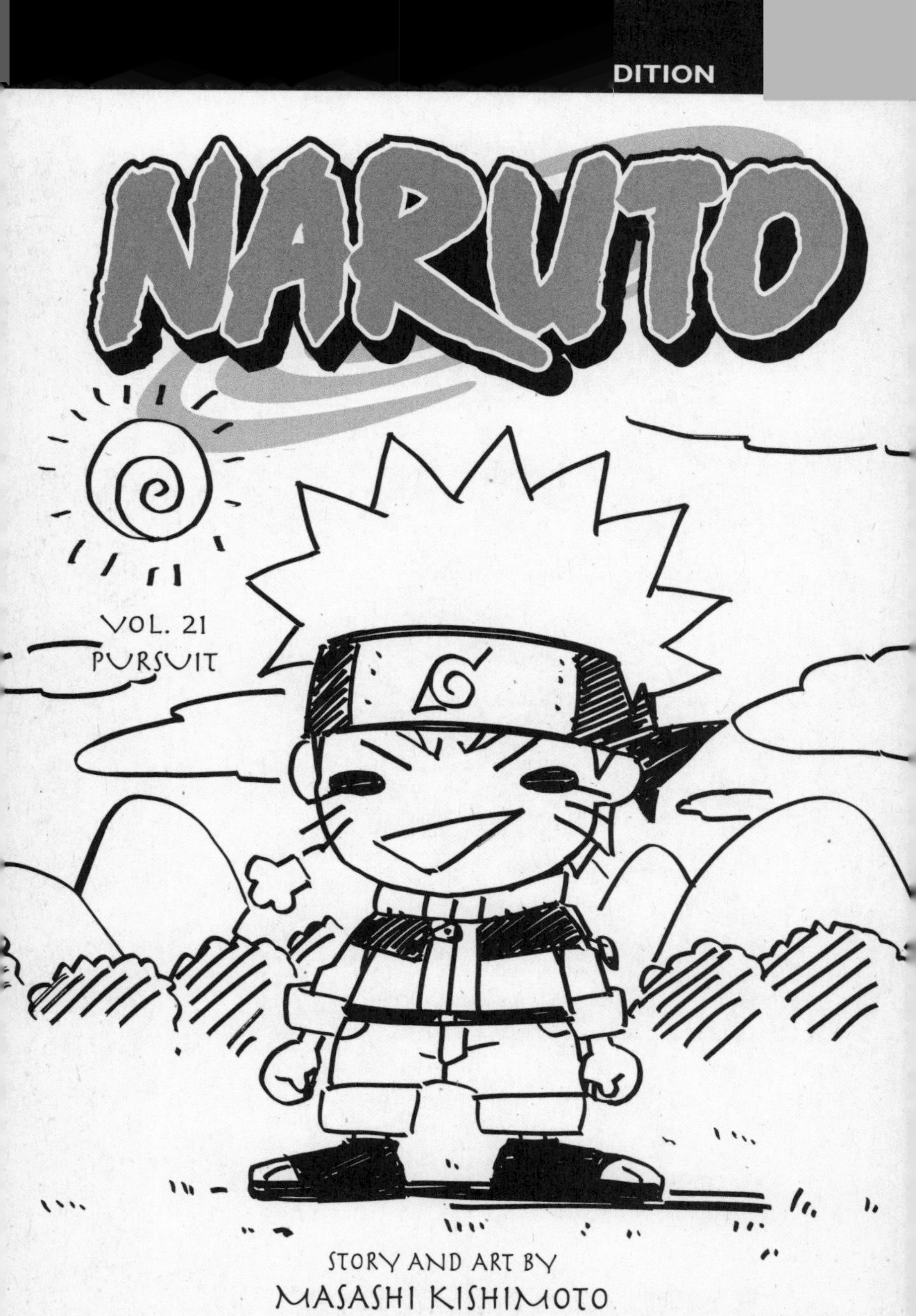

VOL. 21
PURSUIT

STORY AND ART BY
MASASHI KISHIMOTO

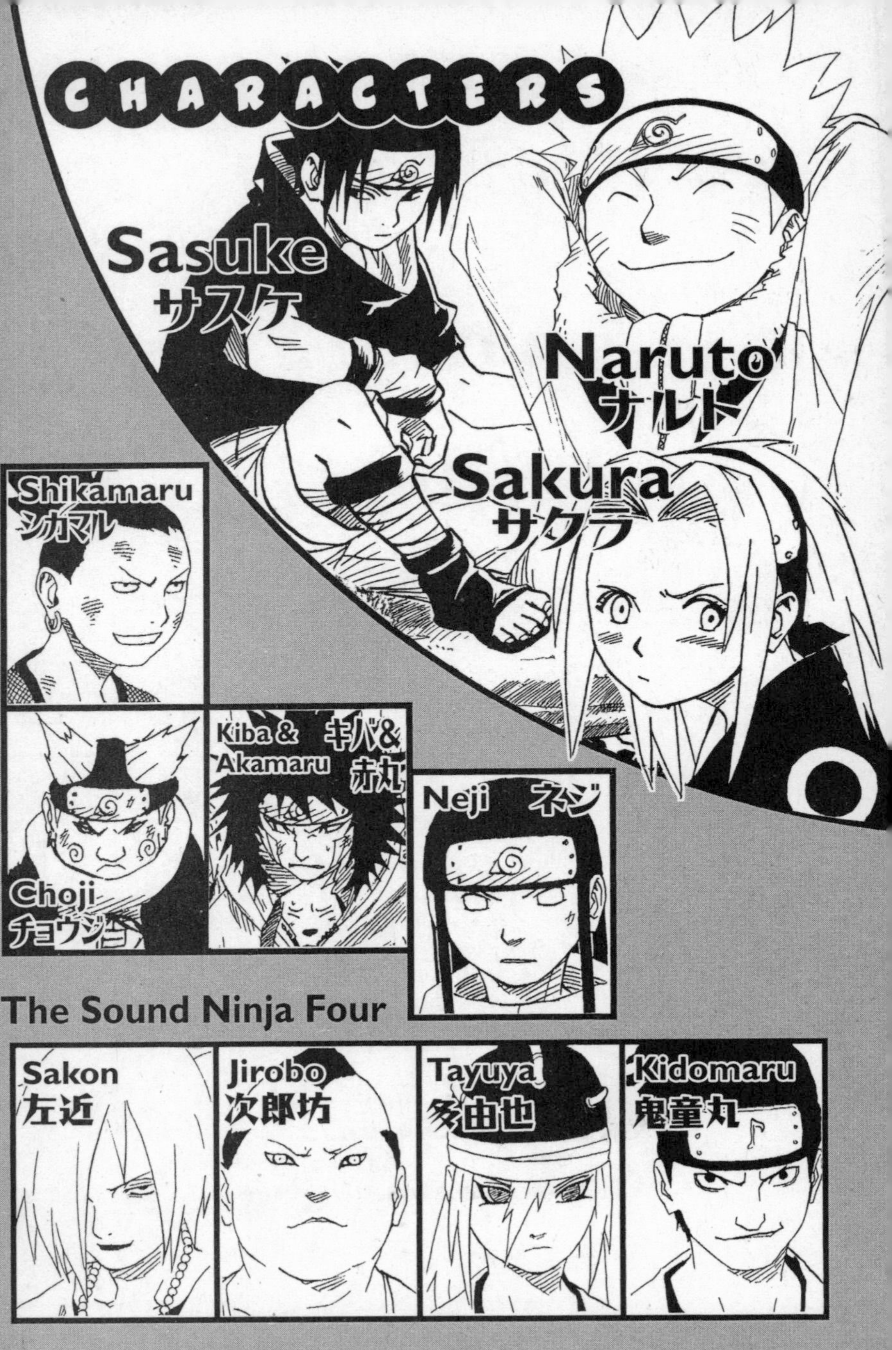
CHARACTERS
Naruto
ナルト
Sasuke
サスケ
Sakura
サクラ
Shikamaru
シカマル
Neji
ネジ
Kiba &
Akamaru
キバ&
赤丸
Choji
チョウジ
The Sound Ninja Four
Kidomaru
鬼童丸
Tayuya
多由也
Jirobo
次郎坊
Sakon
左近

Orochimaru
大蛇丸

Jiraiya
自来也

Rock Lee
ロック・リー

Kakashi
カカシ

Tsunade
綱手

The Story So Far...

Twelve years ago a destructive nine-tailed fox spirit attacked the ninja village of Konohagakure. The Hokage, or village champion, defeated the fox by sealing its soul into the body of a baby boy. Now that boy, Uzumaki Naruto, has grown up to be a ninja-in-training, learning the art of ninjutsu with his teammates Sakura and Sasuke.

Naruto and company take on the Chûnin Selection Exams but suffer a sudden attack from Orochimaru in the Forest of Death. Orochimaru leaves a curse mark on Sasuke's body and vanishes...

...only to return to launch *Operation Destroy Konoha!* The attack appears to be thwarted when Lord Hokage sacrifices his own life.

After the onslaught, Tsunade is elevated to the position of Fifth Hokage. She immediately attends to the medical needs of Sasuke and Rock Lee. Soon after Sasuke's recovery, however, the Sound Ninja Four set upon him. The Four attempt to woo Sasuke away with the power of Orochimaru, but...

NARUTO

VOL. 21
PURSUIT

CONTENTS

NUMBER 181: THE BATTLE BEGINS...!!   7

NUMBER 182: ASSEMBLE!!   27

NUMBER 183: THE PROMISE   47

NUMBER 184: SOUND VS. LEAF!!   67

NUMBER 185: PURSUIT...!!   87

NUMBER 186: FAILURE...?!   107

NUMBER 187: THE PLEA...!!   127

NUMBER 188: THE SHINOBI OF KONOHAGAKURE...!! 147

NUMBER 189: FAITH...!!   171

NUMBER 190: UNFORGIVABLE!!   191

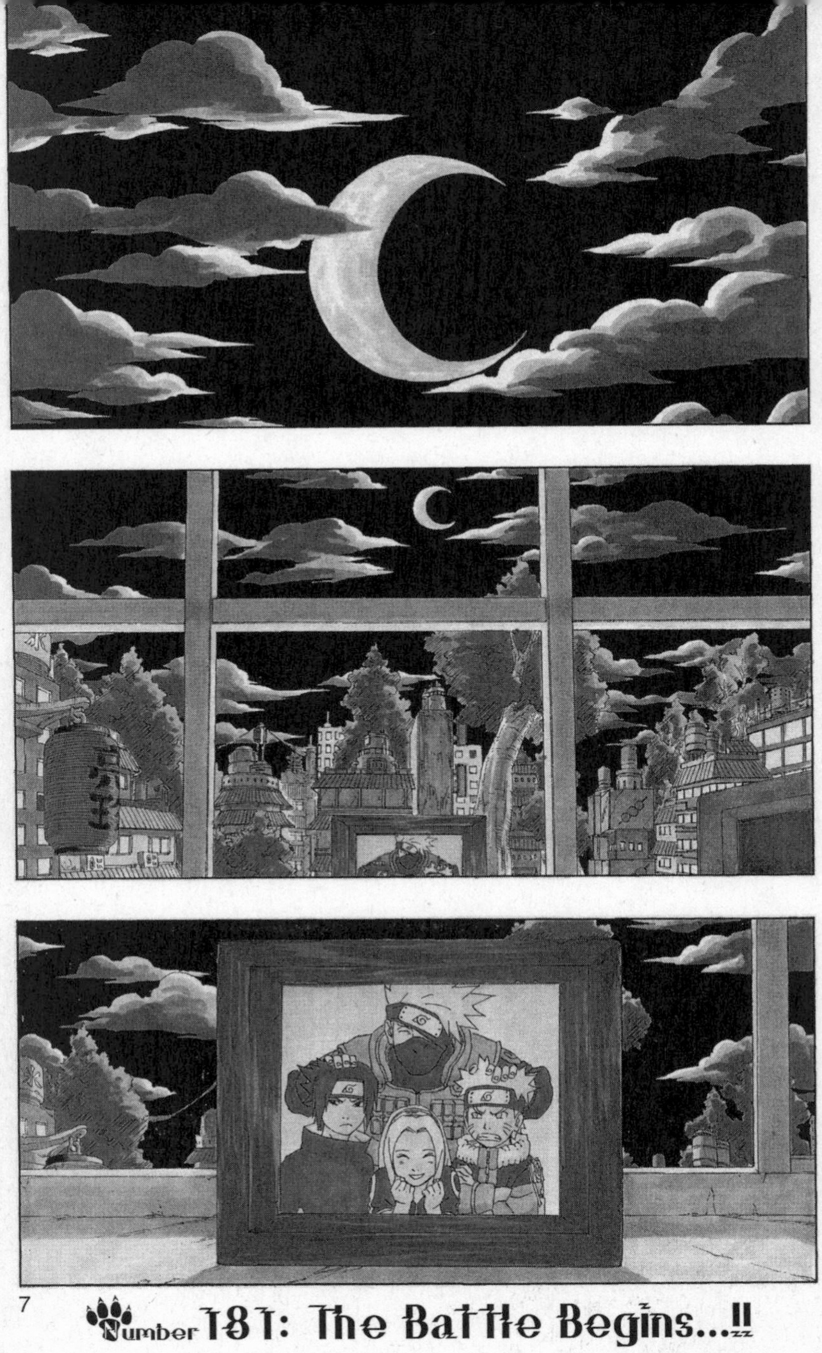

Number 181: The Battle Begins...!!

Number 181: The Battle Begins...!!

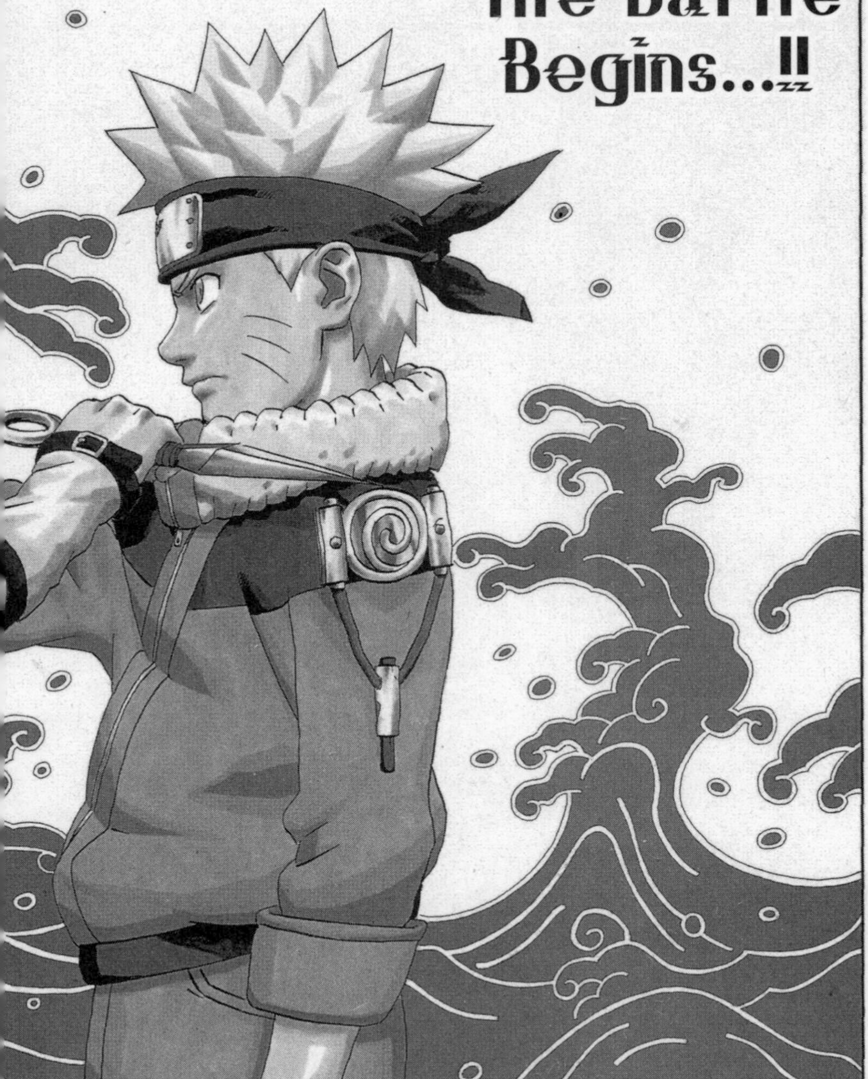

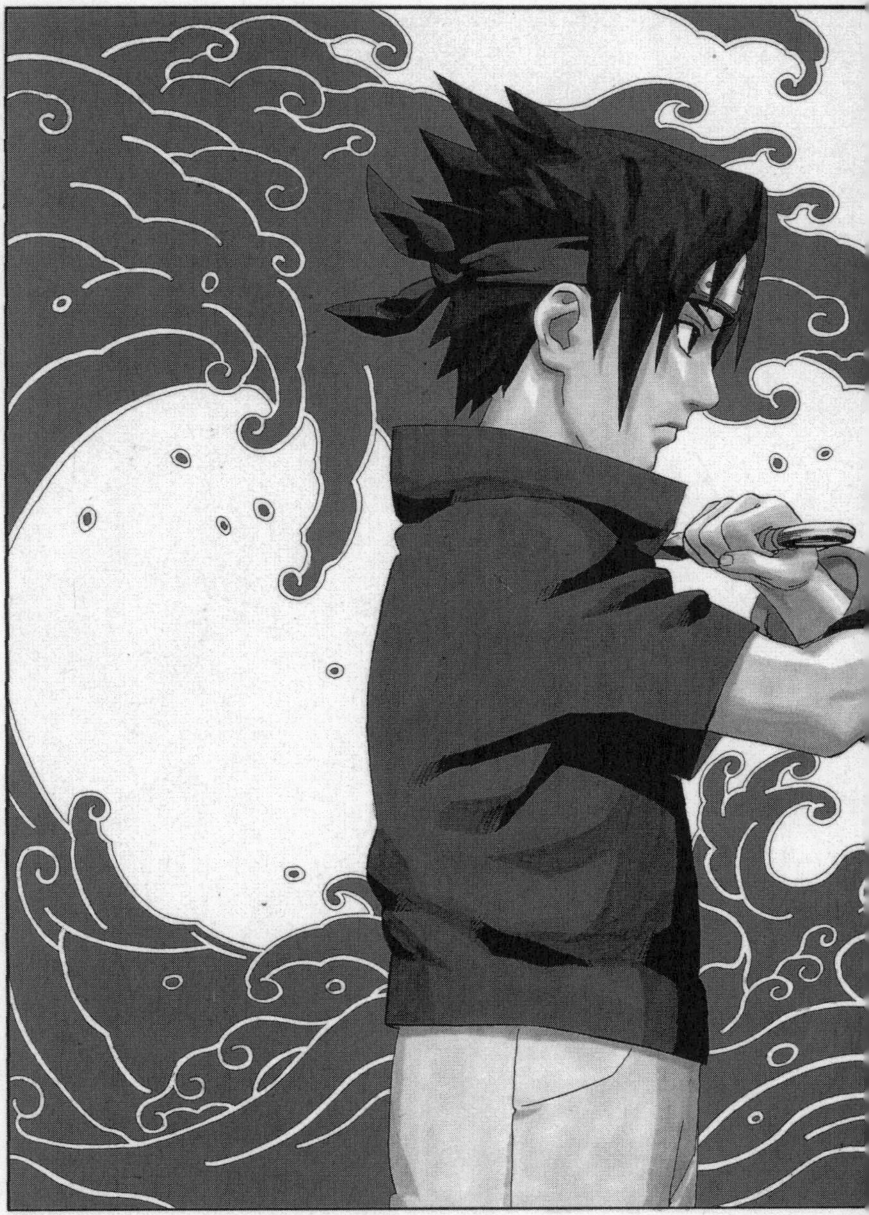

NARUTO

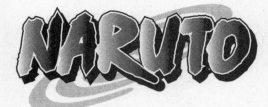

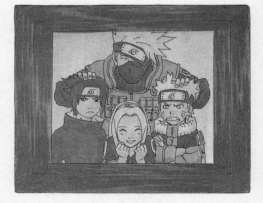

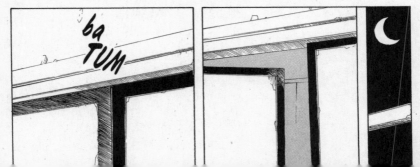

ba
TUM

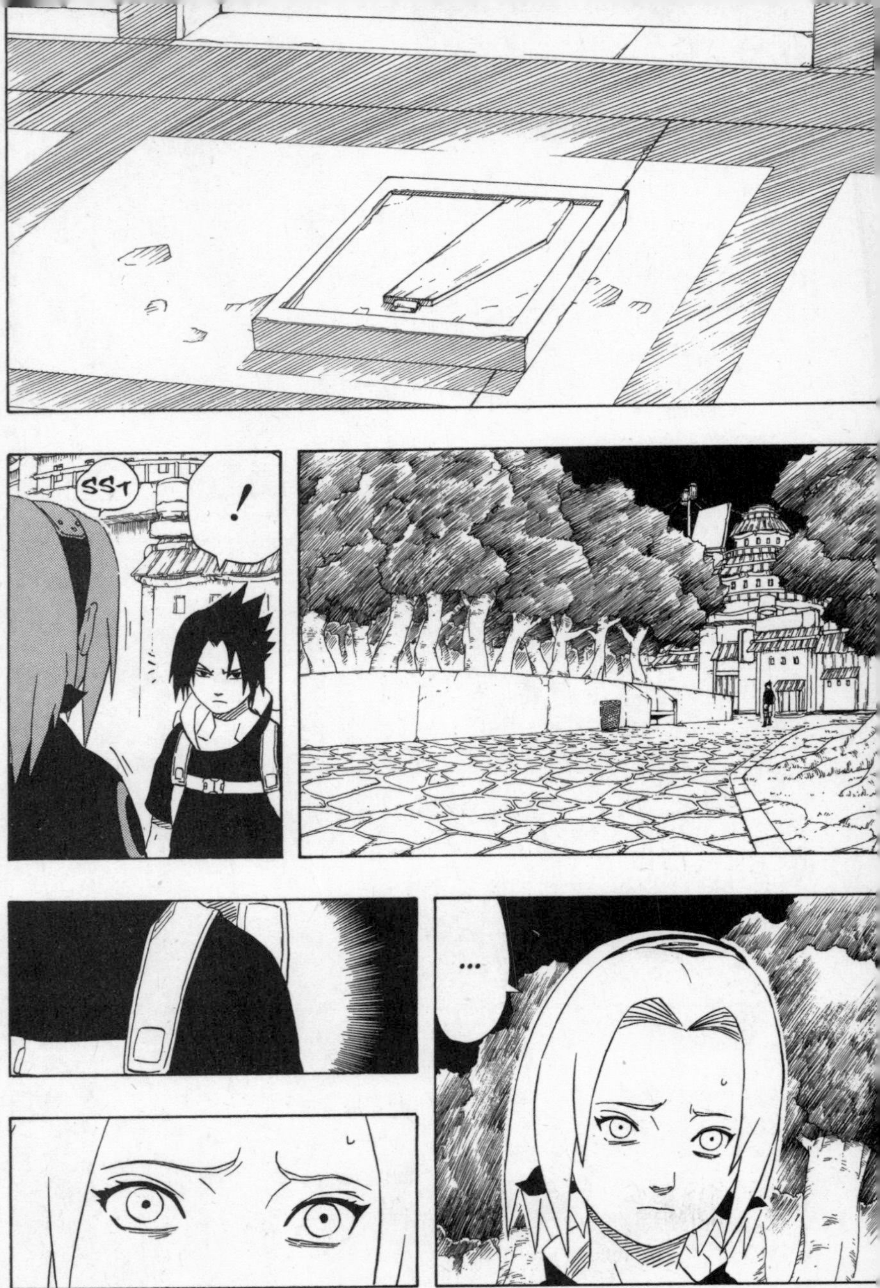
!
SST
...

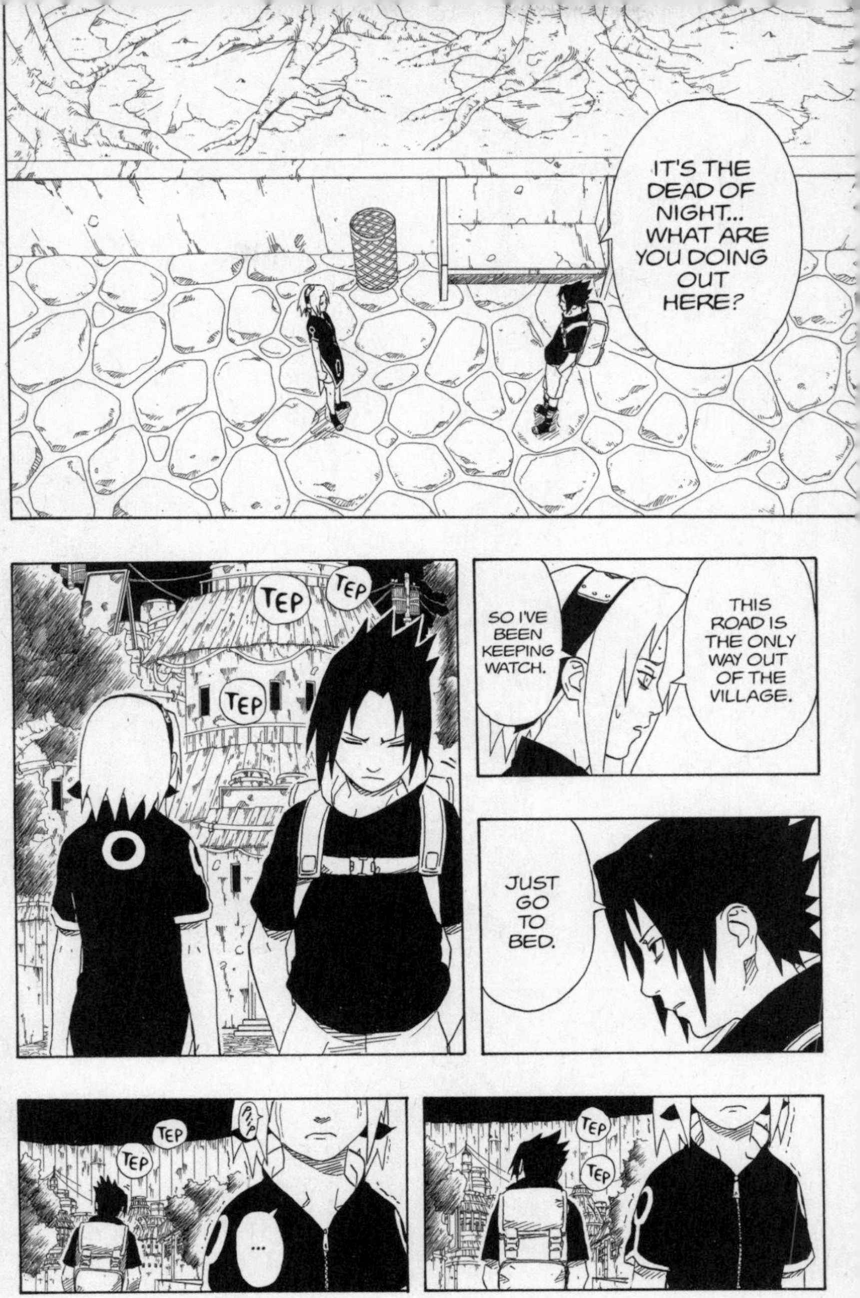
IT'S THE DEAD OF NIGHT... WHAT ARE YOU DOING OUT HERE?
THIS ROAD IS THE ONLY WAY OUT OF THE VILLAGE.
SO I'VE BEEN KEEPING WATCH.
JUST GO TO BED.
TEP
TEP
TEP
TEP
TEP
TEP
TEP
...

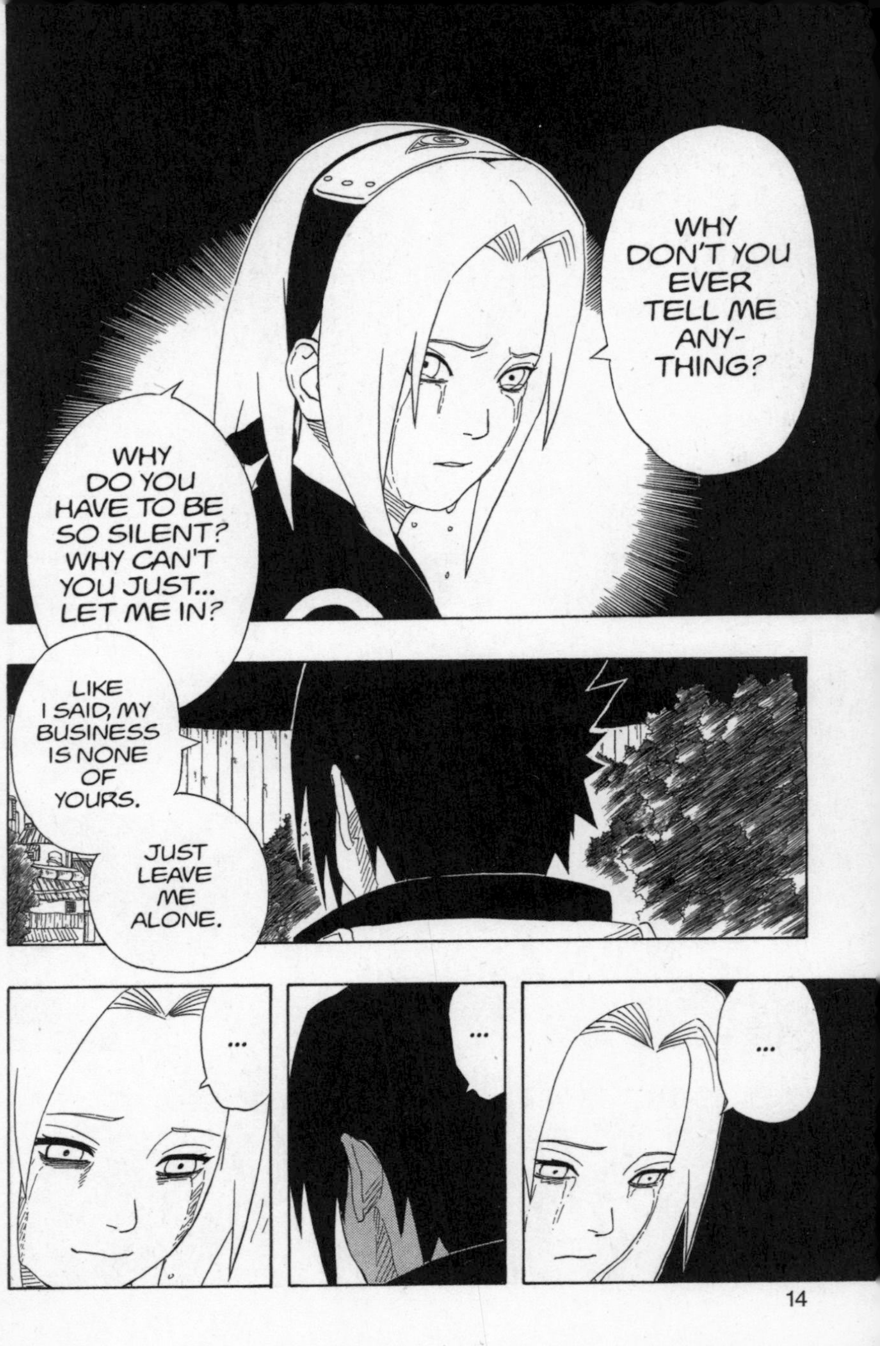
WHY DON'T YOU EVER TELL ME ANY-THING?
WHY DO YOU HAVE TO BE SO SILENT? WHY CAN'T YOU JUST... LET ME IN?
LIKE I SAID, MY BUSINESS IS NONE OF YOURS.
JUST LEAVE ME ALONE.
...
...
...

READ THIS WAY

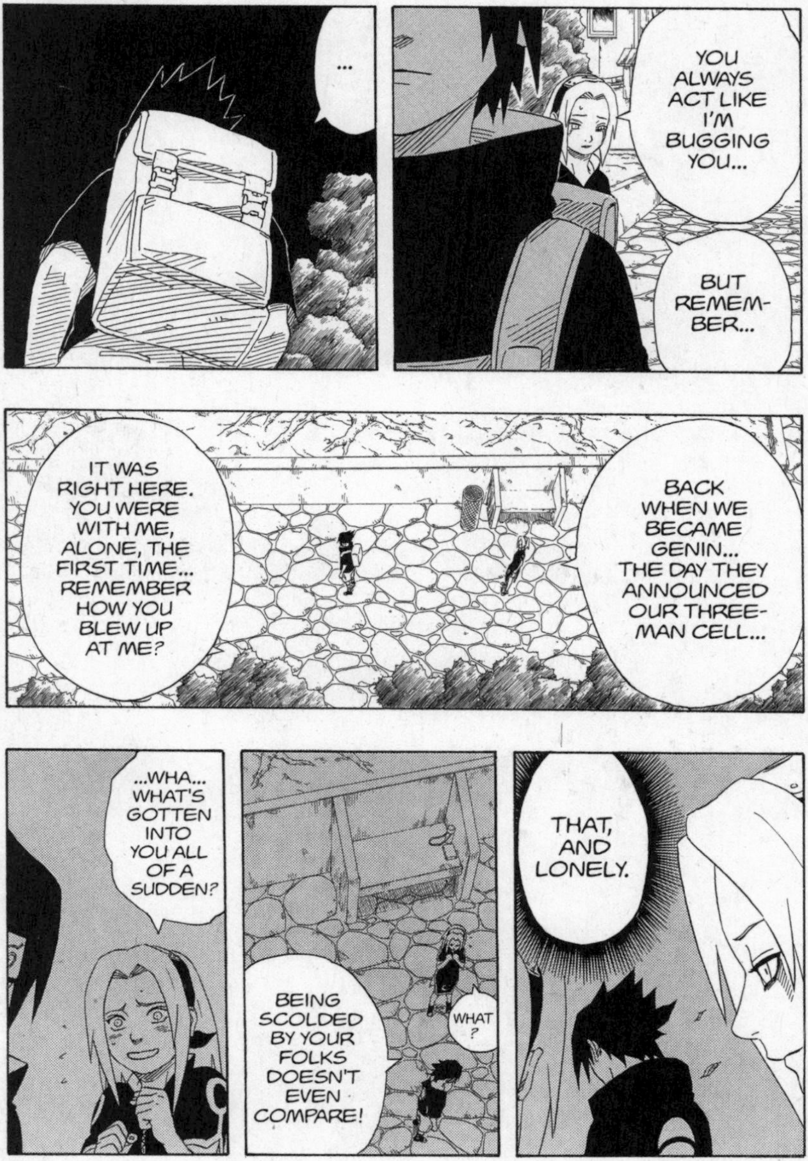
YOU ALWAYS ACT LIKE I'M BUGGING YOU...
BUT REMEMBER...
...
BACK WHEN WE BECAME GENIN... THE DAY THEY ANNOUNCED OUR THREE-MAN CELL...
IT WAS RIGHT HERE. YOU WERE WITH ME, ALONE, THE FIRST TIME... REMEMBER HOW YOU BLEW UP AT ME?
THAT, AND LONELY.
BEING SCOLDED BY YOUR FOLKS DOESN'T EVEN COMPARE!
WHAT?
...WHA... WHAT'S GOTTEN INTO YOU ALL OF A SUDDEN?

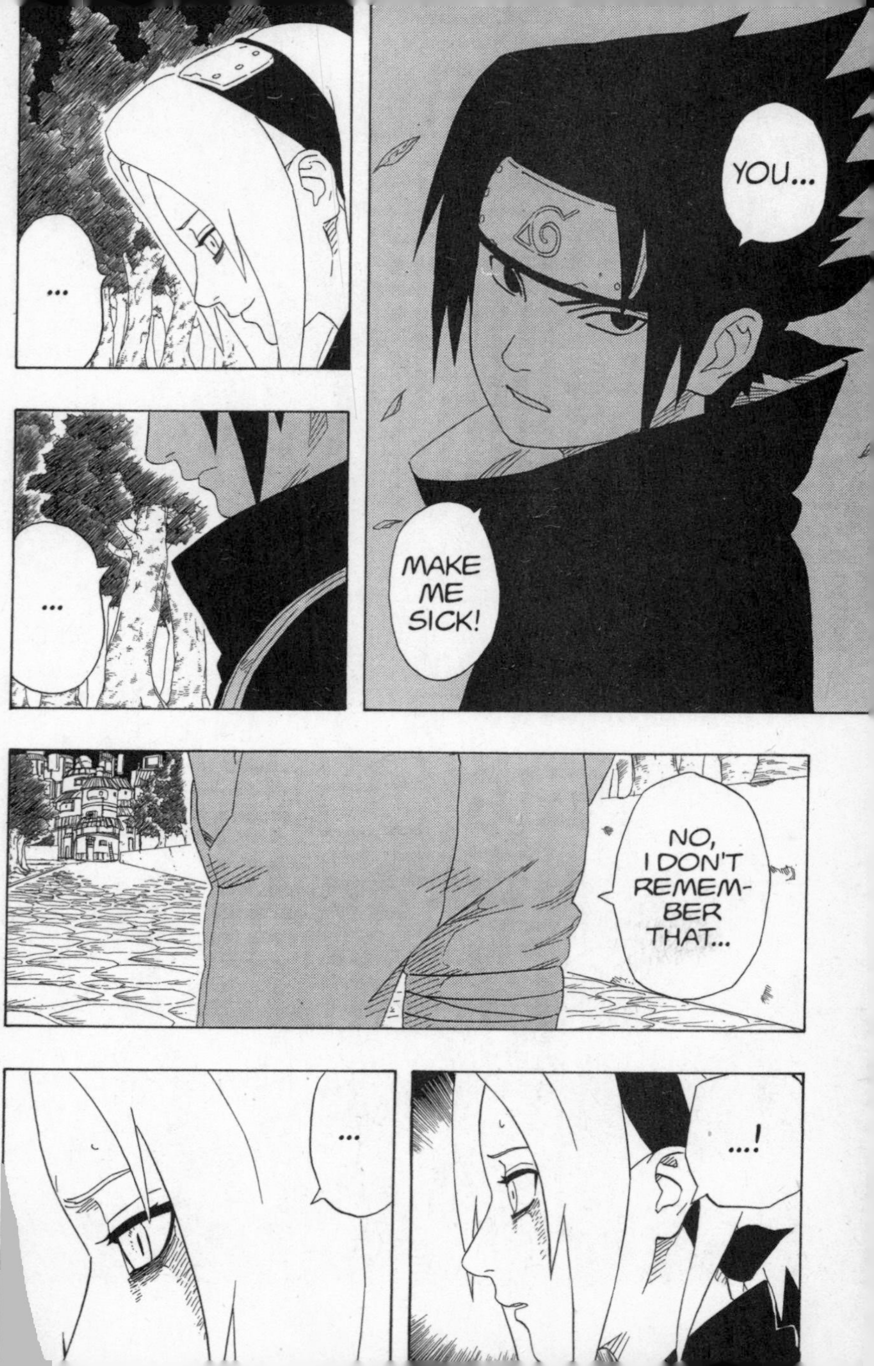
YOU...
MAKE ME SICK!
...
...
NO, I DON'T REMEMBER THAT...
...!
...

READ THIS WAY

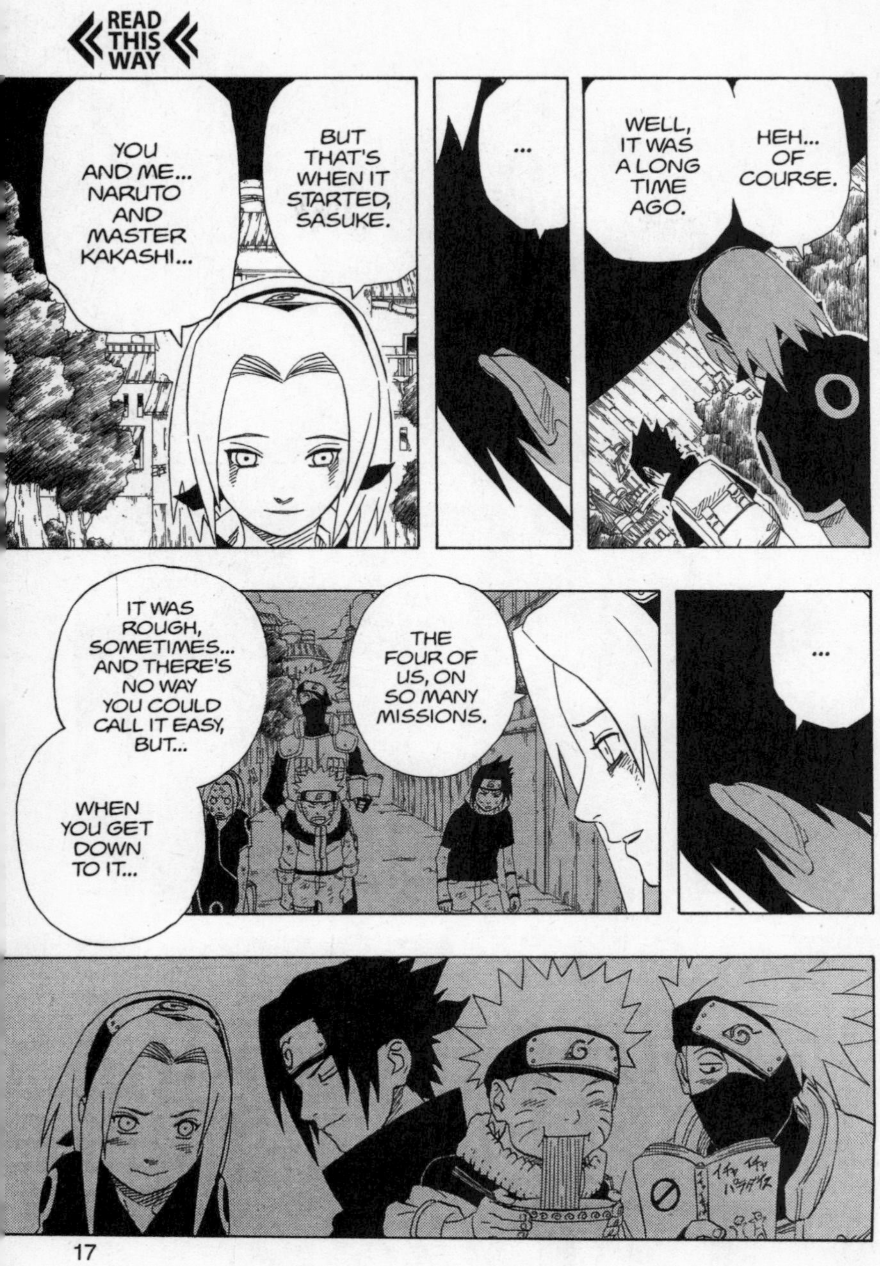
HEH... OF COURSE.
WELL, IT WAS A LONG TIME AGO.
...
BUT THAT'S WHEN IT STARTED, SASUKE.
YOU AND ME... NARUTO AND MASTER KAKASHI...
...
THE FOUR OF US, ON SO MANY MISSIONS.
IT WAS ROUGH, SOMETIMES... AND THERE'S NO WAY YOU COULD CALL IT EASY, BUT...
WHEN YOU GET DOWN TO IT...

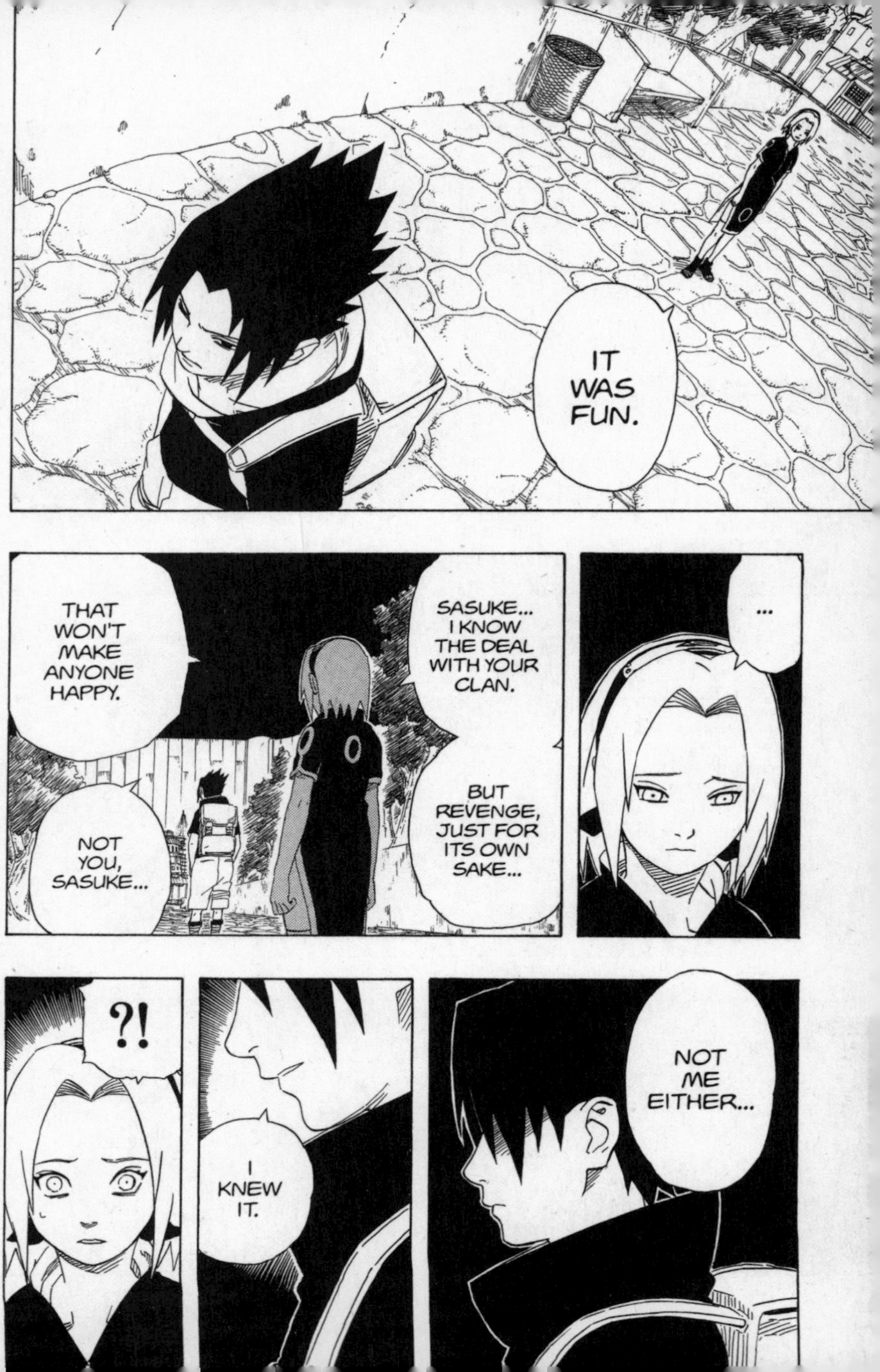
IT WAS FUN.
...
SASUKE... I KNOW THE DEAL WITH YOUR CLAN.
BUT REVENGE, JUST FOR ITS OWN SAKE...
THAT WON'T MAKE ANYONE HAPPY.
NOT YOU, SASUKE...
NOT ME EITHER...
I KNEW IT.
?!

READ THIS WAY

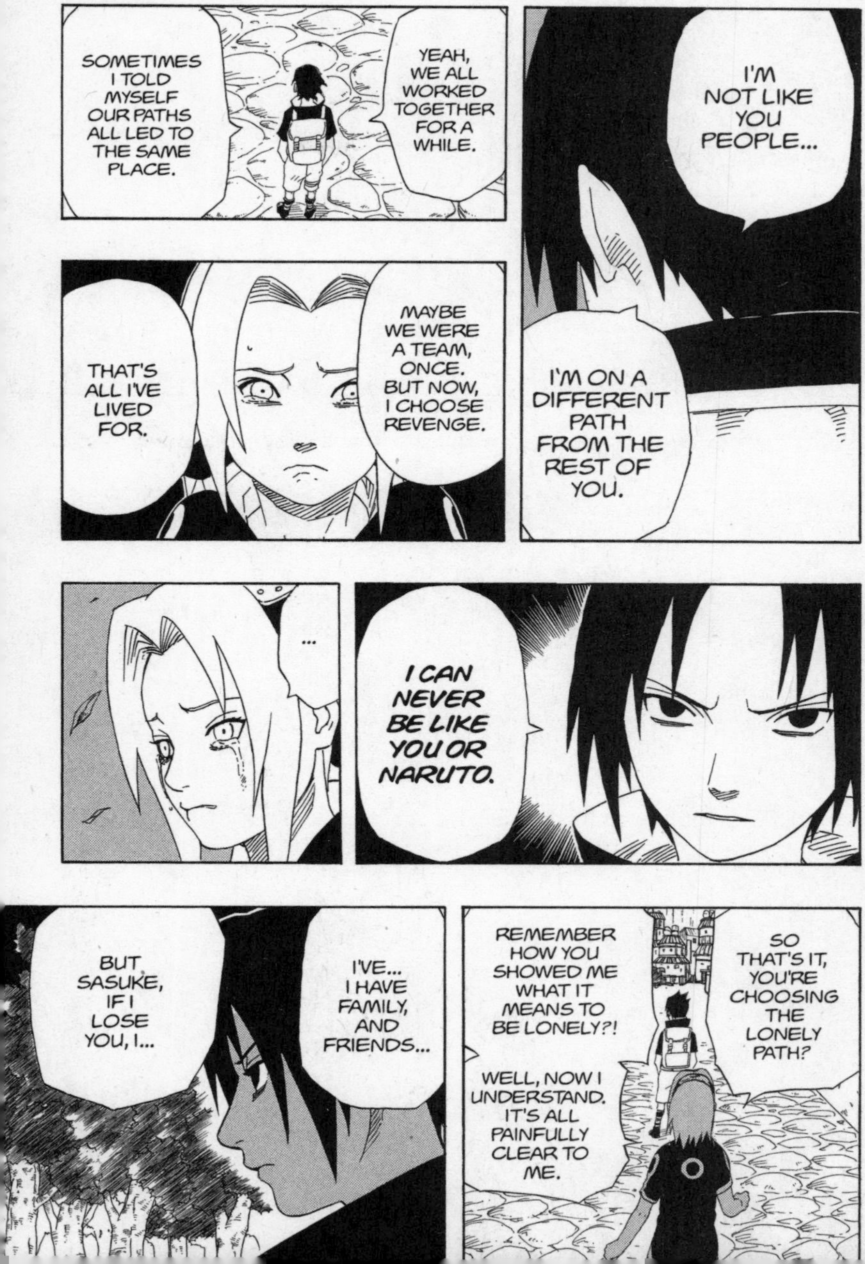
I'M NOT LIKE YOU PEOPLE...
I'M ON A DIFFERENT PATH FROM THE REST OF YOU.
YEAH, WE ALL WORKED TOGETHER FOR A WHILE.
SOMETIMES I TOLD MYSELF OUR PATHS ALL LED TO THE SAME PLACE.
MAYBE WE WERE A TEAM, ONCE. BUT NOW, I CHOOSE REVENGE.
THAT'S ALL I'VE LIVED FOR.
I CAN NEVER BE LIKE YOU OR NARUTO.
...
SO THAT'S IT, YOU'RE CHOOSING THE LONELY PATH?
REMEMBER HOW YOU SHOWED ME WHAT IT MEANS TO BE LONELY?!
WELL, NOW I UNDERSTAND. IT'S ALL PAINFULLY CLEAR TO ME.
I'VE... I HAVE FAMILY, AND FRIENDS...
BUT SASUKE, IF I LOSE YOU, I...

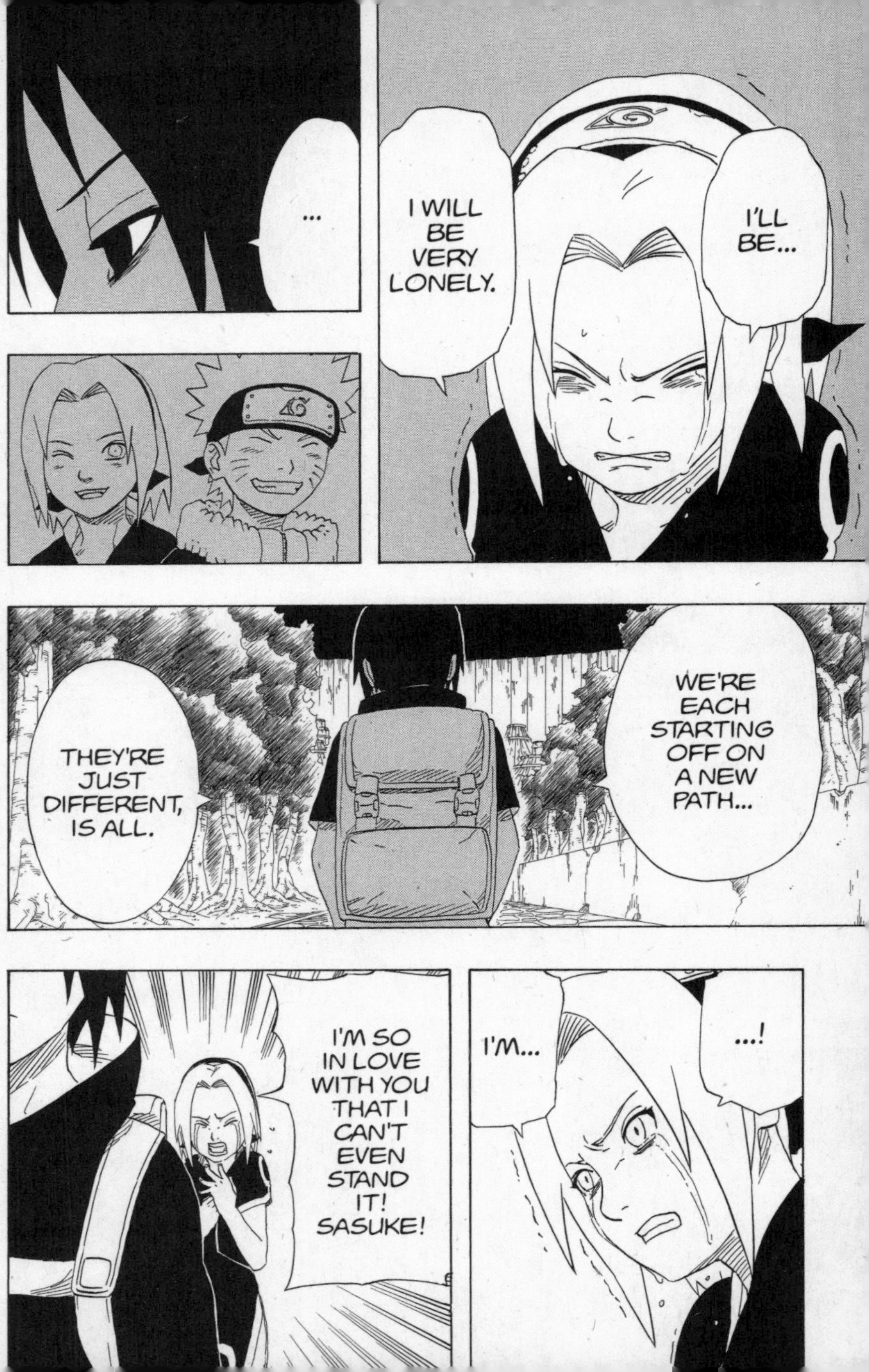
I'LL BE...
I WILL BE VERY LONELY.
...
WE'RE EACH STARTING OFF ON A NEW PATH...
THEY'RE JUST DIFFERENT, IS ALL.
...!
I'M...
I'M SO IN LOVE WITH YOU THAT I CAN'T EVEN STAND IT! SASUKE!

READ THIS WAY

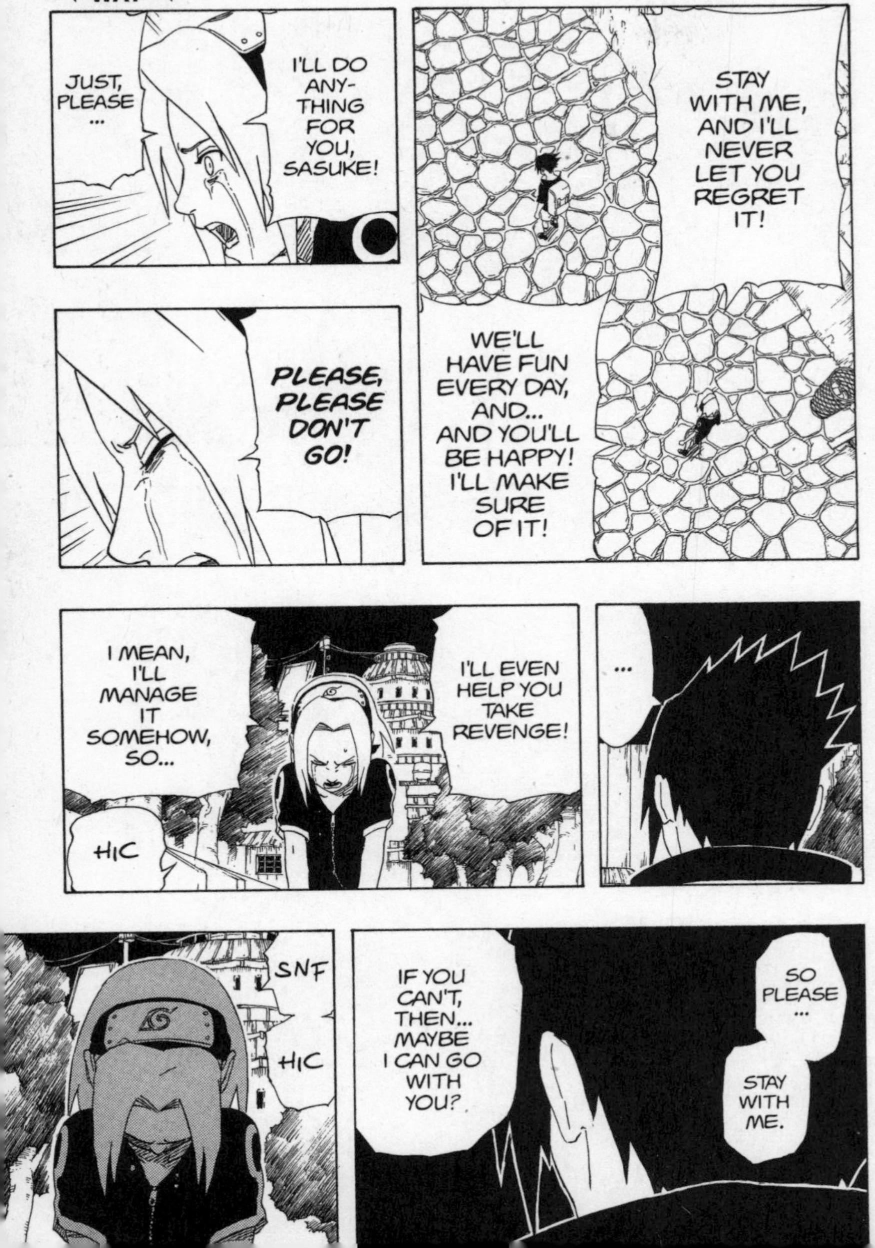
STAY WITH ME, AND I'LL NEVER LET YOU REGRET IT!
WE'LL HAVE FUN EVERY DAY, AND... AND YOU'LL BE HAPPY! I'LL MAKE SURE OF IT!
I'LL DO ANY-THING FOR YOU, SASUKE!
JUST, PLEASE ...
PLEASE, PLEASE DON'T GO!
...
I'LL EVEN HELP YOU TAKE REVENGE!
I MEAN, I'LL MANAGE IT SOMEHOW, SO...
HIC
SO PLEASE ...
STAY WITH ME.
IF YOU CAN'T, THEN... MAYBE I CAN GO WITH YOU?
SNF
HIC

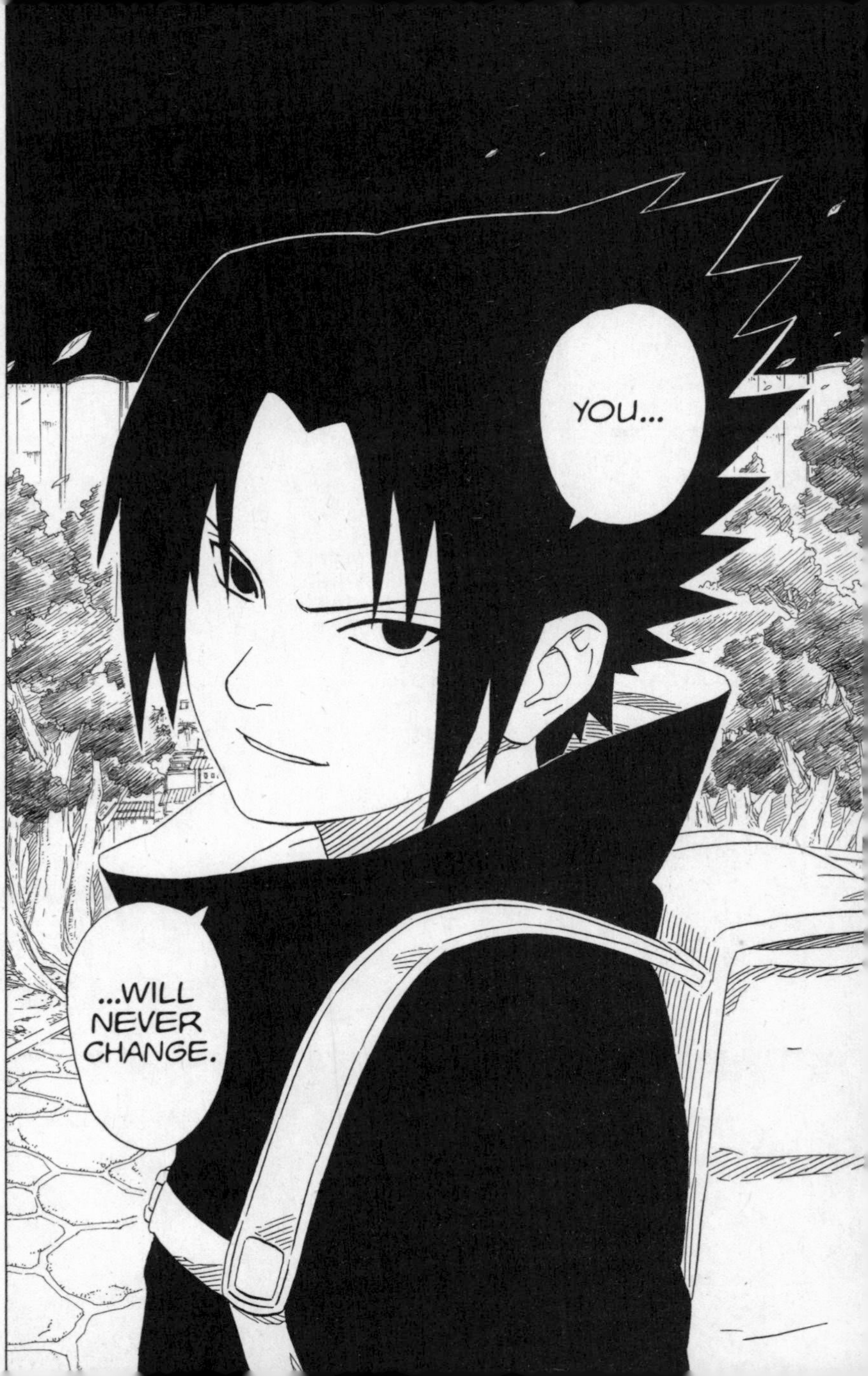
YOU...
...WILL NEVER CHANGE.

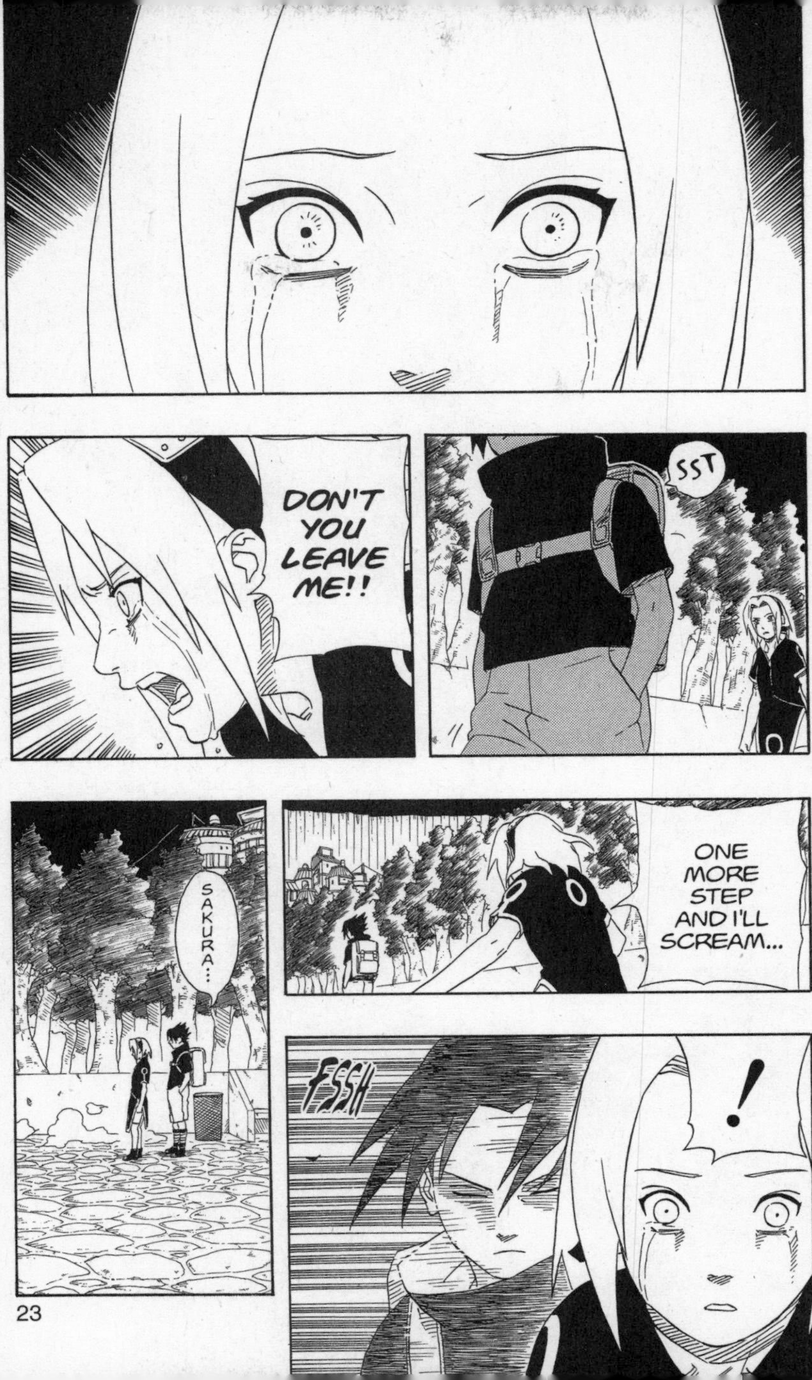
SST
DON'T YOU LEAVE ME!!
ONE MORE STEP AND I'LL SCREAM...
FSSH
!
SAKURA...

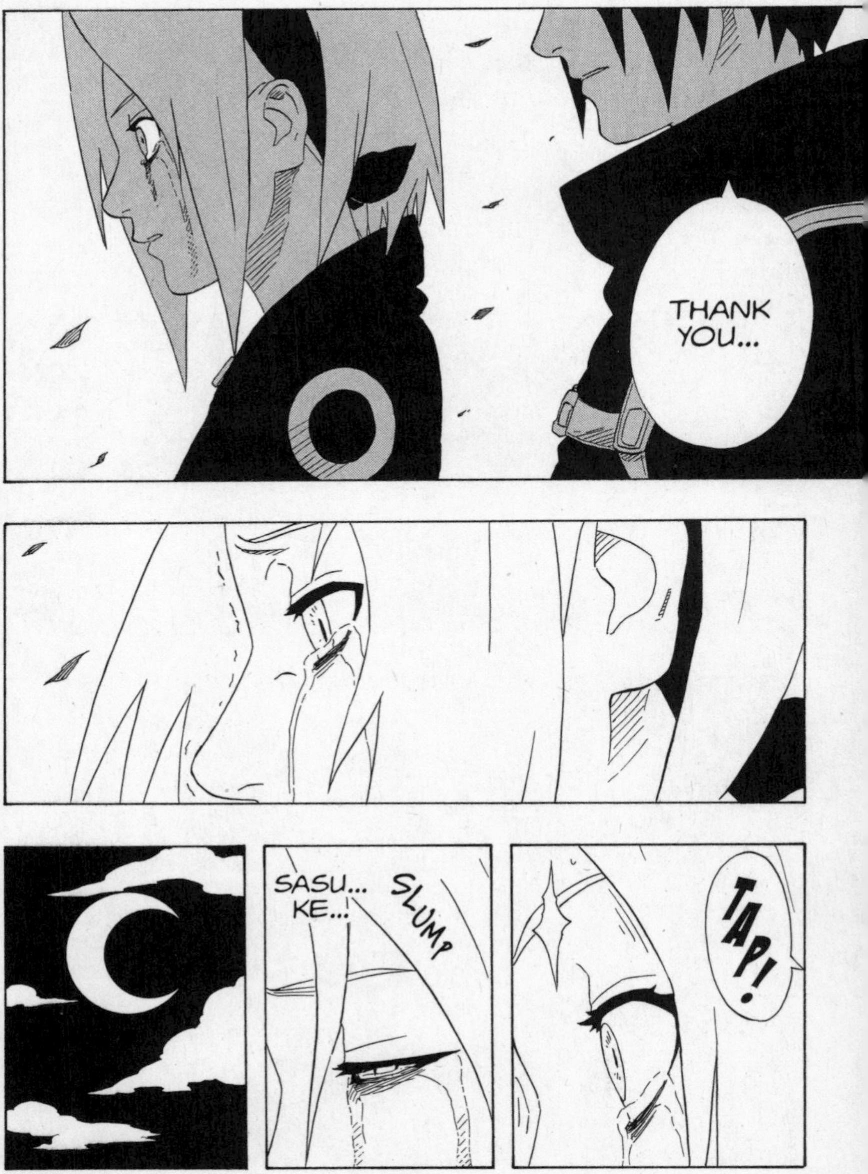
THANK YOU...
TAP!
SASU... KE...!
SLUMP

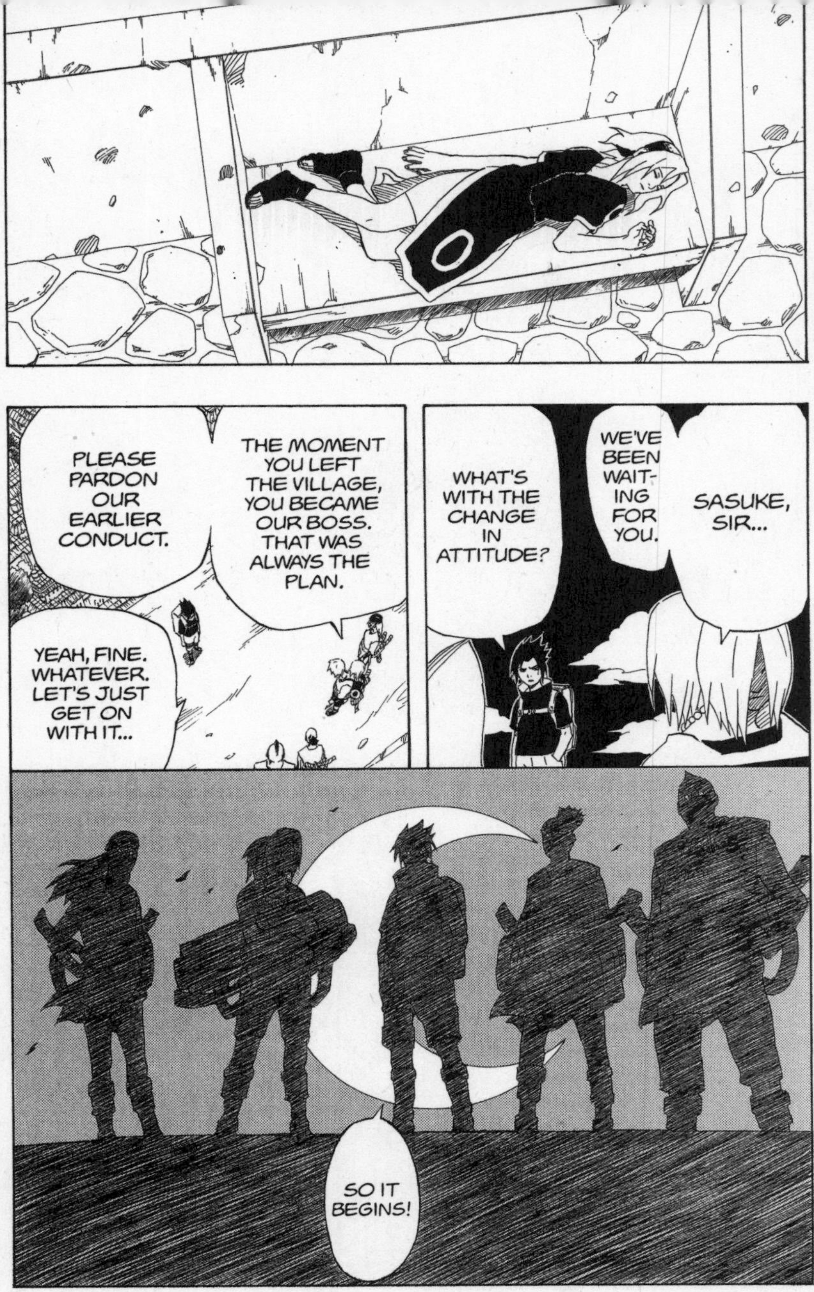
SASUKE, SIR...
WE'VE BEEN WAIT-ING FOR YOU.
WHAT'S WITH THE CHANGE IN ATTITUDE?
THE MOMENT YOU LEFT THE VILLAGE, YOU BECAME OUR BOSS. THAT WAS ALWAYS THE PLAN.
PLEASE PARDON OUR EARLIER CONDUCT.
YEAH, FINE. WHATEVER. LET'S JUST GET ON WITH IT...
SO IT BEGINS!

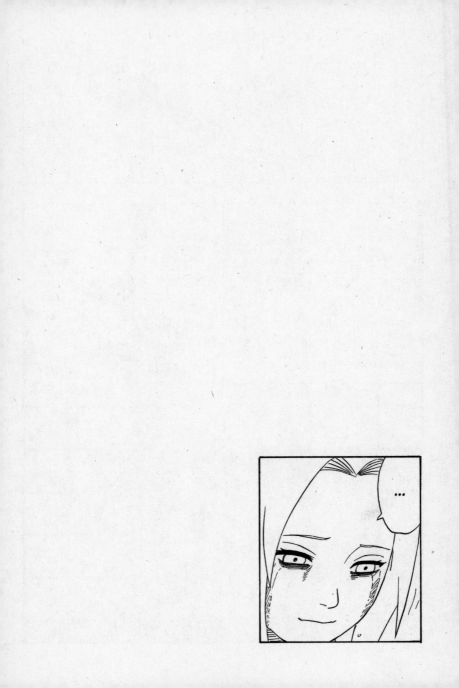

Number 182: Assemble!!

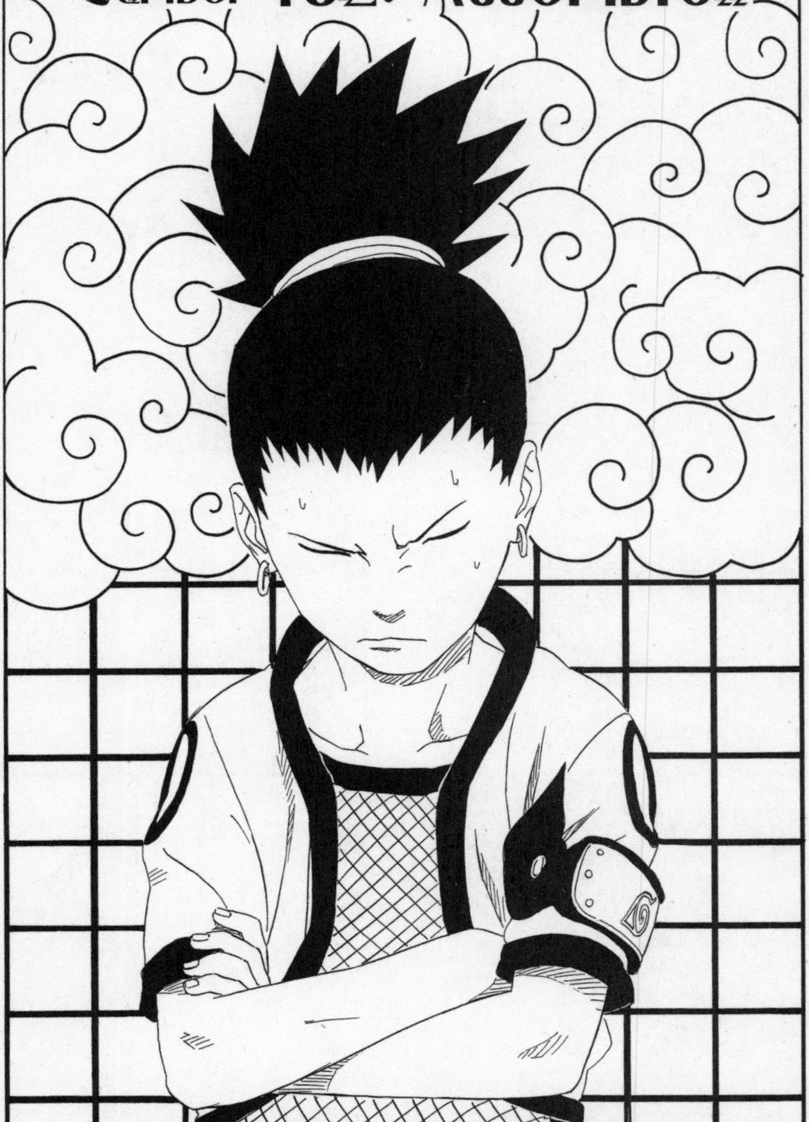

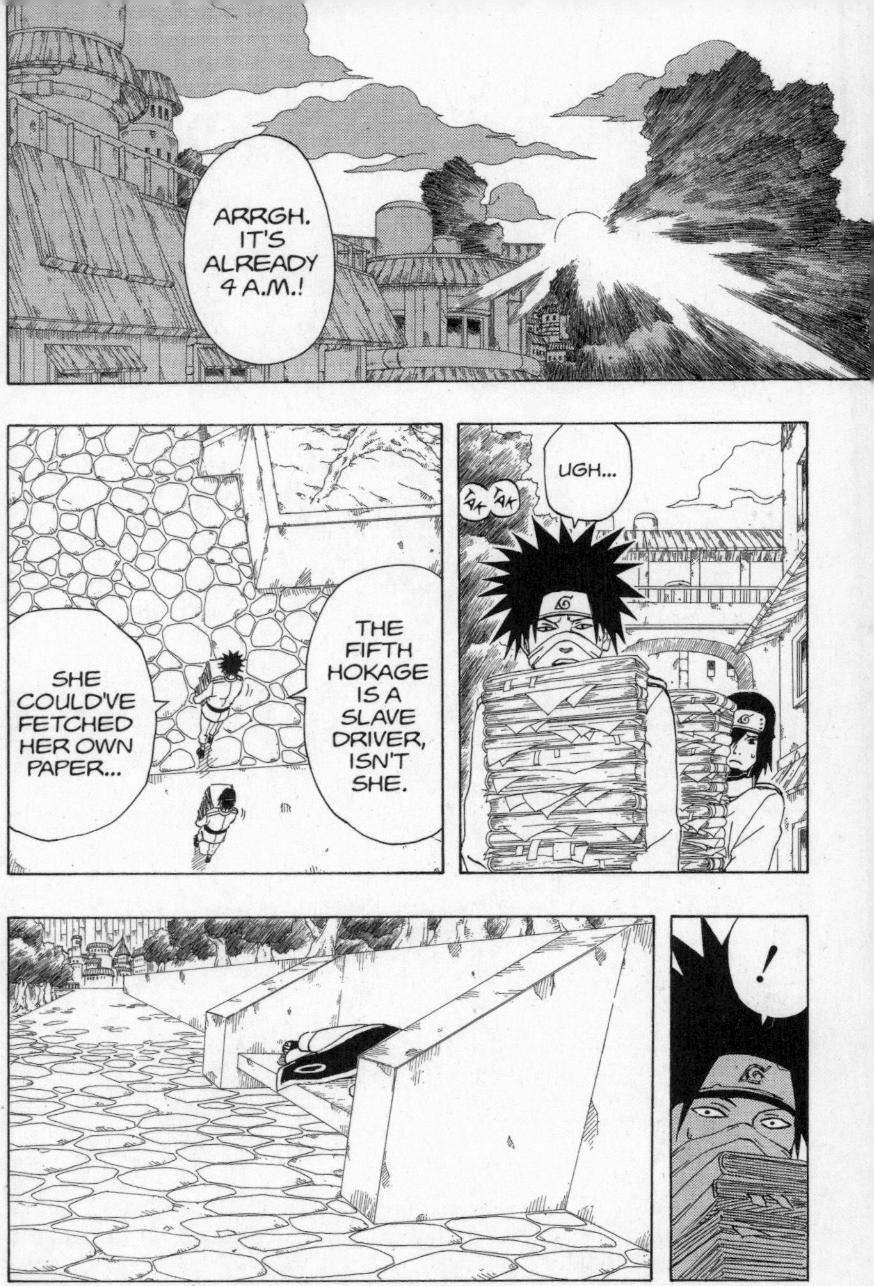
ARRGH. IT'S ALREADY 4 A.M.!
TAK TAK
UGH...
THE FIFTH HOKAGE IS A SLAVE DRIVER, ISN'T SHE.
SHE COULD'VE FETCHED HER OWN PAPER...
!

READ THIS WAY

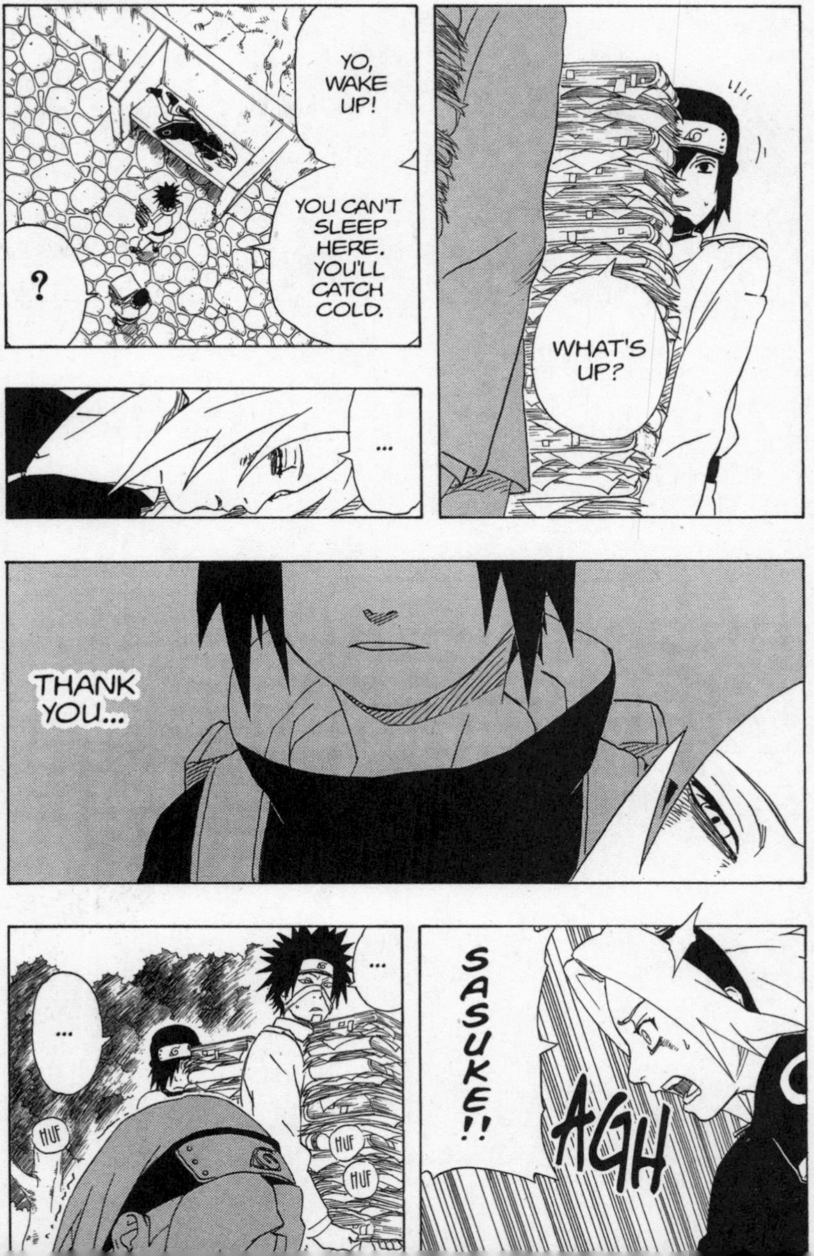
WHAT'S UP?
YO, WAKE UP!
YOU CAN'T SLEEP HERE. YOU'LL CATCH COLD.
?
...
THANK YOU...
SASUKE!!
AGH
...
...
HUF
HUF
HUF

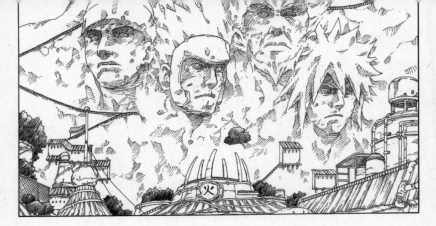

BAM
BAM

ZZZ...
ZZZ...

NGU.H

景 ⊙ 彡

THANKS...

SST

G'CHAK

!

READ THIS WAY

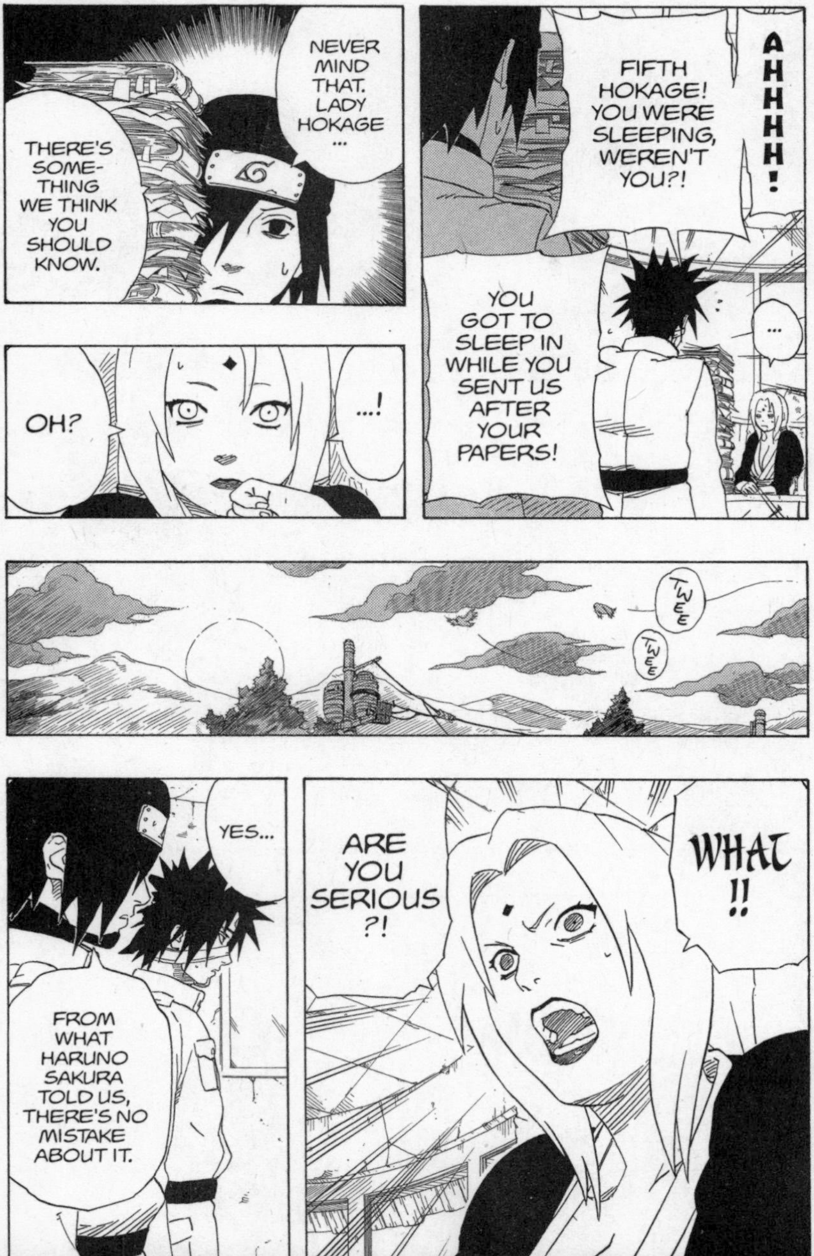
AHHHH!
FIFTH HOKAGE! YOU WERE SLEEPING, WEREN'T YOU?!
YOU GOT TO SLEEP IN WHILE YOU SENT US AFTER YOUR PAPERS!
...
NEVER MIND THAT. LADY HOKAGE ...
THERE'S SOME-THING WE THINK YOU SHOULD KNOW.
...!
OH?
TWEE
TWEE
WHAT!!
ARE YOU SERIOUS?!
YES...
FROM WHAT HARUNO SAKURA TOLD US, THERE'S NO MISTAKE ABOUT IT.

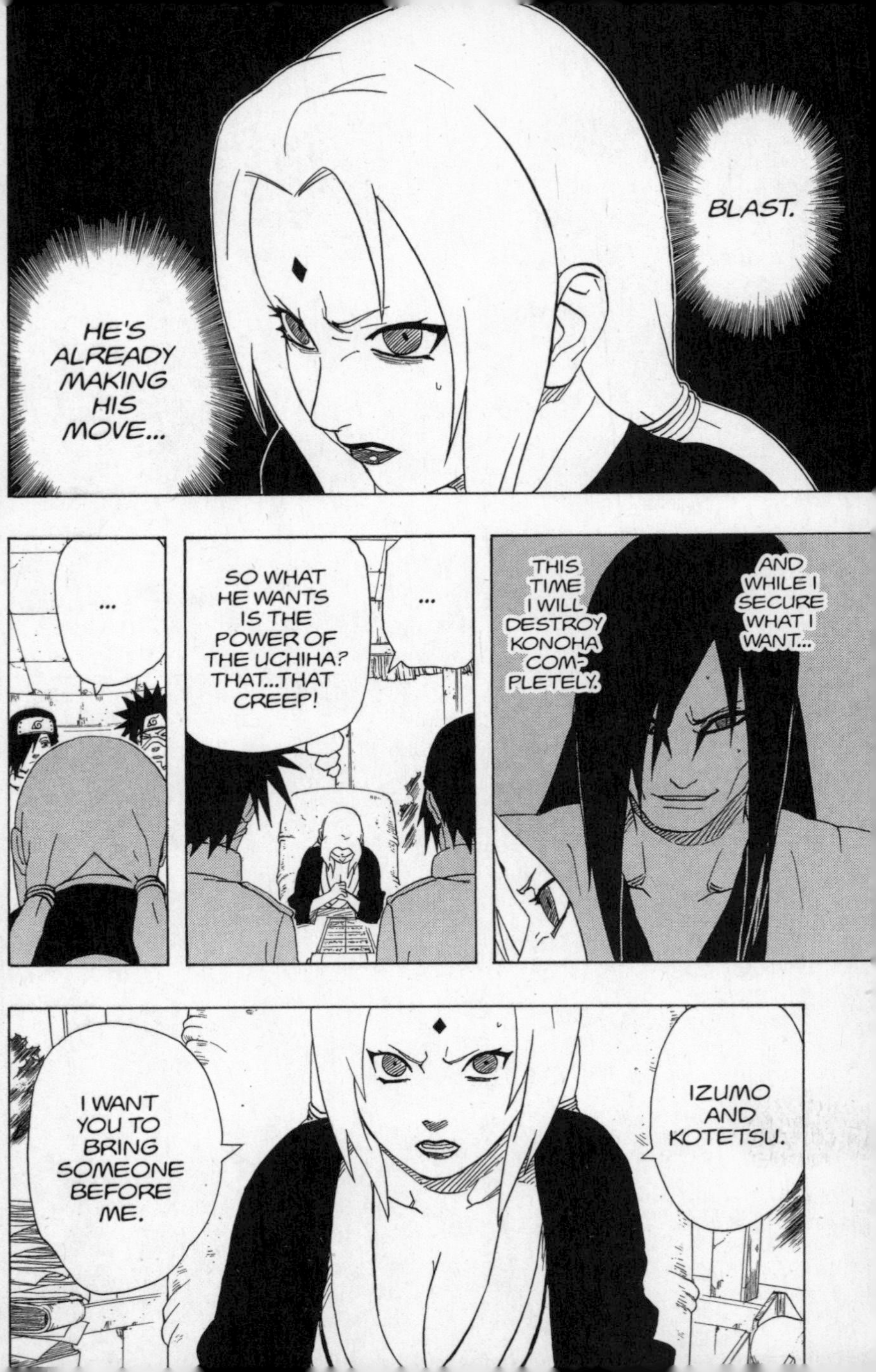
BLAST.
HE'S ALREADY MAKING HIS MOVE...
AND WHILE I SECURE WHAT I WANT...
THIS TIME I WILL DESTROY KONOHA COMPLETELY.
...
SO WHAT HE WANTS IS THE POWER OF THE UCHIHA? THAT...THAT CREEP!
...
IZUMO AND KOTETSU.
I WANT YOU TO BRING SOMEONE BEFORE ME.

READ THIS WAY

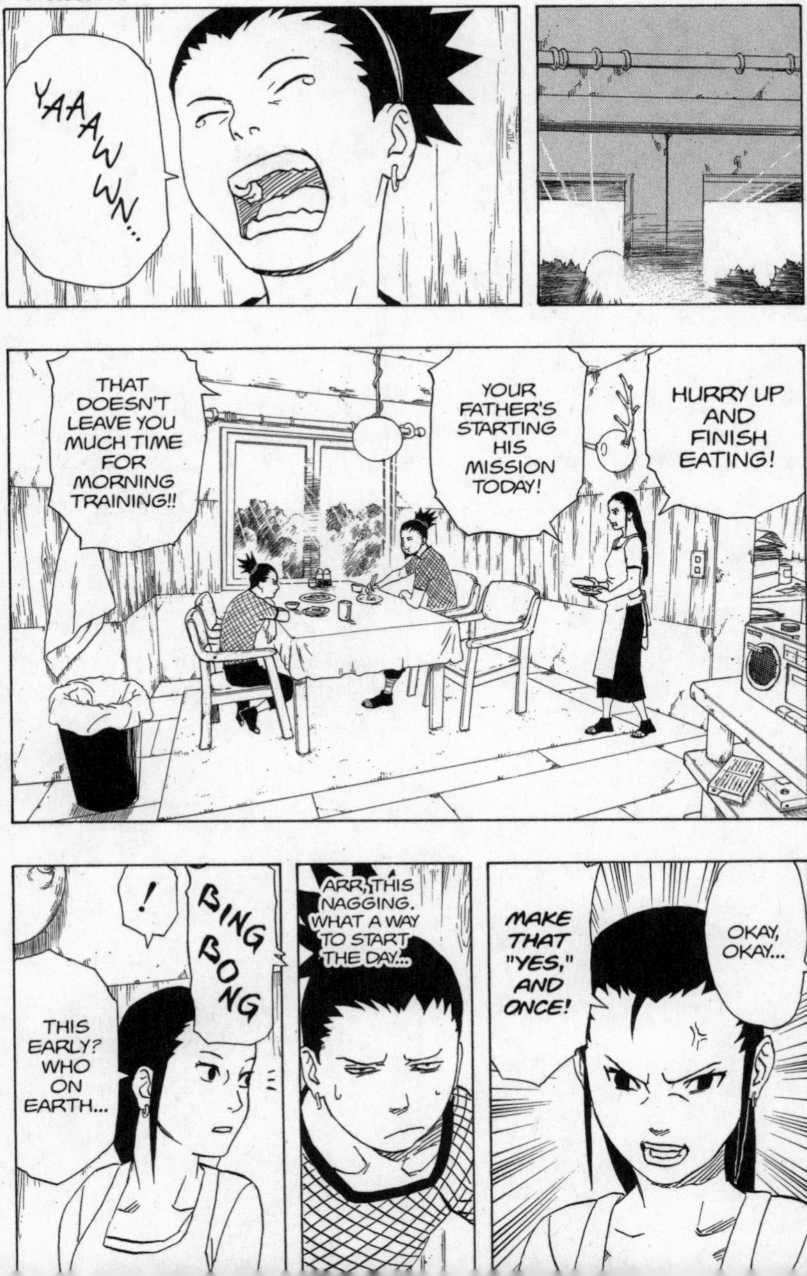
YAAAWWN...
HURRY UP AND FINISH EATING!
YOUR FATHER'S STARTING HIS MISSION TODAY!
THAT DOESN'T LEAVE YOU MUCH TIME FOR MORNING TRAINING!!
OKAY, OKAY...
MAKE THAT "YES," AND ONCE!
ARR, THIS NAGGING. WHAT A WAY TO START THE DAY...
BING BONG
!
THIS EARLY? WHO ON EARTH...

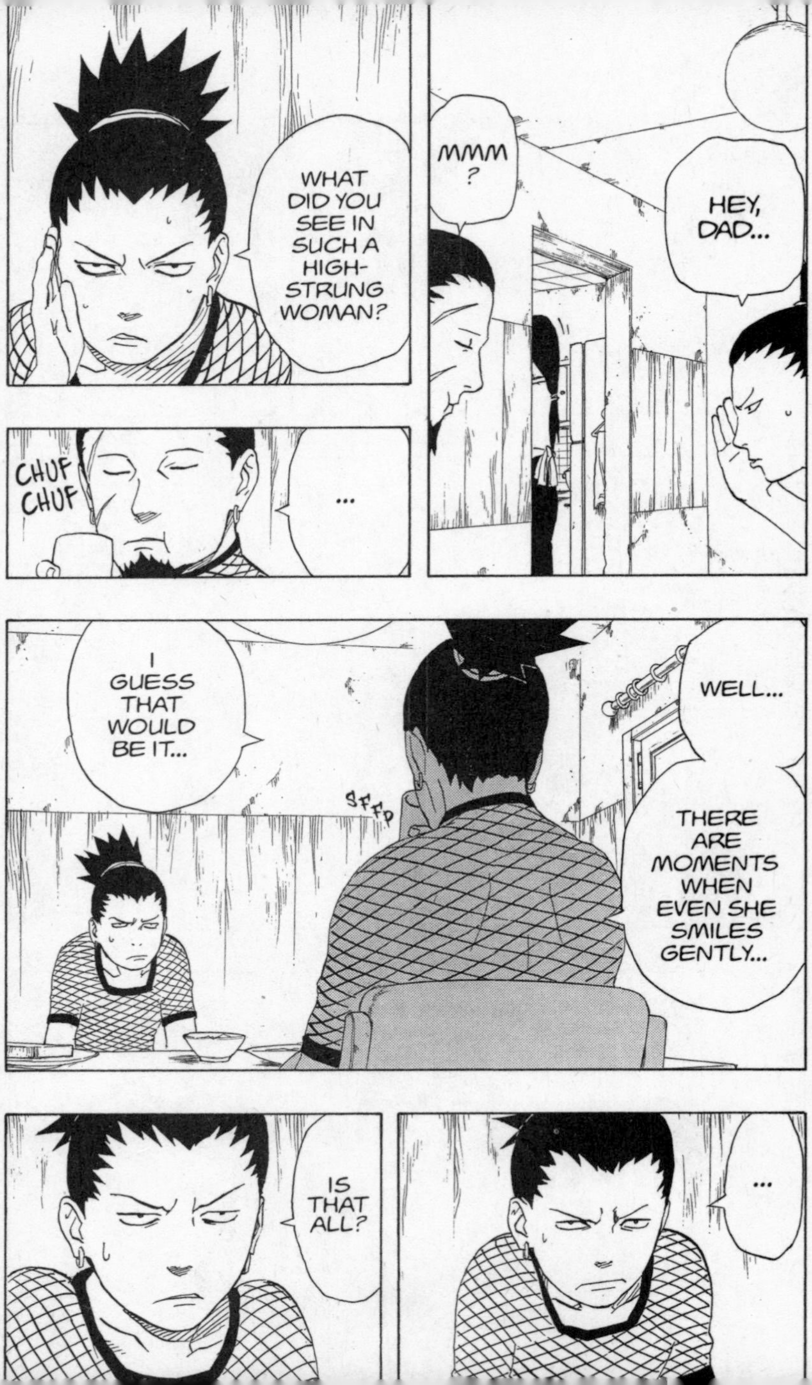
HEY, DAD...
MMM ?
WHAT DID YOU SEE IN SUCH A HIGH-STRUNG WOMAN?
...
CHUF CHUF
WELL...
THERE ARE MOMENTS WHEN EVEN SHE SMILES GENTLY...
I GUESS THAT WOULD BE IT...
SFFP
...
IS THAT ALL?

READ THIS WAY

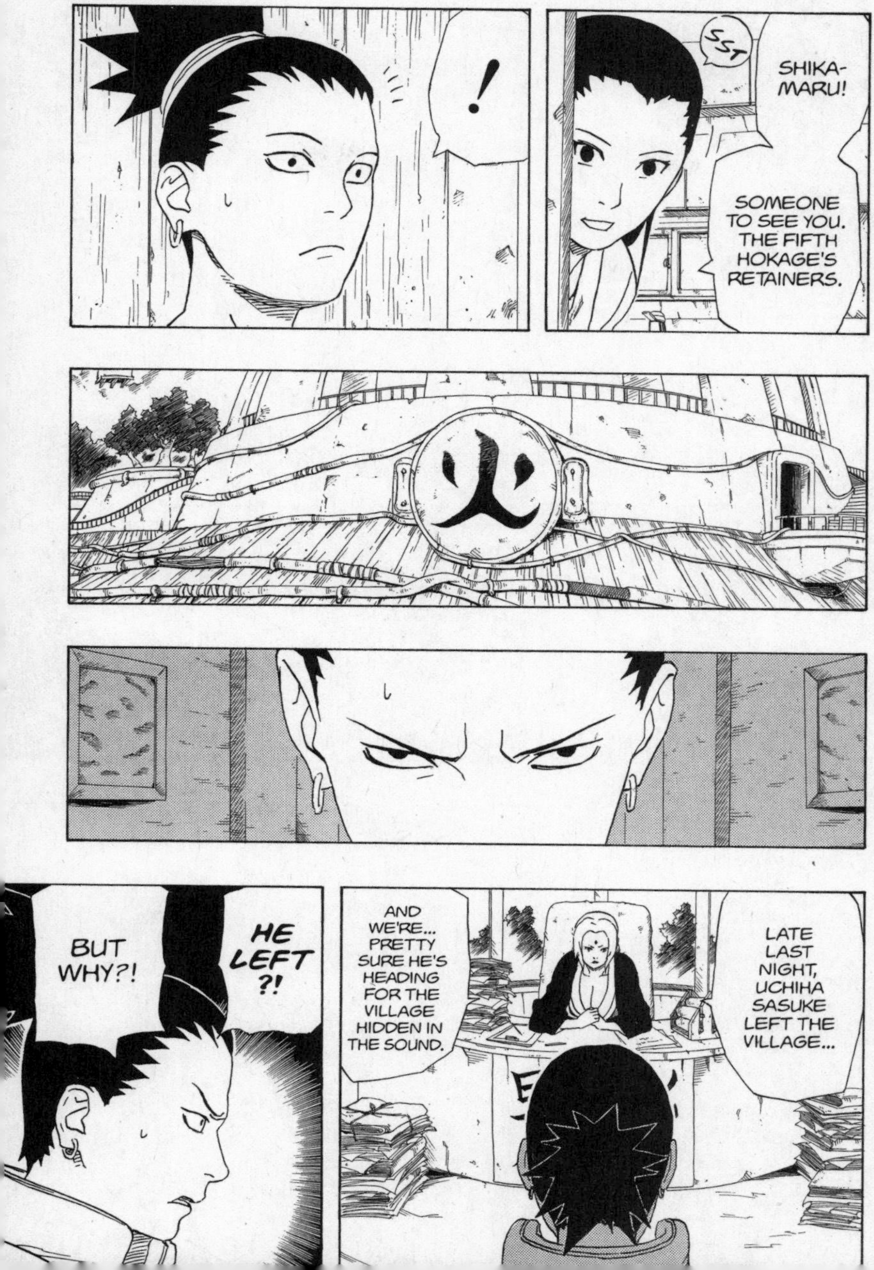
SST
SHIKA-MARU!
SOMEONE TO SEE YOU. THE FIFTH HOKAGE'S RETAINERS.
!
LATE LAST NIGHT, UCHIHA SASUKE LEFT THE VILLAGE...
AND WE'RE... PRETTY SURE HE'S HEADING FOR THE VILLAGE HIDDEN IN THE SOUND.
HE LEFT?!
BUT WHY?!

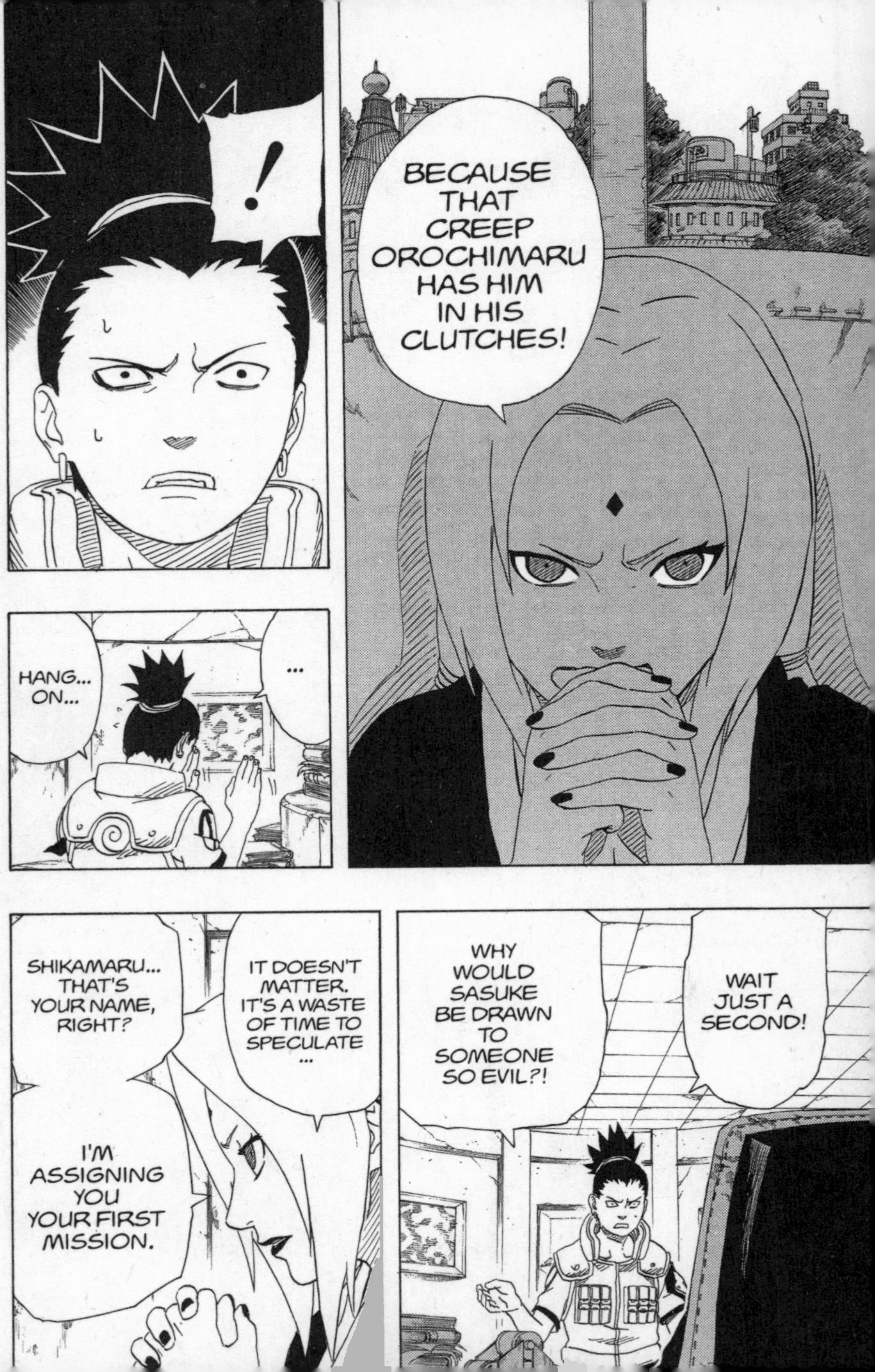
BECAUSE THAT CREEP OROCHIMARU HAS HIM IN HIS CLUTCHES!
!
...
HANG... ON...
WAIT JUST A SECOND!
WHY WOULD SASUKE BE DRAWN TO SOMEONE SO EVIL?!
IT DOESN'T MATTER. IT'S A WASTE OF TIME TO SPECULATE ...
SHIKAMARU... THAT'S YOUR NAME, RIGHT?
I'M ASSIGNING YOU YOUR FIRST MISSION.

READ THIS WAY

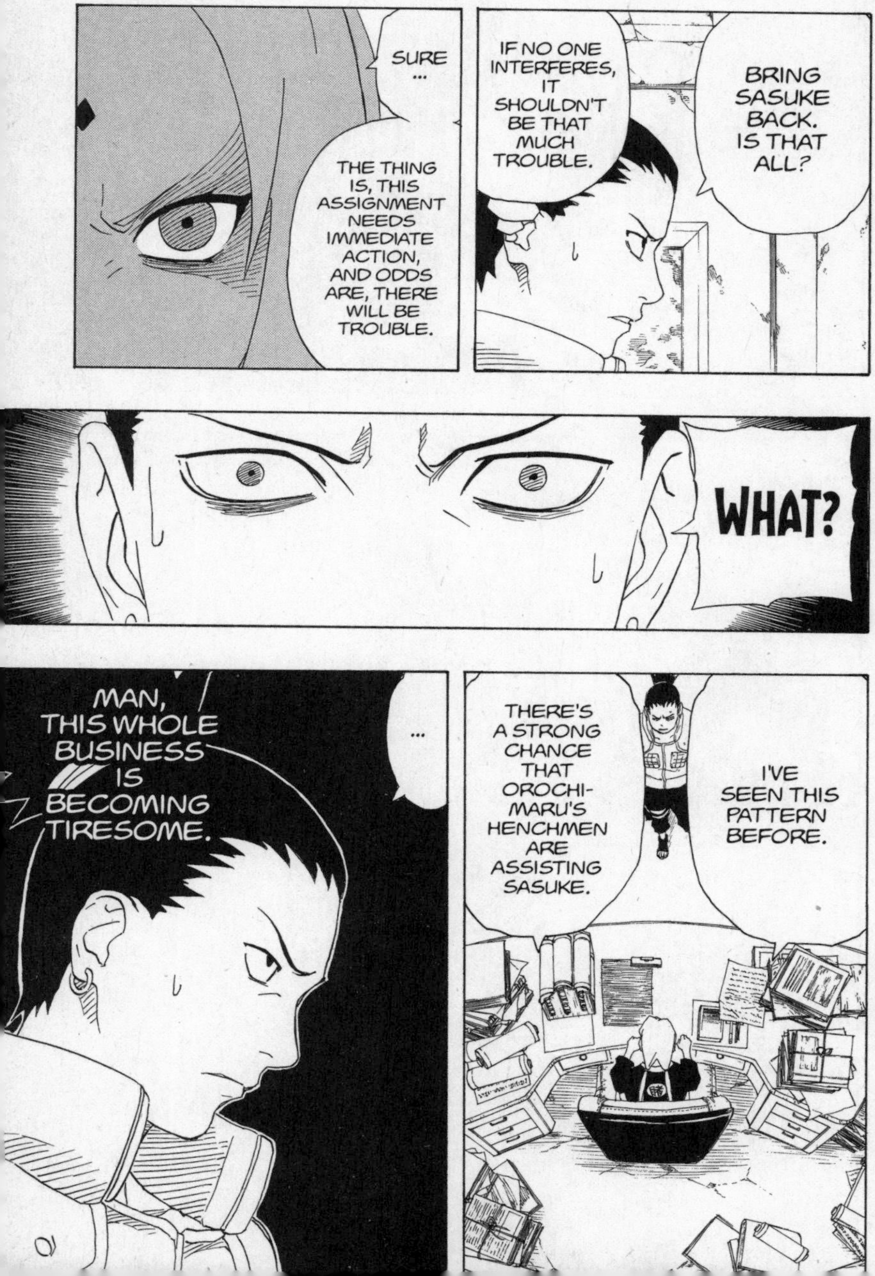
BRING SASUKE BACK. IS THAT ALL?
IF NO ONE INTERFERES, IT SHOULDN'T BE THAT MUCH TROUBLE.
SURE ...
THE THING IS, THIS ASSIGNMENT NEEDS IMMEDIATE ACTION, AND ODDS ARE, THERE WILL BE TROUBLE.
WHAT?
I'VE SEEN THIS PATTERN BEFORE.
THERE'S A STRONG CHANCE THAT OROCHIMARU'S HENCHMEN ARE ASSISTING SASUKE.
...
MAN, THIS WHOLE BUSINESS IS BECOMING TIRESOME.

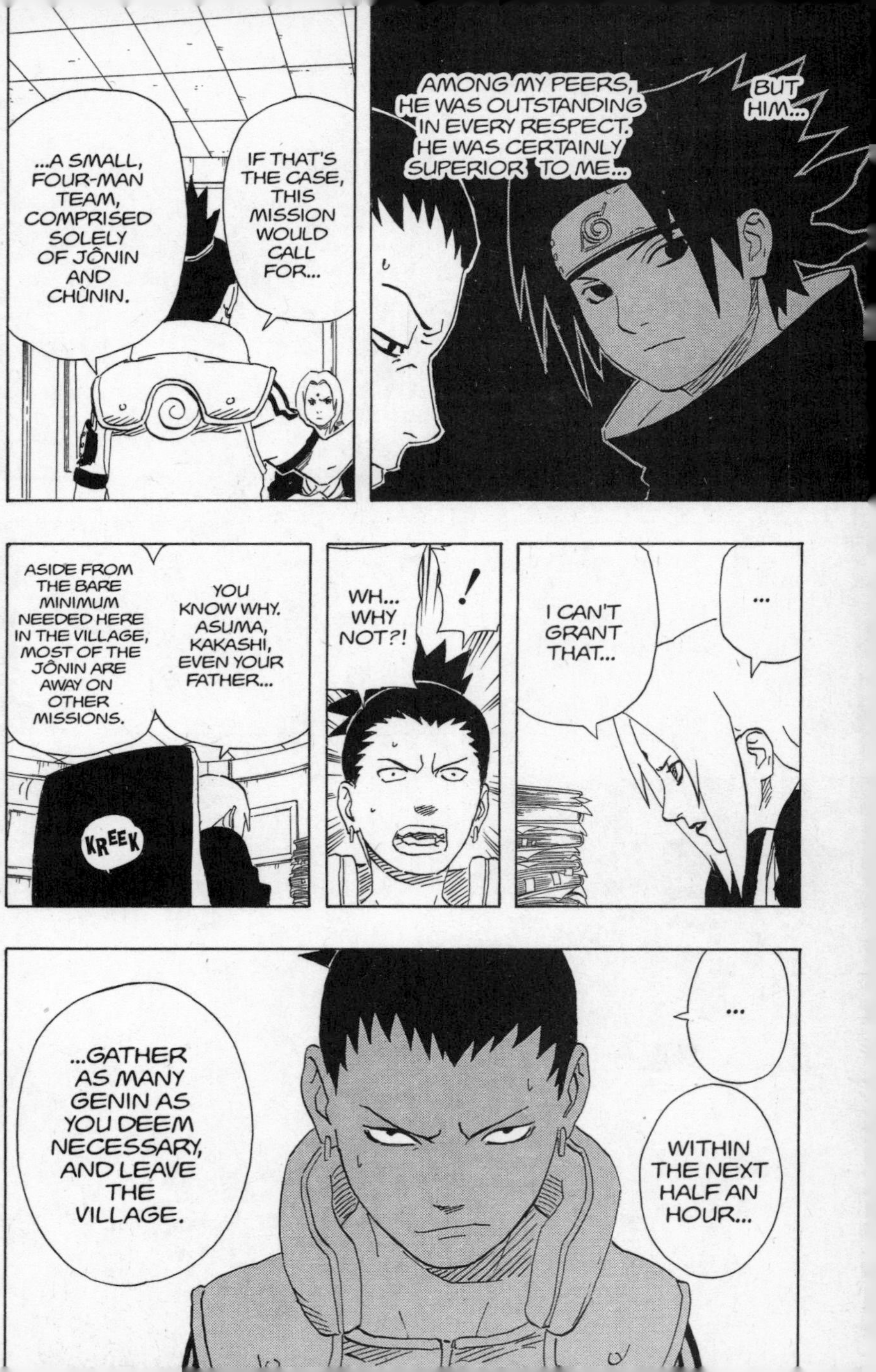
BUT HIM...
AMONG MY PEERS, HE WAS OUTSTANDING IN EVERY RESPECT. HE WAS CERTAINLY SUPERIOR TO ME...
IF THAT'S THE CASE, THIS MISSION WOULD CALL FOR...
...A SMALL, FOUR-MAN TEAM, COMPRISED SOLELY OF JÔNIN AND CHÛNIN.
...
I CAN'T GRANT THAT...
!
WH... WHY NOT?!
YOU KNOW WHY. ASUMA, KAKASHI, EVEN YOUR FATHER...
ASIDE FROM THE BARE MINIMUM NEEDED HERE IN THE VILLAGE, MOST OF THE JÔNIN ARE AWAY ON OTHER MISSIONS.
KREEK
...
WITHIN THE NEXT HALF AN HOUR...
...GATHER AS MANY GENIN AS YOU DEEM NECESSARY, AND LEAVE THE VILLAGE.

READ THIS WAY

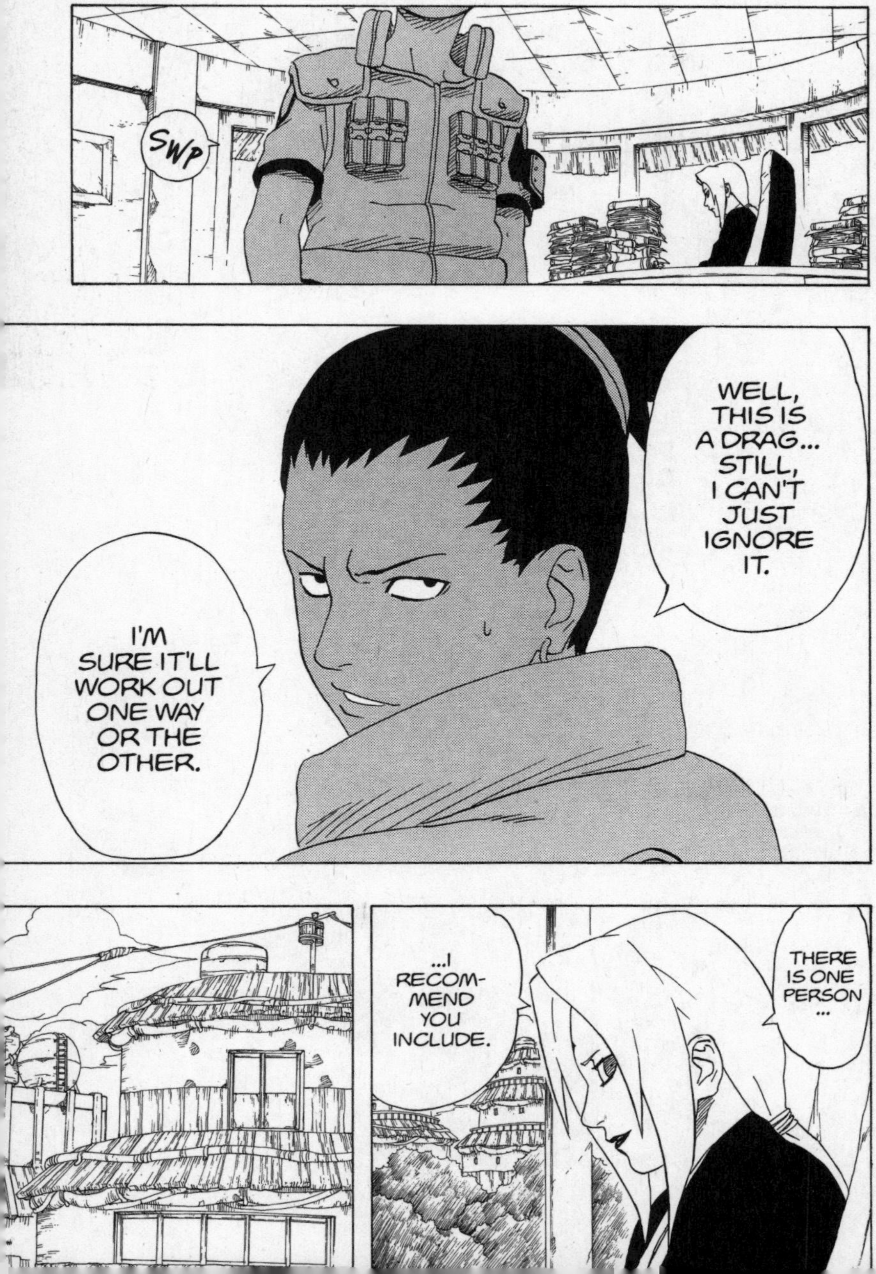
SWP
WELL, THIS IS A DRAG... STILL, I CAN'T JUST IGNORE IT.
I'M SURE IT'LL WORK OUT ONE WAY OR THE OTHER.
THERE IS ONE PERSON...
...I RECOMMEND YOU INCLUDE.

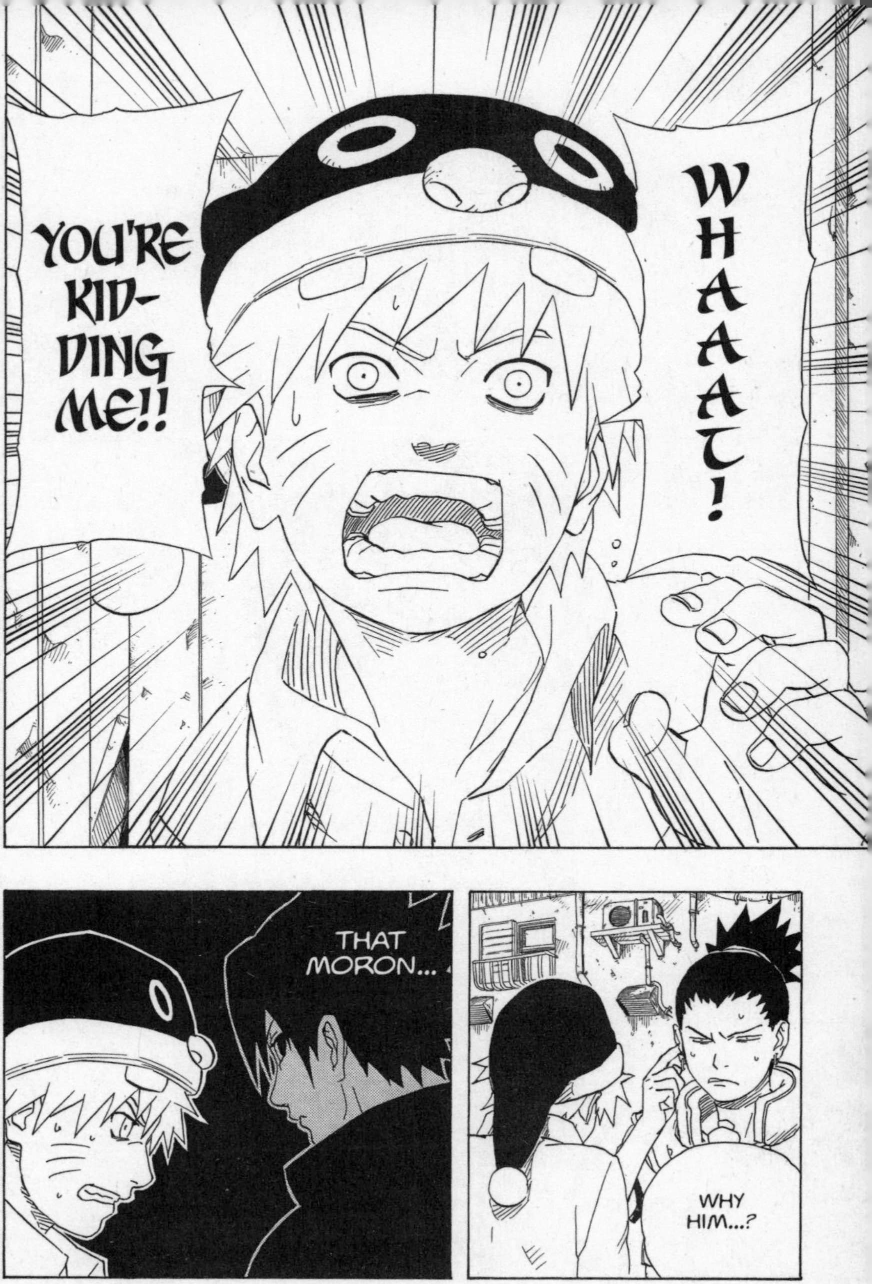
WHAAAT!
YOU'RE KID-DING ME!!
WHY HIM...?
THAT MORON...

WAIT JUST A MINUTE! I'LL JUST CHANGE REAL FAST.

WSSH

ROOSH

ROOSH

SO BESIDES ME, YOU GOT ANY EXCELLENT GENIN IN MIND?

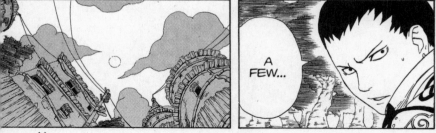

A FEW...

41

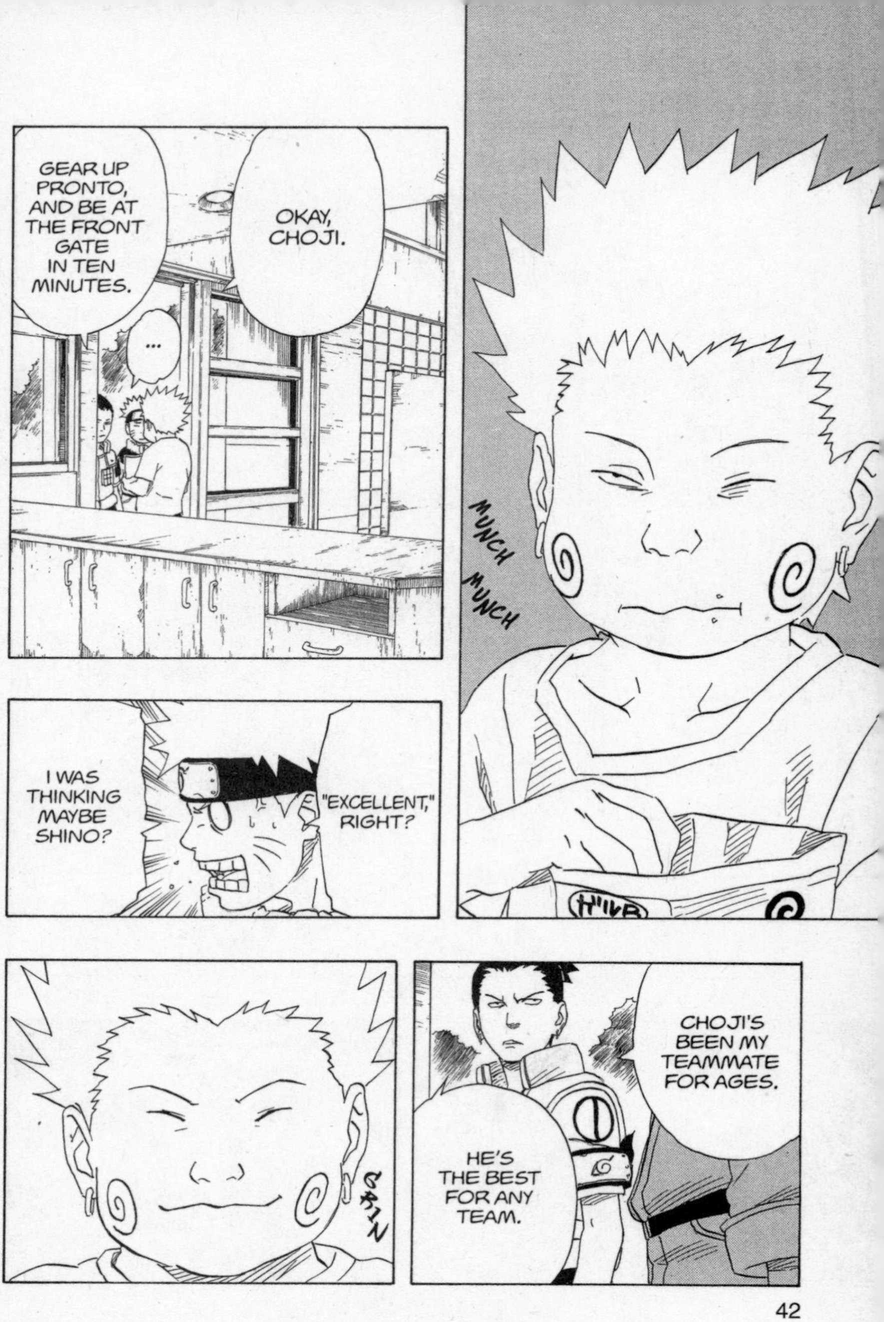
MUNCH MUNCH
OKAY, CHOJI.
GEAR UP PRONTO, AND BE AT THE FRONT GATE IN TEN MINUTES.
...
"EXCELLENT," RIGHT?
I WAS THINKING MAYBE SHINO?
CHOJI'S BEEN MY TEAMMATE FOR AGES.
HE'S THE BEST FOR ANY TEAM.
GRIN

READ THIS WAY

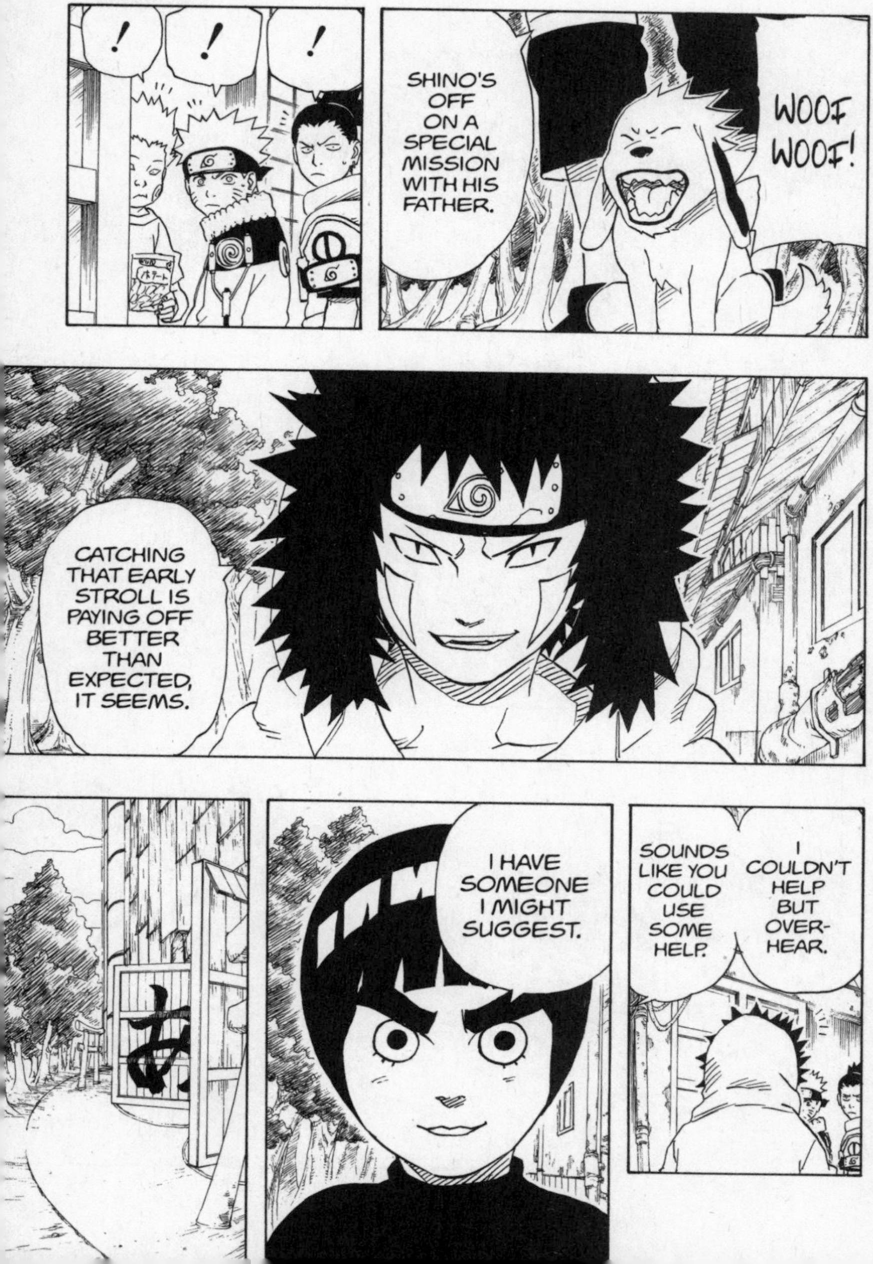

WOOF WOOF!
SHINO'S OFF ON A SPECIAL MISSION WITH HIS FATHER.
!
!
!
CATCHING THAT EARLY STROLL IS PAYING OFF BETTER THAN EXPECTED, IT SEEMS.
I COULDN'T HELP BUT OVER-HEAR.
SOUNDS LIKE YOU COULD USE SOME HELP.
I HAVE SOMEONE I MIGHT SUGGEST.

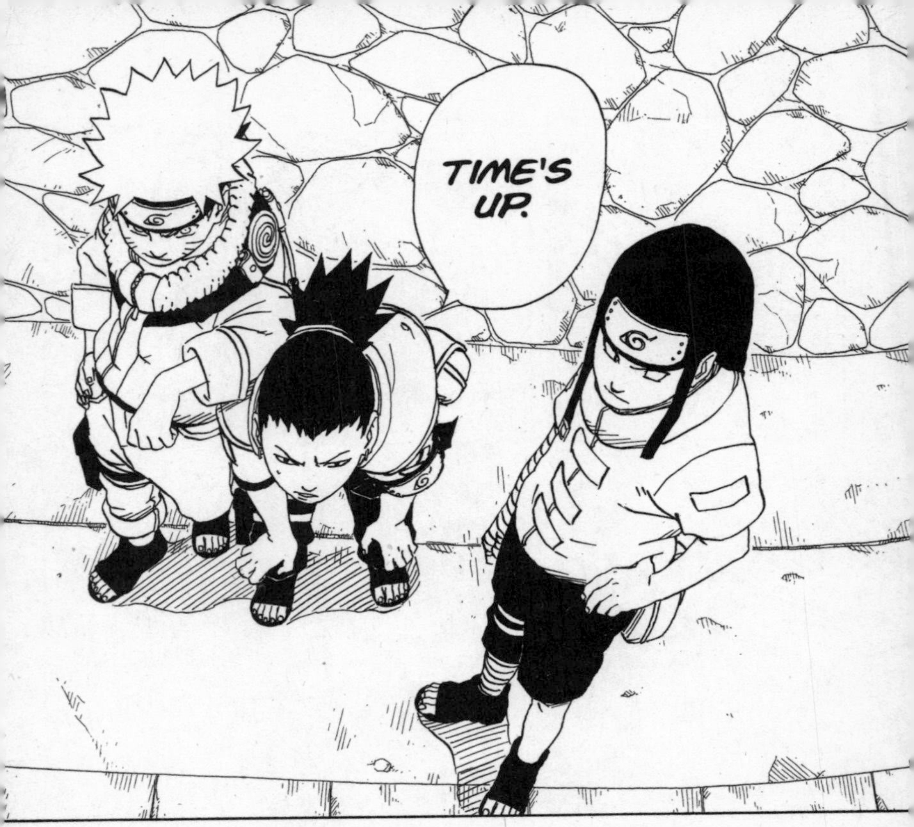
TIME'S UP.
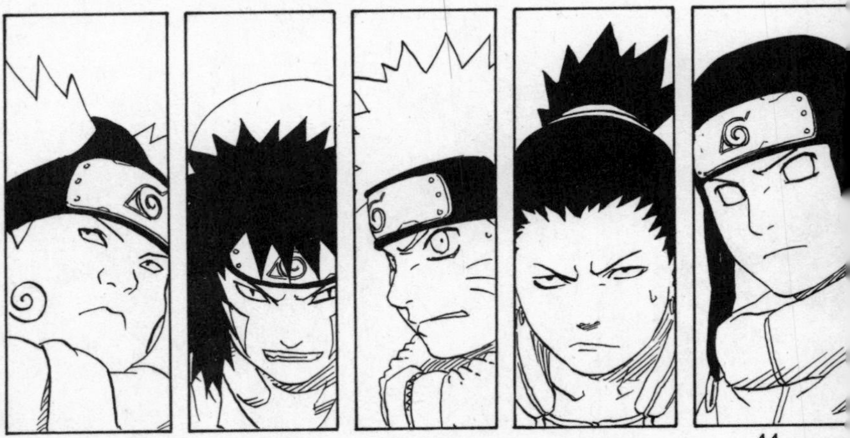

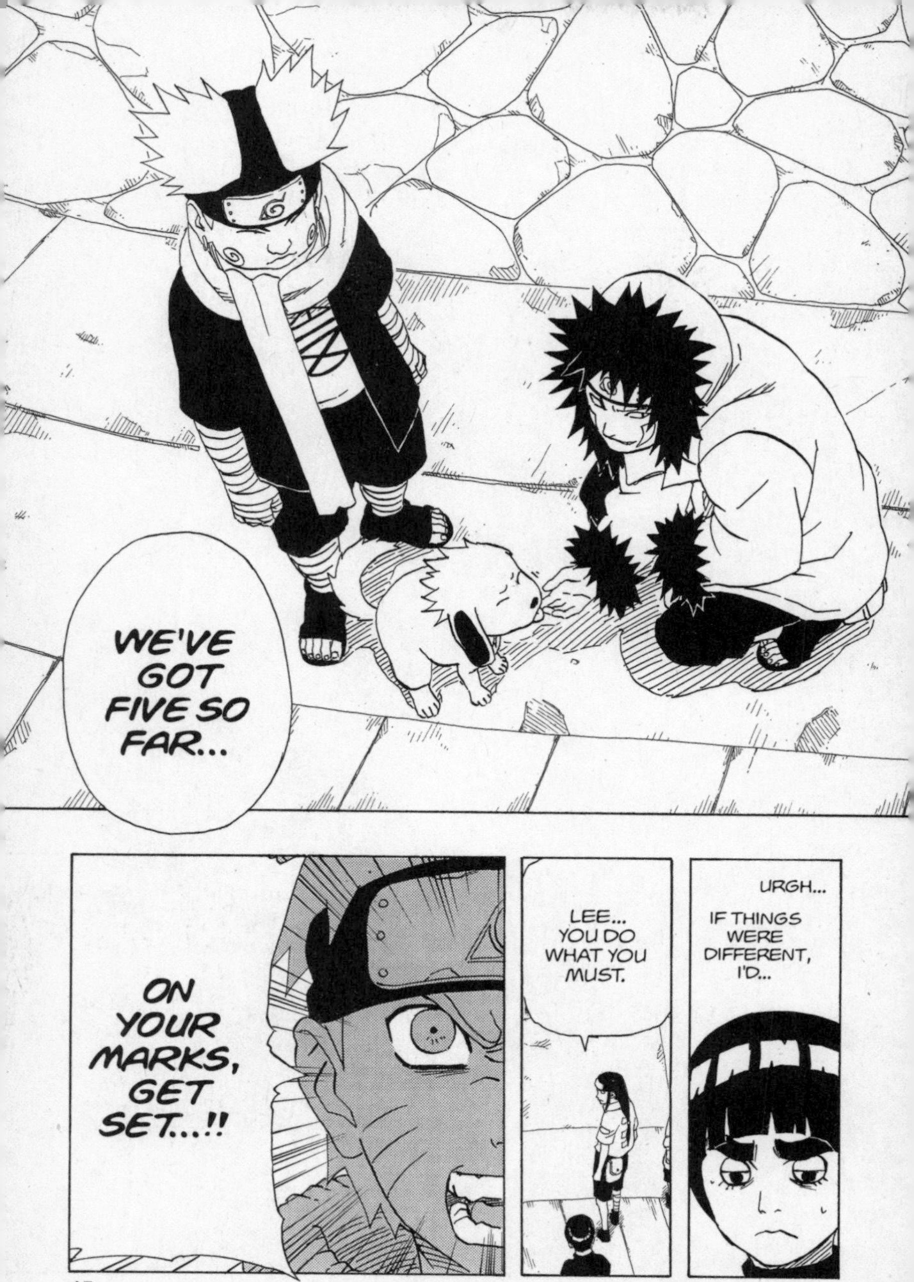
WE'VE GOT FIVE SO FAR...
URGH...
IF THINGS WERE DIFFERENT, I'D...
LEE... YOU DO WHAT YOU MUST.
ON YOUR MARKS, GET SET...!!

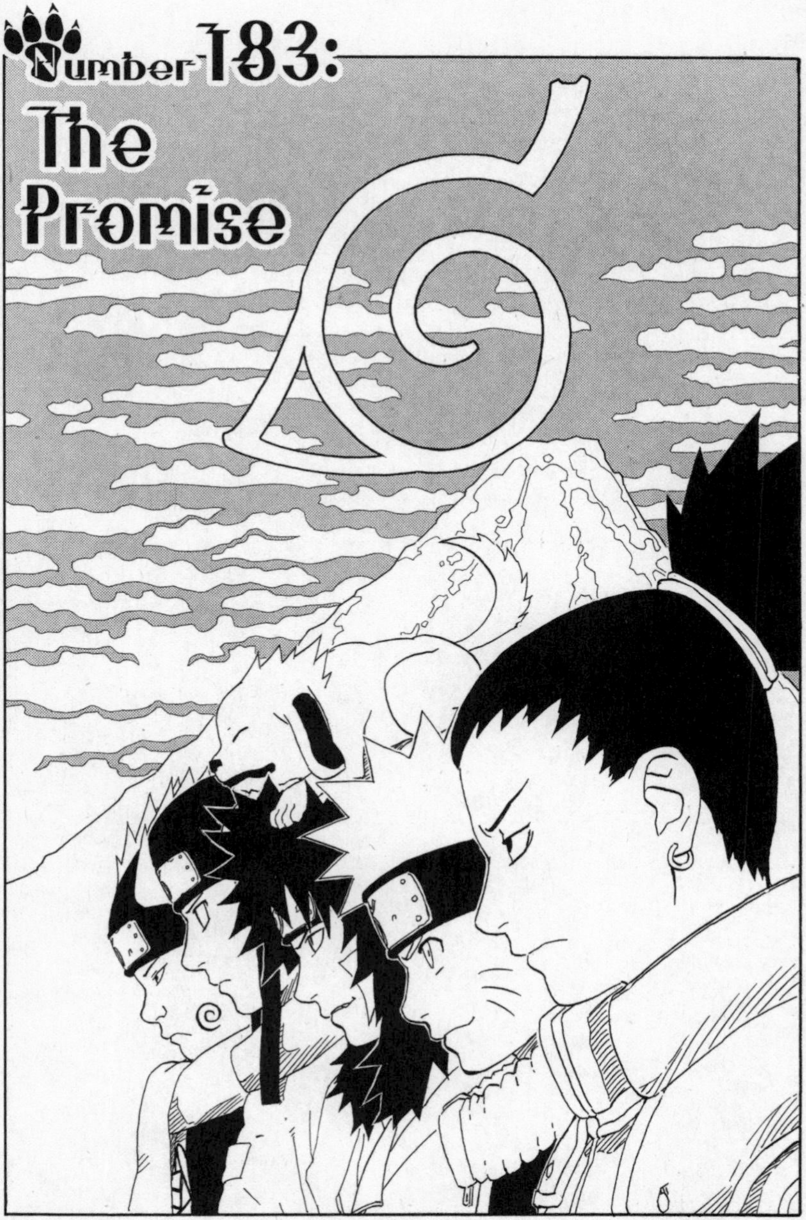
Number 183:
The Promise

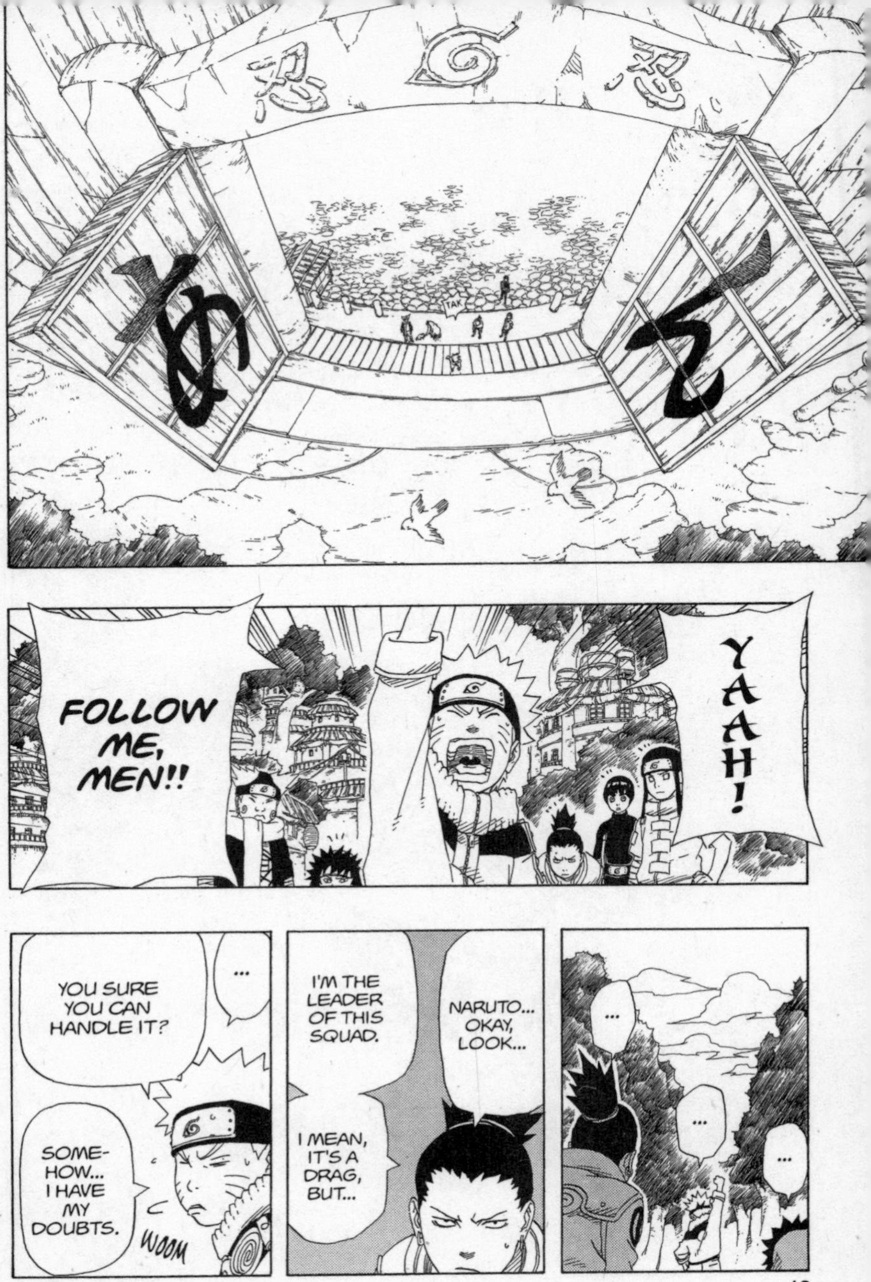
TAK
YAAH!
FOLLOW ME, MEN!!
...
...
...
NARUTO... OKAY, LOOK...
I'M THE LEADER OF THIS SQUAD.
I MEAN, IT'S A DRAG, BUT...
...
YOU SURE YOU CAN HANDLE IT?
SOME-HOW... I HAVE MY DOUBTS.
WOOM

READ THIS WAY

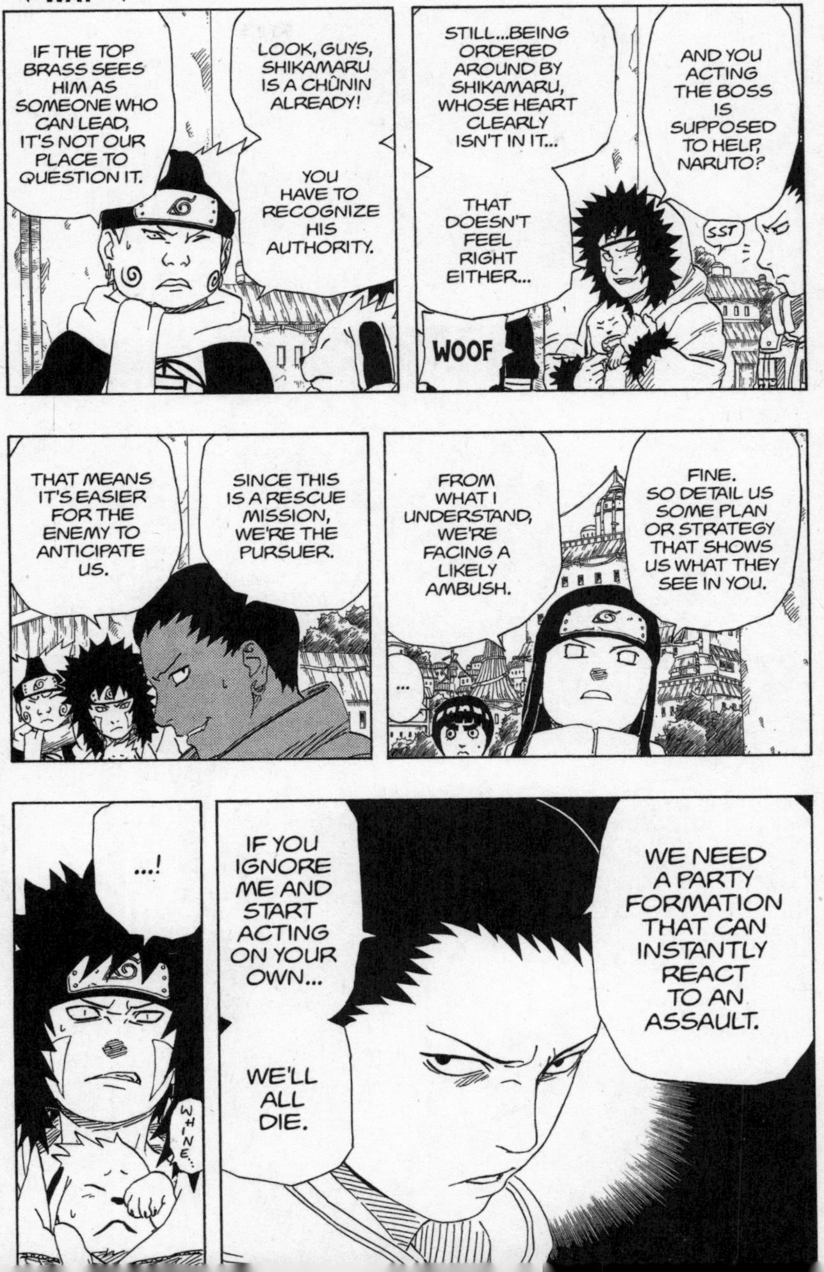
AND YOU ACTING THE BOSS IS SUPPOSED TO HELP, NARUTO?
STILL...BEING ORDERED AROUND BY SHIKAMARU, WHOSE HEART CLEARLY ISN'T IN IT...
THAT DOESN'T FEEL RIGHT EITHER...
SST
WOOF
LOOK, GUYS, SHIKAMARU IS A CHŪNIN ALREADY!
YOU HAVE TO RECOGNIZE HIS AUTHORITY.
IF THE TOP BRASS SEES HIM AS SOMEONE WHO CAN LEAD, IT'S NOT OUR PLACE TO QUESTION IT.
FINE. SO DETAIL US SOME PLAN OR STRATEGY THAT SHOWS US WHAT THEY SEE IN YOU.
FROM WHAT I UNDERSTAND, WE'RE FACING A LIKELY AMBUSH.
...
SINCE THIS IS A RESCUE MISSION, WE'RE THE PURSUER.
THAT MEANS IT'S EASIER FOR THE ENEMY TO ANTICIPATE US.
WE NEED A PARTY FORMATION THAT CAN INSTANTLY REACT TO AN ASSAULT.
IF YOU IGNORE ME AND START ACTING ON YOUR OWN...
WE'LL ALL DIE.
...!
WHINE...

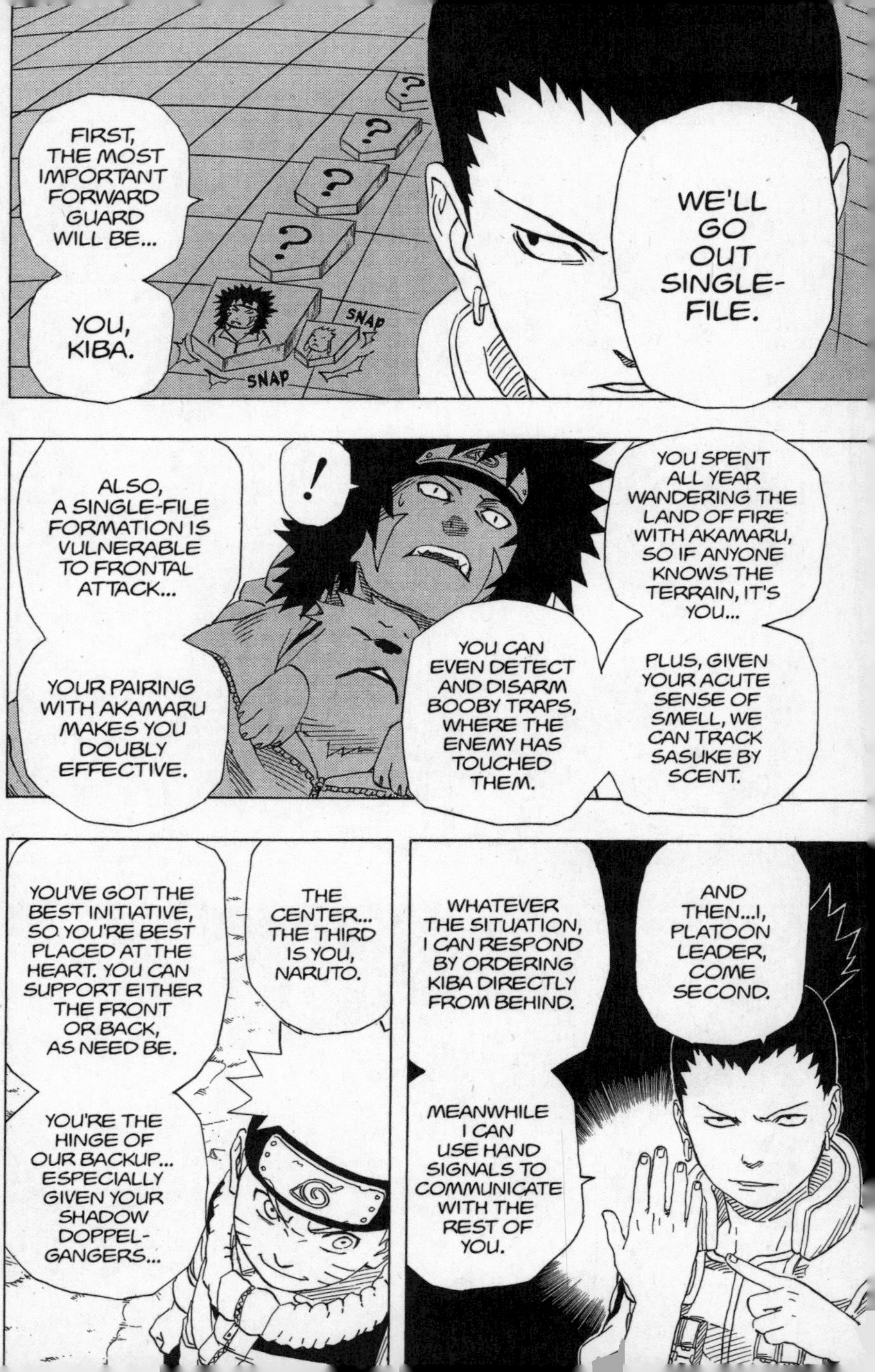
WE'LL GO OUT SINGLE-FILE.
FIRST, THE MOST IMPORTANT FORWARD GUARD WILL BE...
YOU, KIBA.
SNAP
SNAP
!
YOU SPENT ALL YEAR WANDERING THE LAND OF FIRE WITH AKAMARU, SO IF ANYONE KNOWS THE TERRAIN, IT'S YOU...
PLUS, GIVEN YOUR ACUTE SENSE OF SMELL, WE CAN TRACK SASUKE BY SCENT.
YOU CAN EVEN DETECT AND DISARM BOOBY TRAPS, WHERE THE ENEMY HAS TOUCHED THEM.
ALSO, A SINGLE-FILE FORMATION IS VULNERABLE TO FRONTAL ATTACK...
YOUR PAIRING WITH AKAMARU MAKES YOU DOUBLY EFFECTIVE.
AND THEN...I, PLATOON LEADER, COME SECOND.
WHATEVER THE SITUATION, I CAN RESPOND BY ORDERING KIBA DIRECTLY FROM BEHIND.
MEANWHILE I CAN USE HAND SIGNALS TO COMMUNICATE WITH THE REST OF YOU.
THE CENTER... THE THIRD IS YOU, NARUTO.
YOU'VE GOT THE BEST INITIATIVE, SO YOU'RE BEST PLACED AT THE HEART. YOU CAN SUPPORT EITHER THE FRONT OR BACK, AS NEED BE.
YOU'RE THE HINGE OF OUR BACKUP... ESPECIALLY GIVEN YOUR SHADOW DOPPEL-GANGERS...

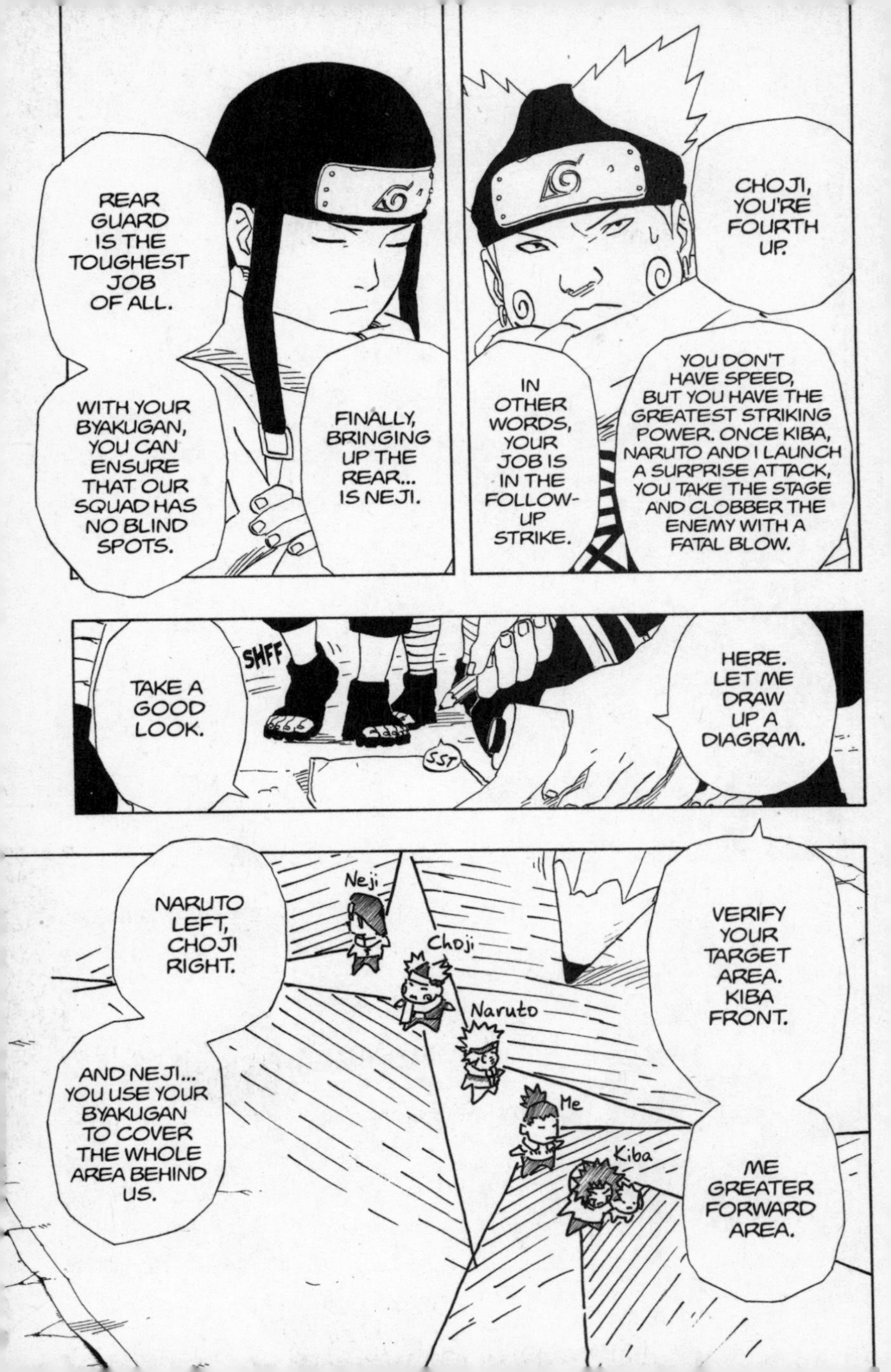
CHOJI, YOU'RE FOURTH UP.
YOU DON'T HAVE SPEED, BUT YOU HAVE THE GREATEST STRIKING POWER. ONCE KIBA, NARUTO AND I LAUNCH A SURPRISE ATTACK, YOU TAKE THE STAGE AND CLOBBER THE ENEMY WITH A FATAL BLOW.
IN OTHER WORDS, YOUR JOB IS IN THE FOLLOW-UP STRIKE.
FINALLY, BRINGING UP THE REAR... IS NEJI.
REAR GUARD IS THE TOUGHEST JOB OF ALL.
WITH YOUR BYAKUGAN, YOU CAN ENSURE THAT OUR SQUAD HAS NO BLIND SPOTS.
HERE. LET ME DRAW UP A DIAGRAM.
SST
SHFF
TAKE A GOOD LOOK.
VERIFY YOUR TARGET AREA. KIBA FRONT.
ME GREATER FORWARD AREA.
Neji
Choji
Naruto
Me
Kiba
NARUTO LEFT, CHOJI RIGHT.
AND NEJI... YOU USE YOUR BYAKUGAN TO COVER THE WHOLE AREA BEHIND US.

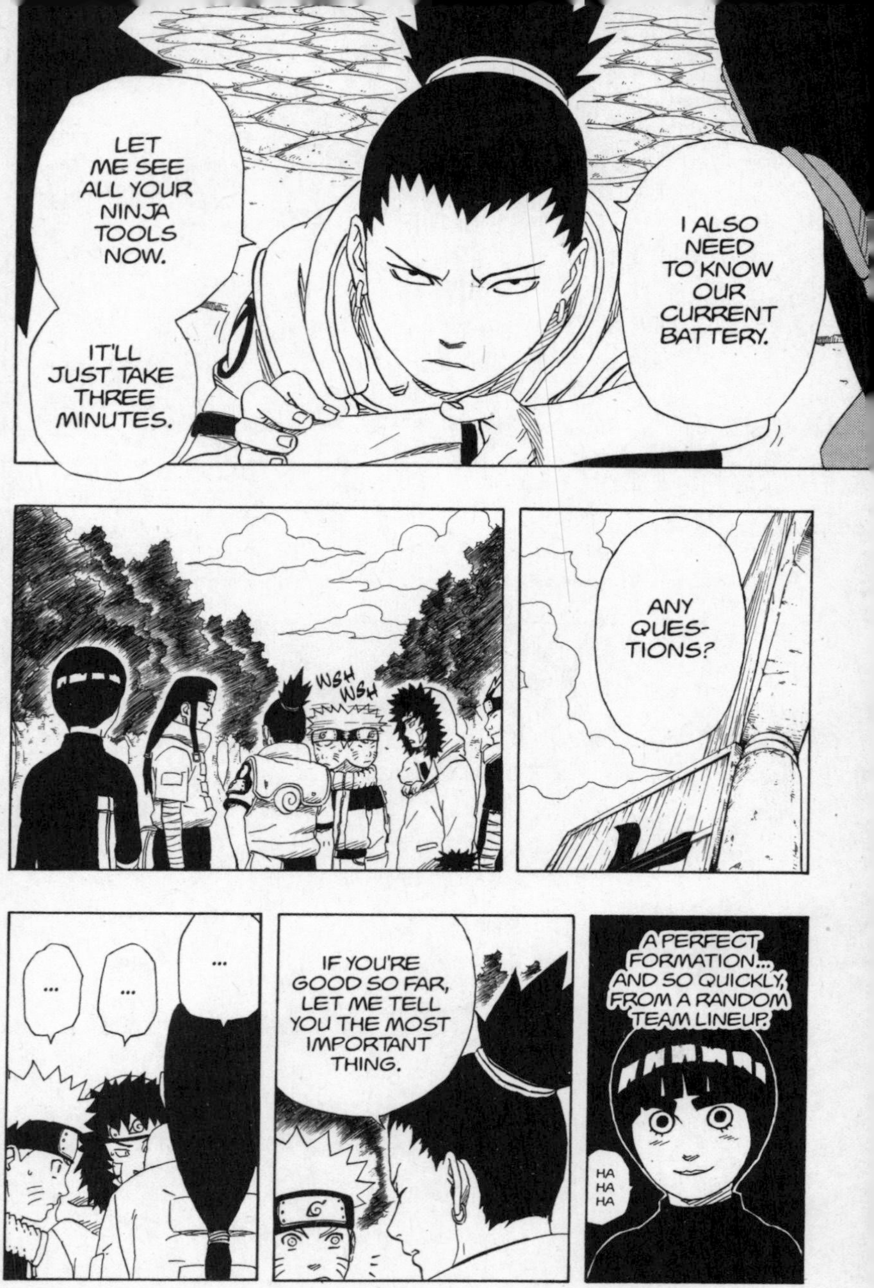
LET ME SEE ALL YOUR NINJA TOOLS NOW.
IT'LL JUST TAKE THREE MINUTES.
I ALSO NEED TO KNOW OUR CURRENT BATTERY.
ANY QUESTIONS?
WSH WSH
A PERFECT FORMATION... AND SO QUICKLY, FROM A RANDOM TEAM LINEUP.
HA HA HA
IF YOU'RE GOOD SO FAR, LET ME TELL YOU THE MOST IMPORTANT THING.
...
...
...

READ THIS WAY

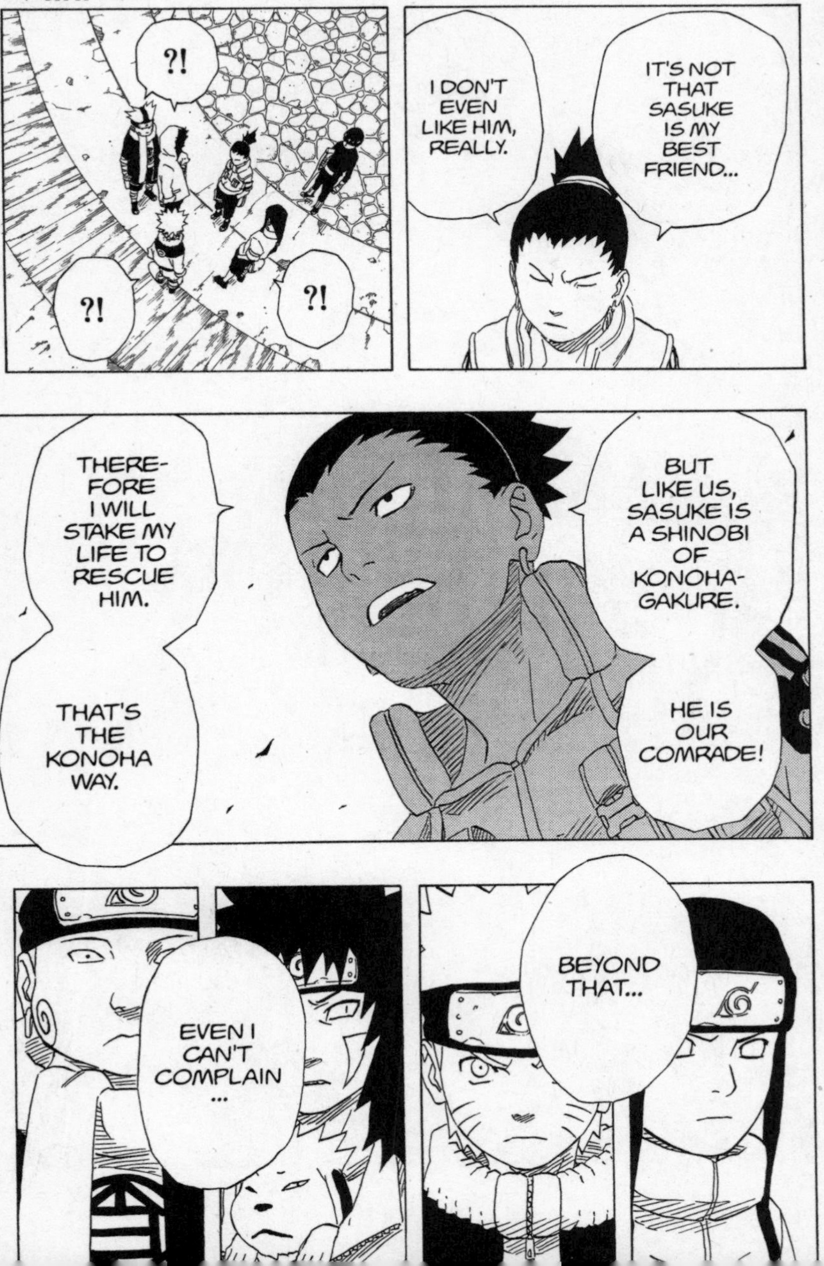

IT'S NOT THAT SASUKE IS MY BEST FRIEND...
I DON'T EVEN LIKE HIM, REALLY.
?!
?!
?!
BUT LIKE US, SASUKE IS A SHINOBI OF KONOHA-GAKURE.
HE IS OUR COMRADE!
THEREFORE I WILL STAKE MY LIFE TO RESCUE HIM.
THAT'S THE KONOHA WAY.
BEYOND THAT...
EVEN I CAN'T COMPLAIN ...

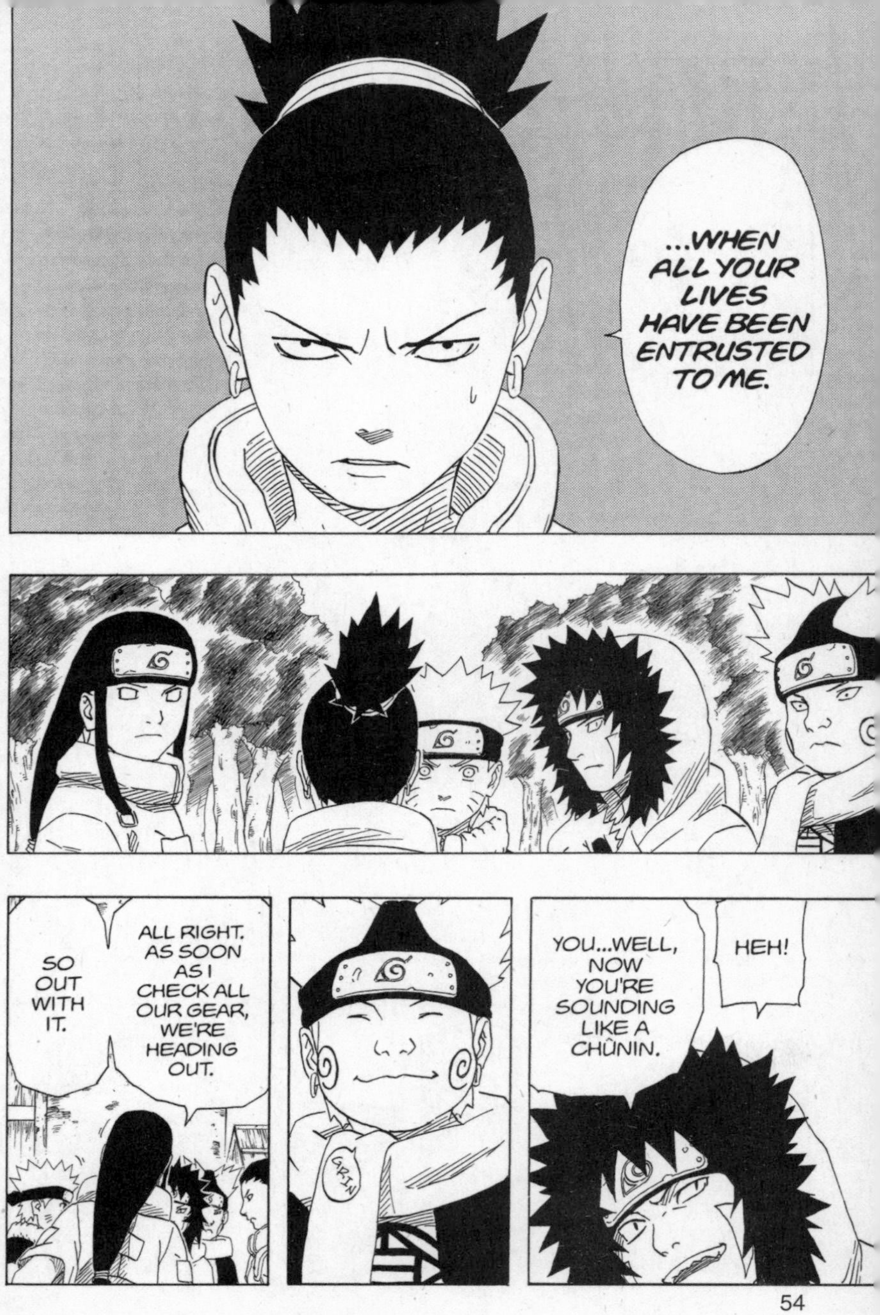
...WHEN ALL YOUR LIVES HAVE BEEN ENTRUSTED TO ME.
HEH!
YOU...WELL, NOW YOU'RE SOUNDING LIKE A CHÛNIN.
GRIN
ALL RIGHT. AS SOON AS I CHECK ALL OUR GEAR, WE'RE HEADING OUT.
SO OUT WITH IT.

READ THIS WAY

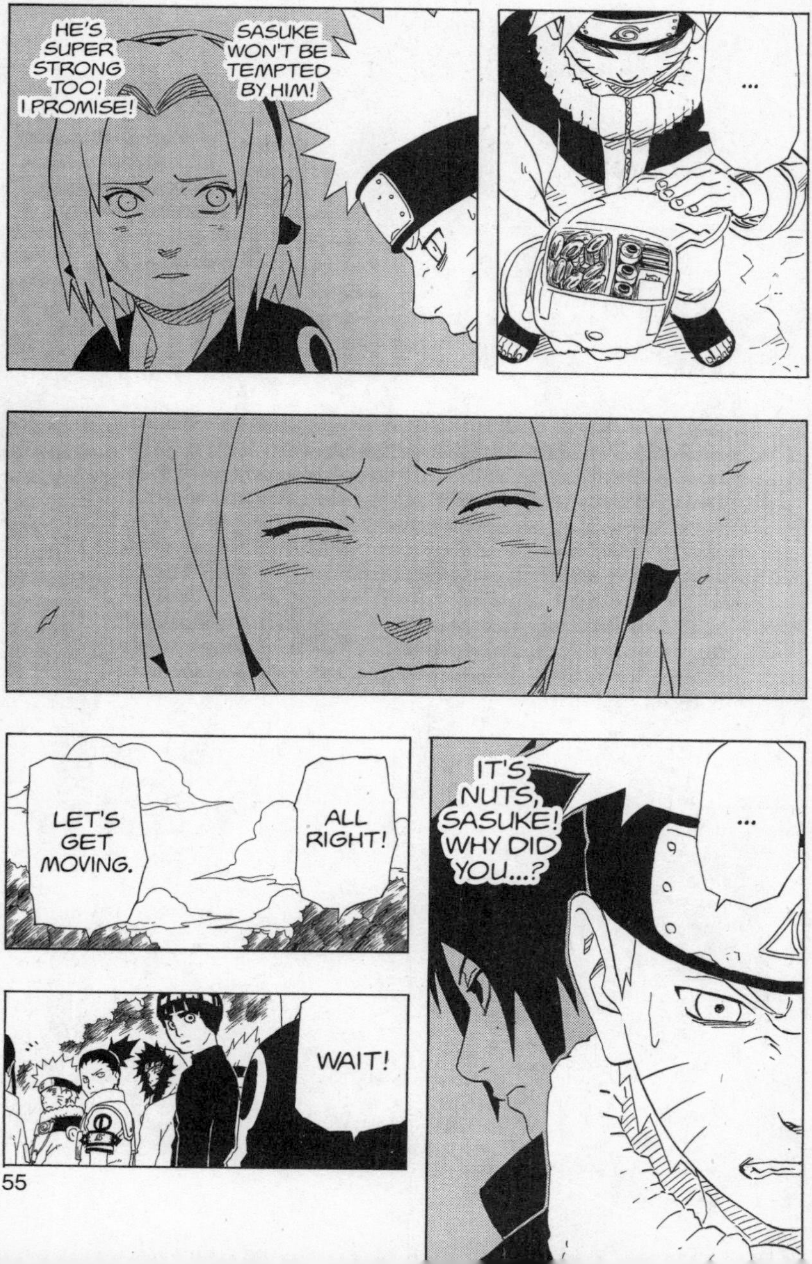

...
SASUKE WON'T BE TEMPTED BY HIM!
HE'S SUPER STRONG TOO! I PROMISE!
...
IT'S NUTS, SASUKE! WHY DID YOU...?
ALL RIGHT!
LET'S GET MOVING.
WAIT!

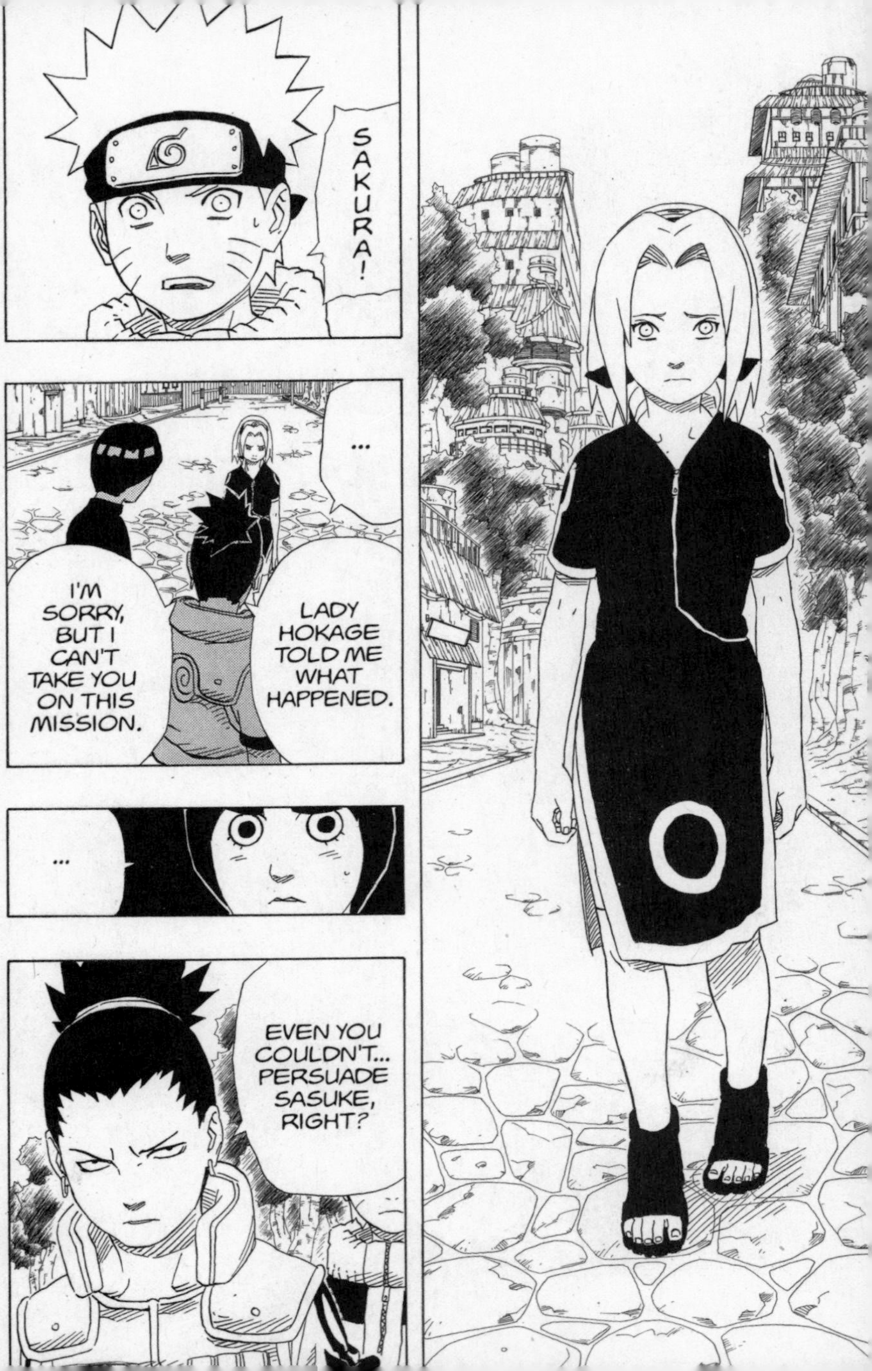
SAKURA!
...
LADY HOKAGE TOLD ME WHAT HAPPENED.
I'M SORRY, BUT I CAN'T TAKE YOU ON THIS MISSION.
...
EVEN YOU COULDN'T... PERSUADE SASUKE, RIGHT?

READ THIS WAY

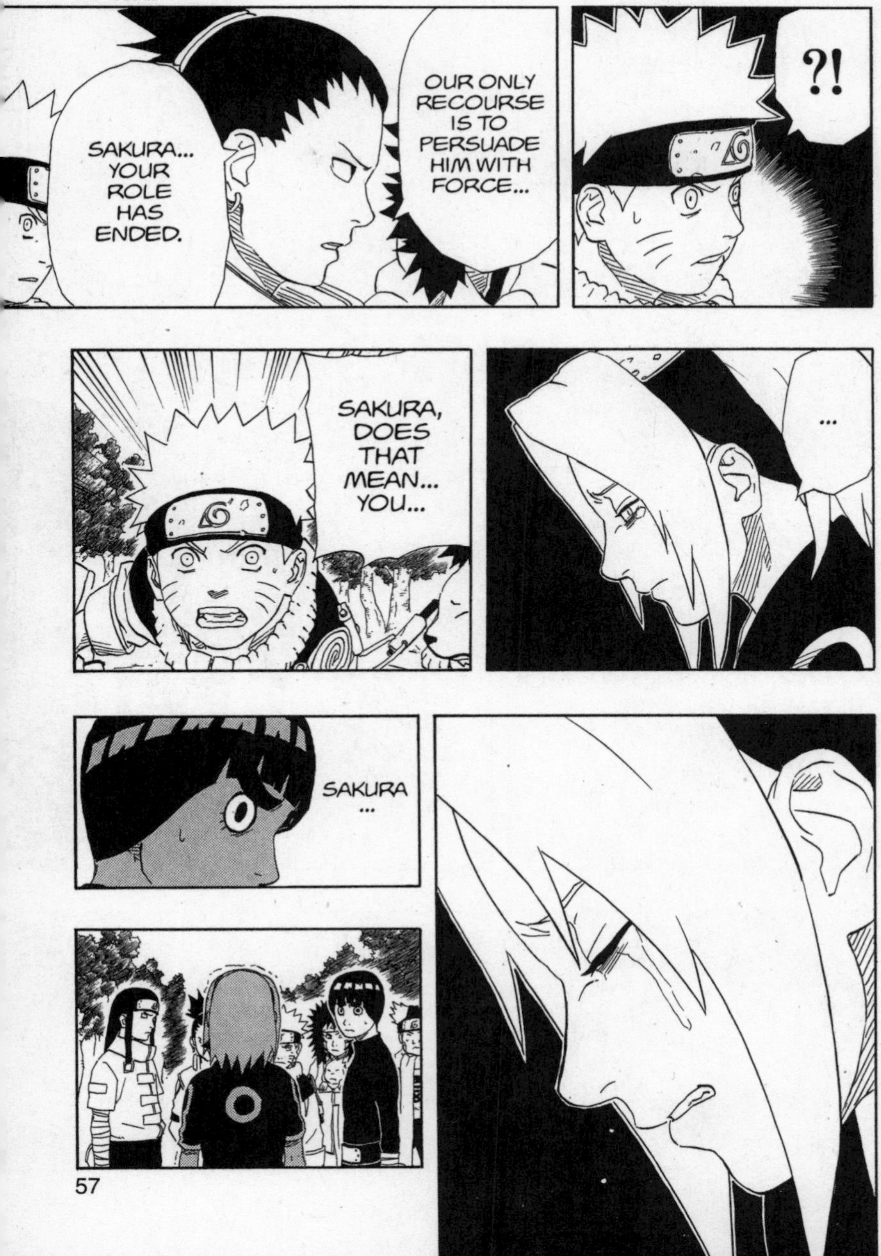
?!
OUR ONLY RECOURSE IS TO PERSUADE HIM WITH FORCE...
SAKURA... YOUR ROLE HAS ENDED.
...
SAKURA, DOES THAT MEAN... YOU...
SAKURA ...

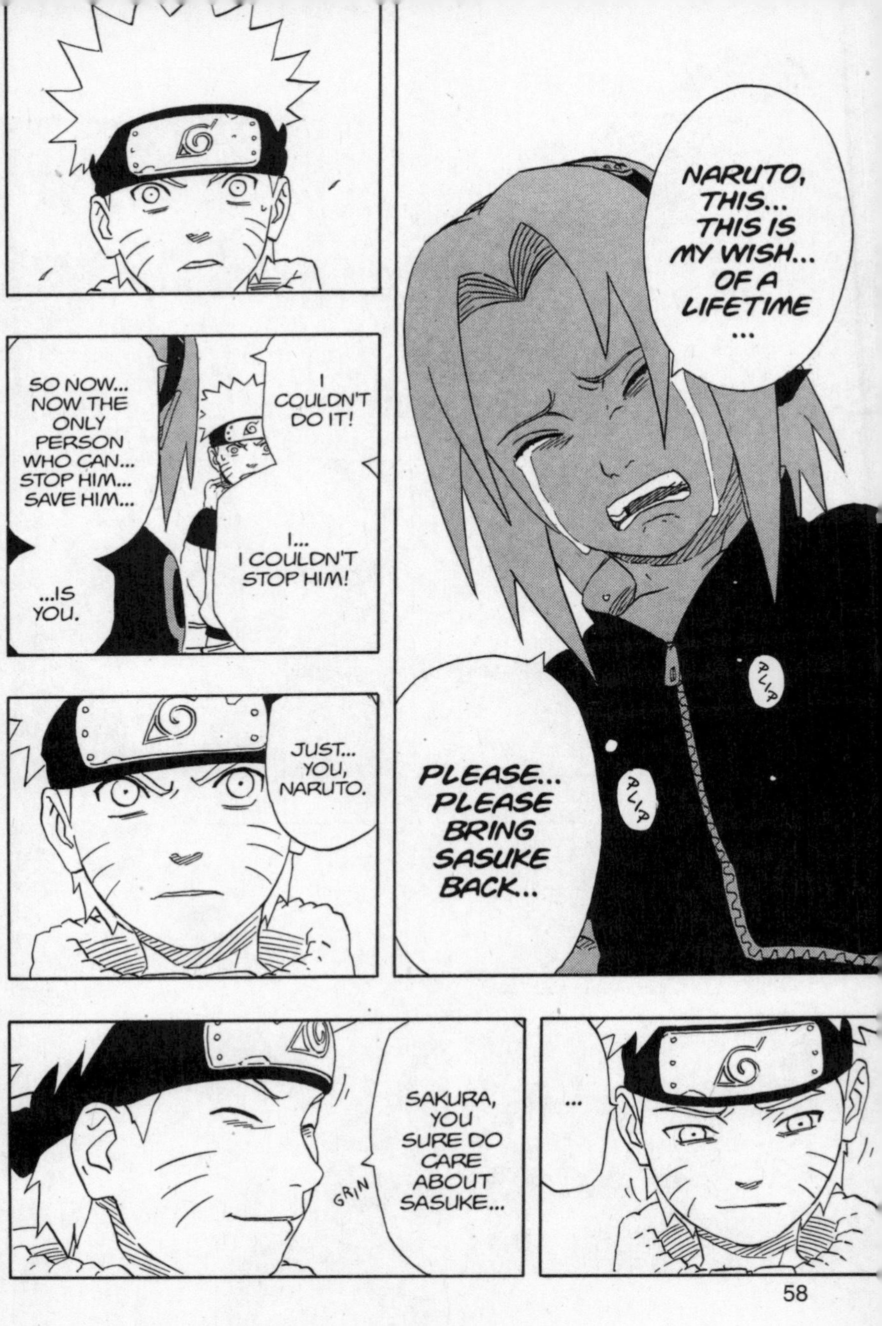
NARUTO, THIS... THIS IS MY WISH... OF A LIFETIME...
PLEASE... PLEASE BRING SASUKE BACK..
FLIP
FLIP
I COULDN'T DO IT!
I... I COULDN'T STOP HIM!
SO NOW... NOW THE ONLY PERSON WHO CAN... STOP HIM... SAVE HIM...
...IS YOU.
JUST... YOU, NARUTO.
...
SAKURA, YOU SURE DO CARE ABOUT SASUKE...
GRIN

READ THIS WAY

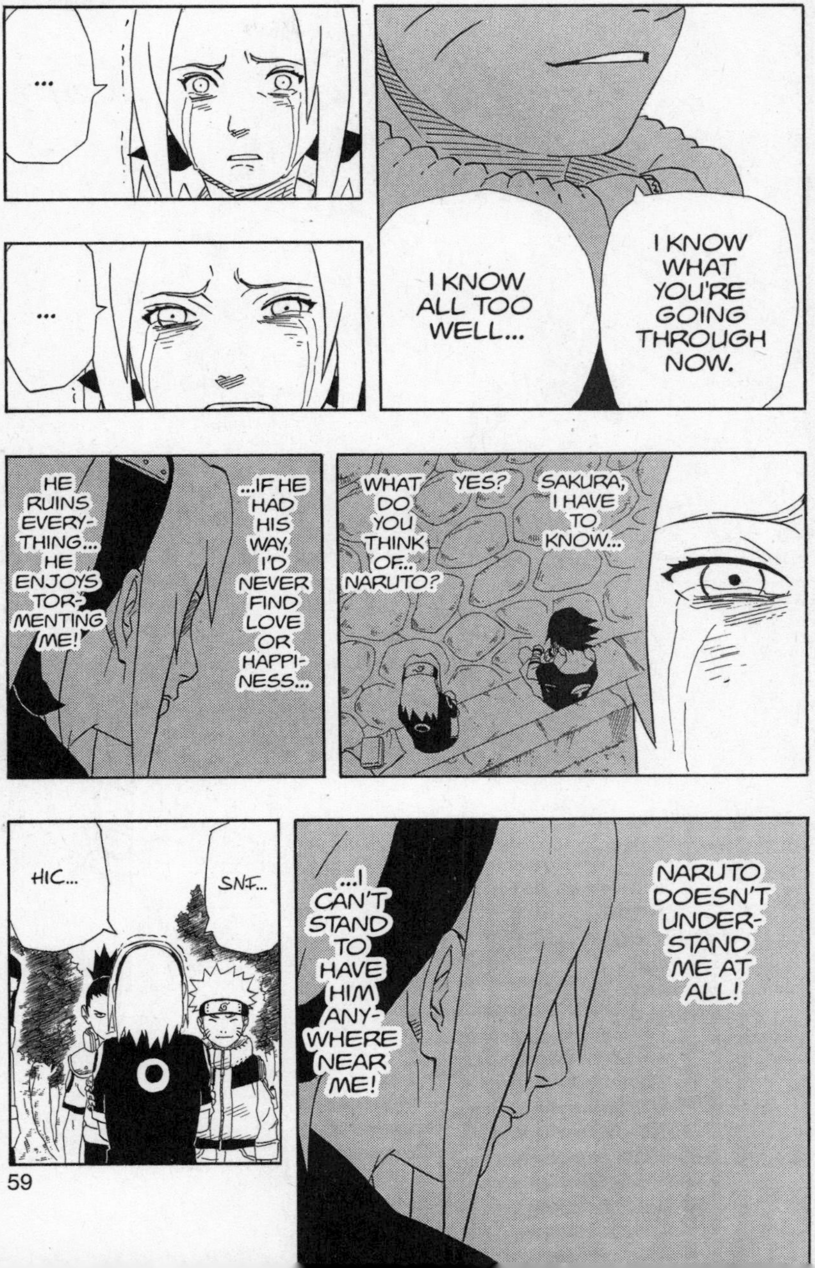

I KNOW WHAT YOU'RE GOING THROUGH NOW.
I KNOW ALL TOO WELL...
...
...
SAKURA, I HAVE TO KNOW...
YES?
WHAT DO YOU THINK OF... NARUTO?
...IF HE HAD HIS WAY, I'D NEVER FIND LOVE OR HAPPINESS...
HE RUINS EVERYTHING... HE ENJOYS TORMENTING ME!
NARUTO DOESN'T UNDERSTAND ME AT ALL!
...I CAN'T STAND TO HAVE HIM ANYWHERE NEAR ME!
SNF...
HIC...

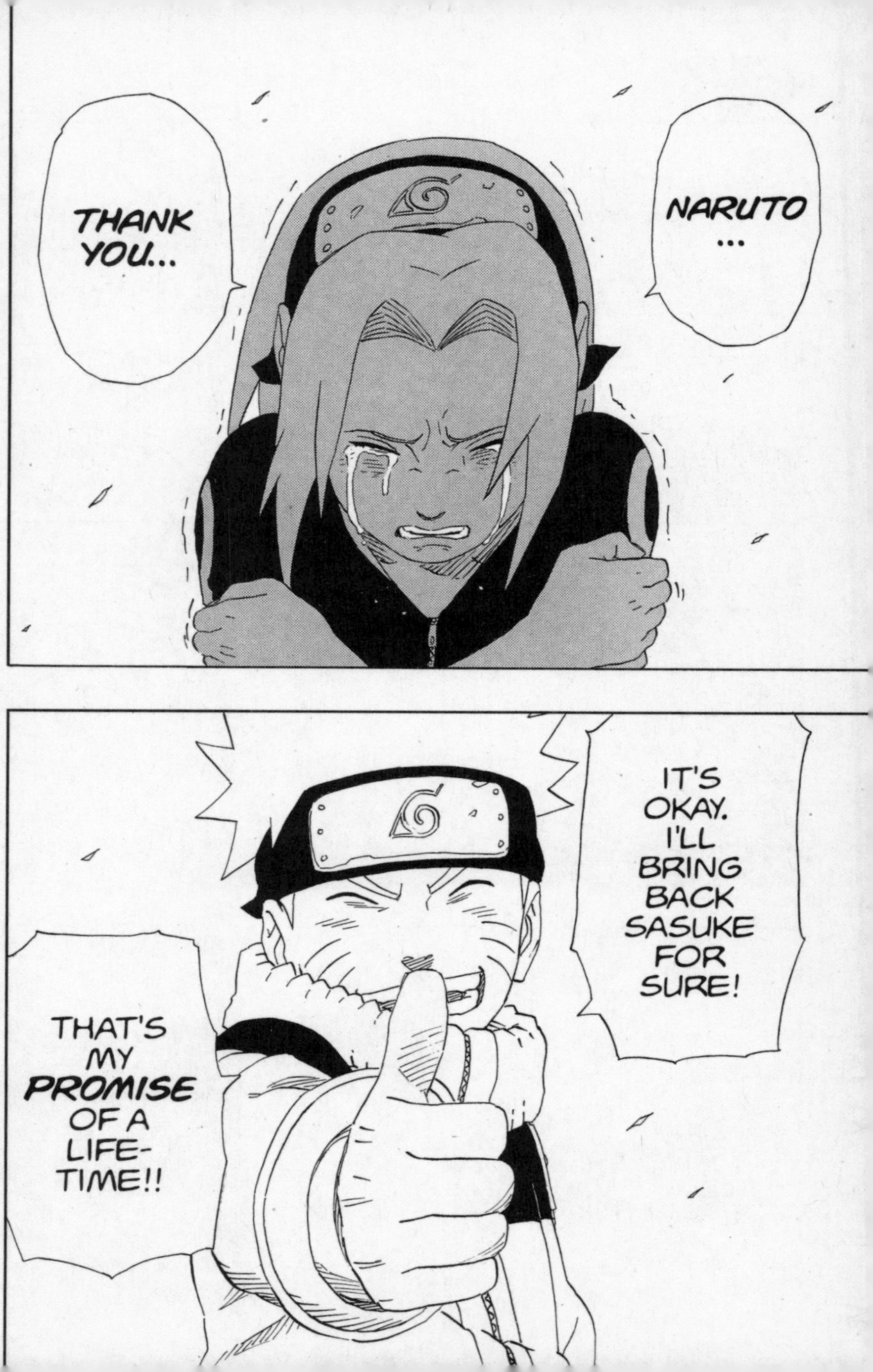
NARUTO ...
THANK YOU...
IT'S OKAY. I'LL BRING BACK SASUKE FOR SURE!
THAT'S MY PROMISE OF A LIFE-TIME!!

READ THIS WAY

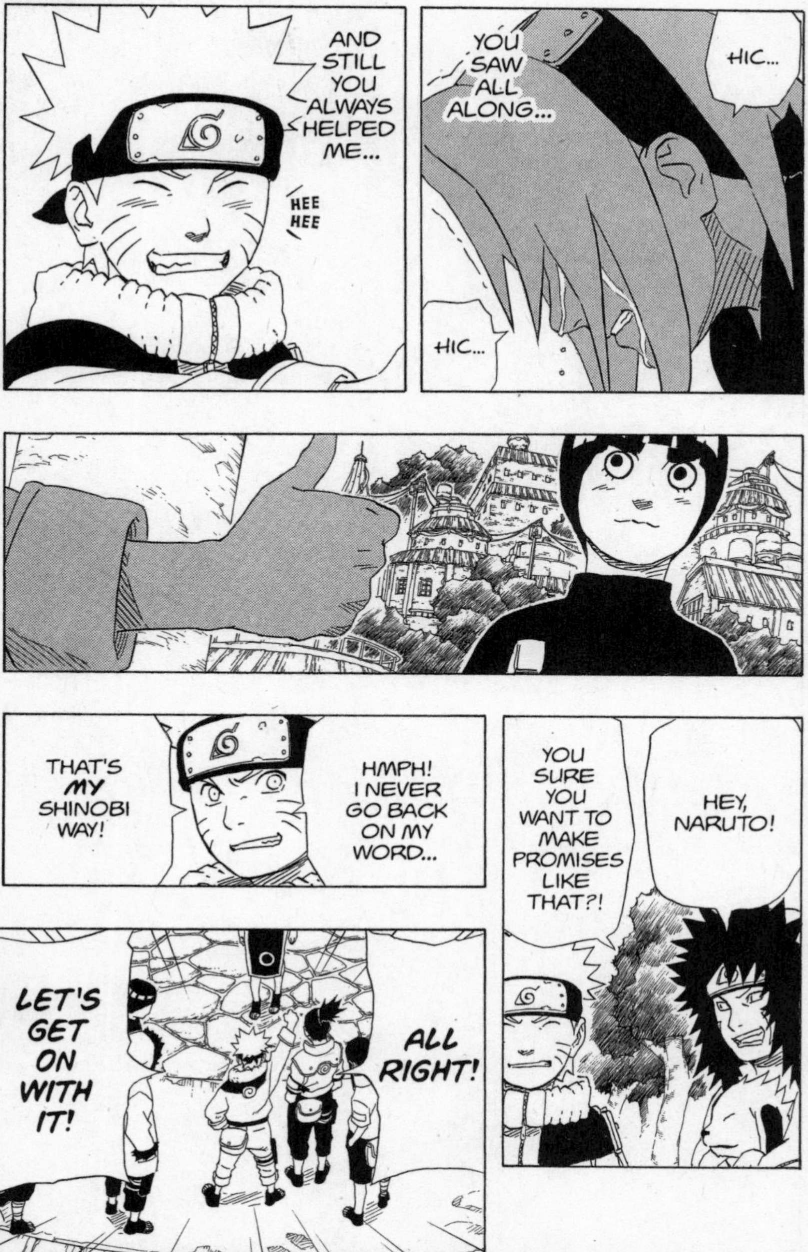

HIC...
YOU SAW ALL ALONG...
HIC...
AND STILL YOU ALWAYS HELPED ME...
HEE HEE
HEY, NARUTO!
YOU SURE YOU WANT TO MAKE PROMISES LIKE THAT?!
HMPH! I NEVER GO BACK ON MY WORD...
THAT'S *MY* SHINOBI WAY!
ALL RIGHT!
LET'S GET ON WITH IT!

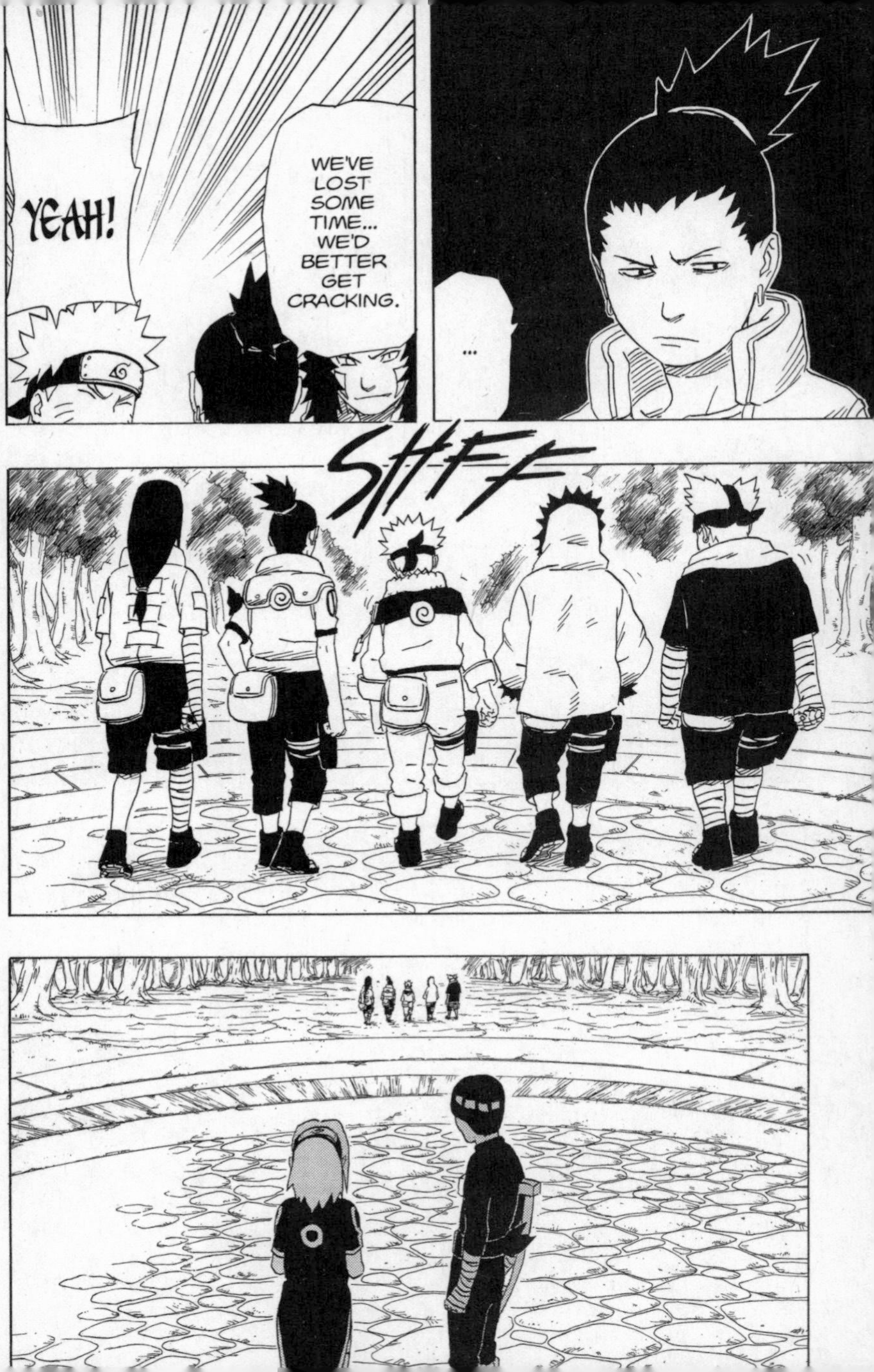
...
WE'VE LOST SOME TIME... WE'D BETTER GET CRACKING.
YEAH!
SHFF

READ THIS WAY

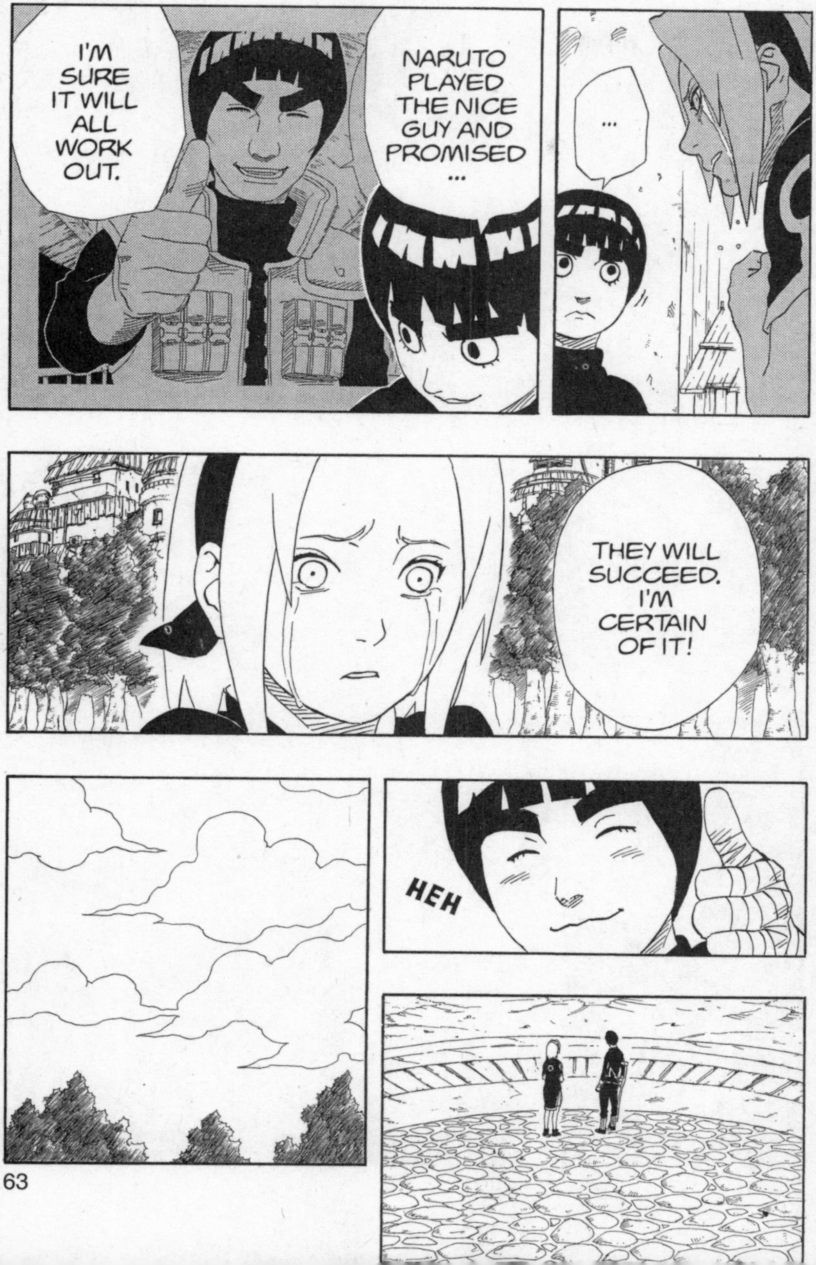

...
NARUTO PLAYED THE NICE GUY AND PROMISED ...
I'M SURE IT WILL ALL WORK OUT.
THEY WILL SUCCEED. I'M CERTAIN OF IT!
HEH

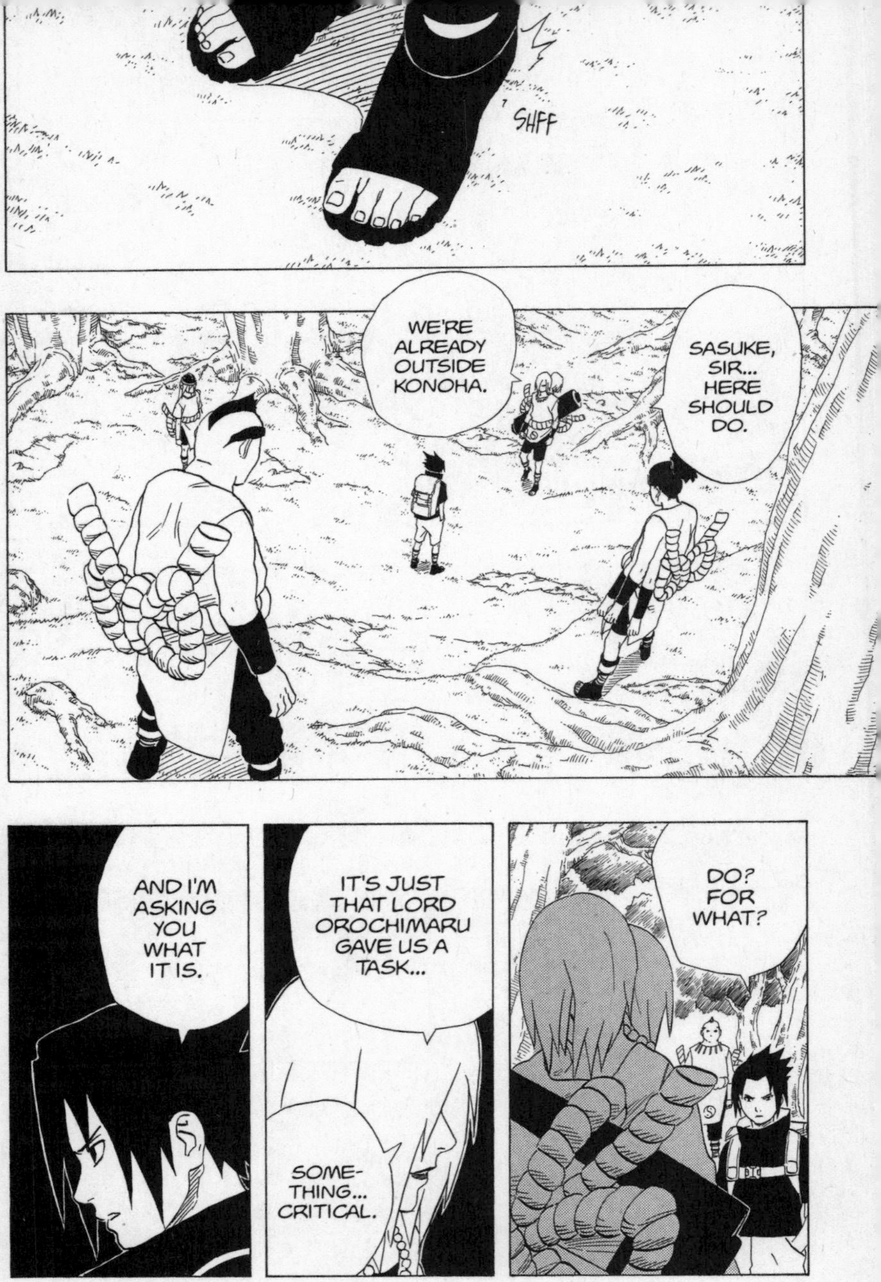
SHFF
SASUKE, SIR... HERE SHOULD DO.
WE'RE ALREADY OUTSIDE KONOHA.
DO? FOR WHAT?
IT'S JUST THAT LORD OROCHIMARU GAVE US A TASK...
SOME-THING... CRITICAL.
AND I'M ASKING YOU WHAT IT IS.

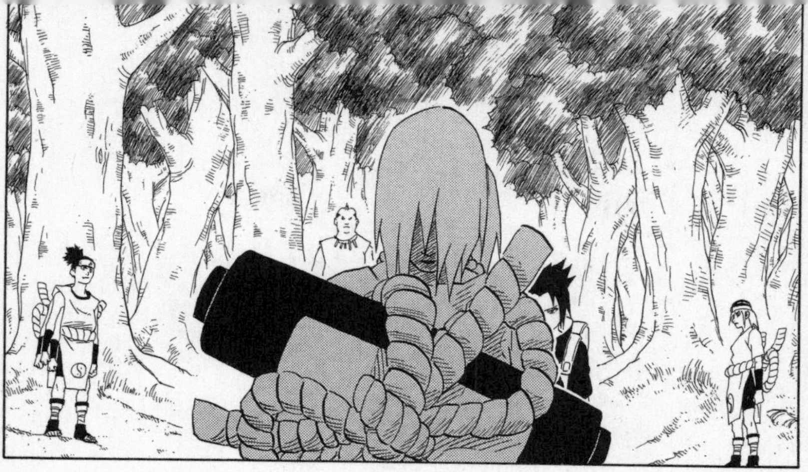

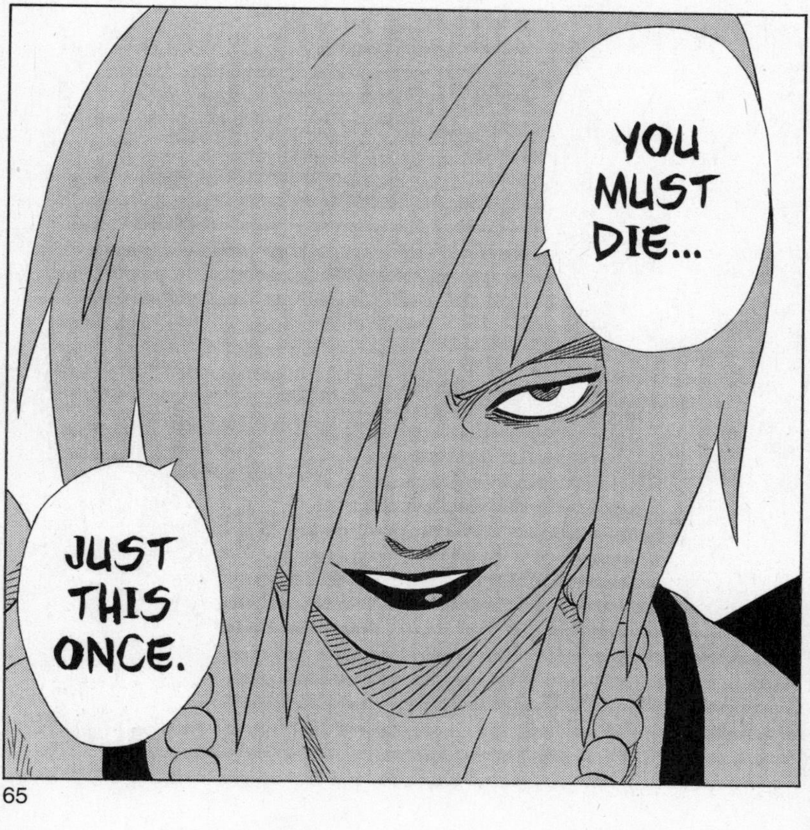
YOU MUST DIE...
JUST THIS ONCE.

Number 184: Sound Vs. Leaf!!

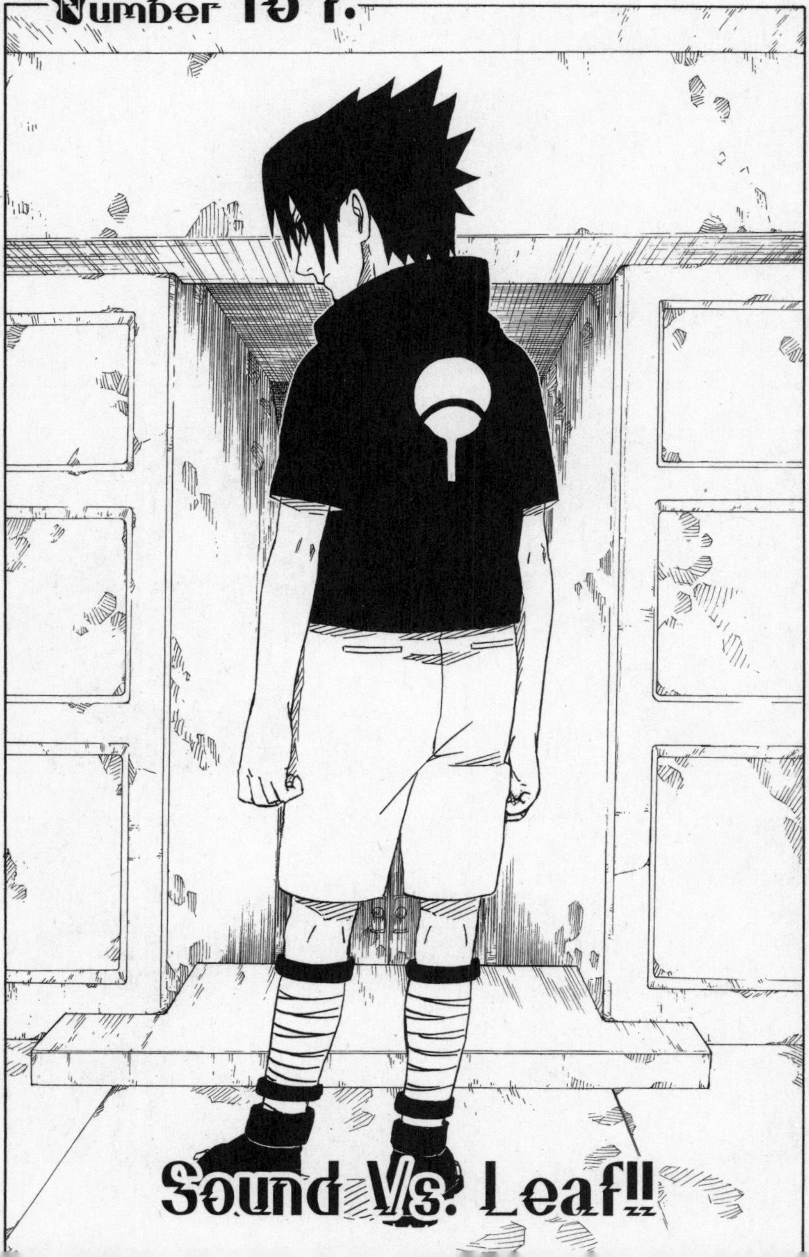

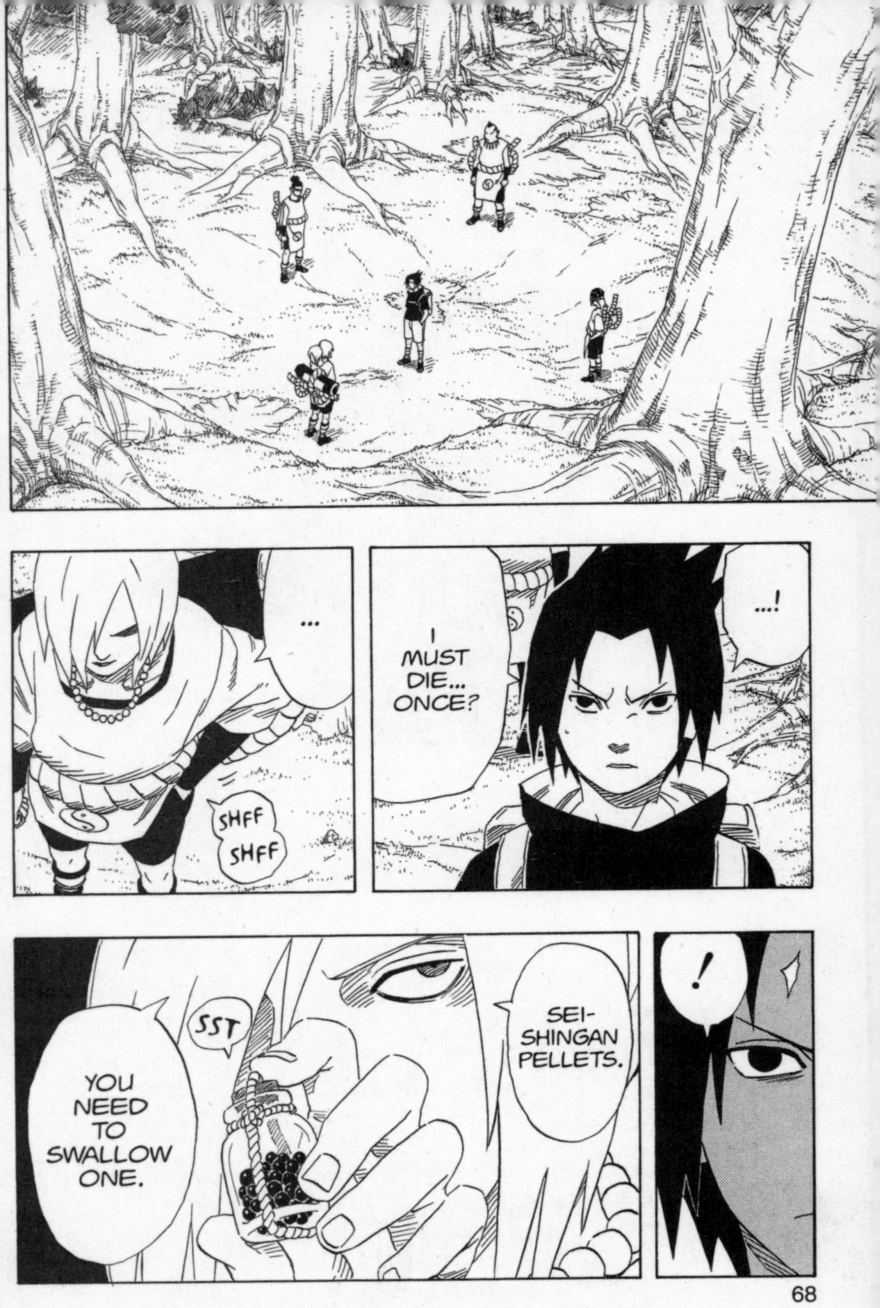
...!
I MUST DIE... ONCE?
...
SHFF SHFF
!
SEI-SHINGAN PELLETS.
SST
YOU NEED TO SWALLOW ONE.

READ THIS WAY

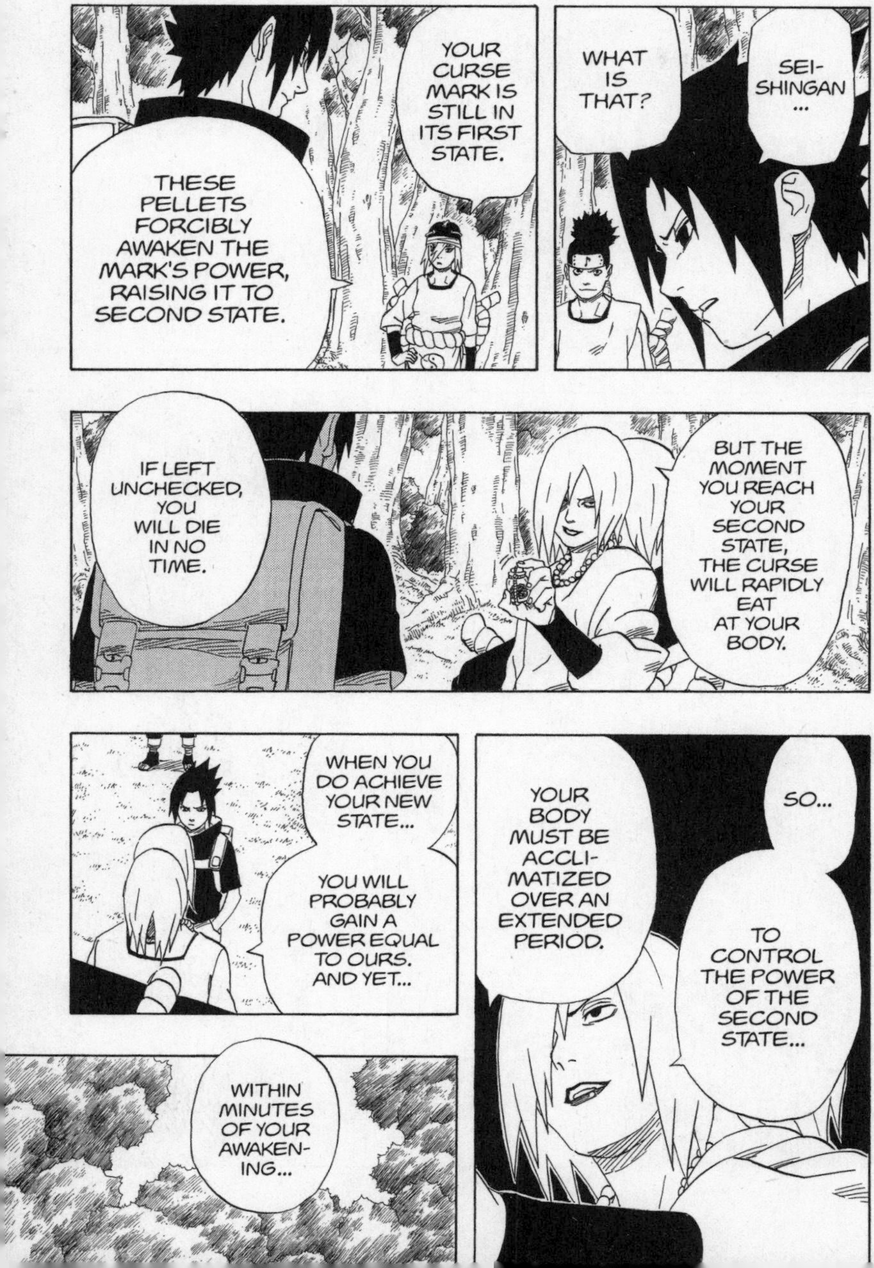
SEI-SHINGAN...
WHAT IS THAT?
YOUR CURSE MARK IS STILL IN ITS FIRST STATE.
THESE PELLETS FORCIBLY AWAKEN THE MARK'S POWER, RAISING IT TO SECOND STATE.
BUT THE MOMENT YOU REACH YOUR SECOND STATE, THE CURSE WILL RAPIDLY EAT AT YOUR BODY.
IF LEFT UNCHECKED, YOU WILL DIE IN NO TIME.
SO...
YOUR BODY MUST BE ACCLIMATIZED OVER AN EXTENDED PERIOD.
TO CONTROL THE POWER OF THE SECOND STATE...
WHEN YOU DO ACHIEVE YOUR NEW STATE...
YOU WILL PROBABLY GAIN A POWER EQUAL TO OURS. AND YET...
WITHIN MINUTES OF YOUR AWAKENING...

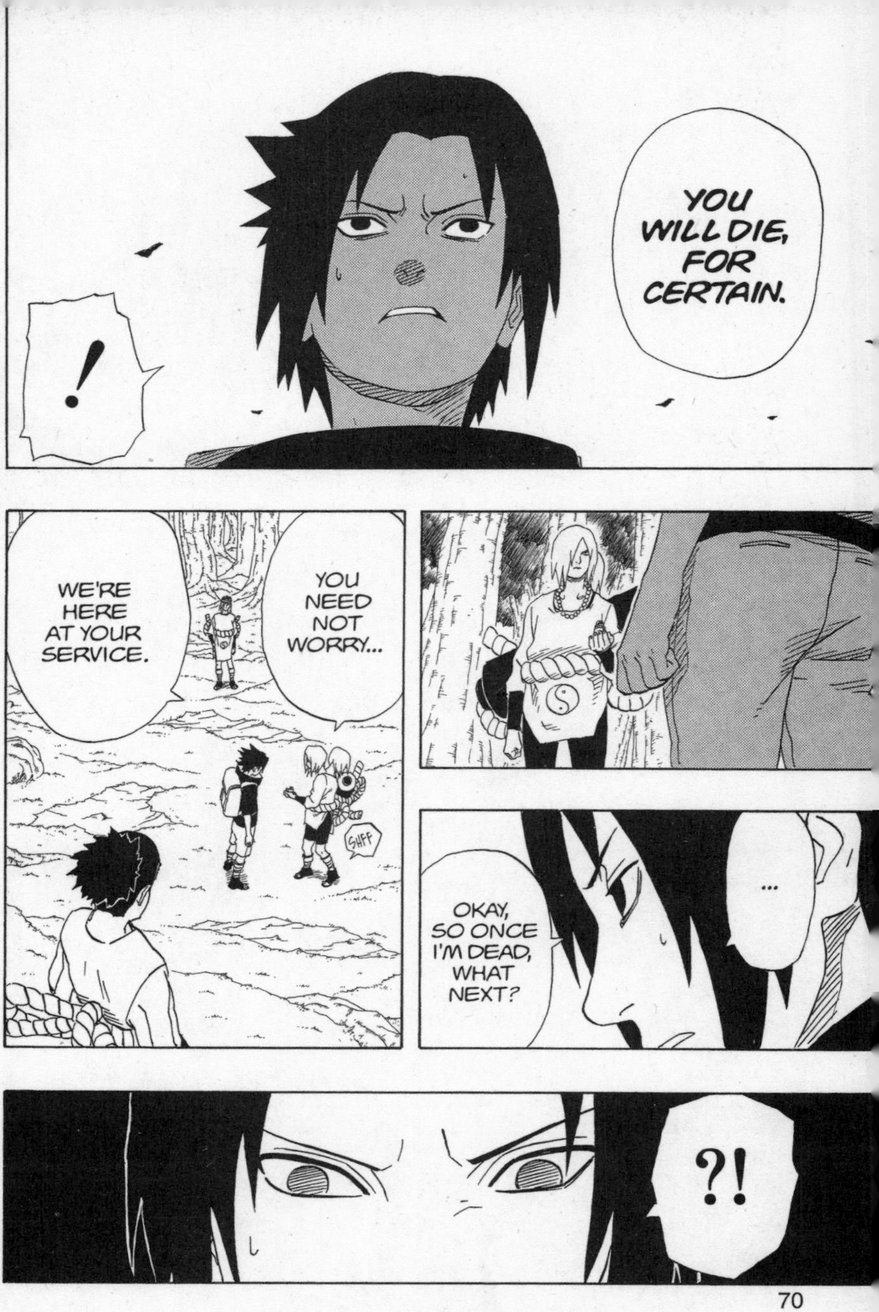
YOU WILL DIE, FOR CERTAIN.
!
...
OKAY, SO ONCE I'M DEAD, WHAT NEXT?
YOU NEED NOT WORRY...
WE'RE HERE AT YOUR SERVICE.
SNIFF
?!

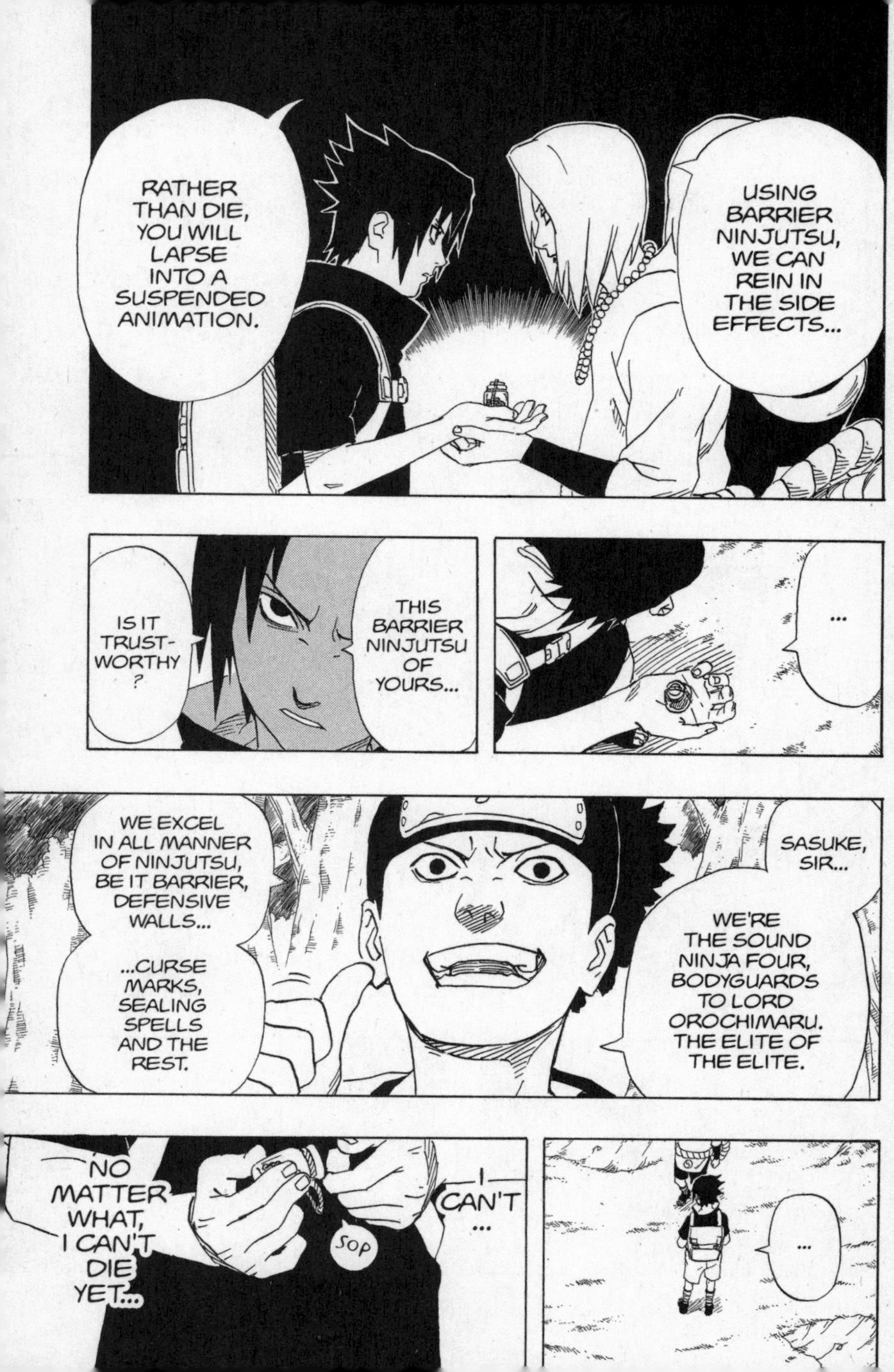
USING BARRIER NINJUTSU, WE CAN REIN IN THE SIDE EFFECTS...
RATHER THAN DIE, YOU WILL LAPSE INTO A SUSPENDED ANIMATION.
...
THIS BARRIER NINJUTSU OF YOURS...
IS IT TRUSTWORTHY?
SASUKE, SIR...
WE'RE THE SOUND NINJA FOUR, BODYGUARDS TO LORD OROCHIMARU. THE ELITE OF THE ELITE.
WE EXCEL IN ALL MANNER OF NINJUTSU, BE IT BARRIER, DEFENSIVE WALLS...
...CURSE MARKS, SEALING SPELLS AND THE REST.
...
I CAN'T...
SOP
NO MATTER WHAT, I CAN'T DIE YET...

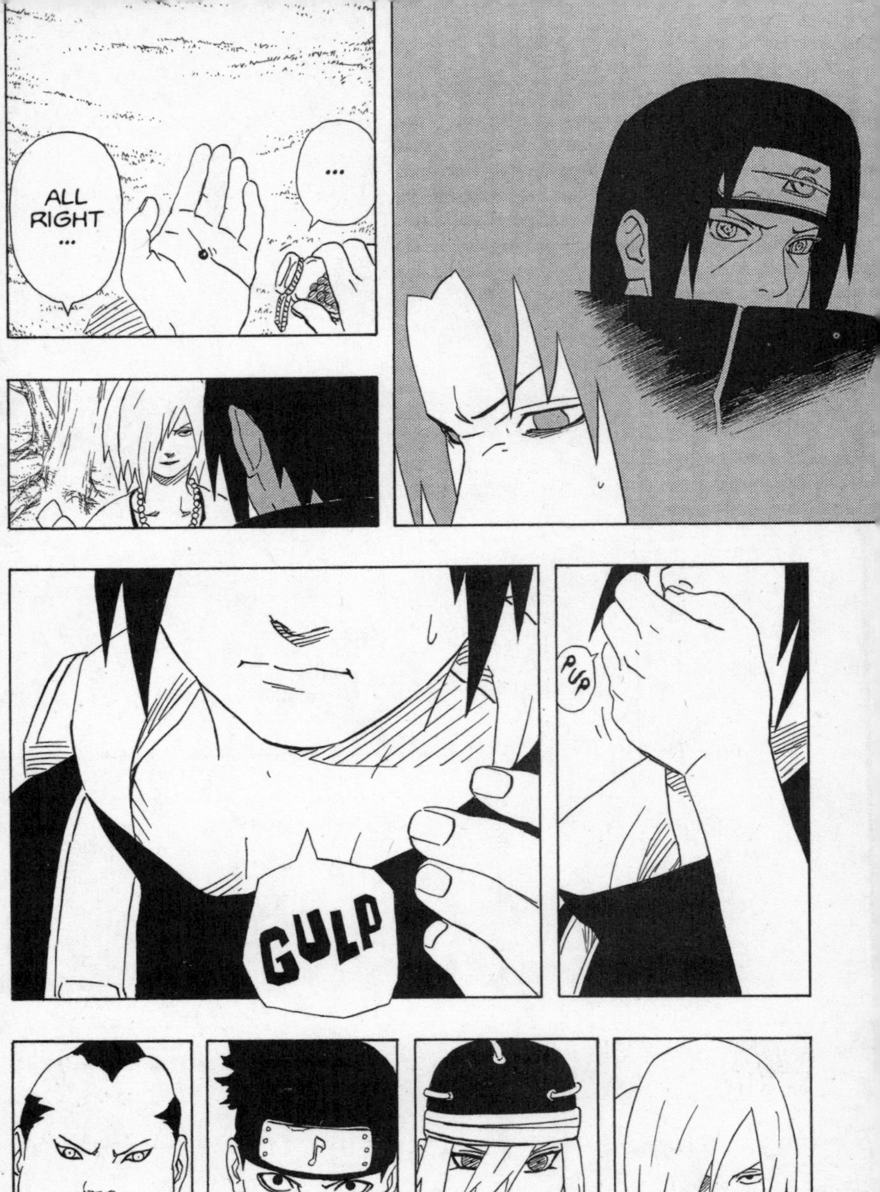
...
ALL RIGHT ...
PUP
GULP

READ THIS WAY

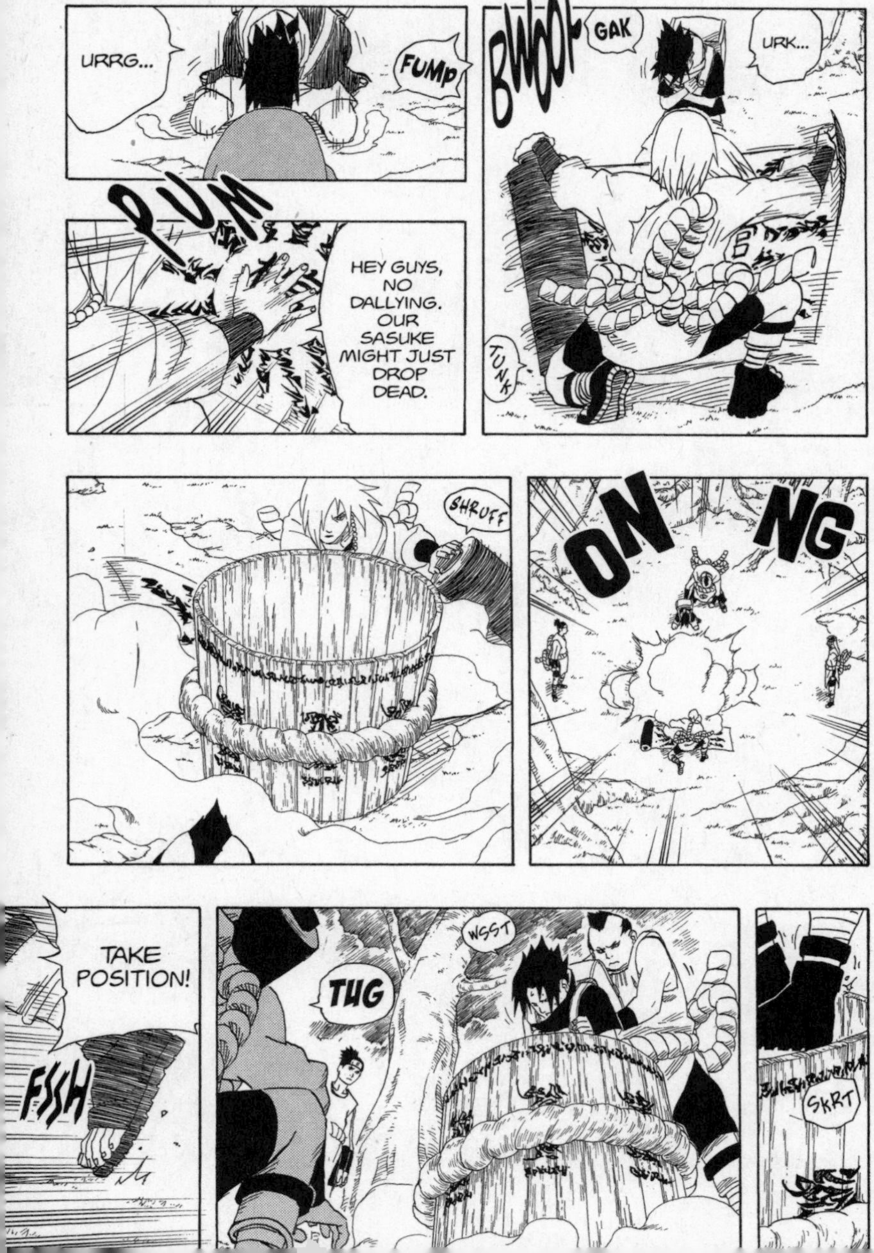
URK...
GAK
BWOOF
TUNK
FUMP
URRG...
HEY GUYS, NO DALLYING. OUR SASUKE MIGHT JUST DROP DEAD.
PUM
ON NG
SHRUFF
SKRT
WSST
TUG
TAKE POSITION!
FSSH

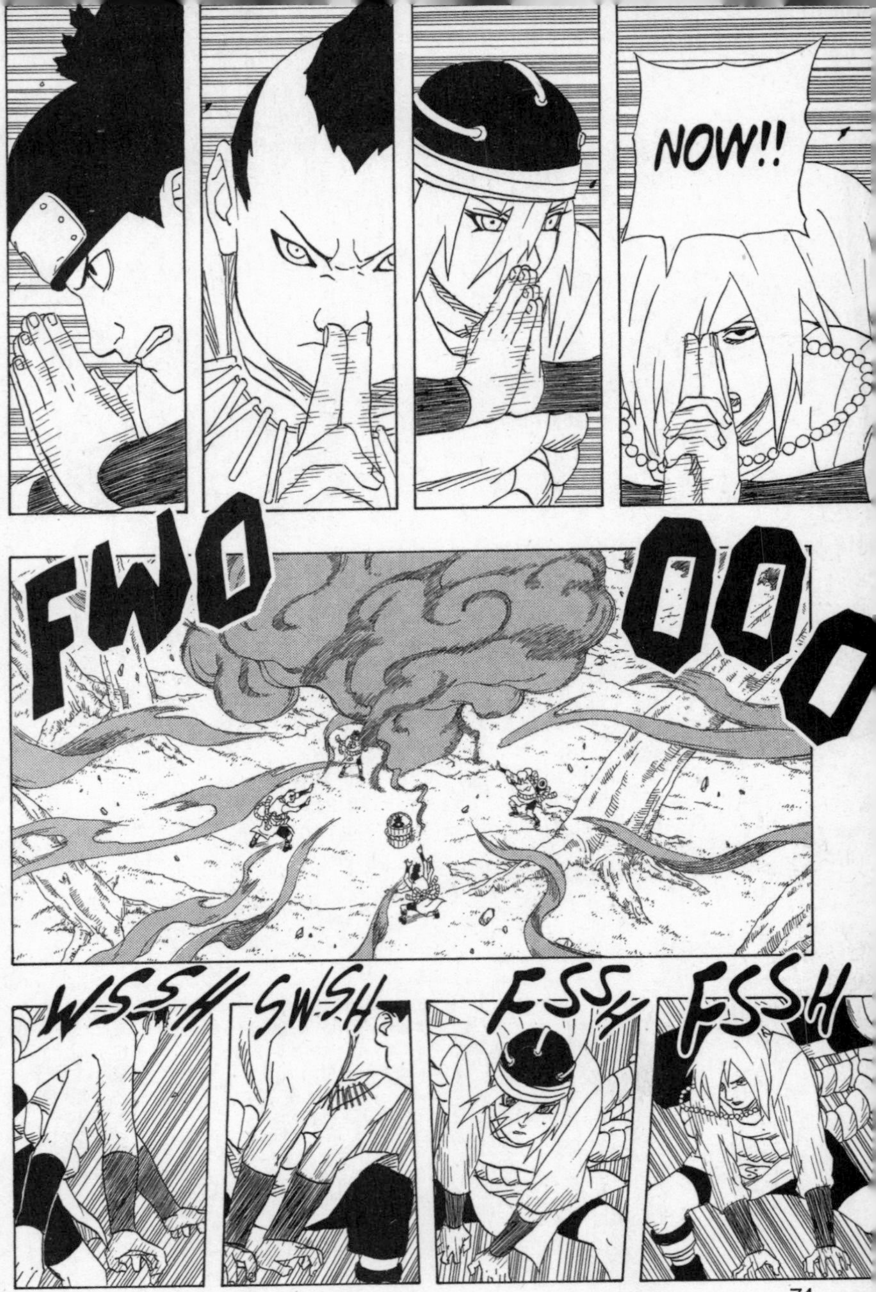
NOW!!
FWOOOO
FSSH
FSSH
SWSH
WSSH

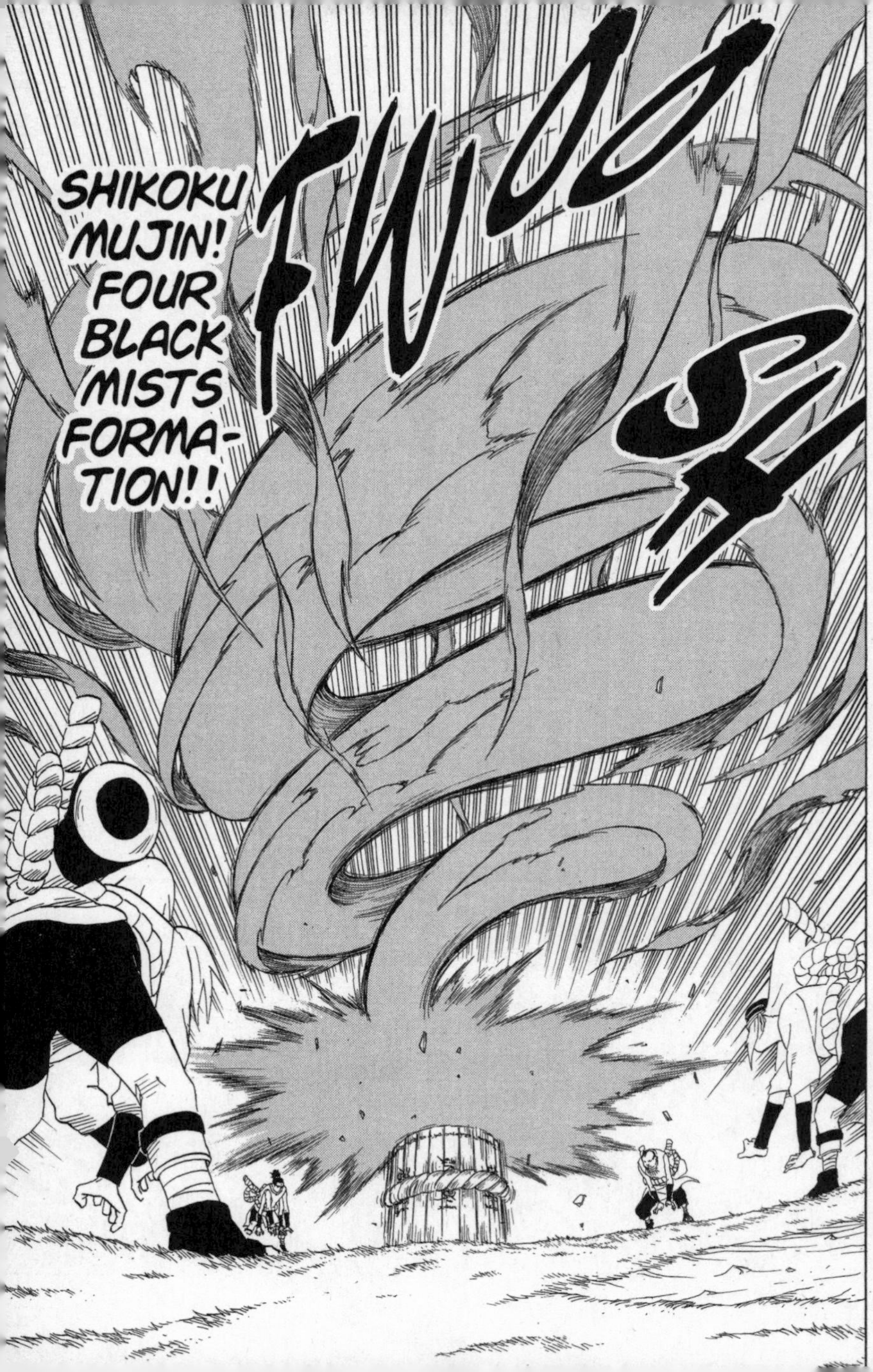
SHIKOKU MUJIN! FOUR BLACK MISTS FORMATION!!
FWOOSH

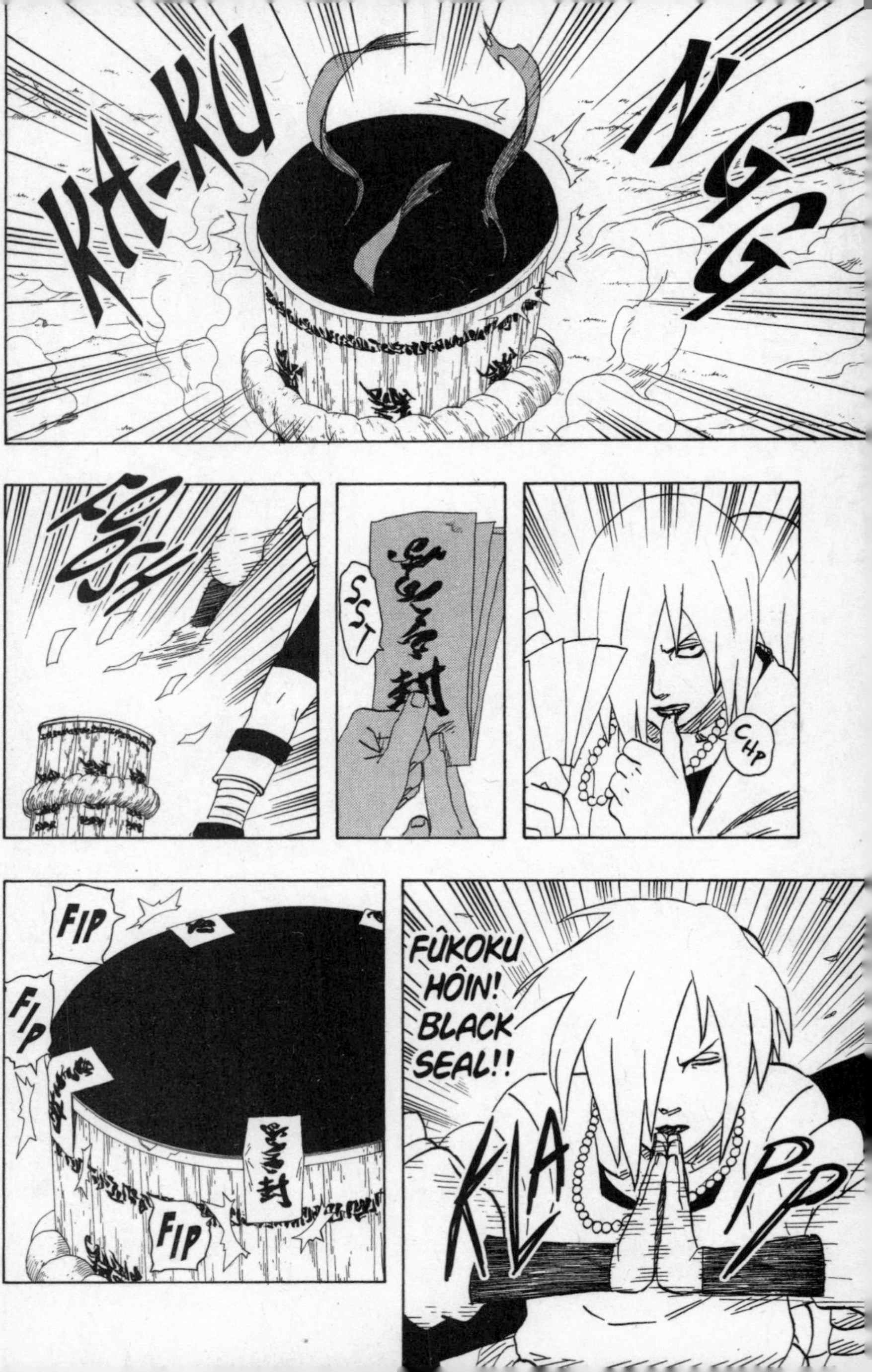
KA-KU
NGG
CHP
SST
FOOSH
FÛKOKU HÔIN! BLACK SEAL!!
KLAPP
FIP
FIP
FIP

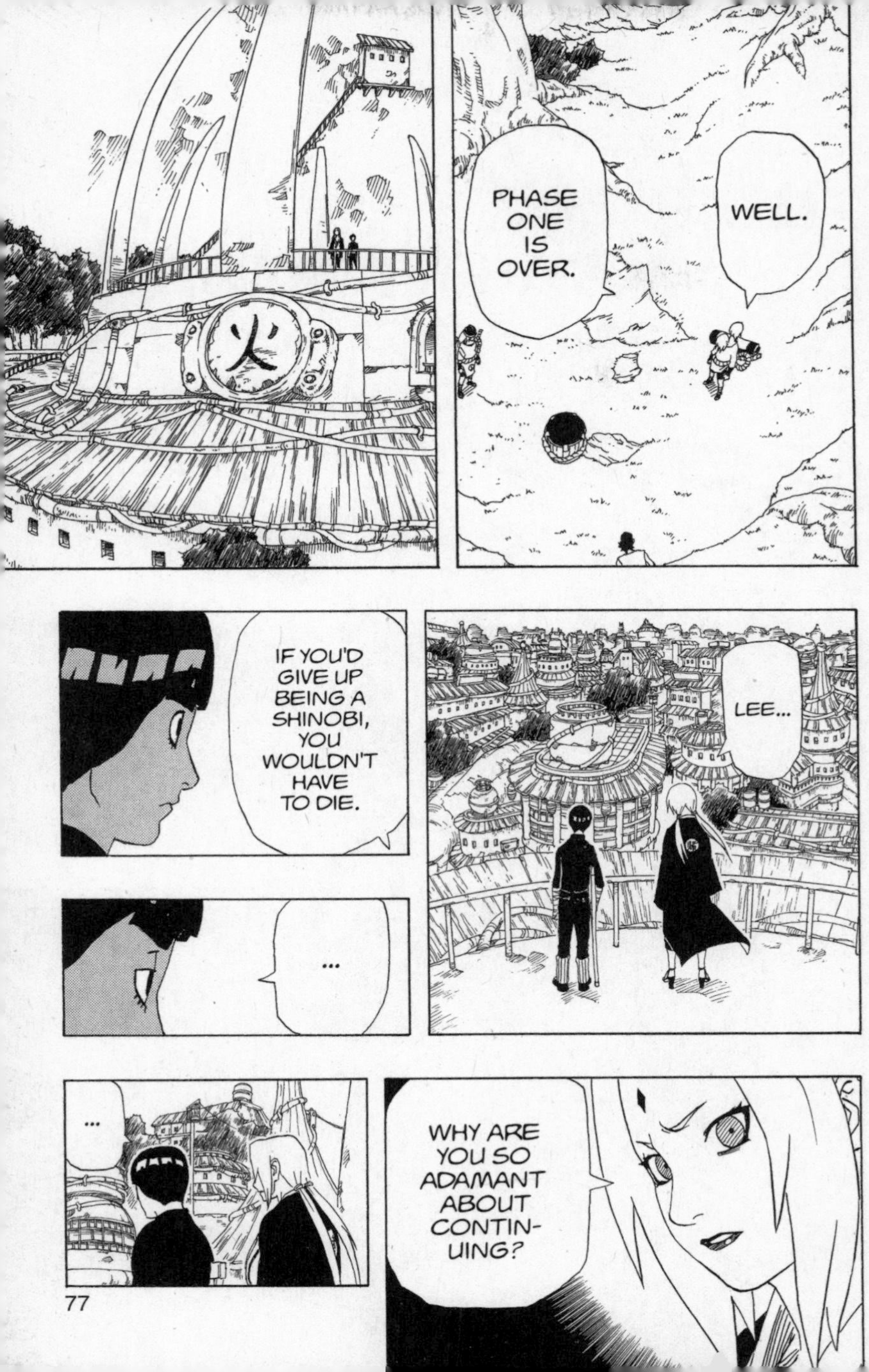
WELL.
PHASE ONE IS OVER.
LEE...
IF YOU'D GIVE UP BEING A SHINOBI, YOU WOULDN'T HAVE TO DIE.
...
WHY ARE YOU SO ADAMANT ABOUT CONTIN-UING?
...

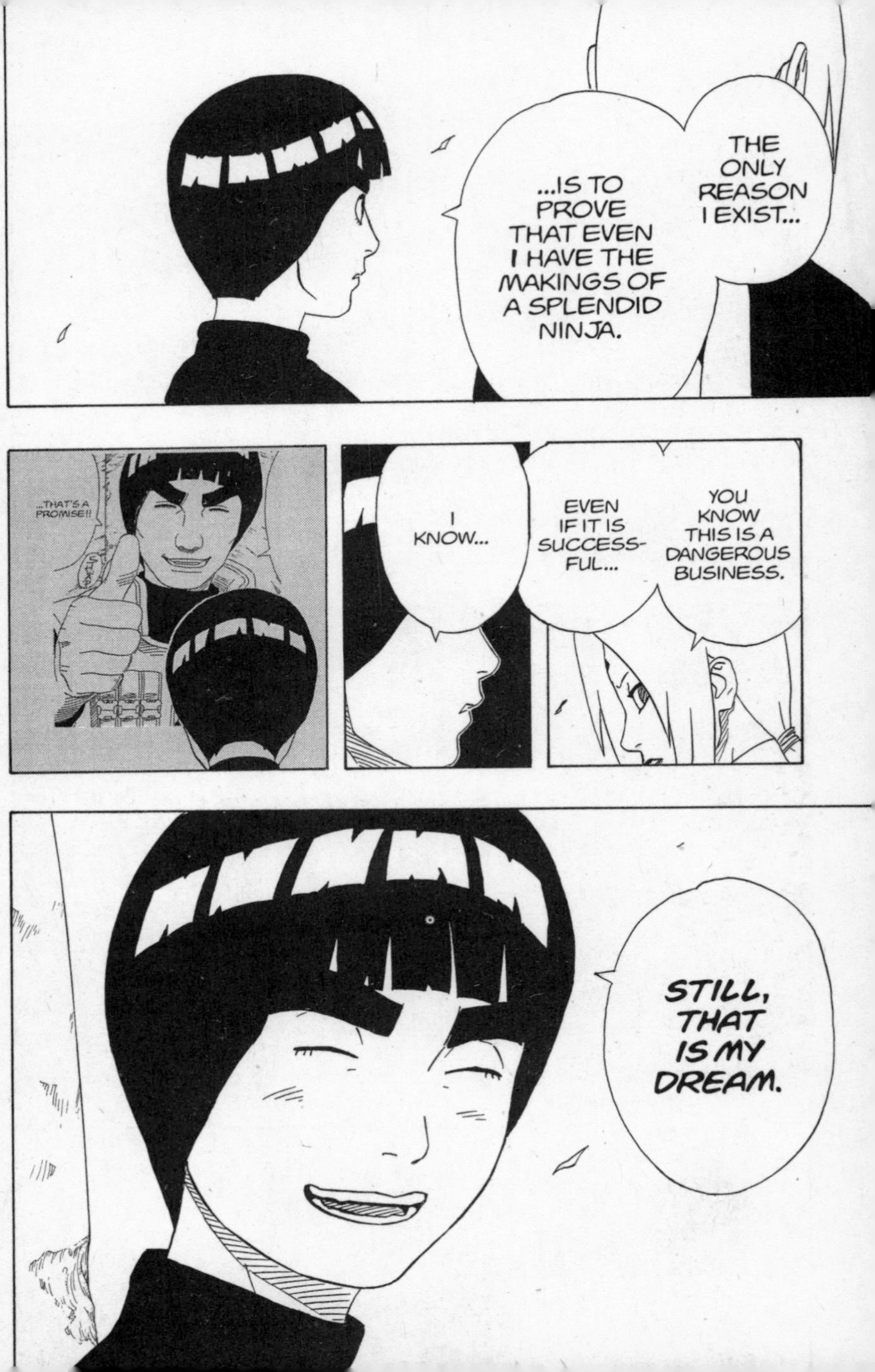
THE ONLY REASON I EXIST...
...IS TO PROVE THAT EVEN I HAVE THE MAKINGS OF A SPLENDID NINJA.
YOU KNOW THIS IS A DANGEROUS BUSINESS.
EVEN IF IT IS SUCCESSFUL...
I KNOW...
...THAT'S A PROMISE!!
STILL, THAT IS MY DREAM.

READ THIS WAY

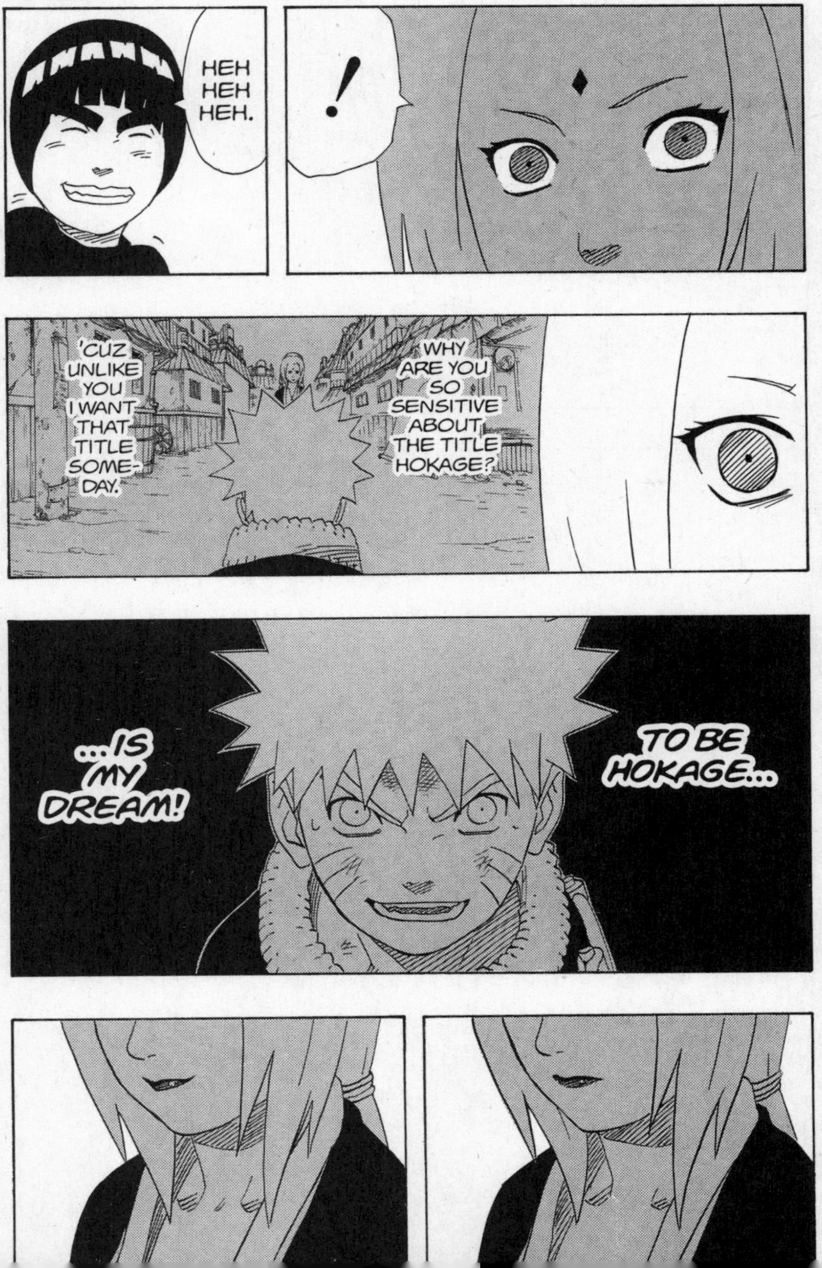
!
HEH HEH HEH.
WHY ARE YOU SO SENSITIVE ABOUT THE TITLE HOKAGE?
'CUZ UNLIKE YOU I WANT THAT TITLE SOMEDAY.
TO BE HOKAGE...
...IS MY DREAM!

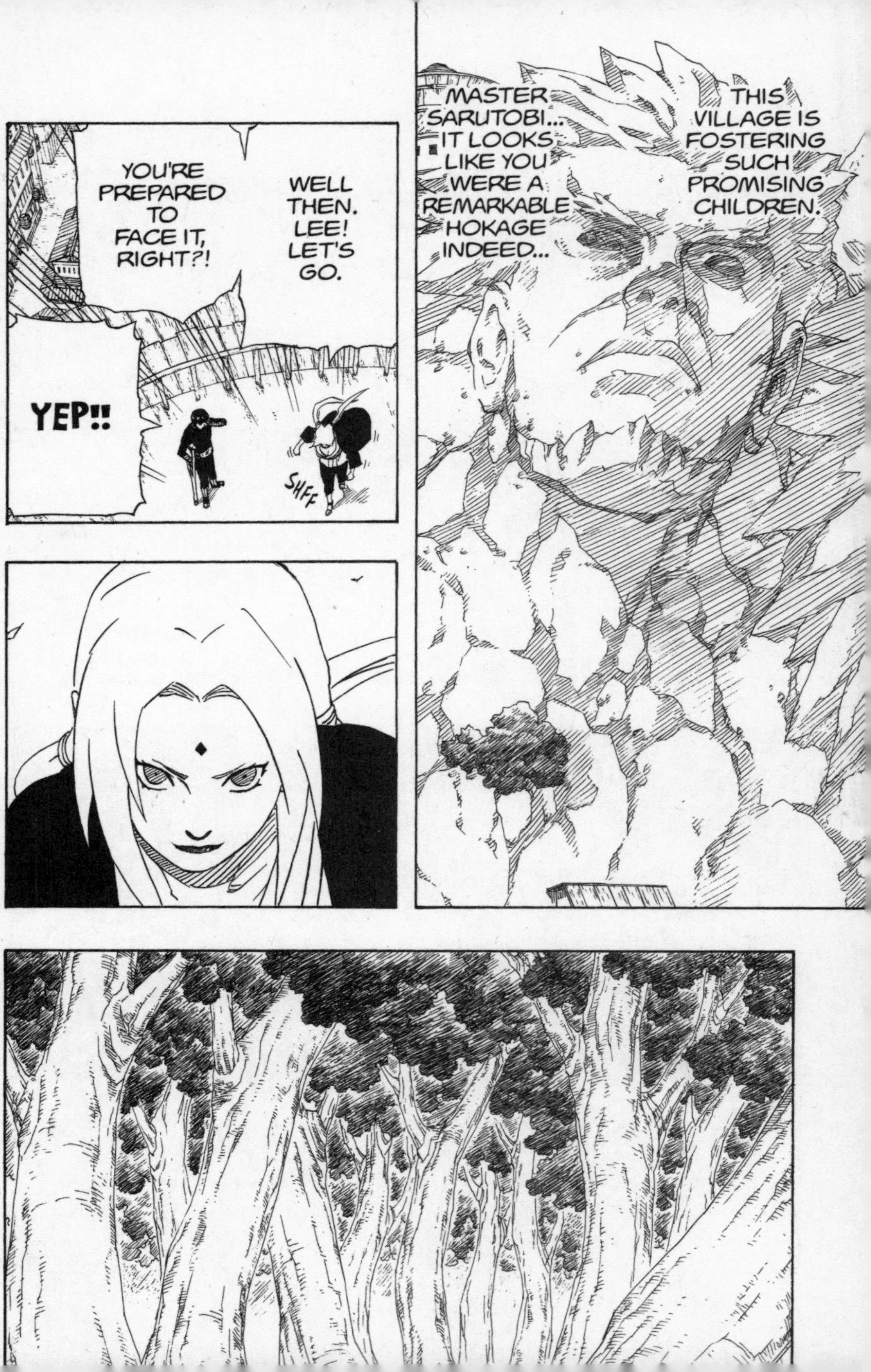
THIS VILLAGE IS FOSTERING SUCH PROMISING CHILDREN.
MASTER SARUTOBI... IT LOOKS LIKE YOU WERE A REMARKABLE HOKAGE INDEED...
WELL THEN. LEE! LET'S GO.
YOU'RE PREPARED TO FACE IT, RIGHT?!
YEP!!
SHFF

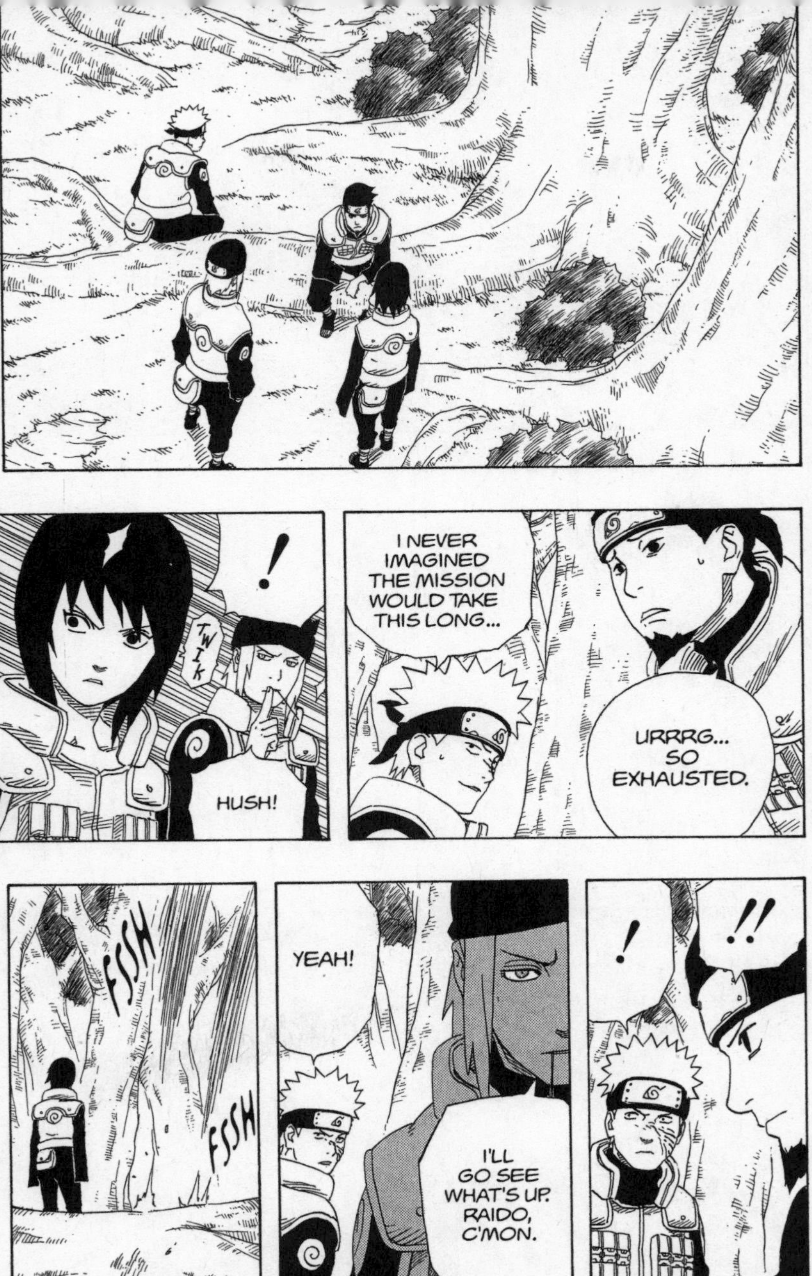
I NEVER IMAGINED THE MISSION WOULD TAKE THIS LONG...
URRRG... SO EXHAUSTED.
!
TWIK
HUSH!
!!
!
YEAH!
I'LL GO SEE WHAT'S UP. RAIDO, C'MON.
FSSH
FSSH

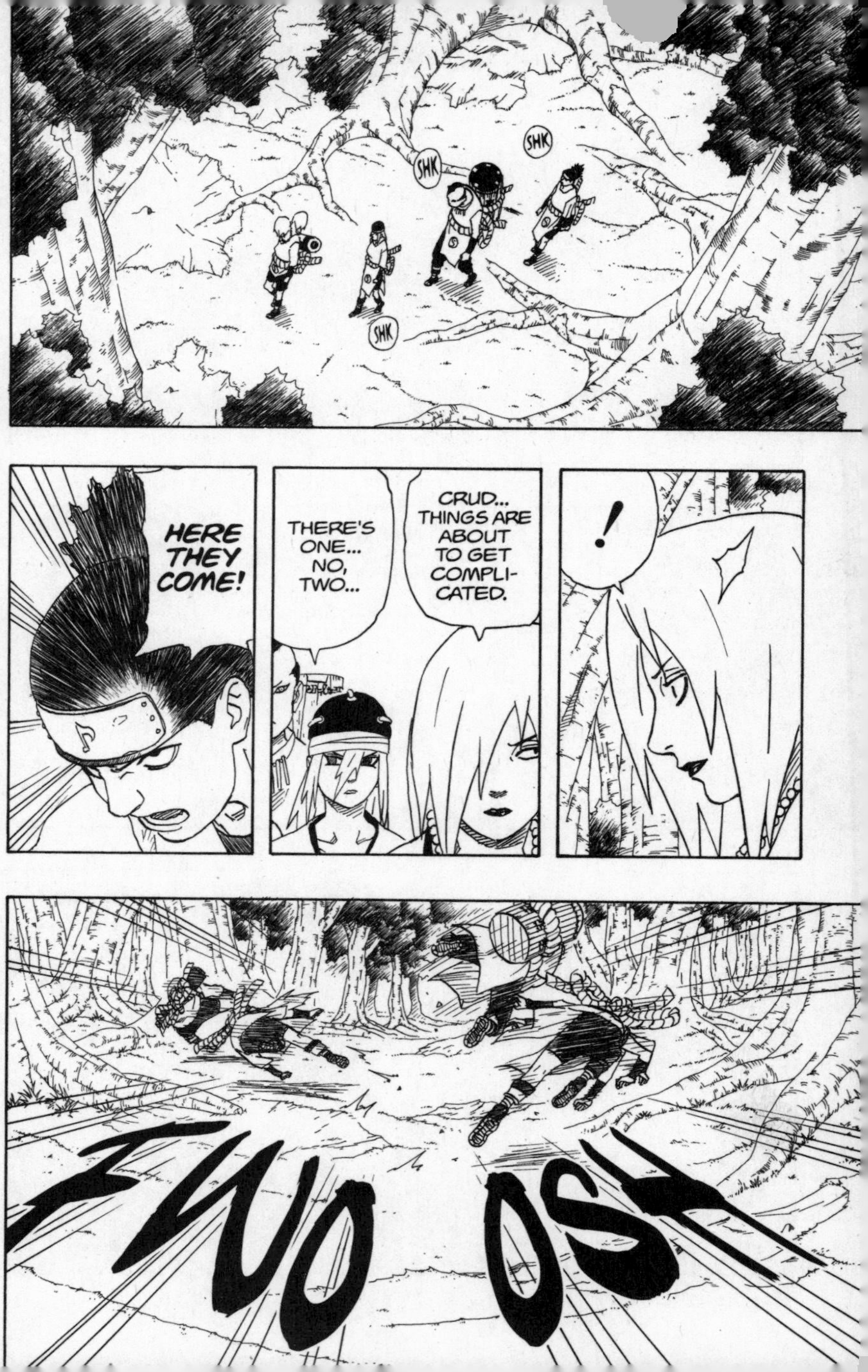
SHK
SHK
SHK
!
CRUD... THINGS ARE ABOUT TO GET COMPLICATED.
THERE'S ONE... NO, TWO...
HERE THEY COME!
WHOOSH

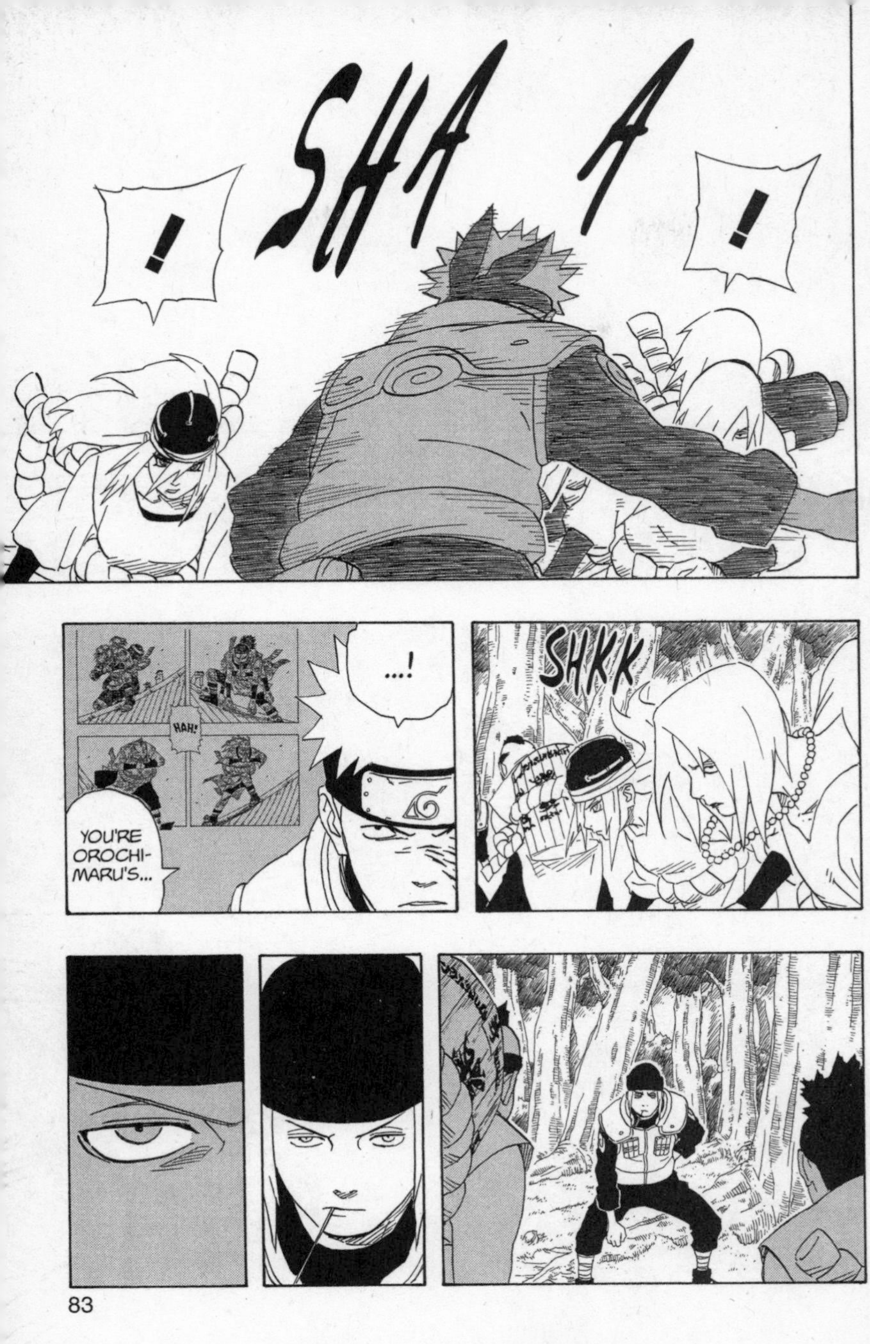
SHA A
!
!
SHKK
...!
HAH!
YOU'RE OROCHI-MARU'S...

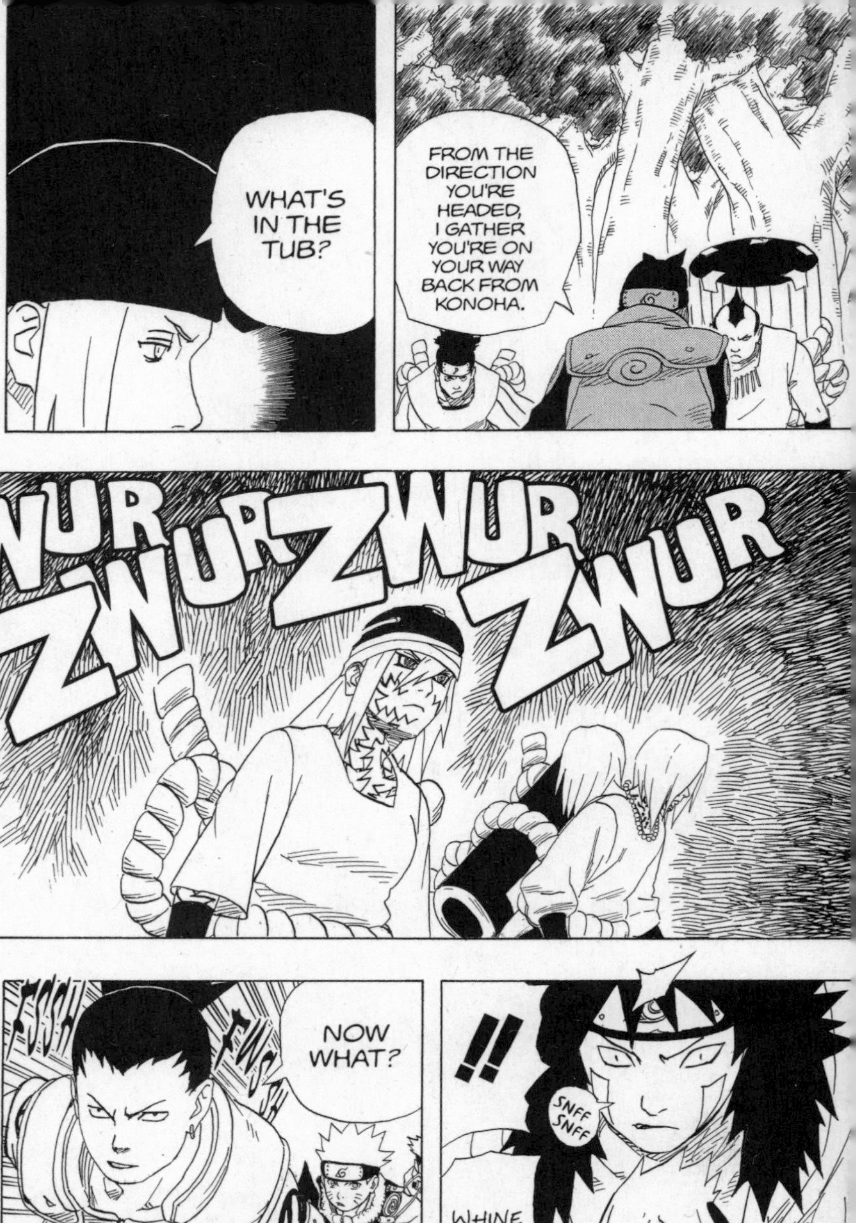
FROM THE DIRECTION YOU'RE HEADED, I GATHER YOU'RE ON YOUR WAY BACK FROM KONOHA.
WHAT'S IN THE TUB?
ZWUR ZWUR ZWUR ZWUR ZWUR
!!
SNFF SNFF
WHINE
NOW WHAT?

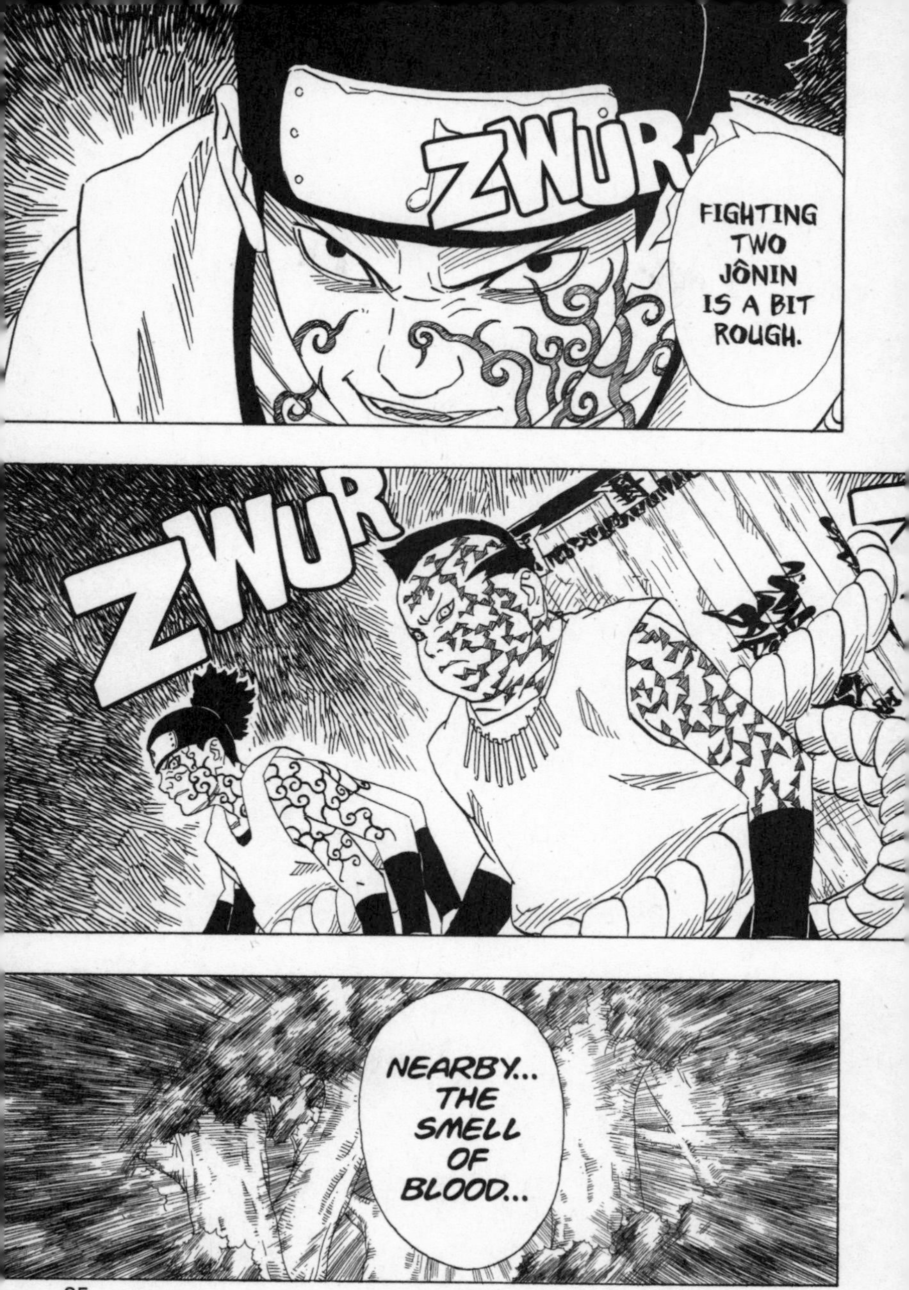
ZWUR
FIGHTING TWO JÔNIN IS A BIT ROUGH.
ZWUR
NEARBY... THE SMELL OF BLOOD...

Number 185: Pursuit...!!

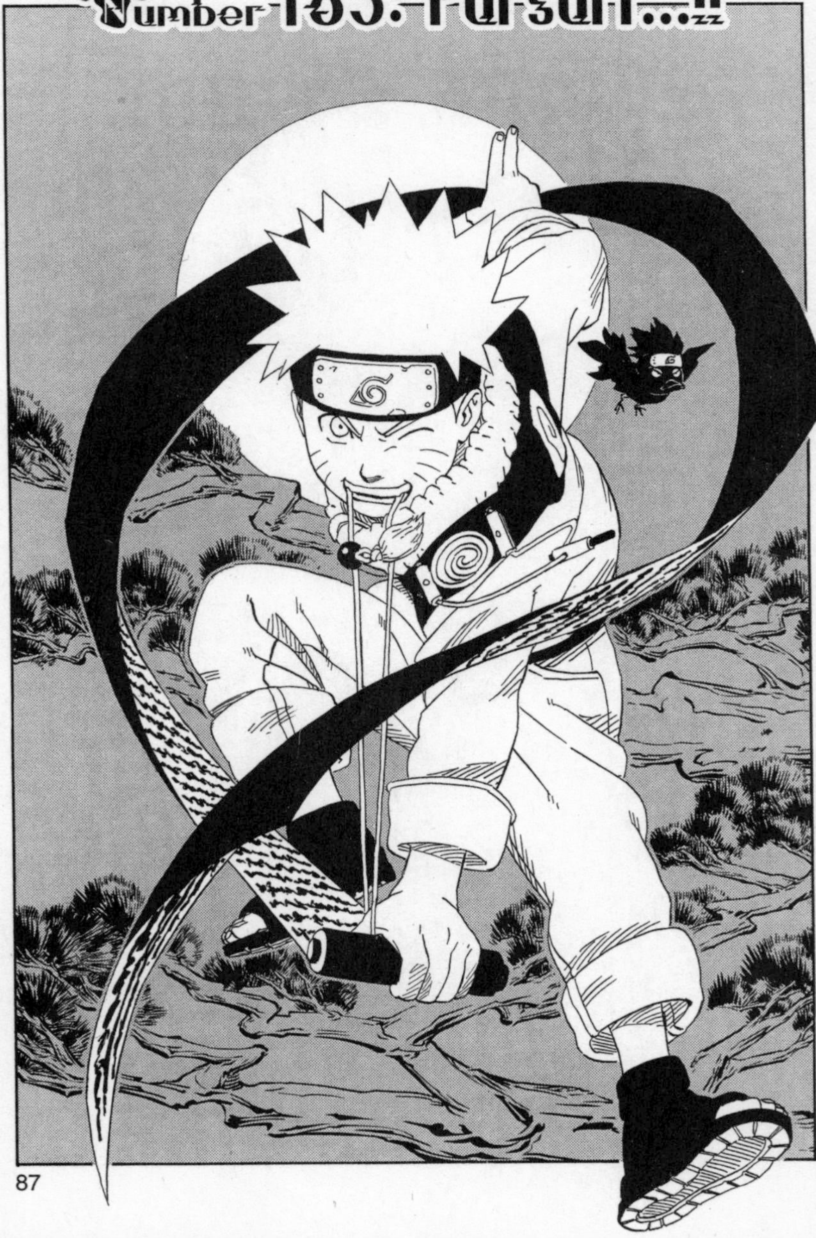

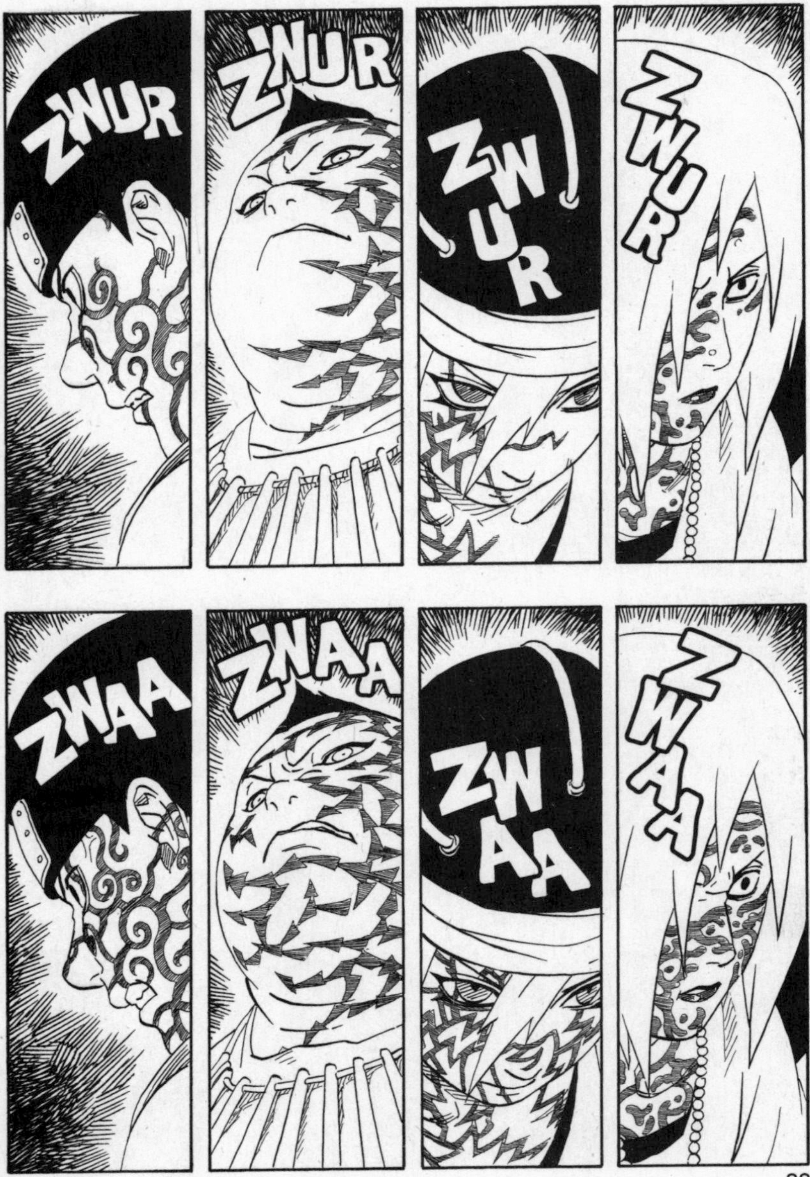
ZWUR
ZWUR
ZWUR
ZWUR
ZWAA
ZWAA
ZWAA
ZWAA

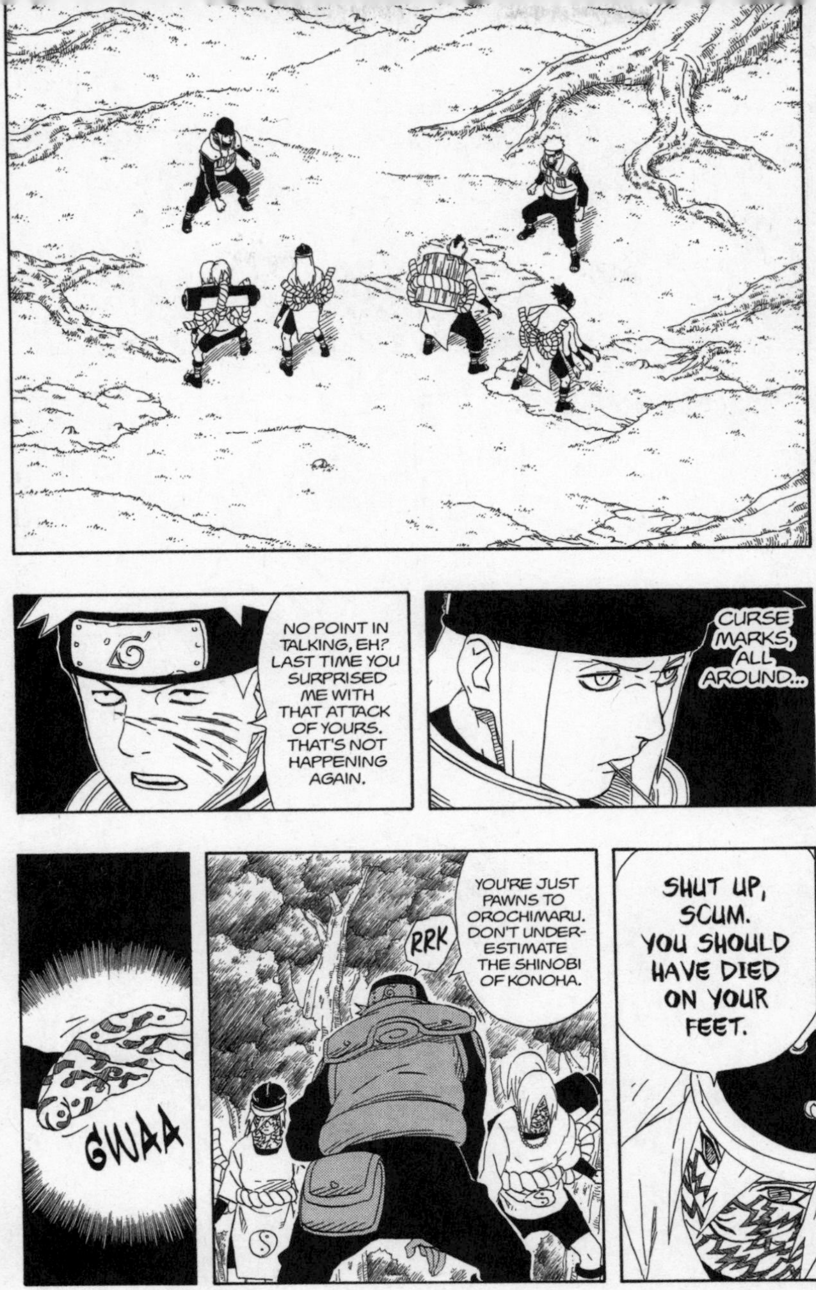
CURSE MARKS, ALL AROUND...
NO POINT IN TALKING, EH? LAST TIME YOU SURPRISED ME WITH THAT ATTACK OF YOURS. THAT'S NOT HAPPENING AGAIN.
SHUT UP, SCUM. YOU SHOULD HAVE DIED ON YOUR FEET.
YOU'RE JUST PAWNS TO OROCHIMARU. DON'T UNDER-ESTIMATE THE SHINOBI OF KONOHA.
RRK
GWAA

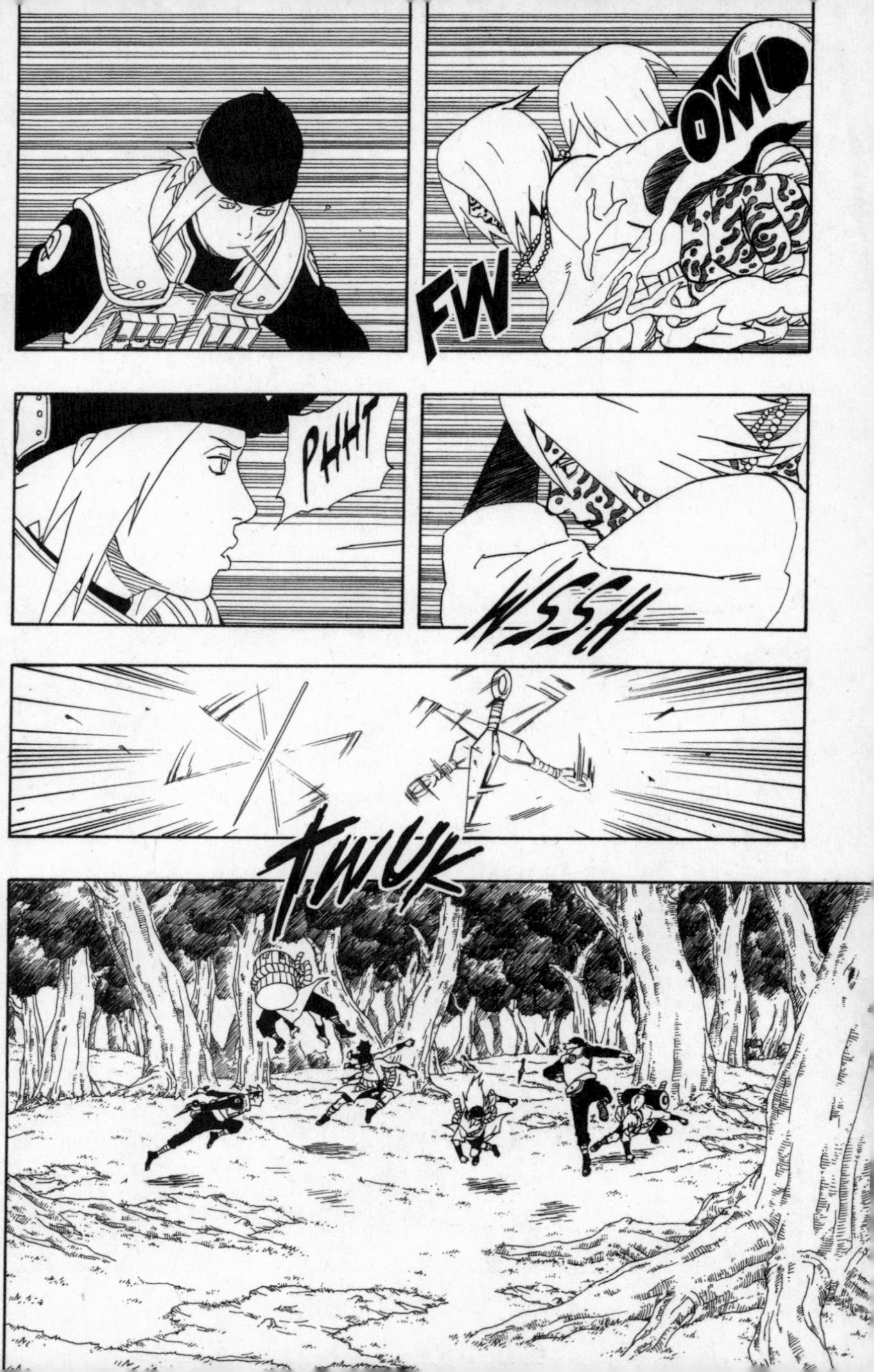
FWOMP
WSSH
PHHT
TWUK

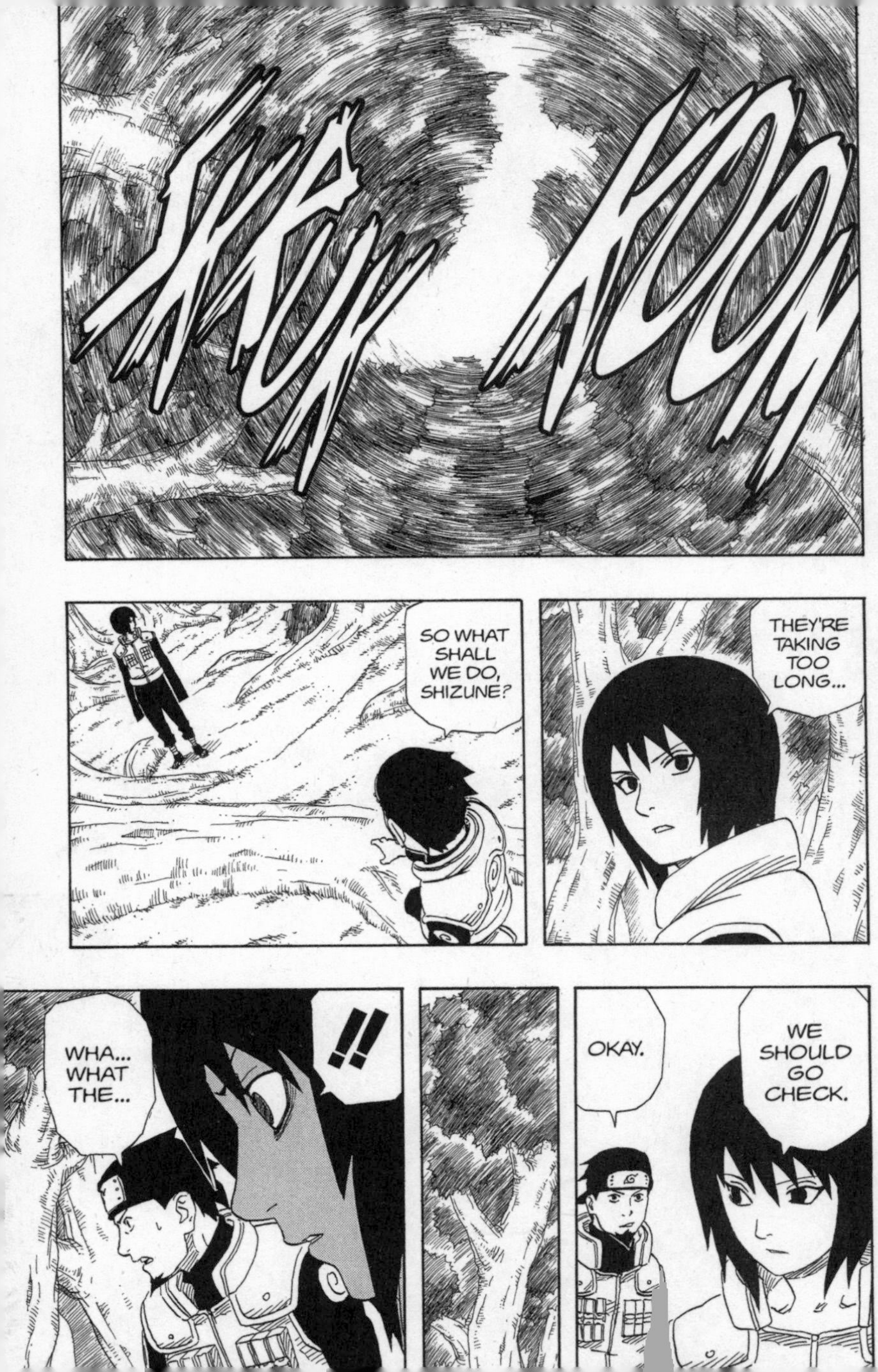
THEY'RE TAKING TOO LONG...
SO WHAT SHALL WE DO, SHIZUNE?
WE SHOULD GO CHECK.
OKAY.
!!
WHA... WHAT THE...

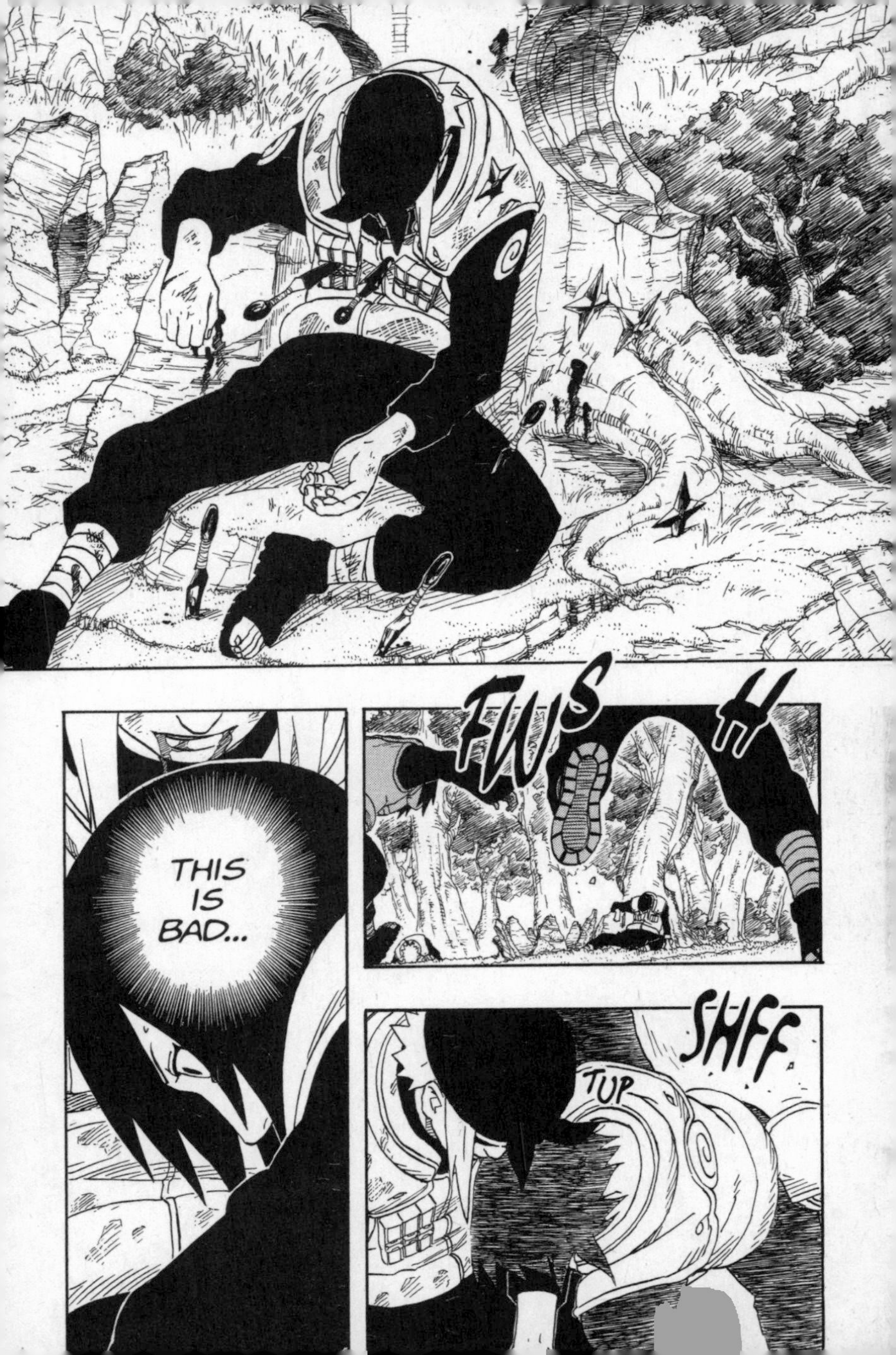
FWSH
SHFF
TUP
THIS IS BAD...

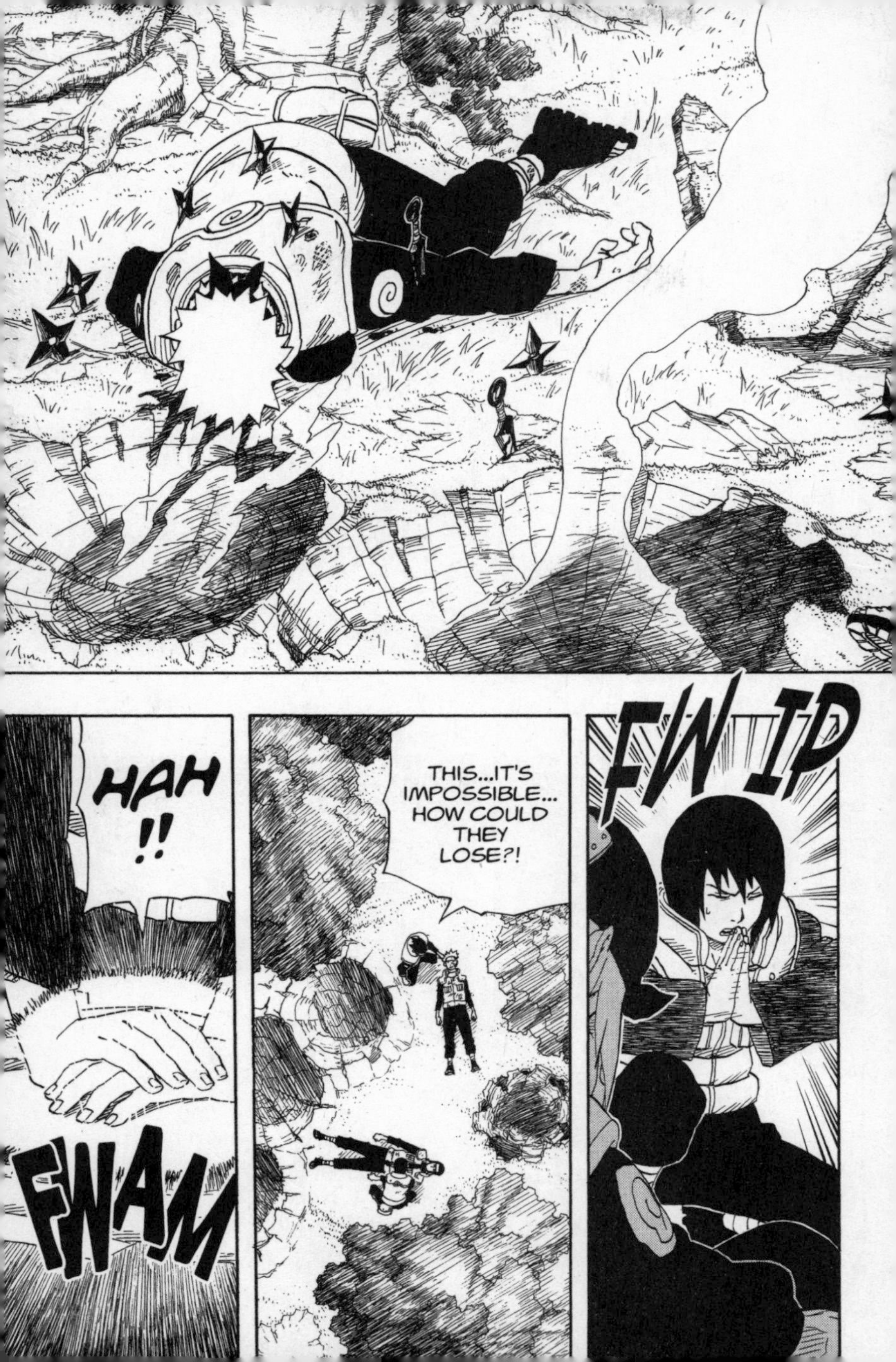
FWIP
THIS...IT'S IMPOSSIBLE... HOW COULD THEY LOSE?!
HAH !!
FWAM

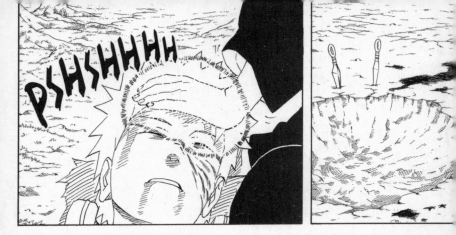

PSHSHHHH

URK...

DON'T!

FIRST AID IS ALL I CAN DO NOW...

I'M HEADING AFTER THEM!

SHIZUNE.

READ THIS WAY

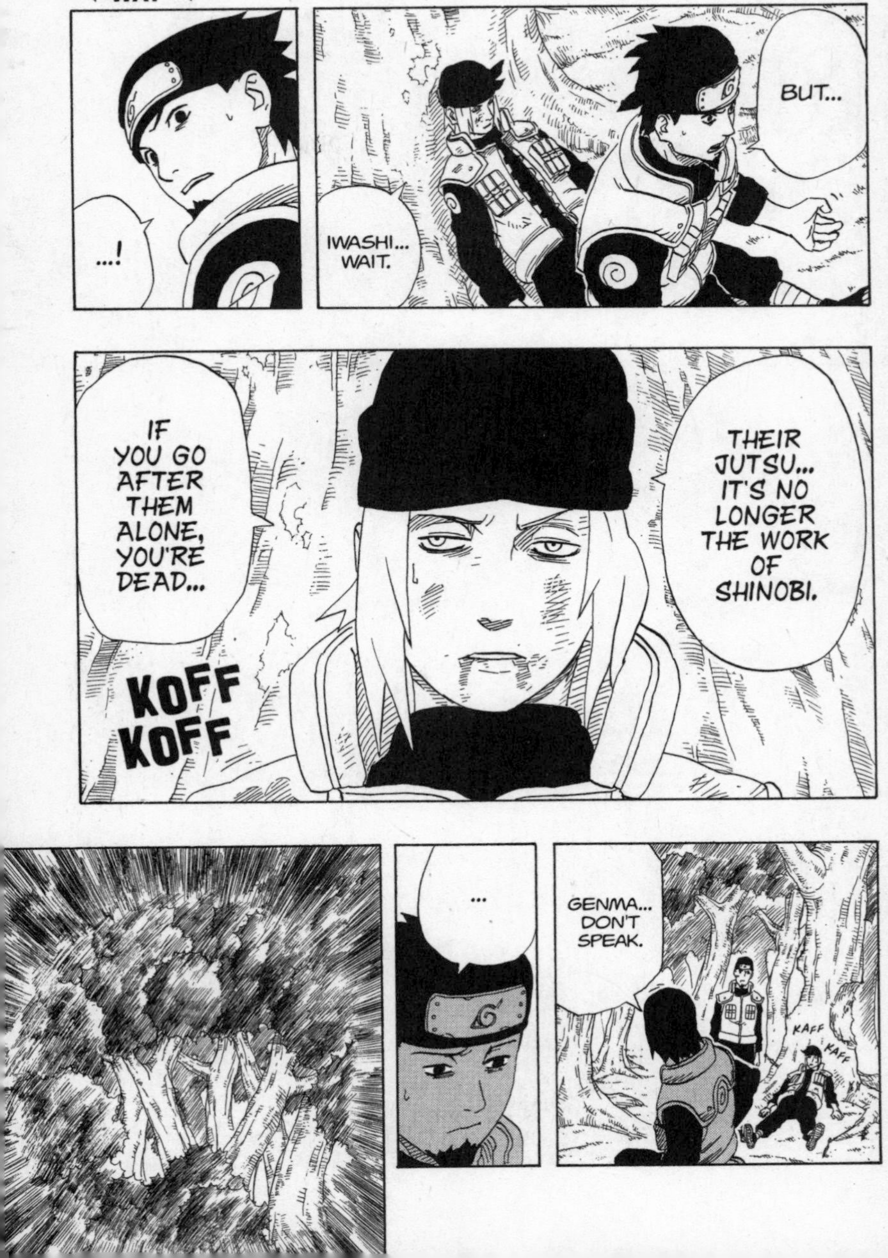
BUT...
IWASHI... WAIT.
...!
THEIR JUTSU... IT'S NO LONGER THE WORK OF SHINOBI.
IF YOU GO AFTER THEM ALONE, YOU'RE DEAD...
KOFF KOFF
GENMA... DON'T SPEAK.
KAFF KAFF
...

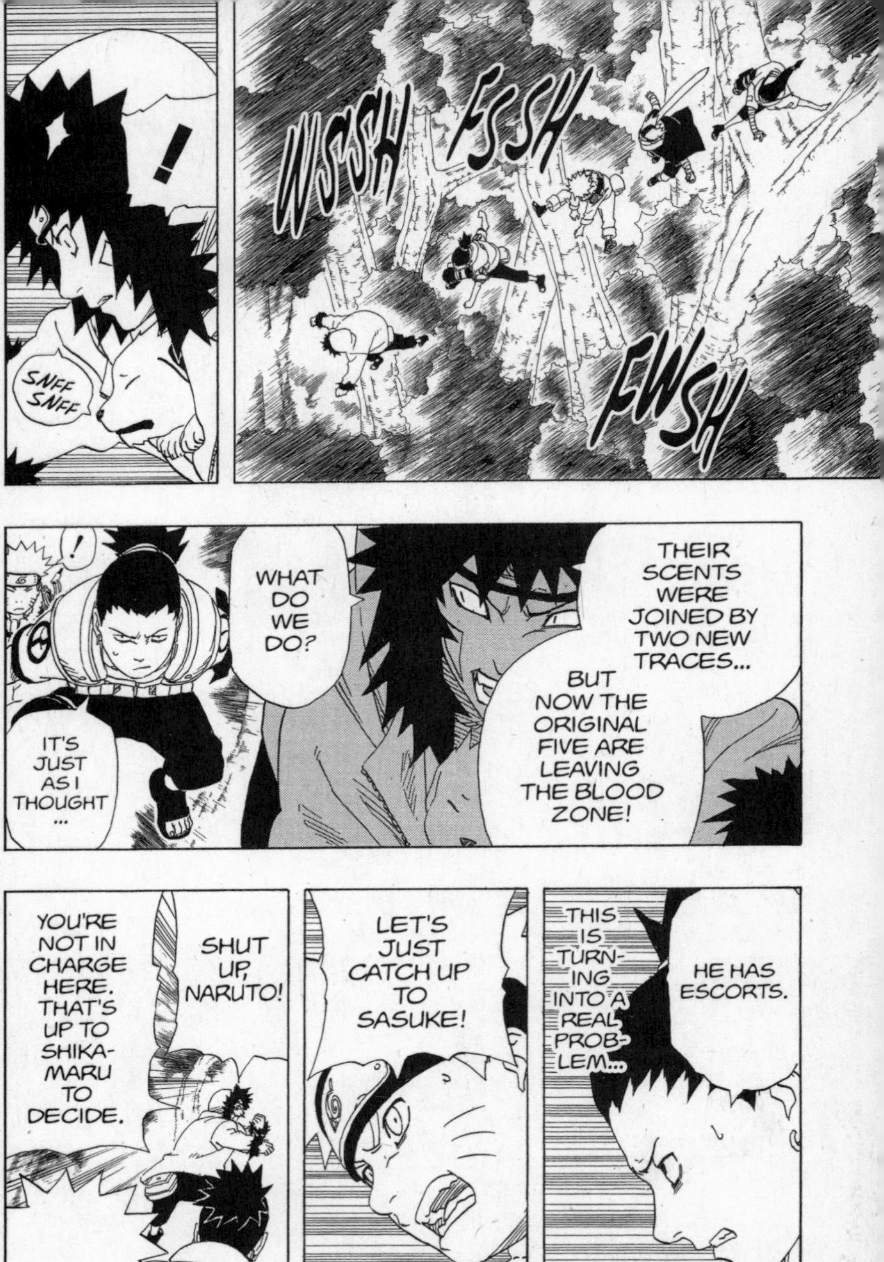
FSSH
WSSH
FWSH
!
SNFF SNFF
THEIR SCENTS WERE JOINED BY TWO NEW TRACES...
BUT NOW THE ORIGINAL FIVE ARE LEAVING THE BLOOD ZONE!
WHAT DO WE DO?
!
IT'S JUST AS I THOUGHT ...
HE HAS ESCORTS.
THIS IS TURNING INTO A REAL PROBLEM...
LET'S JUST CATCH UP TO SASUKE!
SHUT UP, NARUTO!
YOU'RE NOT IN CHARGE HERE. THAT'S UP TO SHIKAMARU TO DECIDE.

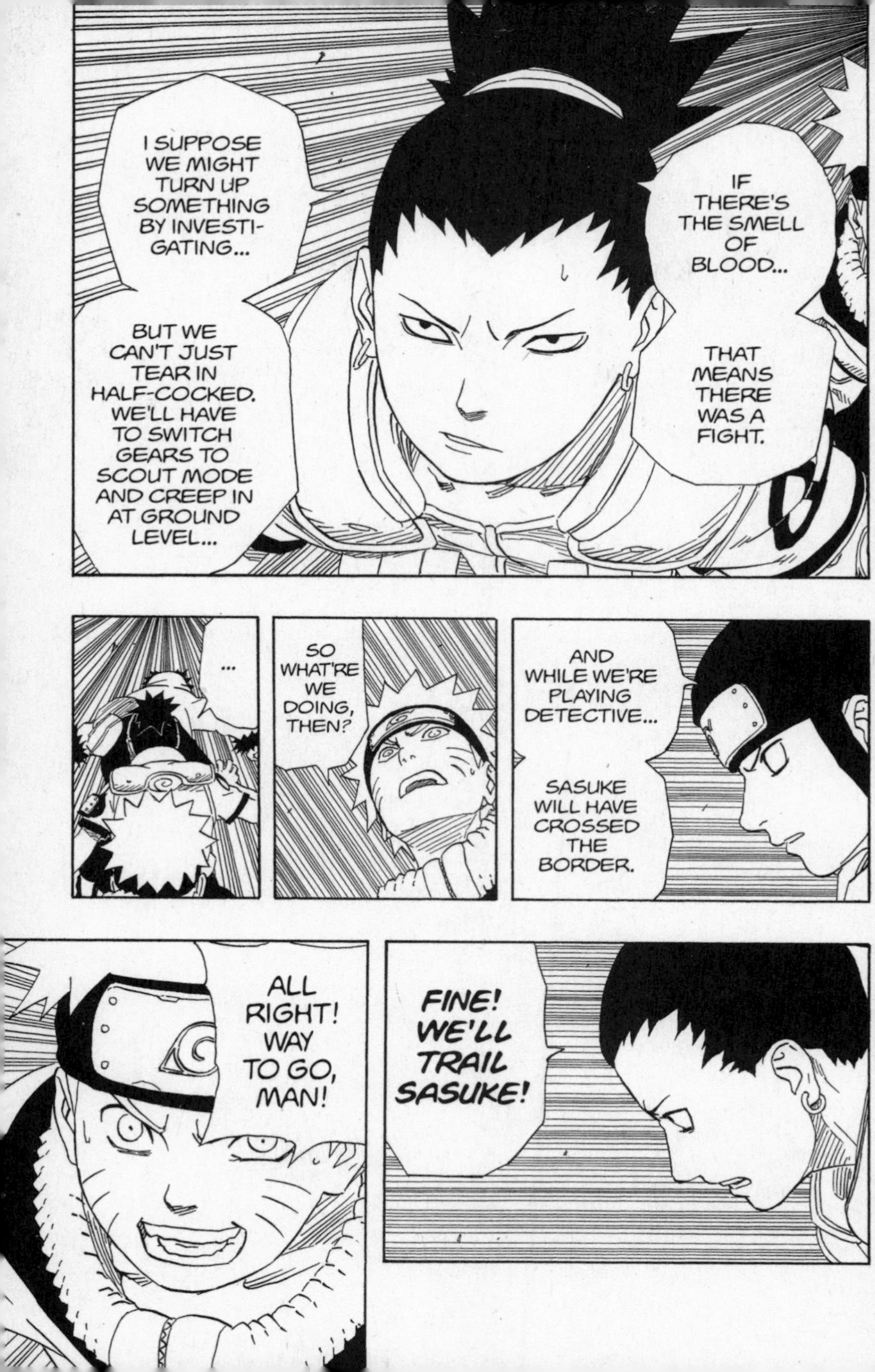
IF THERE'S THE SMELL OF BLOOD...
THAT MEANS THERE WAS A FIGHT.
I SUPPOSE WE MIGHT TURN UP SOMETHING BY INVESTI-GATING...
BUT WE CAN'T JUST TEAR IN HALF-COCKED. WE'LL HAVE TO SWITCH GEARS TO SCOUT MODE AND CREEP IN AT GROUND LEVEL...
AND WHILE WE'RE PLAYING DETECTIVE...
SASUKE WILL HAVE CROSSED THE BORDER.
SO WHAT'RE WE DOING, THEN?
...
FINE! WE'LL TRAIL SASUKE!
ALL RIGHT! WAY TO GO, MAN!

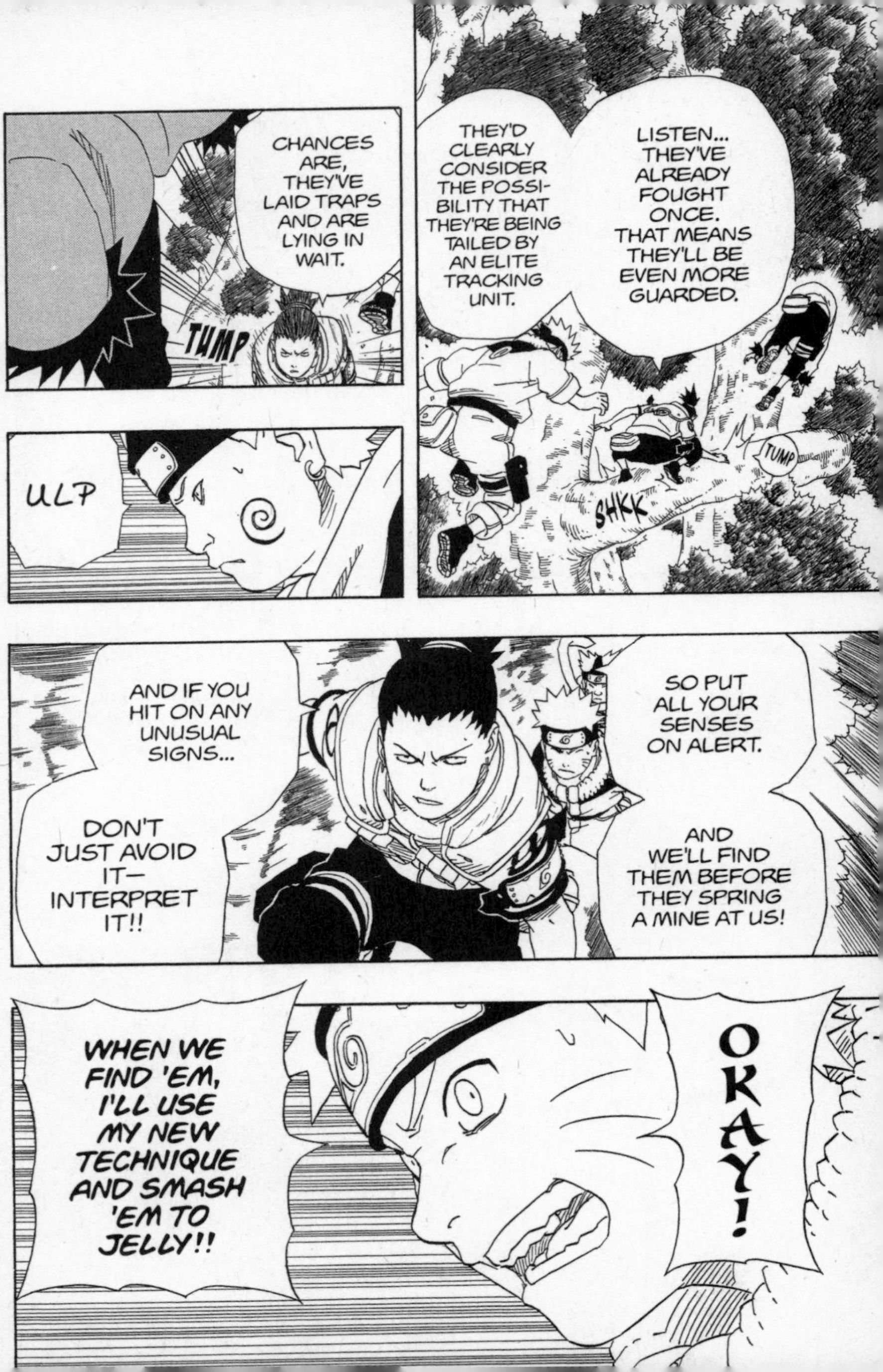
LISTEN... THEY'VE ALREADY FOUGHT ONCE. THAT MEANS THEY'LL BE EVEN MORE GUARDED.
THEY'D CLEARLY CONSIDER THE POSSI-BILITY THAT THEY'RE BEING TAILED BY AN ELITE TRACKING UNIT.
TUMP
SHKK
CHANCES ARE, THEY'VE LAID TRAPS AND ARE LYING IN WAIT.
TUMP
ULP
SO PUT ALL YOUR SENSES ON ALERT.
AND IF YOU HIT ON ANY UNUSUAL SIGNS...
DON'T JUST AVOID IT— INTERPRET IT!!
AND WE'LL FIND THEM BEFORE THEY SPRING A MINE AT US!
OKAY!
WHEN WE FIND 'EM, I'LL USE MY NEW TECHNIQUE AND SMASH 'EM TO JELLY!!

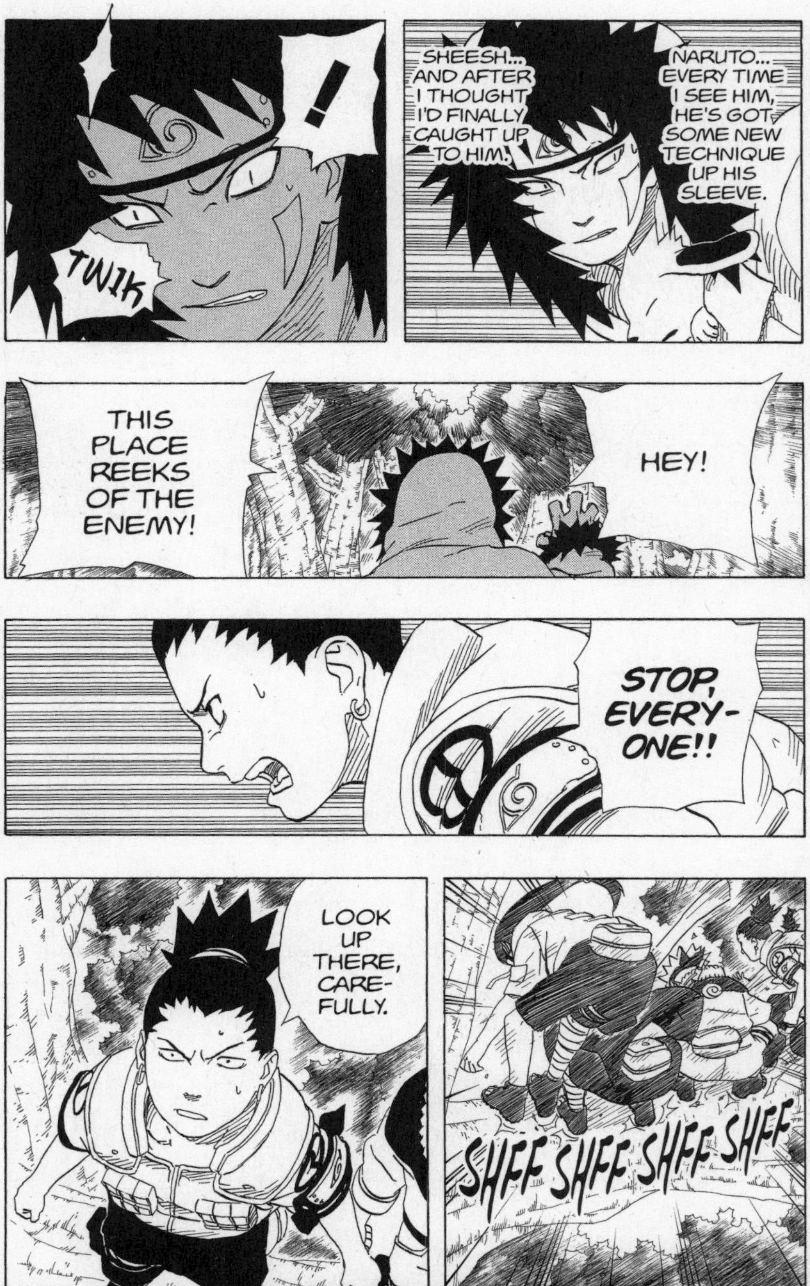
NARUTO... EVERY TIME I SEE HIM, HE'S GOT SOME NEW TECHNIQUE UP HIS SLEEVE.
SHEESH... AND AFTER I THOUGHT I'D FINALLY CAUGHT UP TO HIM.
!
TWIK
HEY!
THIS PLACE REEKS OF THE ENEMY!
STOP, EVERY-ONE!!
SHFF SHFF SHFF SHFF
LOOK UP THERE, CARE-FULLY.

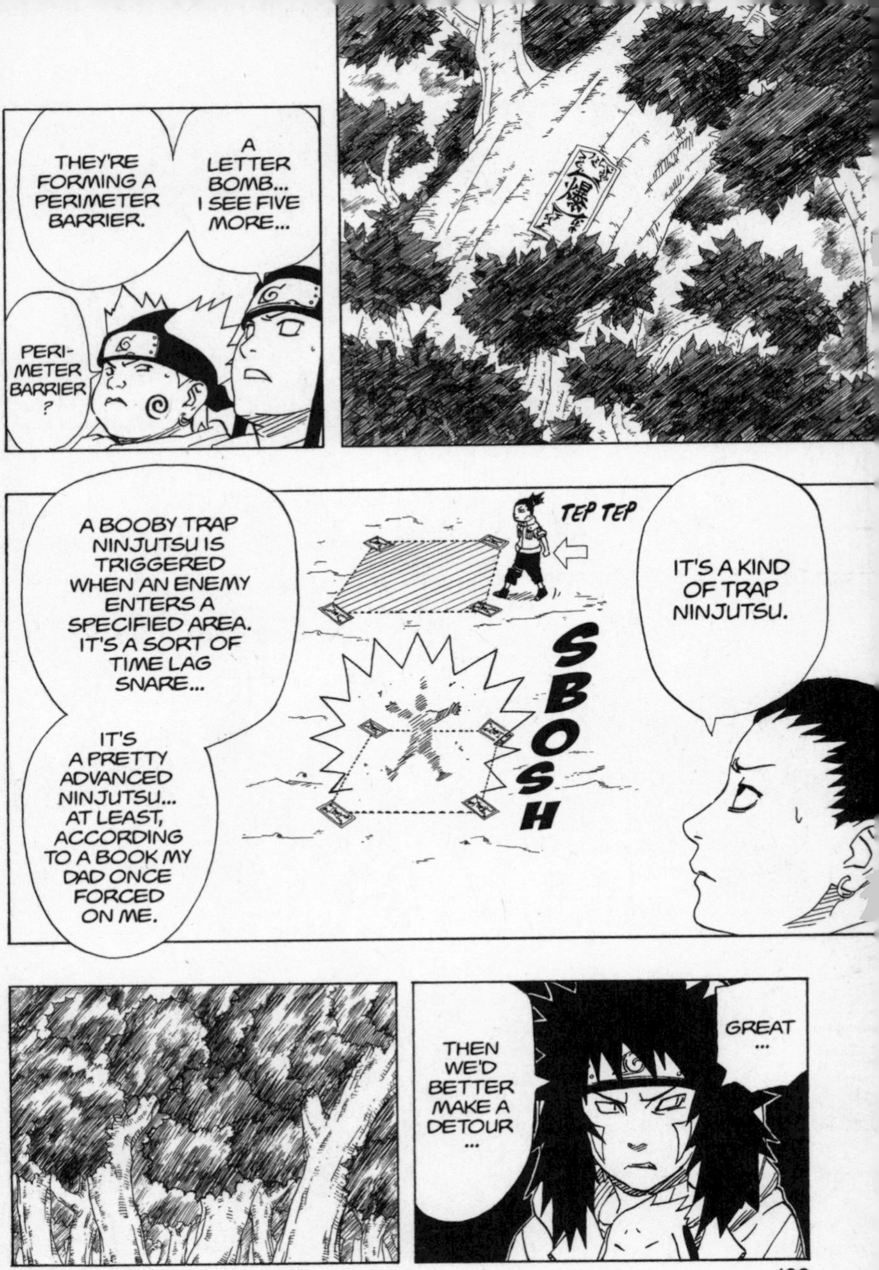
A LETTER BOMB... I SEE FIVE MORE...
THEY'RE FORMING A PERIMETER BARRIER.
PERI-METER BARRIER?
IT'S A KIND OF TRAP NINJUTSU.
TEP TEP
SBOSH
A BOOBY TRAP NINJUTSU IS TRIGGERED WHEN AN ENEMY ENTERS A SPECIFIED AREA. IT'S A SORT OF TIME LAG SNARE...
IT'S A PRETTY ADVANCED NINJUTSU... AT LEAST, ACCORDING TO A BOOK MY DAD ONCE FORCED ON ME.
GREAT...
THEN WE'D BETTER MAKE A DETOUR...

READ THIS WAY

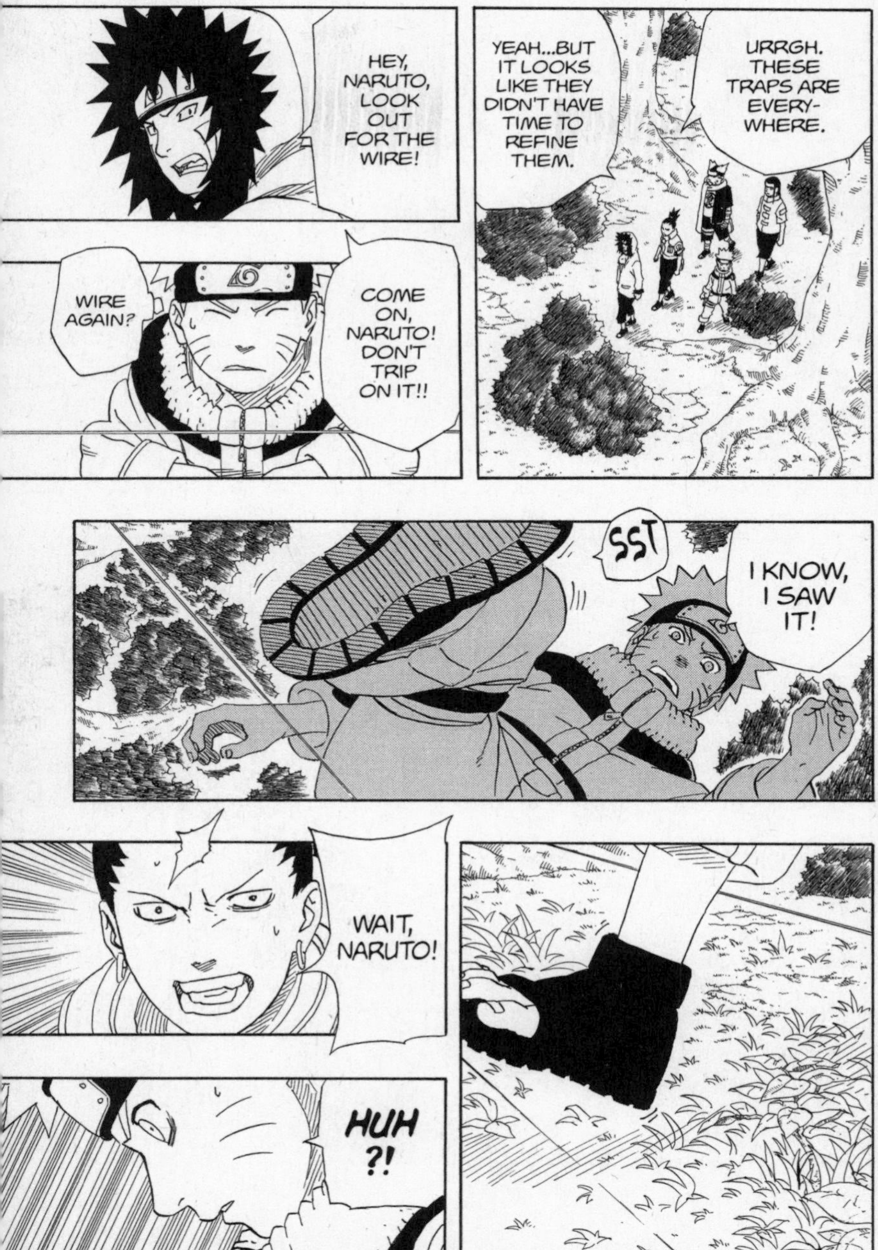
URRGH. THESE TRAPS ARE EVERY-WHERE.
YEAH...BUT IT LOOKS LIKE THEY DIDN'T HAVE TIME TO REFINE THEM.
HEY, NARUTO, LOOK OUT FOR THE WIRE!
COME ON, NARUTO! DON'T TRIP ON IT!!
WIRE AGAIN?
I KNOW, I SAW IT!
SST
WAIT, NARUTO!
HUH ?!

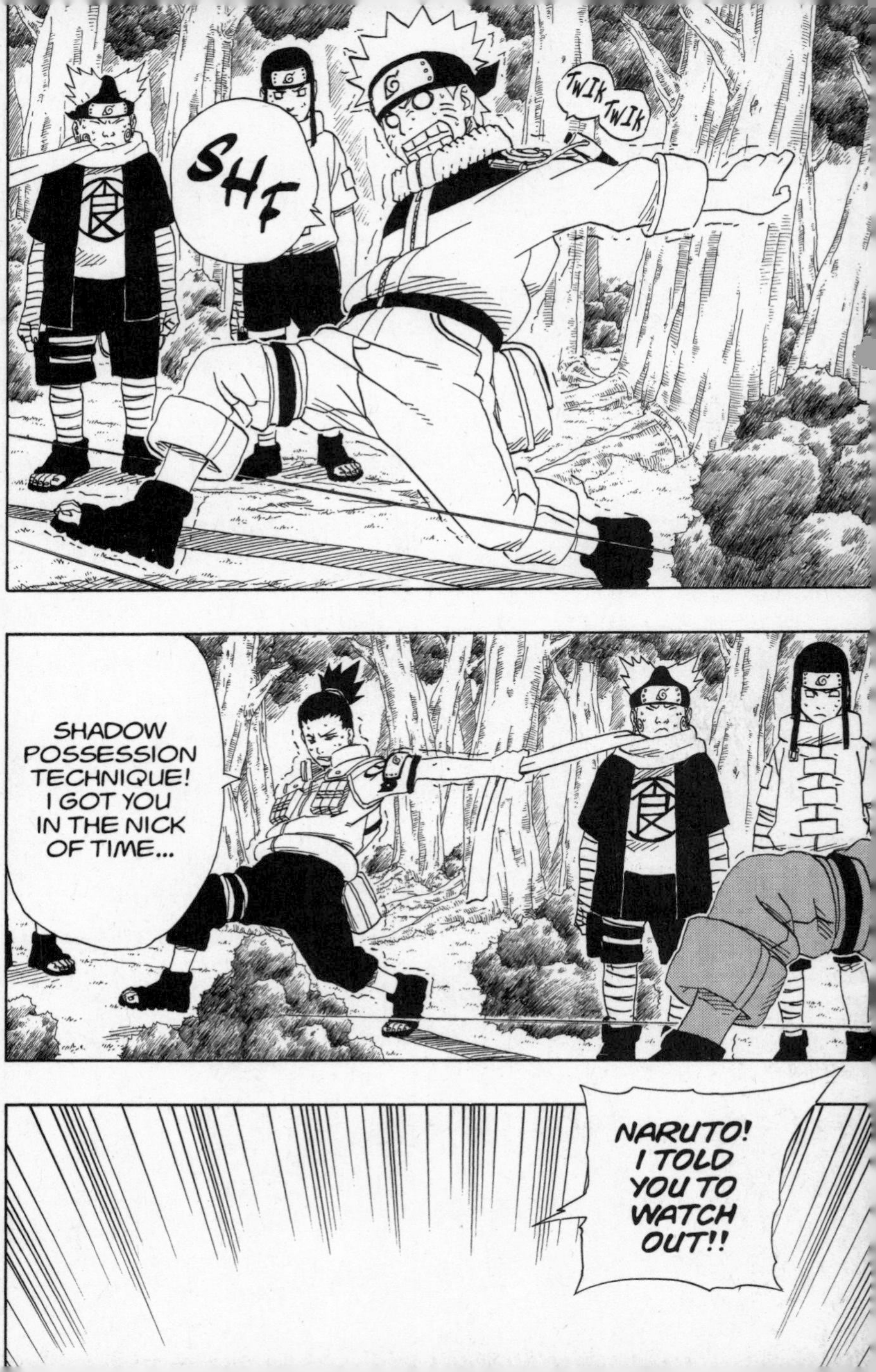
TWIK TWIK
SHF
SHADOW POSSESSION TECHNIQUE! I GOT YOU IN THE NICK OF TIME...
NARUTO! I TOLD YOU TO WATCH OUT!!

READ THIS WAY

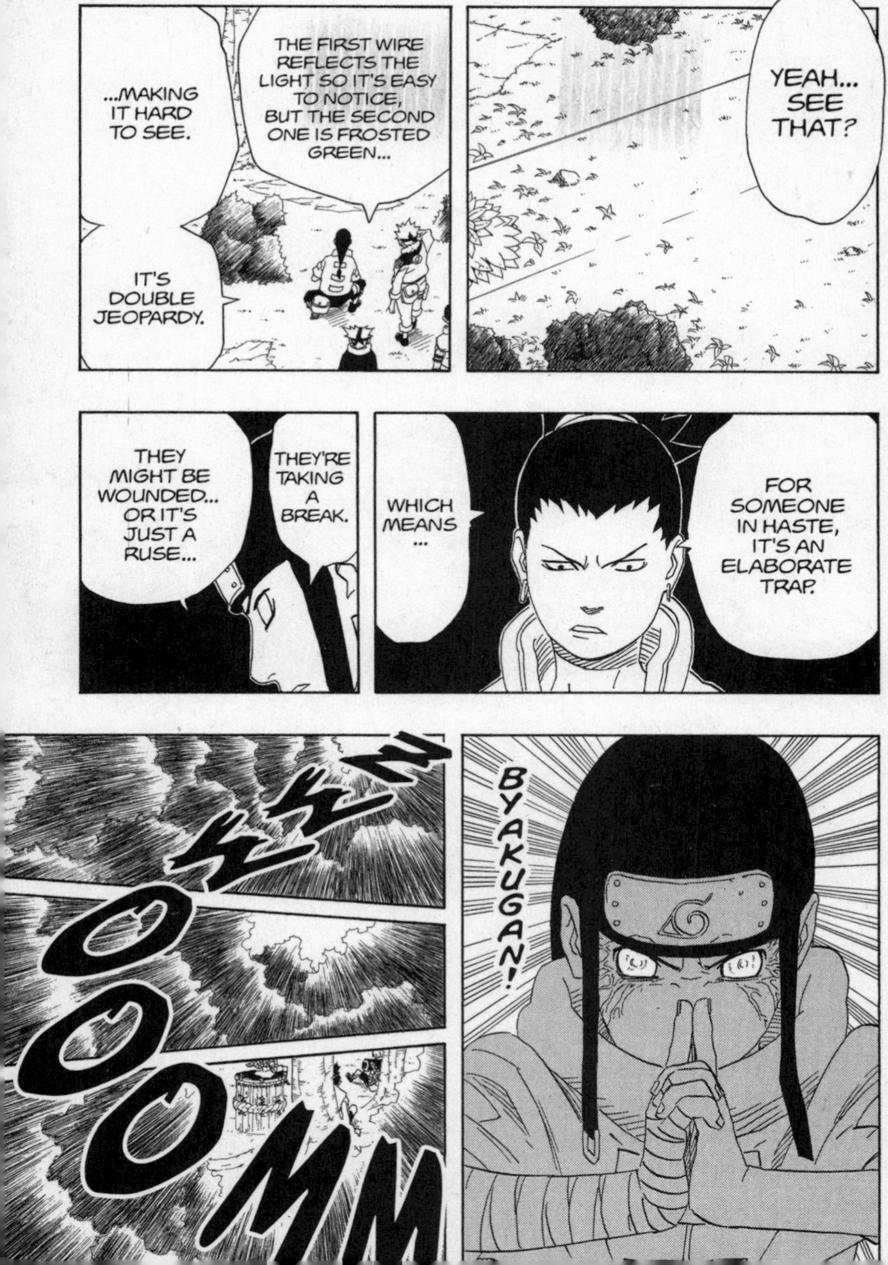
YEAH... SEE THAT?
THE FIRST WIRE REFLECTS THE LIGHT SO IT'S EASY TO NOTICE, BUT THE SECOND ONE IS FROSTED GREEN...
...MAKING IT HARD TO SEE.
IT'S DOUBLE JEOPARDY.
FOR SOMEONE IN HASTE, IT'S AN ELABORATE TRAP.
WHICH MEANS ...
THEY'RE TAKING A BREAK.
THEY MIGHT BE WOUNDED... OR IT'S JUST A RUSE...
BYAKUGAN!

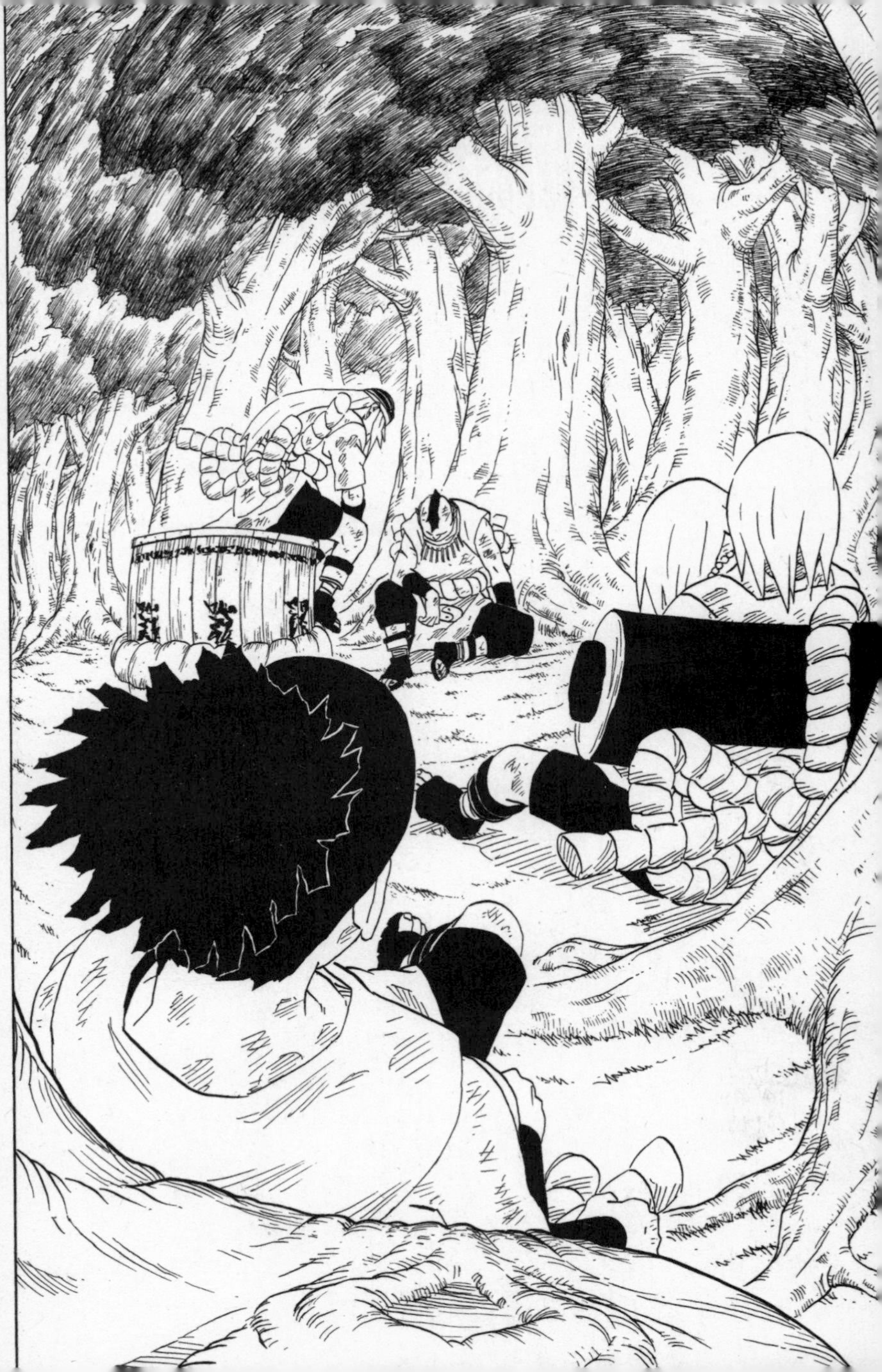

READ THIS WAY

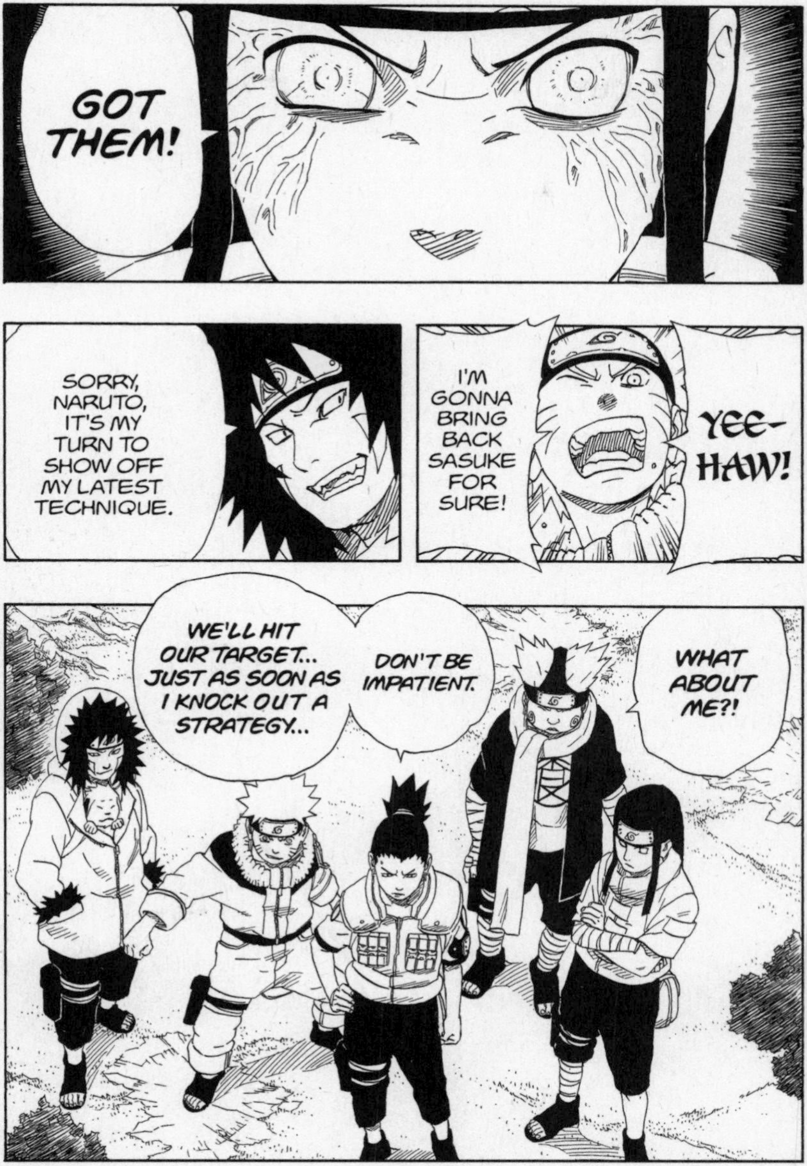
GOT THEM!
YEE-HAW!
I'M GONNA BRING BACK SASUKE FOR SURE!
SORRY, NARUTO, IT'S MY TURN TO SHOW OFF MY LATEST TECHNIQUE.
WHAT ABOUT ME?!
DON'T BE IMPATIENT.
WE'LL HIT OUR TARGET... JUST AS SOON AS I KNOCK OUT A STRATEGY...

Number 186: Failure...?!

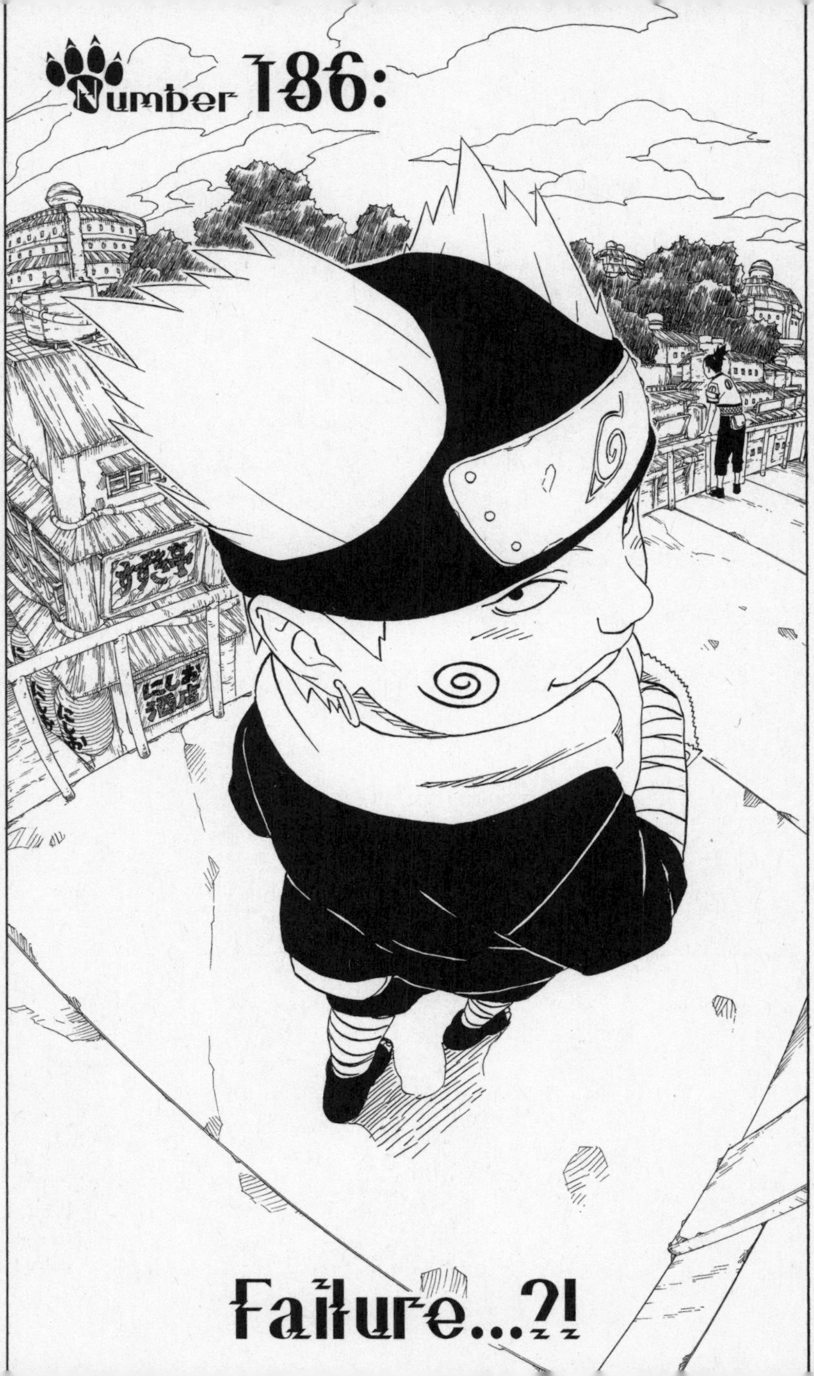

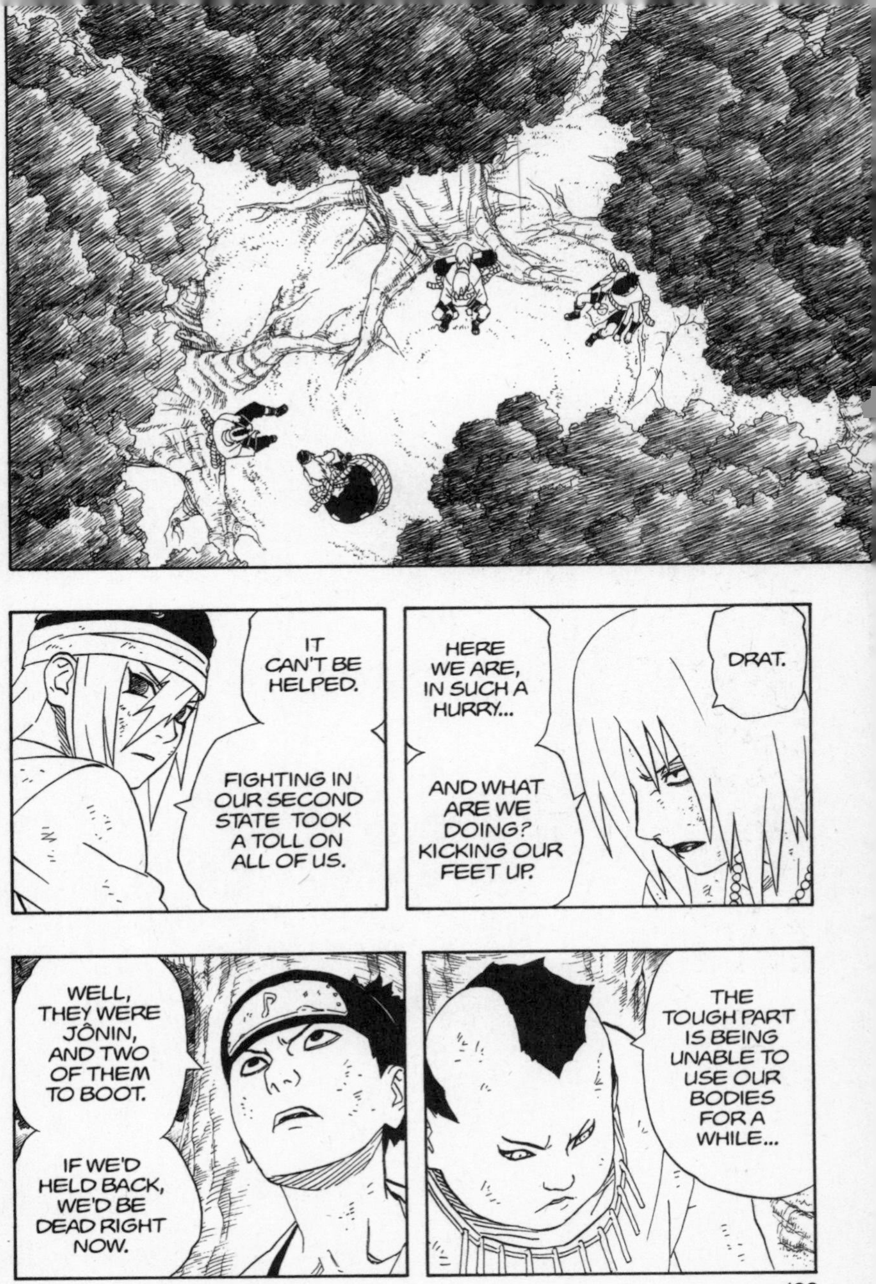
DRAT.
HERE WE ARE, IN SUCH A HURRY...
AND WHAT ARE WE DOING? KICKING OUR FEET UP.
IT CAN'T BE HELPED.
FIGHTING IN OUR SECOND STATE TOOK A TOLL ON ALL OF US.
THE TOUGH PART IS BEING UNABLE TO USE OUR BODIES FOR A WHILE...
WELL, THEY WERE JÔNIN, AND TWO OF THEM TO BOOT.
IF WE'D HELD BACK, WE'D BE DEAD RIGHT NOW.

READ THIS WAY

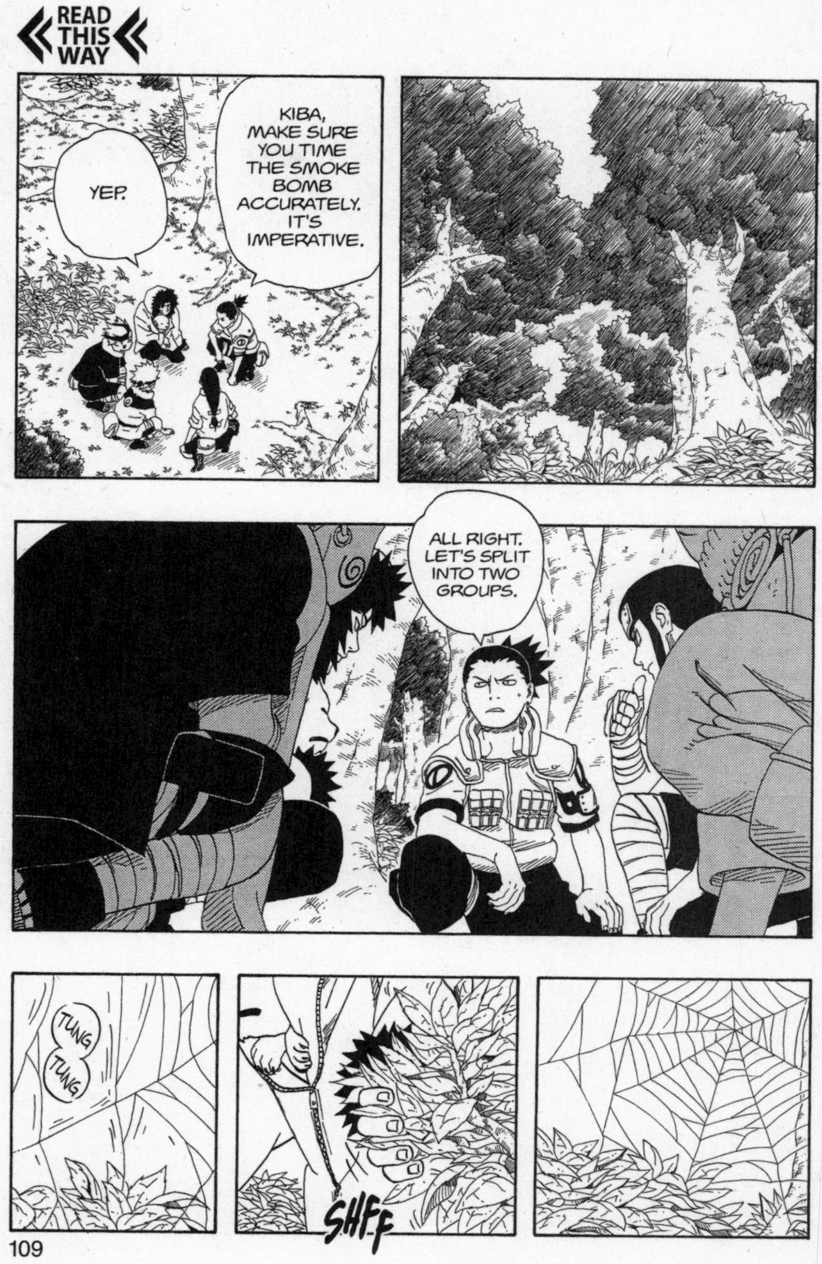
KIBA, MAKE SURE YOU TIME THE SMOKE BOMB ACCURATELY. IT'S IMPERATIVE.
YEP.
ALL RIGHT. LET'S SPLIT INTO TWO GROUPS.
SHFF
TUNG TUNG

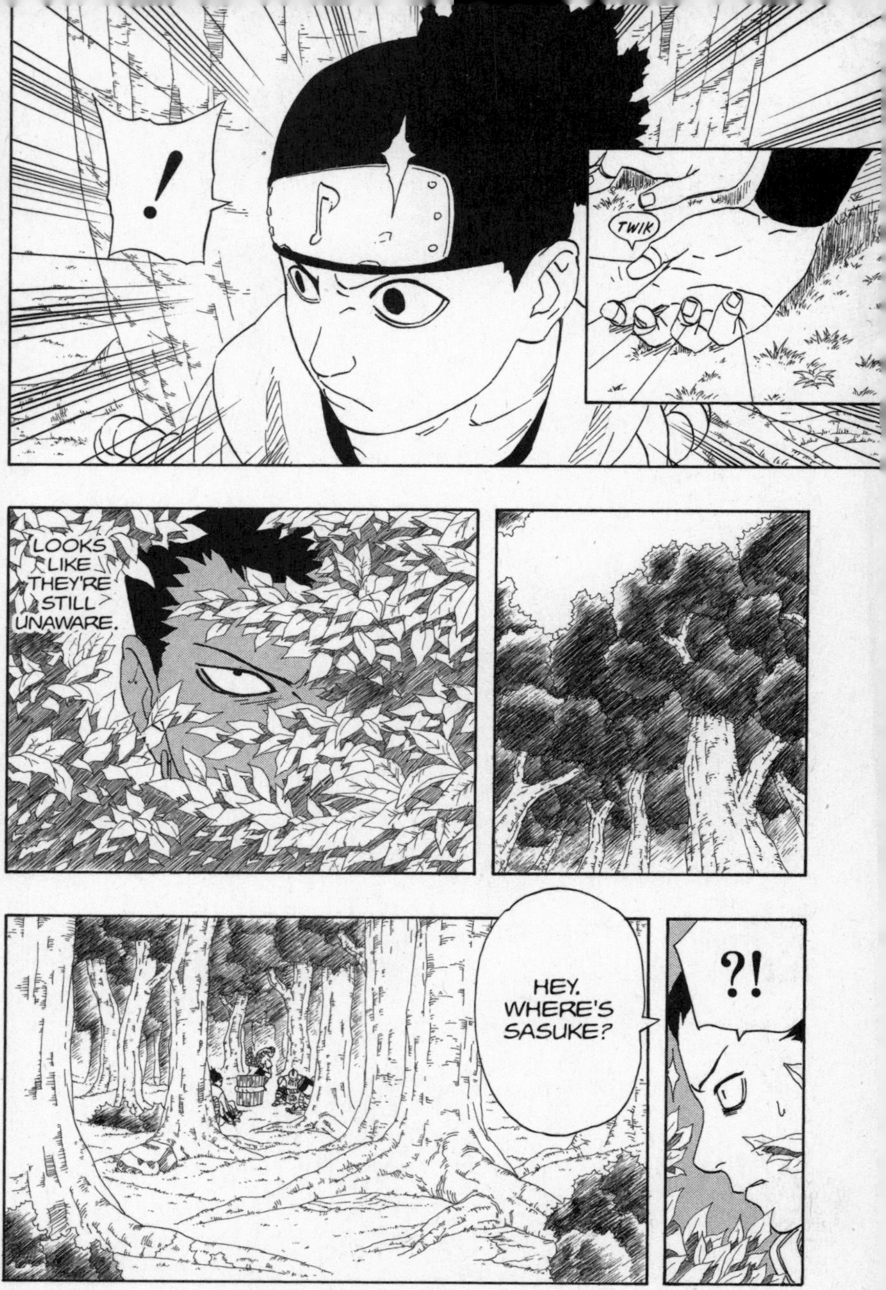
TWIK
!
LOOKS LIKE THEY'RE STILL UNAWARE.
?!
HEY. WHERE'S SASUKE?

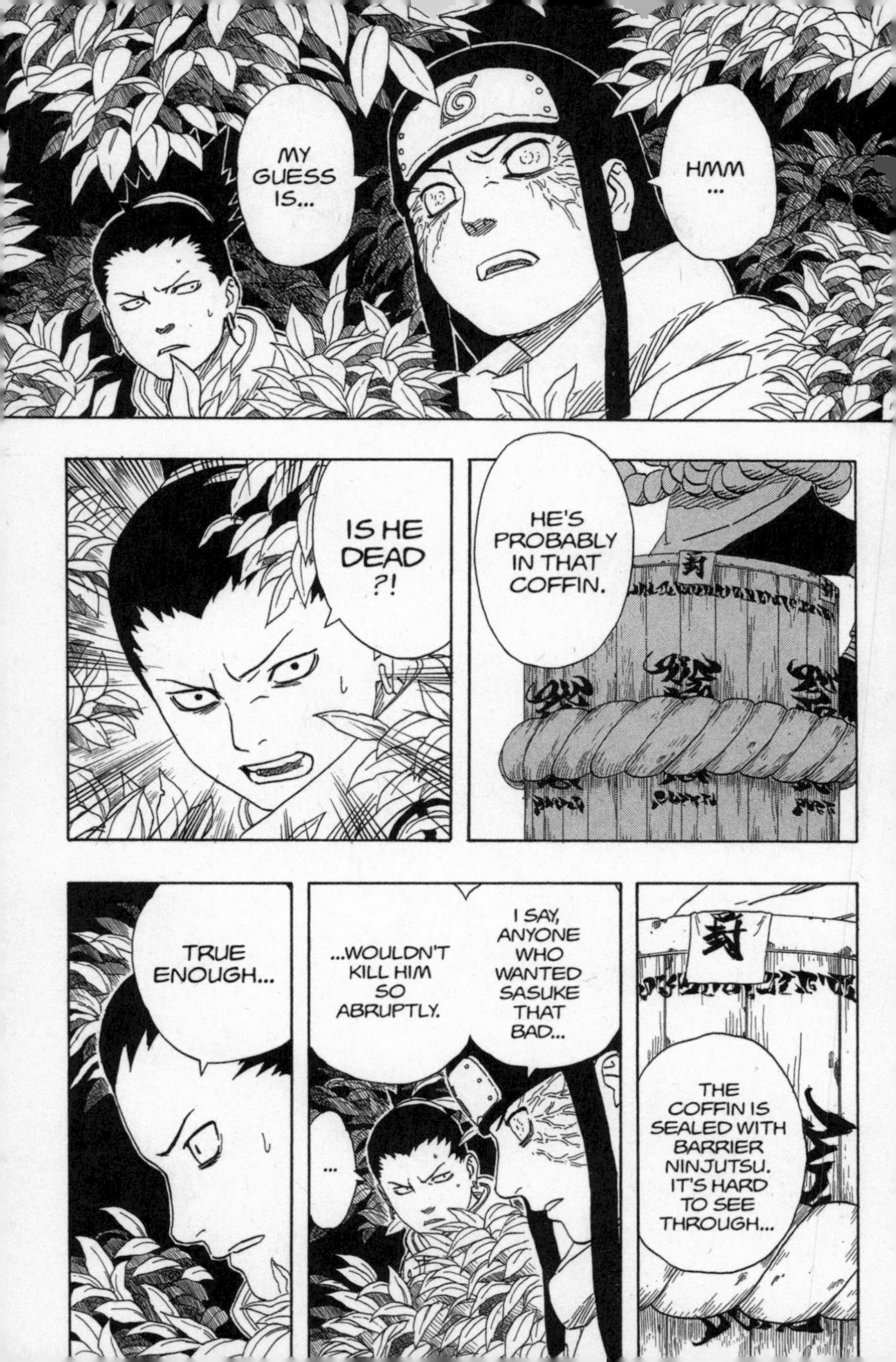
HMM...
MY GUESS IS...
HE'S PROBABLY IN THAT COFFIN.
IS HE DEAD?!
THE COFFIN IS SEALED WITH BARRIER NINJUTSU. IT'S HARD TO SEE THROUGH...
I SAY, ANYONE WHO WANTED SASUKE THAT BAD...
...WOULDN'T KILL HIM SO ABRUPTLY.
...
TRUE ENOUGH...

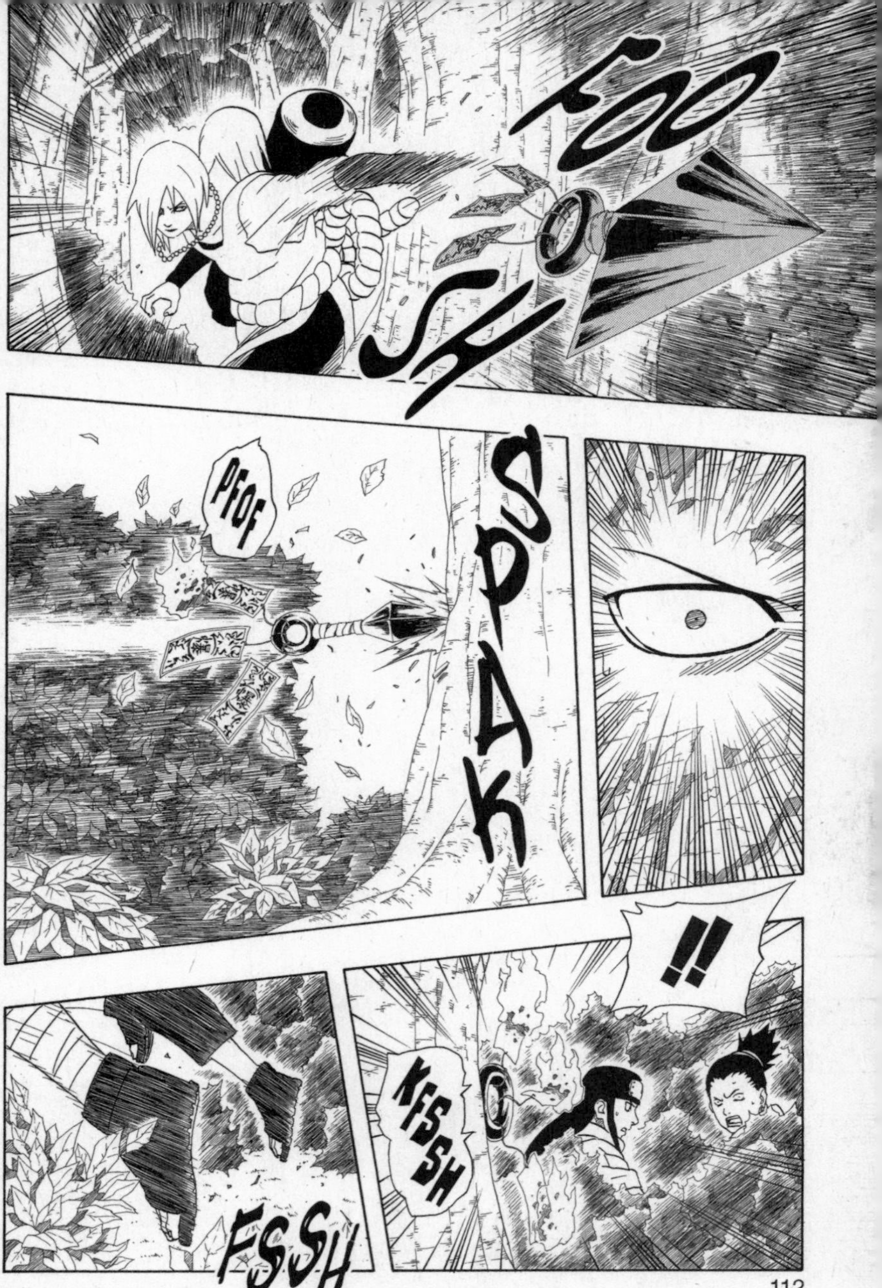
FOOSH
SPAK
PFOF
!!
KFSSH
FSSH

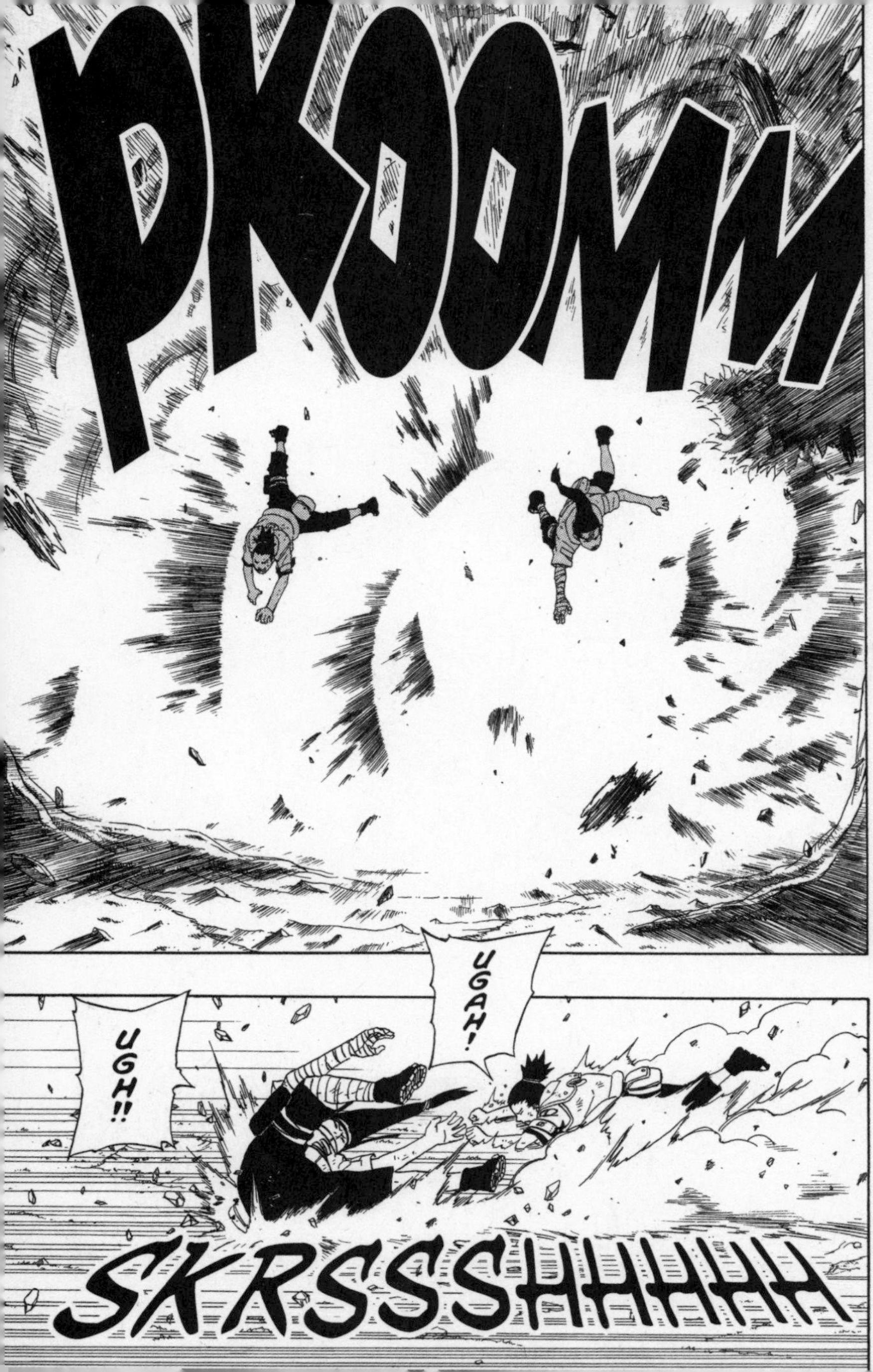
PKOOM
UGAH!
UGH!!
SKRSSHHHHH

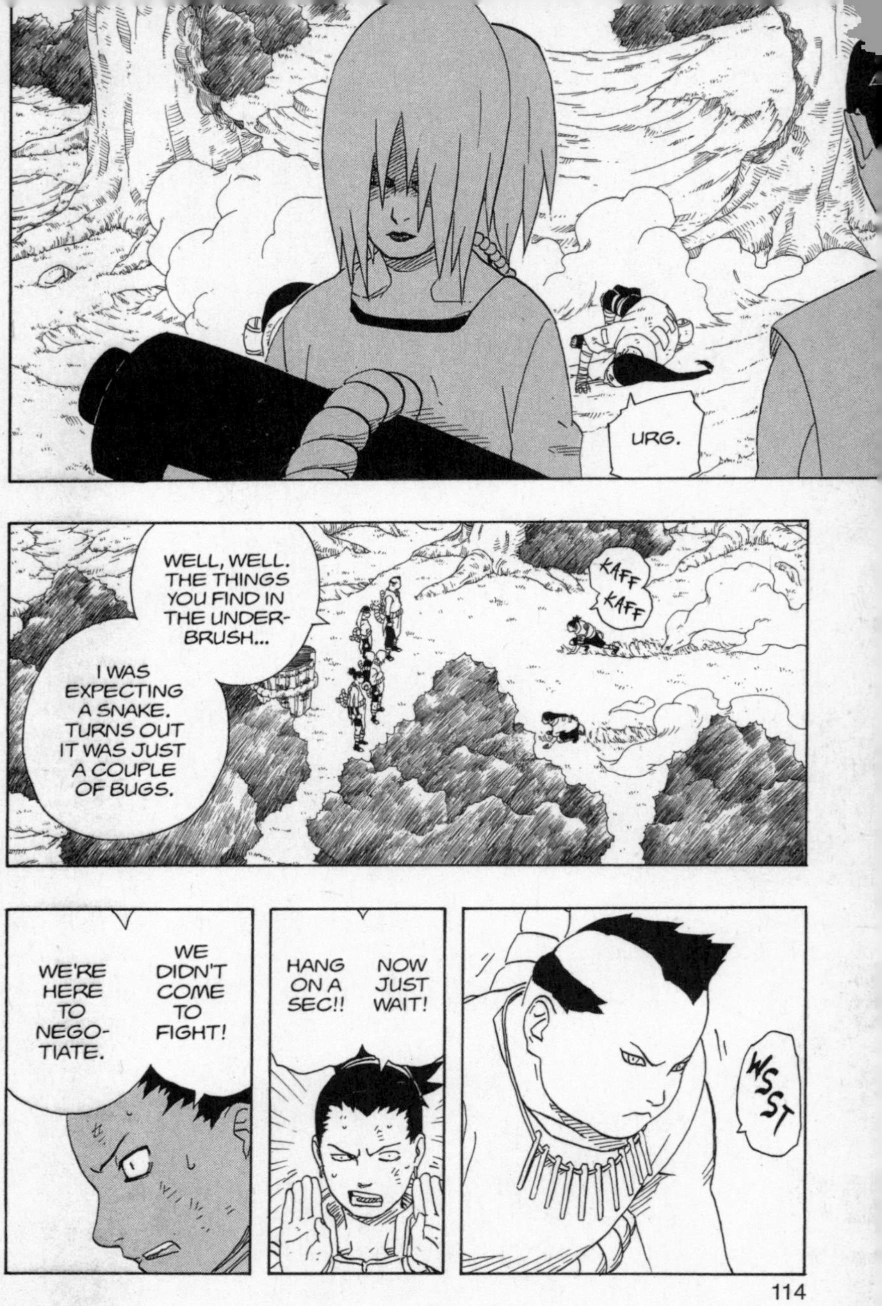
URG.
KAFF KAFF
WELL, WELL. THE THINGS YOU FIND IN THE UNDER-BRUSH...
I WAS EXPECTING A SNAKE. TURNS OUT IT WAS JUST A COUPLE OF BUGS.
WSST
NOW JUST WAIT!
HANG ON A SEC!!
WE DIDN'T COME TO FIGHT!
WE'RE HERE TO NEGO-TIATE.

READ THIS WAY

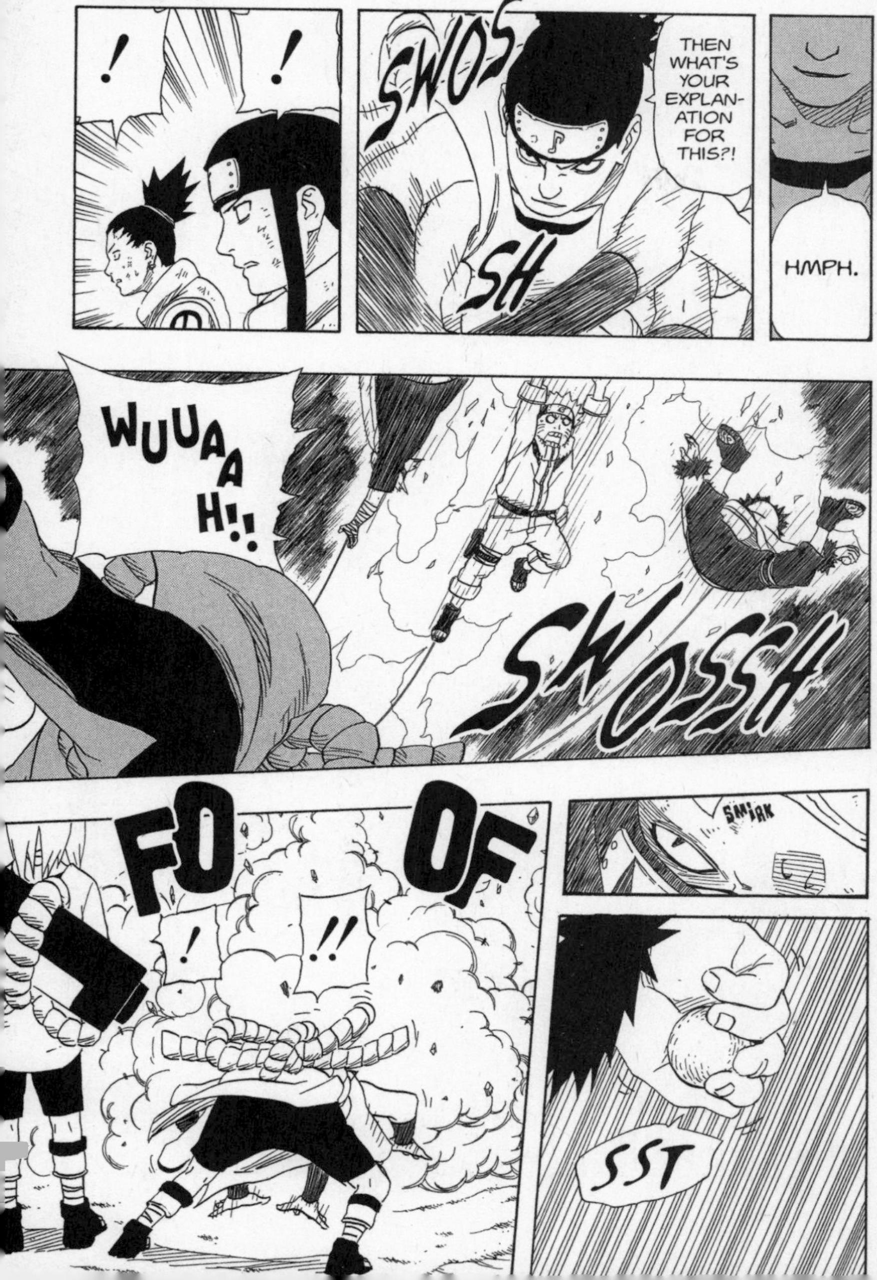
HMPH.
THEN WHAT'S YOUR EXPLANATION FOR THIS?!
SWOS
SH
!
!
WUUAAH!!
SKWOSSH
SMIRK
SST
FOOF
!
!!

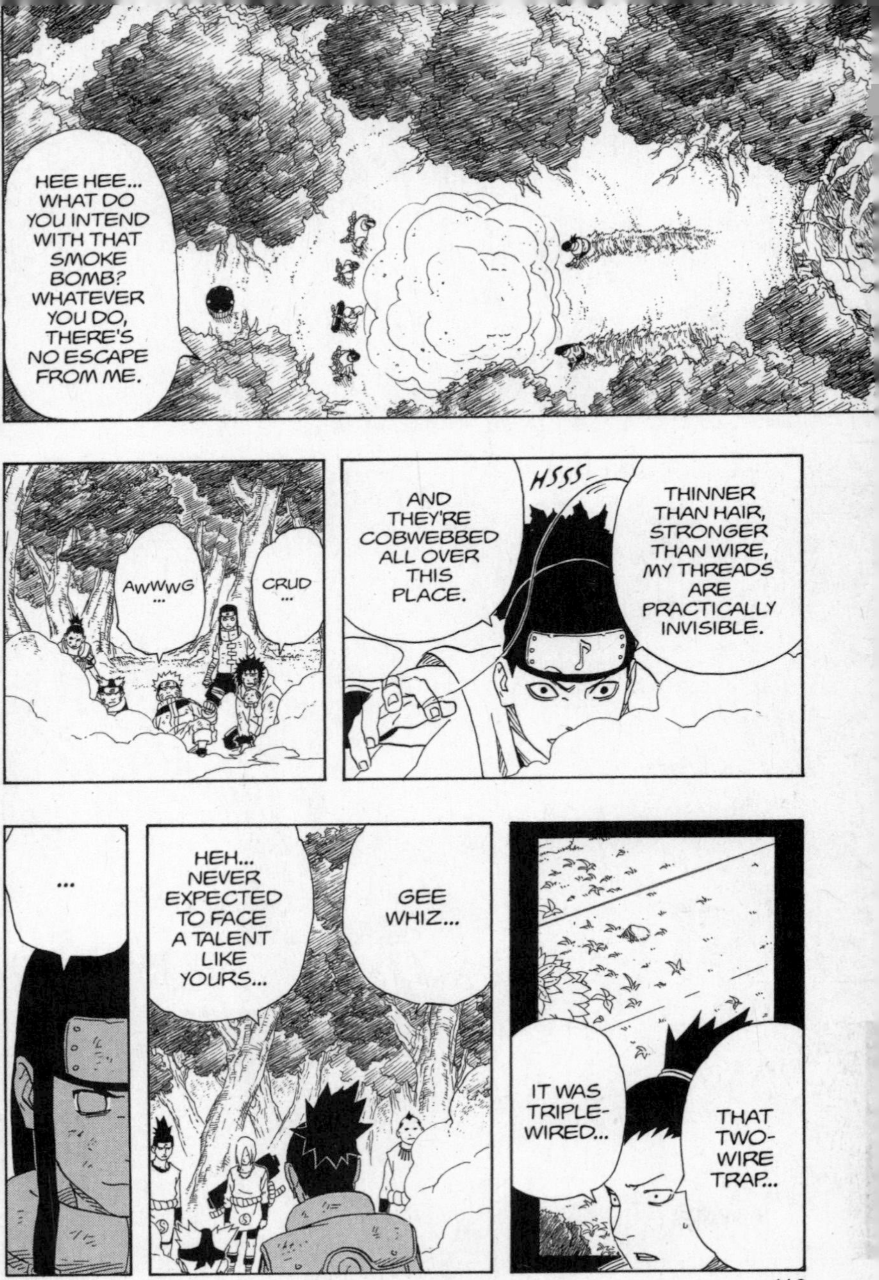
HEE HEE... WHAT DO YOU INTEND WITH THAT SMOKE BOMB? WHATEVER YOU DO, THERE'S NO ESCAPE FROM ME.
THINNER THAN HAIR, STRONGER THAN WIRE, MY THREADS ARE PRACTICALLY INVISIBLE.
HSSS
AND THEY'RE COBWEBBED ALL OVER THIS PLACE.
CRUD...
AWWWG...
THAT TWO-WIRE TRAP...
IT WAS TRIPLE-WIRED...
GEE WHIZ...
HEH... NEVER EXPECTED TO FACE A TALENT LIKE YOURS...
...

READ THIS WAY

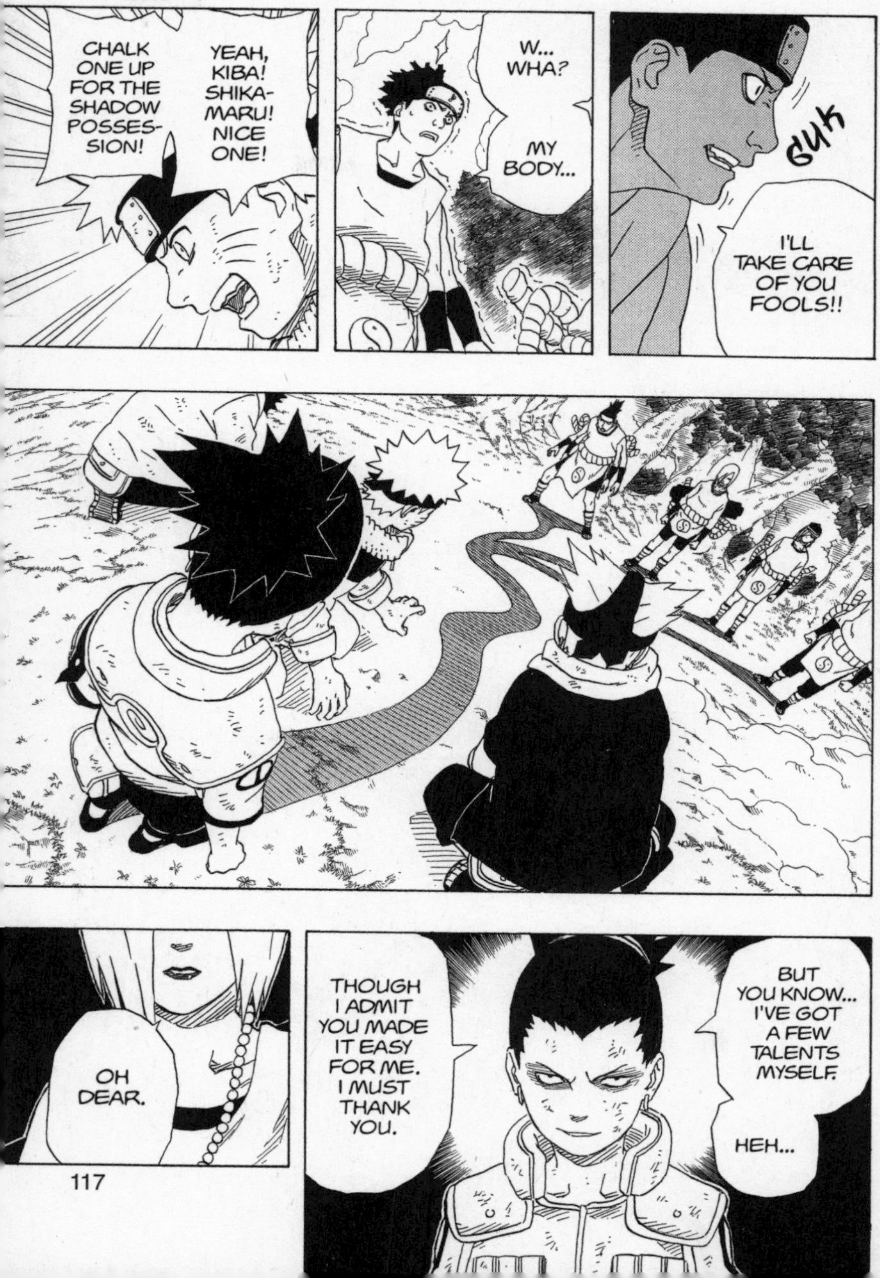
GUK
I'LL TAKE CARE OF YOU FOOLS!!
W... WHA?
MY BODY...
YEAH, KIBA! SHIKA-MARU! NICE ONE!
CHALK ONE UP FOR THE SHADOW POSSES-SION!
BUT YOU KNOW... I'VE GOT A FEW TALENTS MYSELF.
HEH...
THOUGH I ADMIT YOU MADE IT EASY FOR ME. I MUST THANK YOU.
OH DEAR.

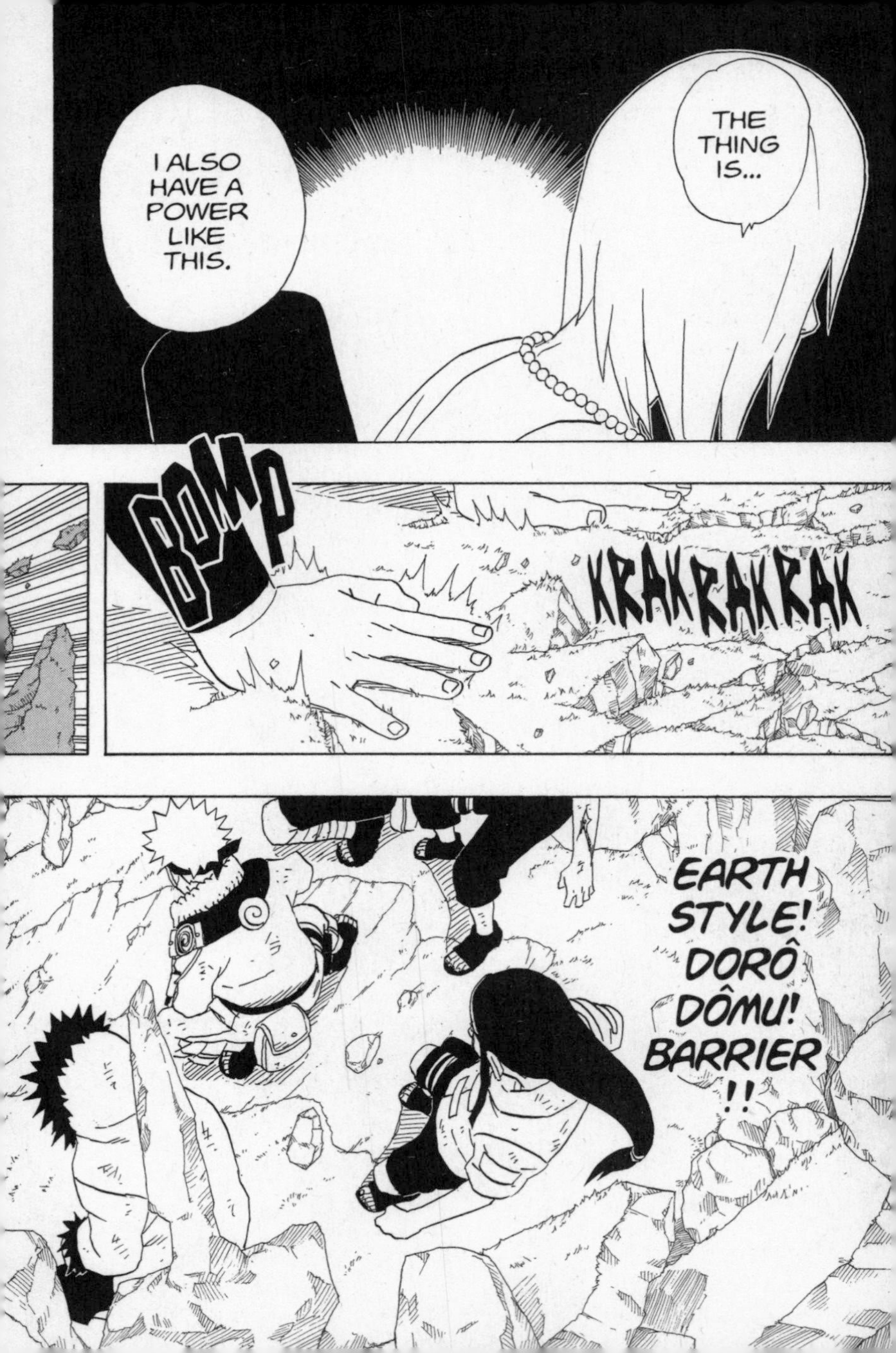
THE THING IS...
I ALSO HAVE A POWER LIKE THIS.
BOMP
KRAKRAKRAK
EARTH STYLE! DORÔ DÔMU! BARRIER!!

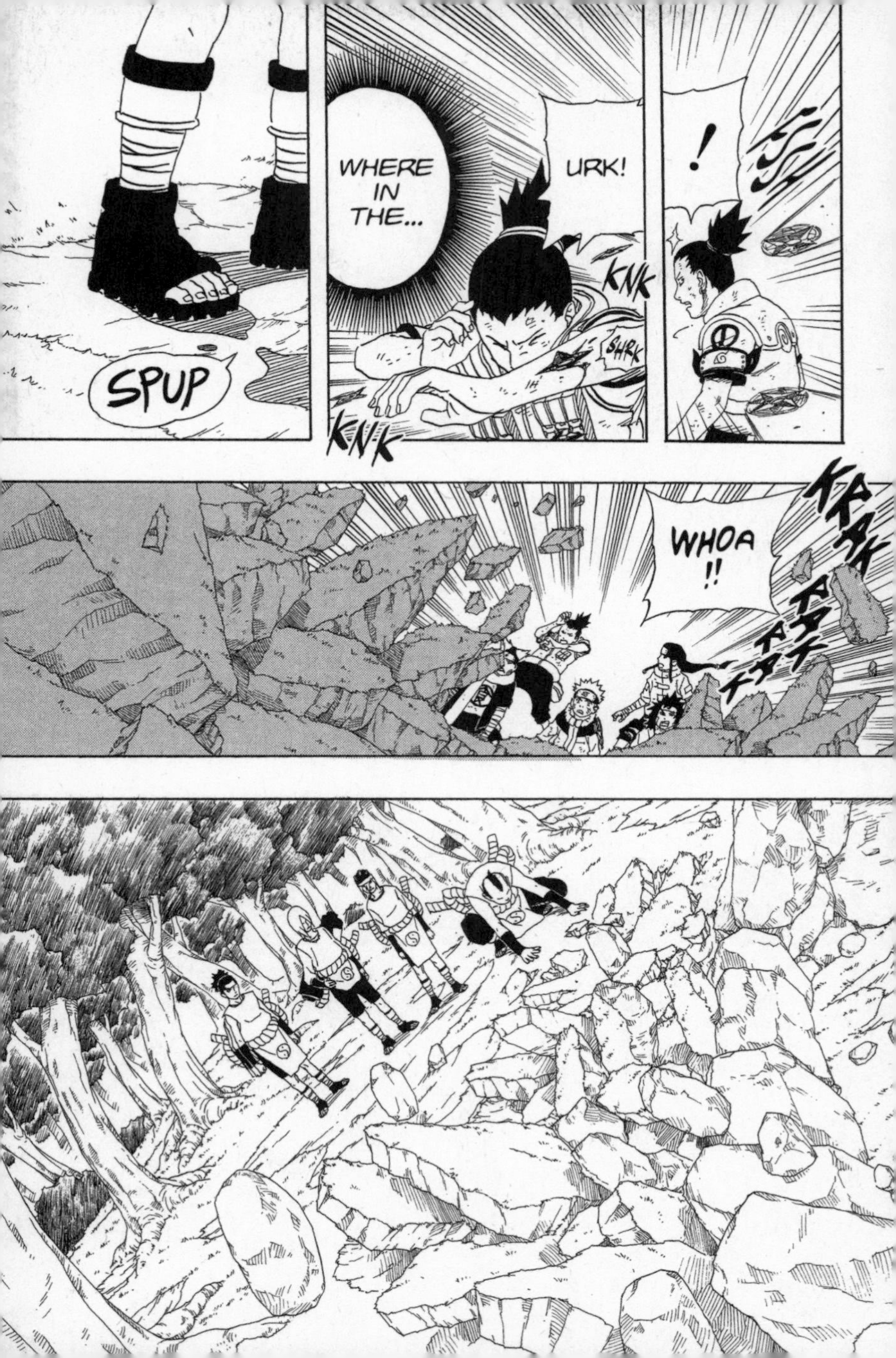
FSSH
!
URK!
WHERE IN THE...
KNK
SHRK
KNK
SPUP
KRAK KRAK KRAK
WHOA!!

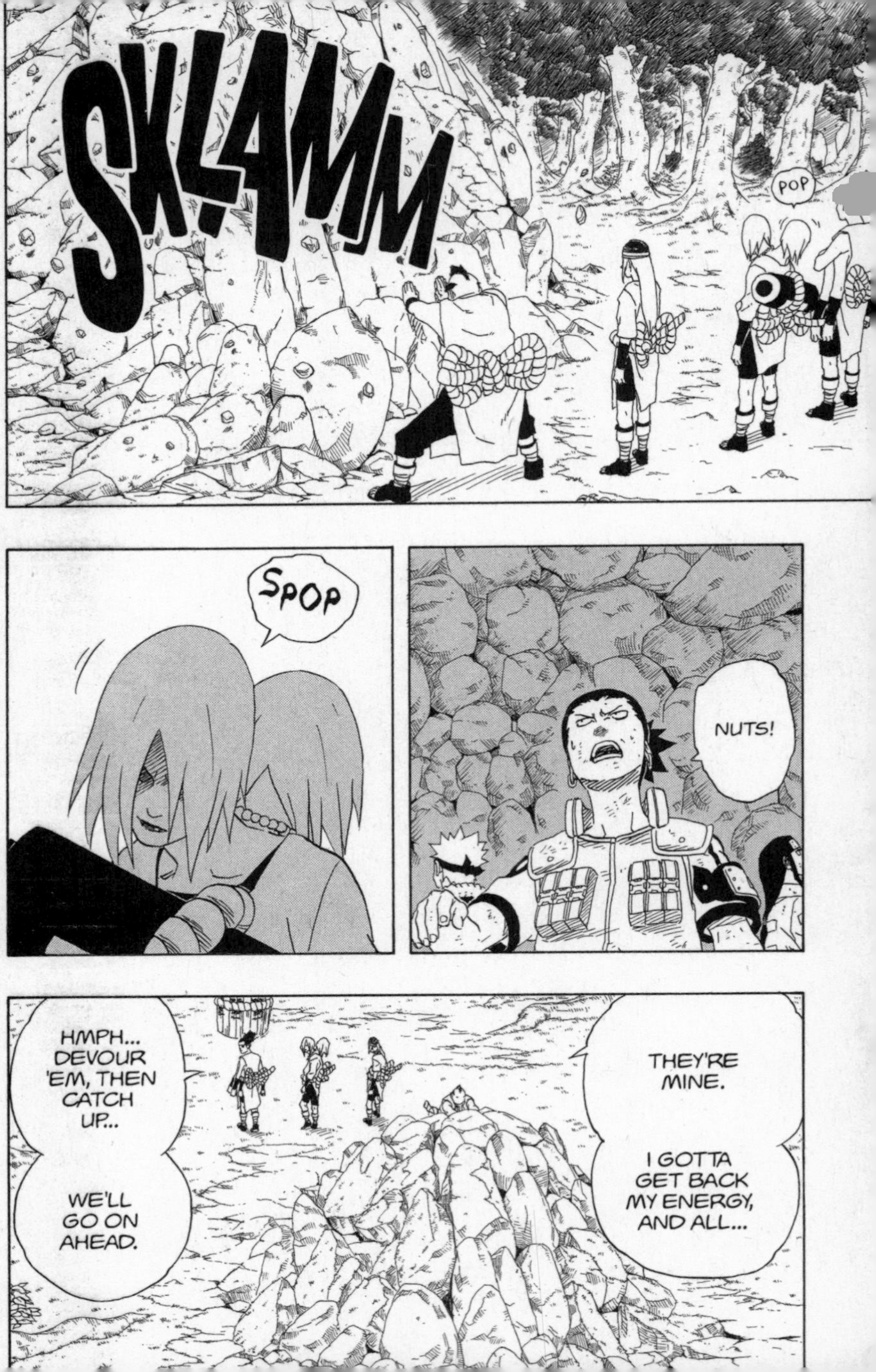
SKLAMM
POP
NUTS!
SPOP
THEY'RE MINE.
I GOTTA GET BACK MY ENERGY, AND ALL...
HMPH... DEVOUR 'EM, THEN CATCH UP...
WE'LL GO ON AHEAD.

READ THIS WAY

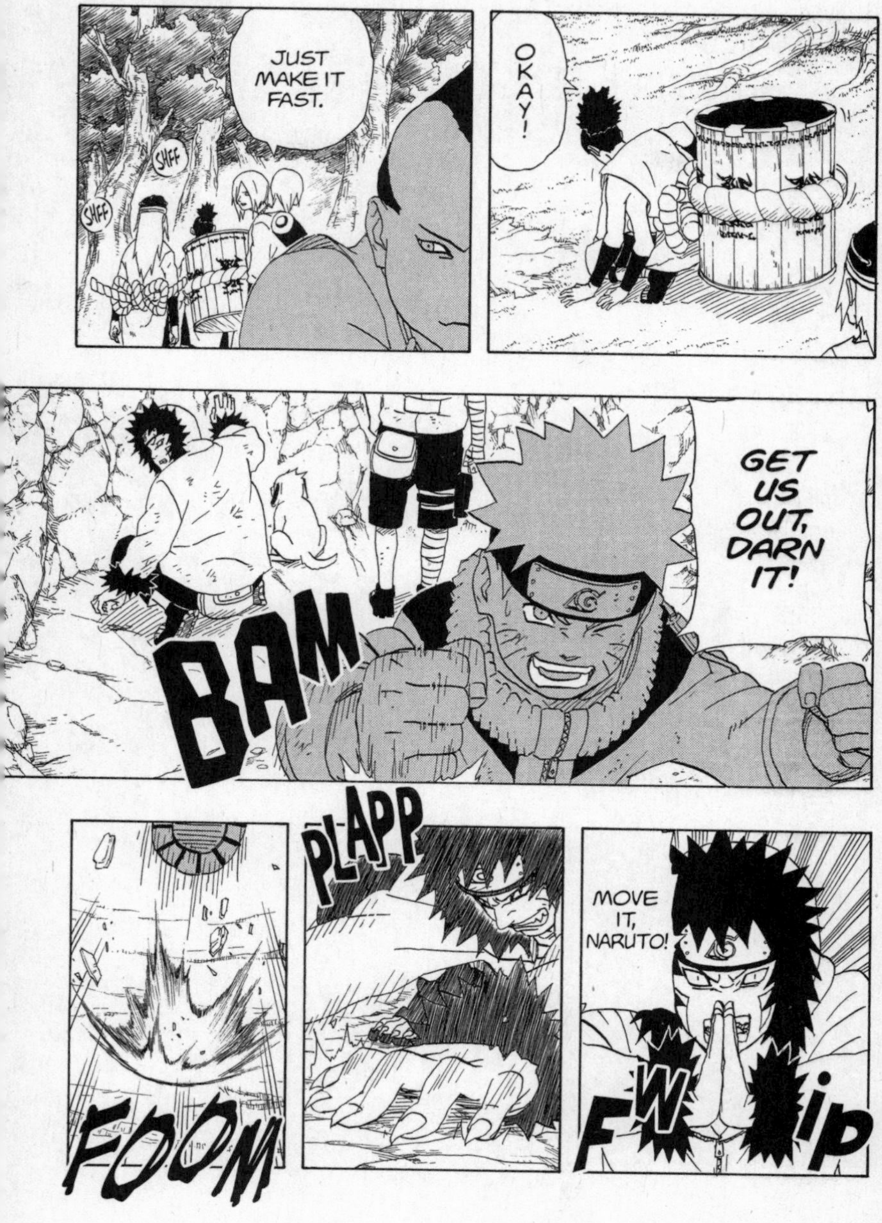
OKAY!
JUST MAKE IT FAST.
SHFF
SHFF
GET US OUT, DARN IT!
BAM
MOVE IT, NARUTO!
FWip
PLAPP
FOOM

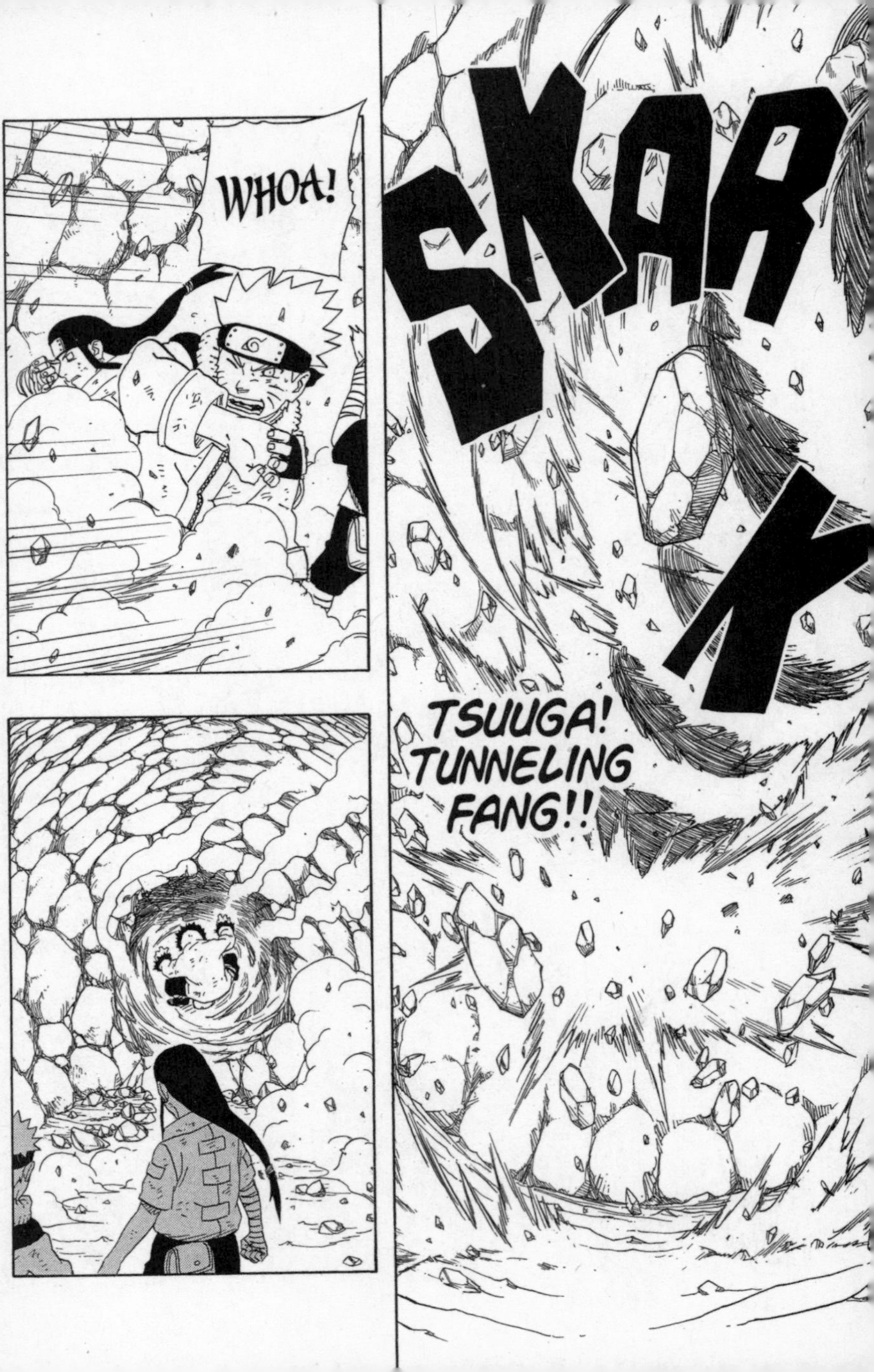
SKARK
TSUUGA! TUNNELING FANG!!
WHOA!

READ THIS WAY

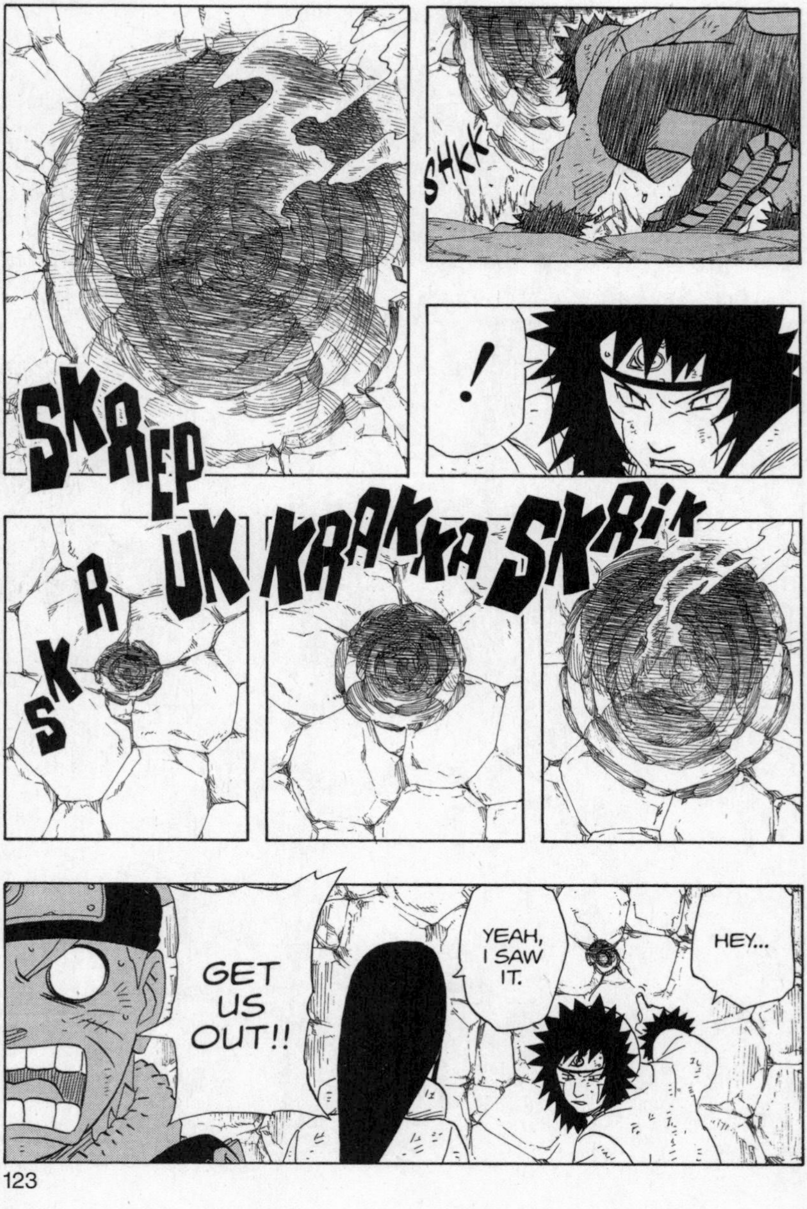
SHKK
!
SKREP
SKRIK
KRAKKA
SKRUK
HEY...
YEAH, I SAW IT.
GET US OUT!!

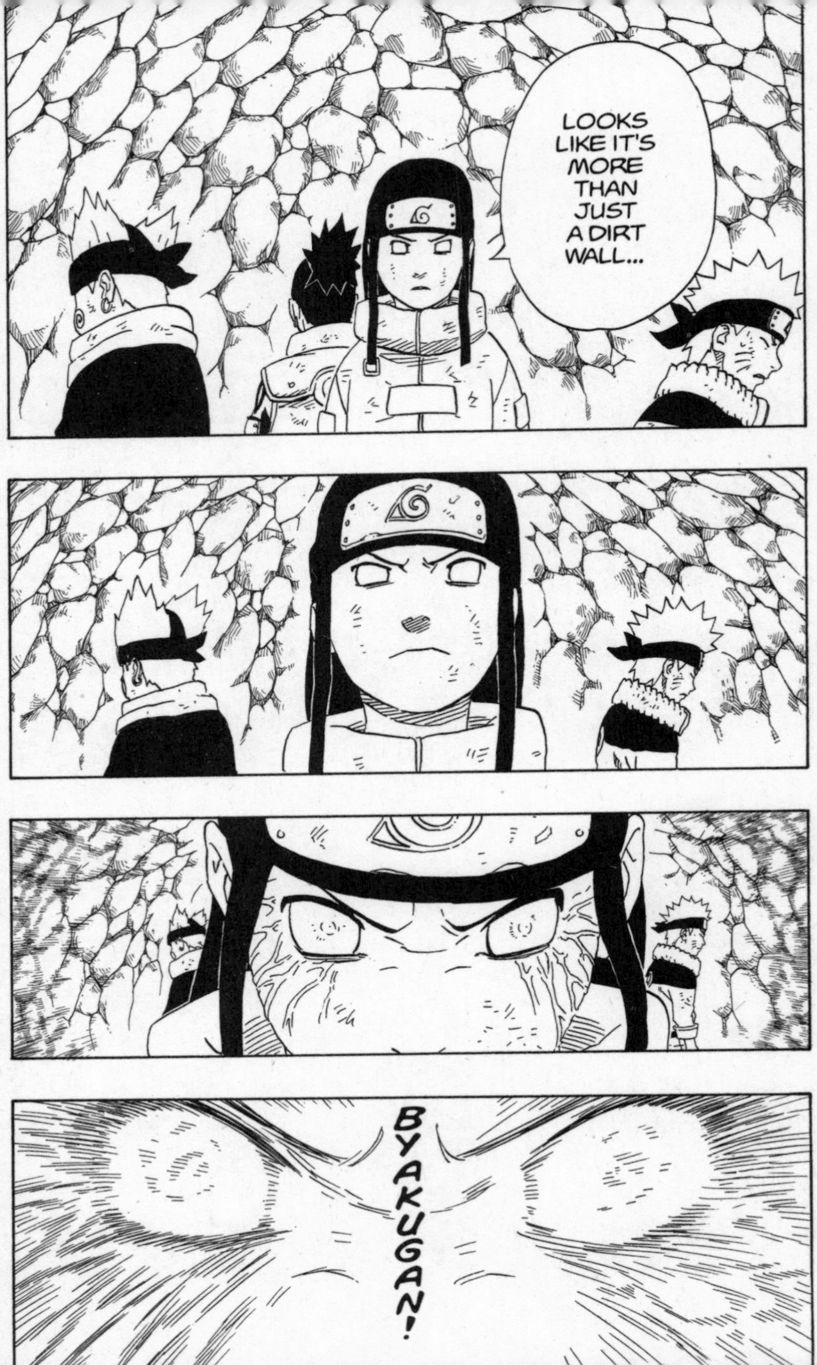
LOOKS LIKE IT'S MORE THAN JUST A DIRT WALL...
BYAKUGAN!

READ THIS WAY

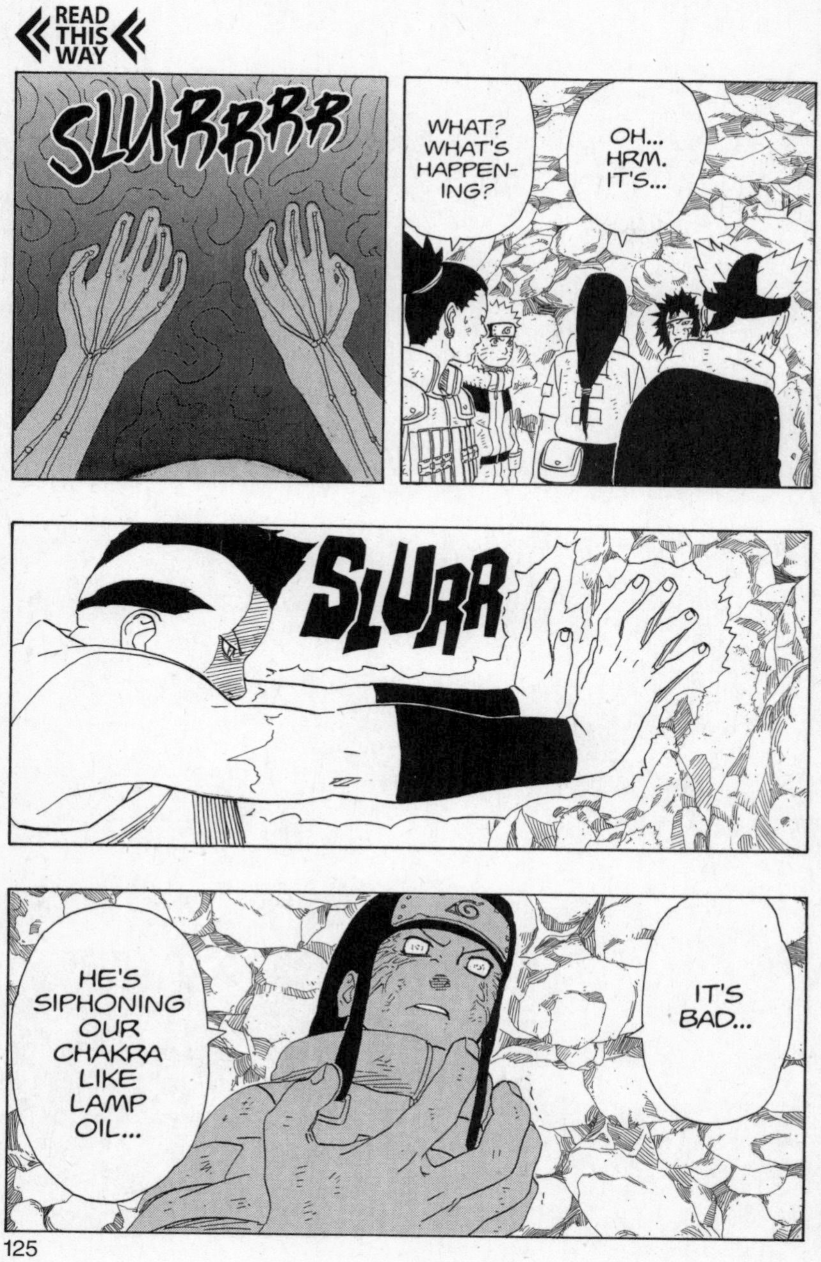
OH... HRM. IT'S...
WHAT? WHAT'S HAPPEN-ING?
SLURRRR
SLURR
IT'S BAD...
HE'S SIPHONING OUR CHAKRA LIKE LAMP OIL...

Number 187: The Plea...!!

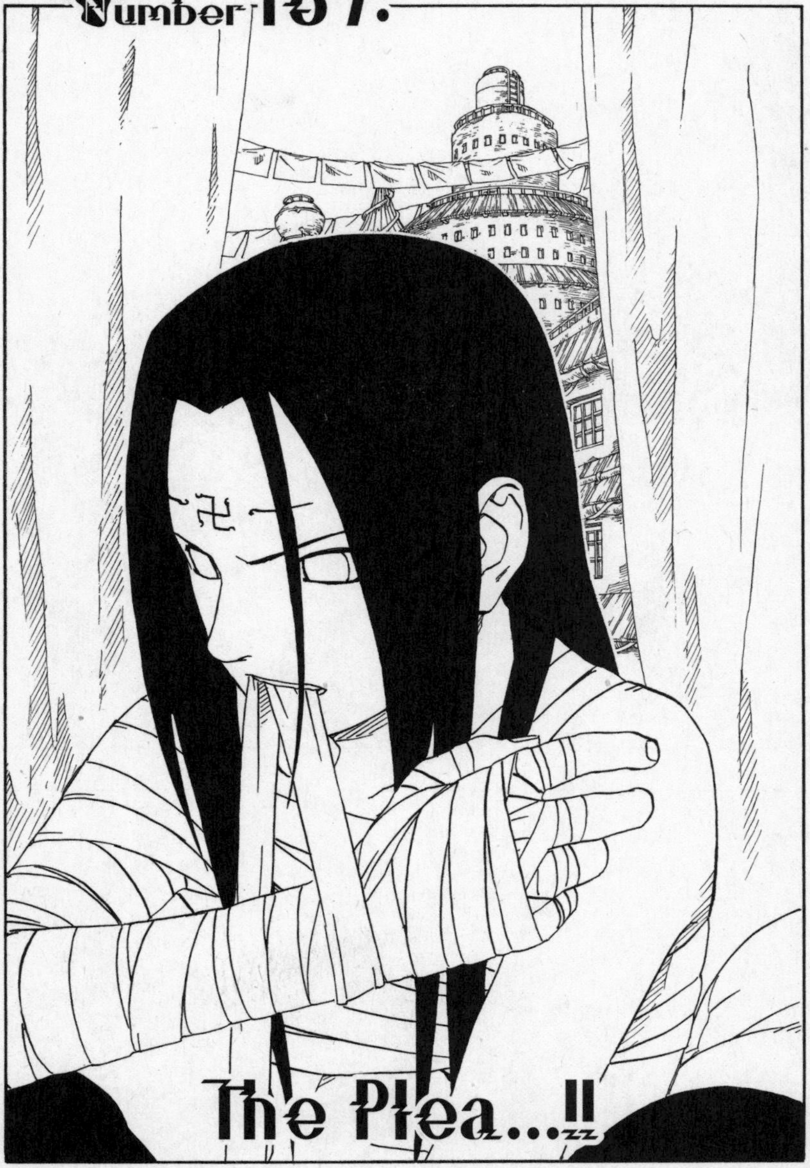

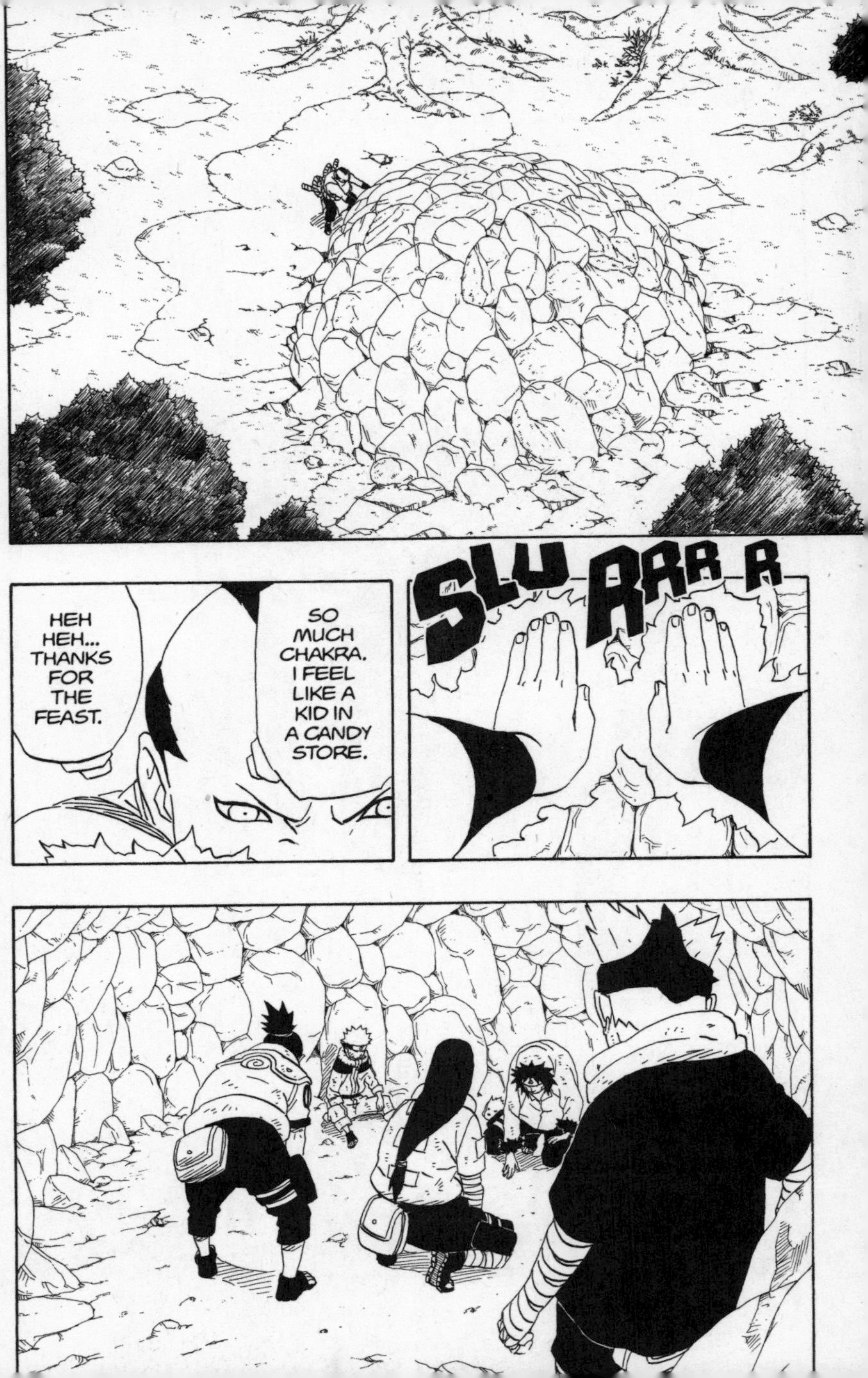
SLURRRR
SO MUCH CHAKRA. I FEEL LIKE A KID IN A CANDY STORE.
HEH HEH... THANKS FOR THE FEAST.

READ THIS WAY

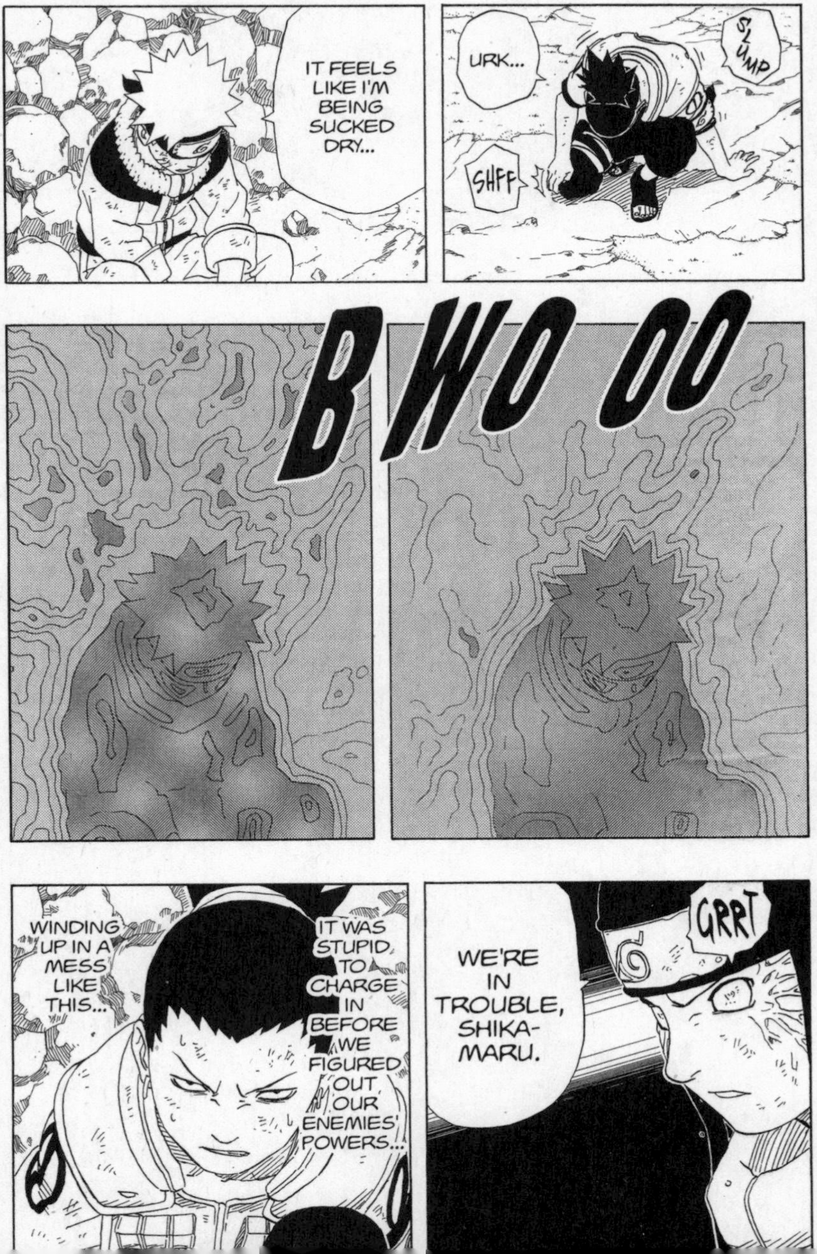
SLUMP
URK...
SHFF
IT FEELS LIKE I'M BEING SUCKED DRY...
BWOOO
GRRT
WE'RE IN TROUBLE, SHIKAMARU.
IT WAS STUPID TO CHARGE IN BEFORE WE FIGURED OUT OUR ENEMIES' POWERS...
WINDING UP IN A MESS LIKE THIS...

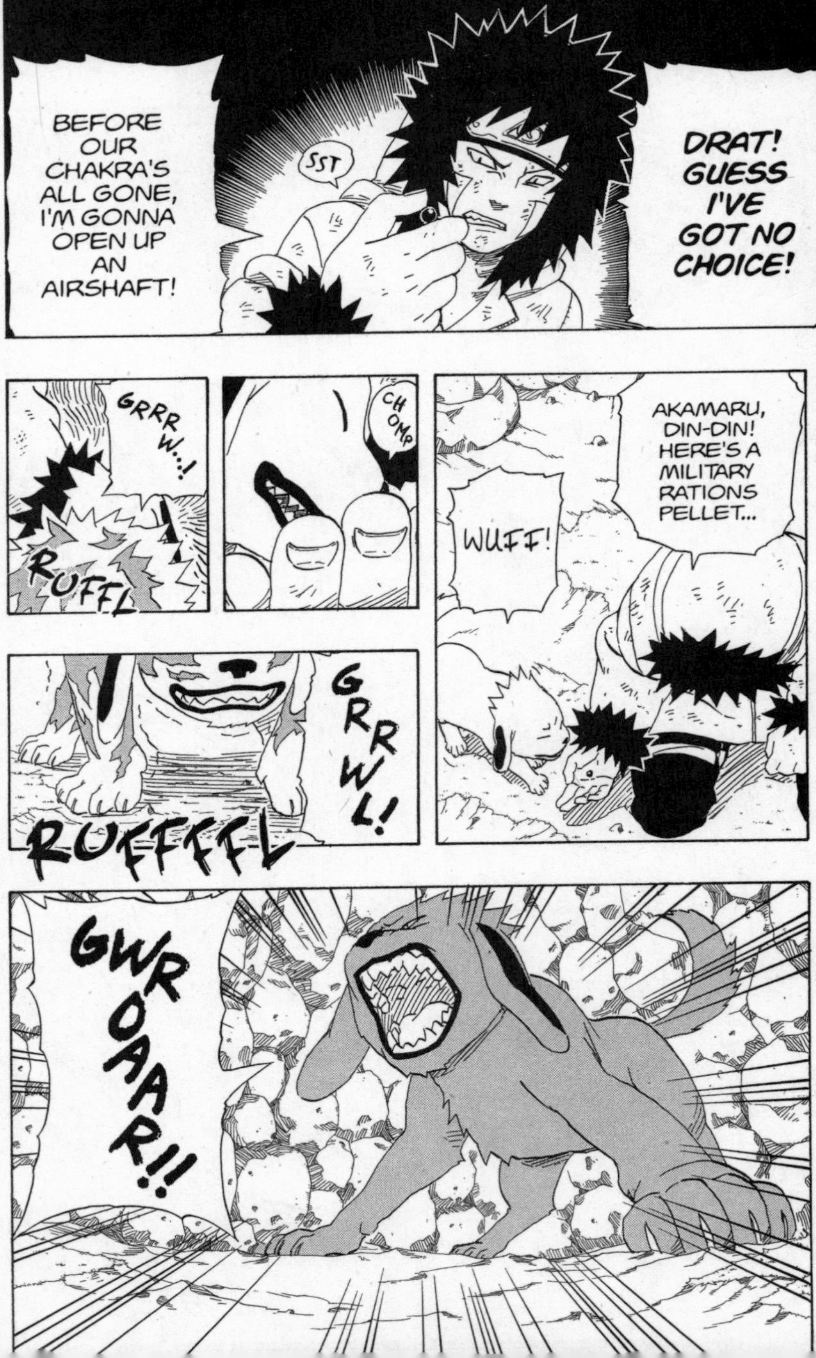
DRAT! GUESS I'VE GOT NO CHOICE!
SST
BEFORE OUR CHAKRA'S ALL GONE, I'M GONNA OPEN UP AN AIRSHAFT!
AKAMARU, DIN-DIN! HERE'S A MILITARY RATIONS PELLET...
WUFF!
CHOMP
GRRRW...!
RUFFL
GRRWL!
RUFFFFL
GWROAAR!!

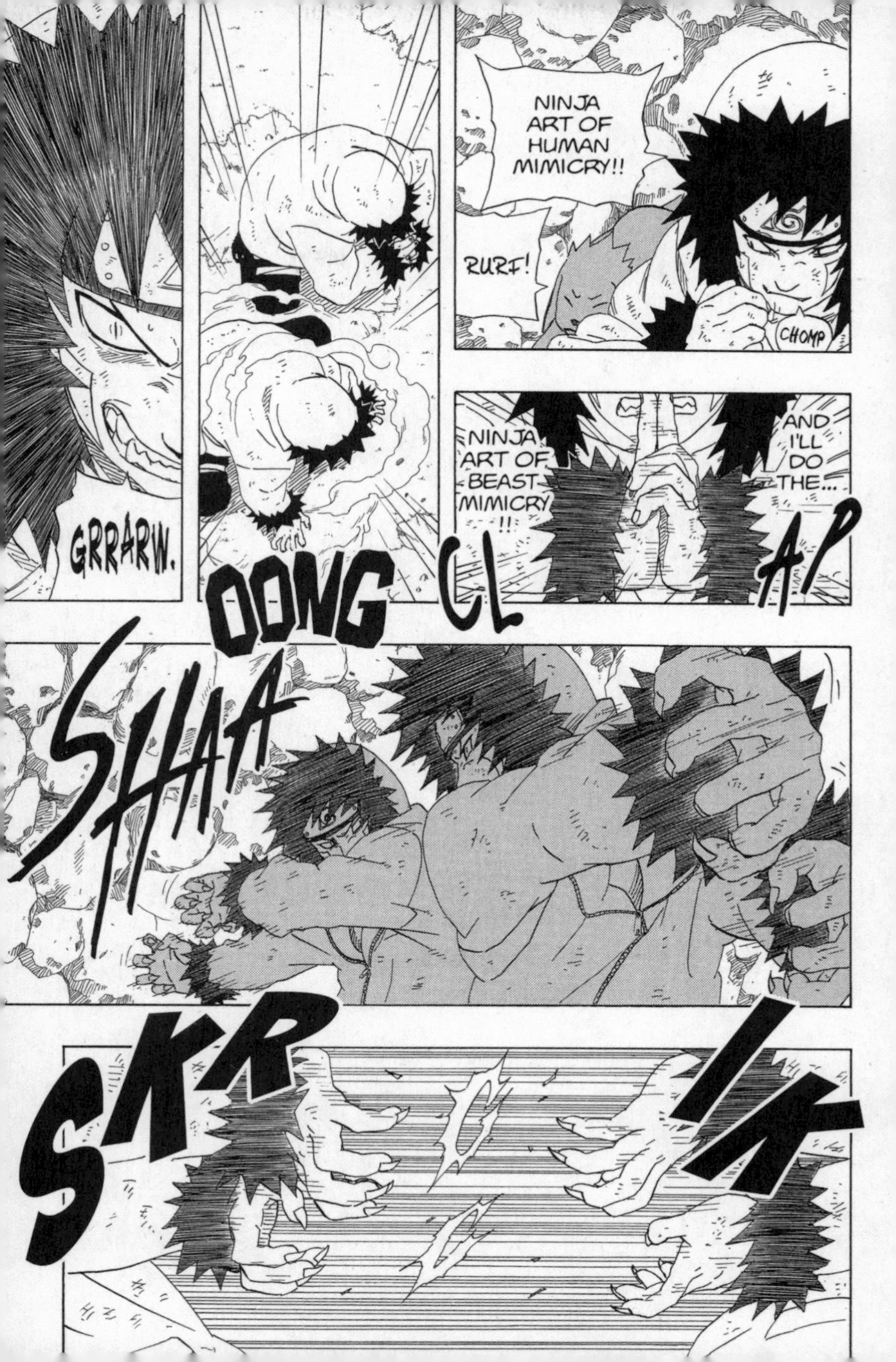
NINJA ART OF HUMAN MIMICRY!!
RURF!
CHOMP
AND I'LL DO THE...
NINJA ART OF BEAST MIMICRY!!
CL AP
OONG
GRRARW.
SHAA
SKR IIK

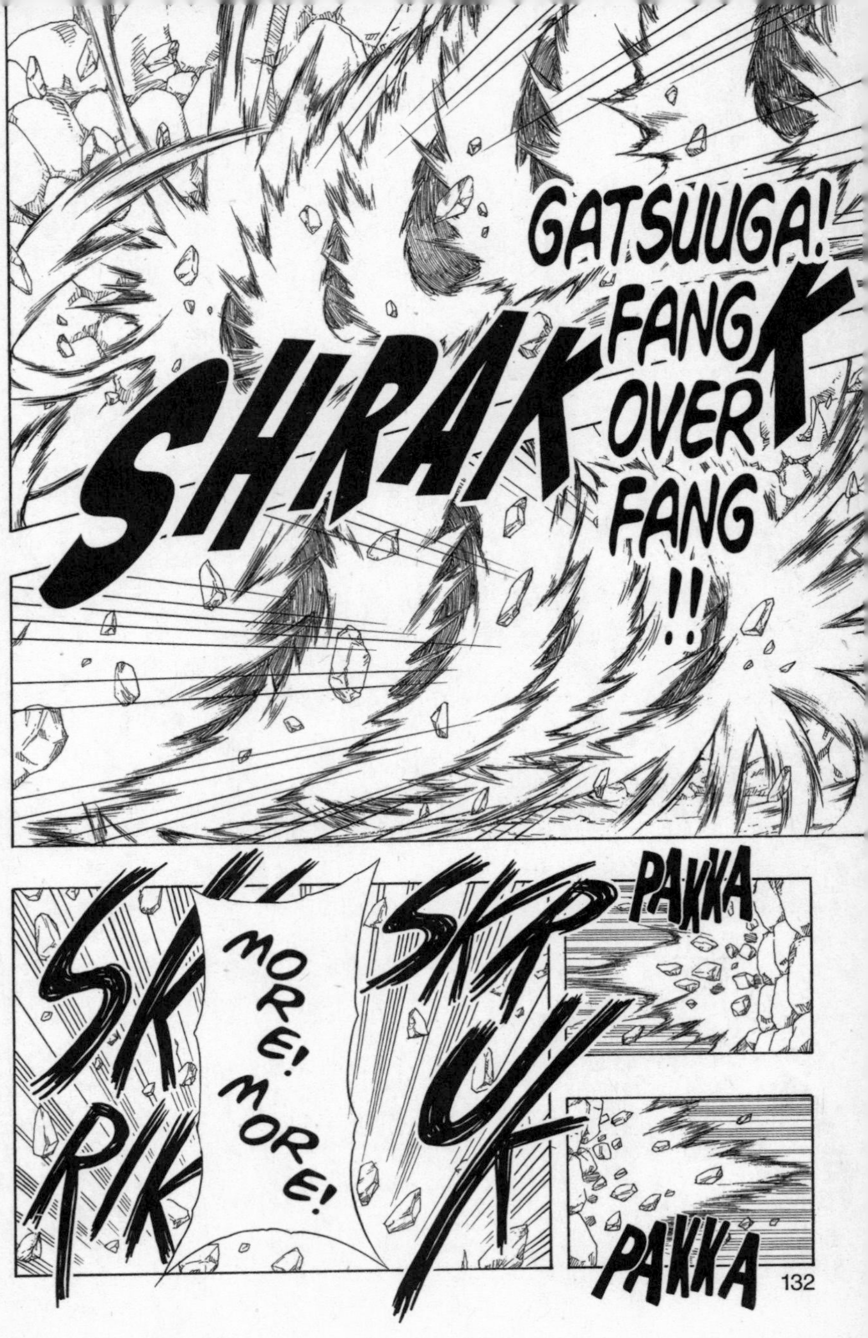
GATSUUGA! FANG OVER FANG!!
SHRAKK
PAKKA
PAKKA
SKRUK
MORE! MORE! MORE!
SKRIK

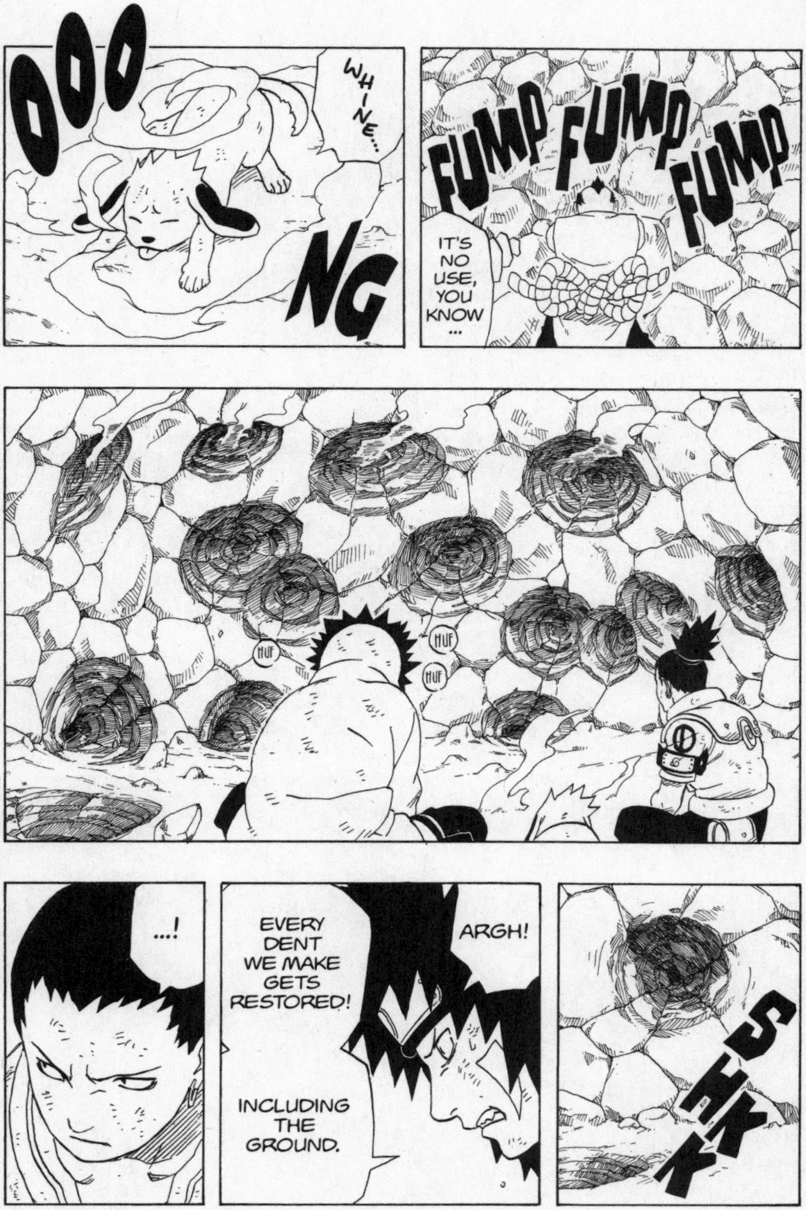
FUMP FUMP FUMP FUMP
IT'S NO USE, YOU KNOW...
WHINE...
OOO
NG
HUF
HUF
HUF
SHKK
ARGH!
EVERY DENT WE MAKE GETS RESTORED!
INCLUDING THE GROUND.
...!

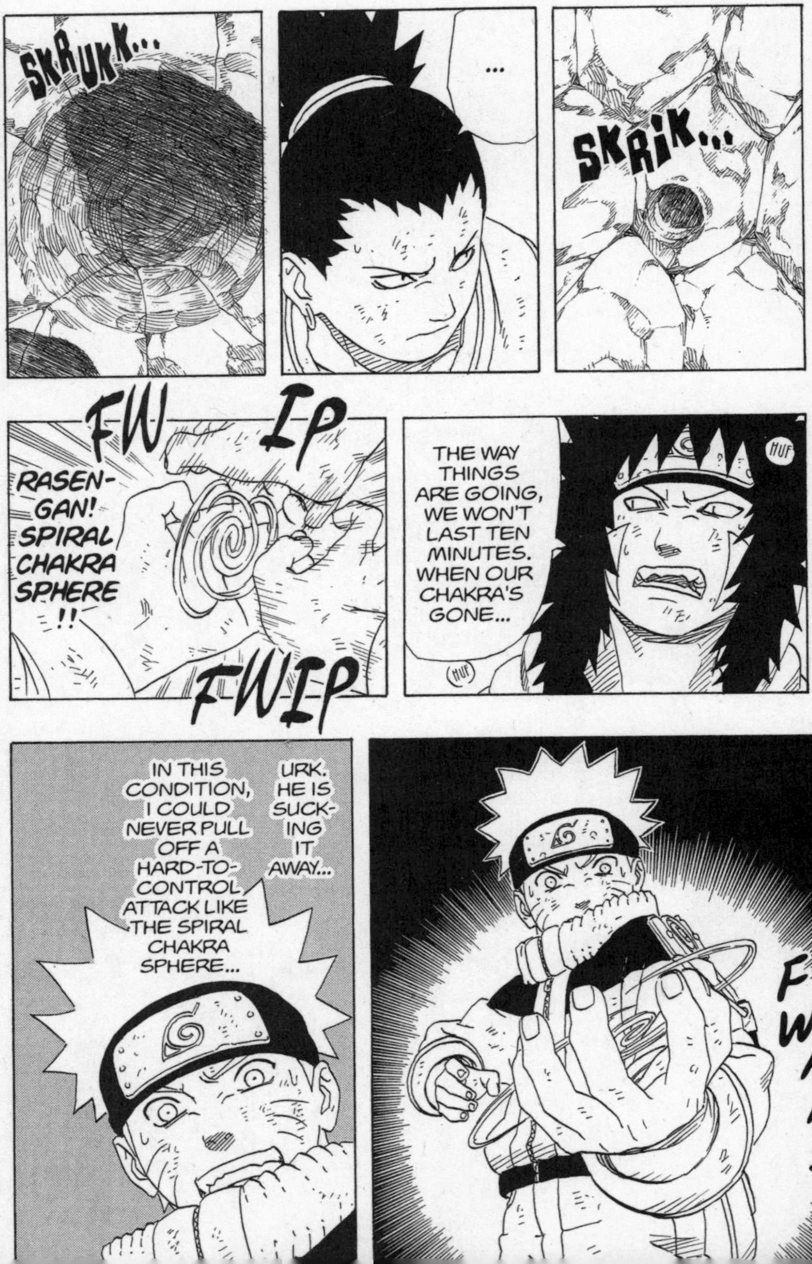
SKRIK...
...
SKRUKK...
HUF
THE WAY THINGS ARE GOING, WE WON'T LAST TEN MINUTES. WHEN OUR CHAKRA'S GONE...
HUF
FWIP
RASEN-GAN! SPIRAL CHAKRA SPHERE!!
FWIP
FWAA...
URK. HE IS SUCK-ING IT AWAY...
IN THIS CONDITION, I COULD NEVER PULL OFF A HARD-TO-CONTROL ATTACK LIKE THE SPIRAL CHAKRA SPHERE...

READ THIS WAY

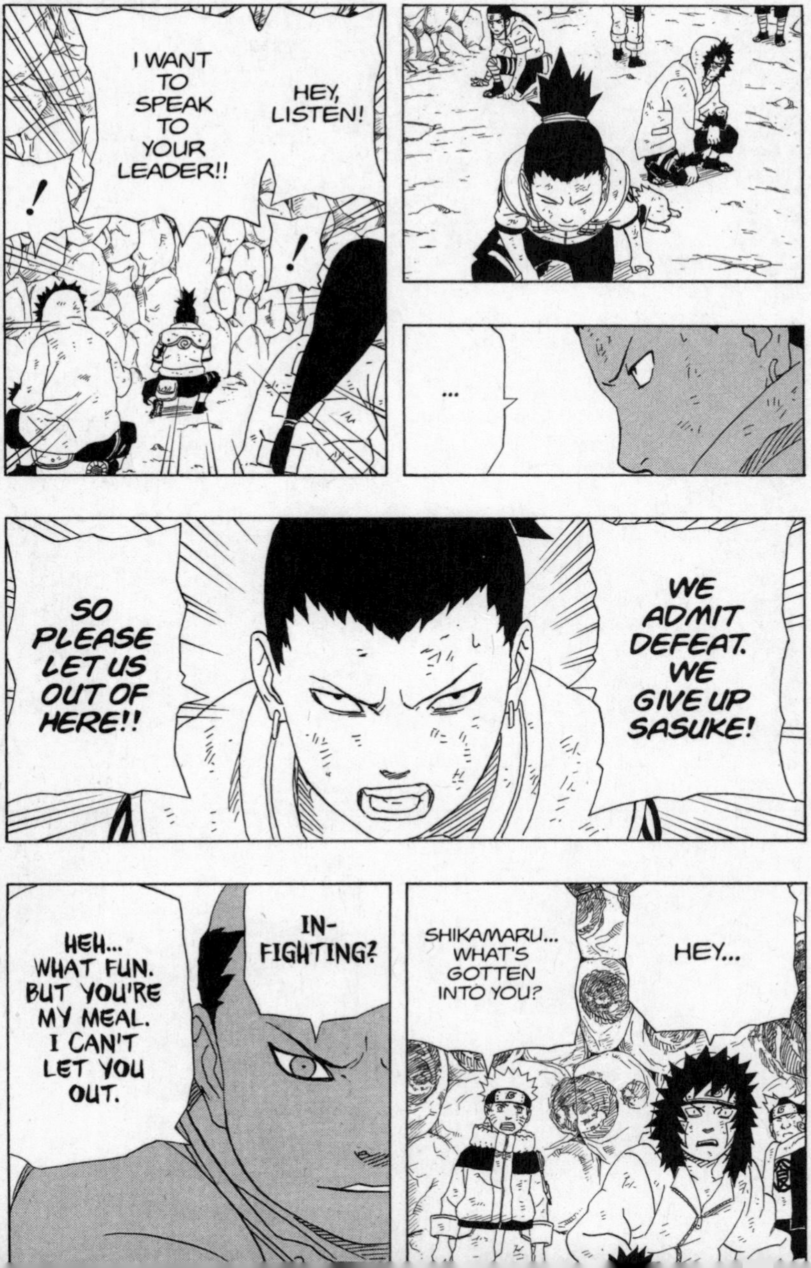
...
HEY, LISTEN!
I WANT TO SPEAK TO YOUR LEADER!!
!
!
WE ADMIT DEFEAT. WE GIVE UP SASUKE!
SO PLEASE LET US OUT OF HERE!!
HEY...
SHIKAMARU... WHAT'S GOTTEN INTO YOU?
IN-FIGHTING?
HEH... WHAT FUN. BUT YOU'RE MY MEAL. I CAN'T LET YOU OUT.

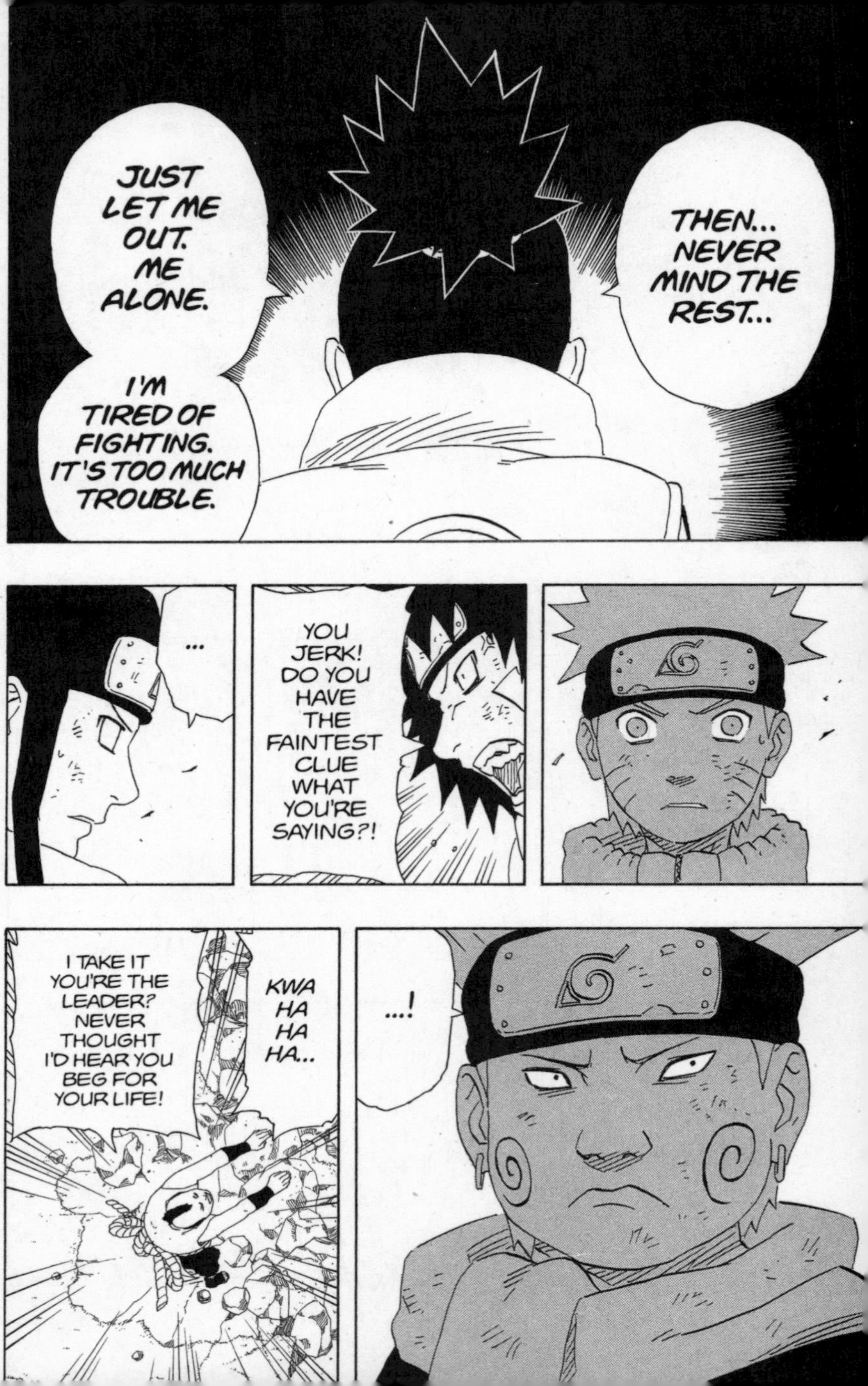
THEN... NEVER MIND THE REST...
JUST LET ME OUT. ME ALONE.
I'M TIRED OF FIGHTING. IT'S TOO MUCH TROUBLE.
YOU JERK! DO YOU HAVE THE FAINTEST CLUE WHAT YOU'RE SAYING?!
...
...!
KWA HA HA HA...
I TAKE IT YOU'RE THE LEADER? NEVER THOUGHT I'D HEAR YOU BEG FOR YOUR LIFE!

READ THIS WAY

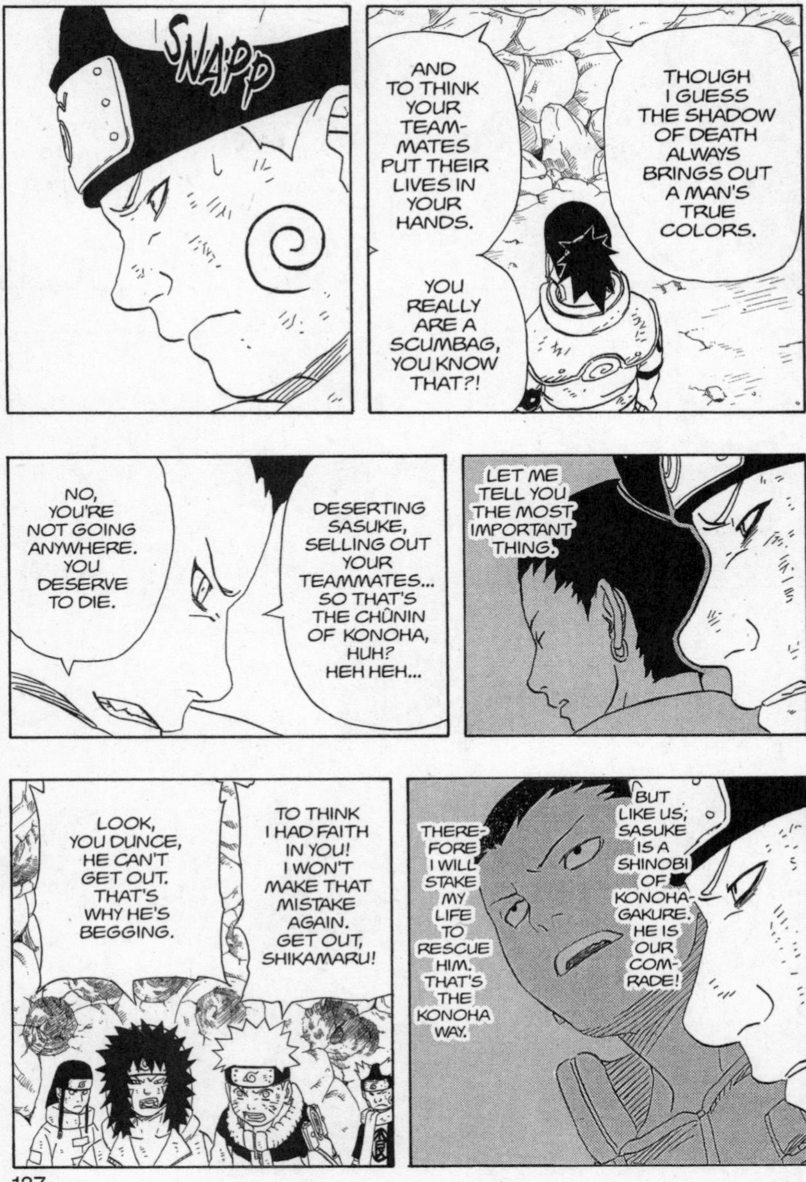
THOUGH I GUESS THE SHADOW OF DEATH ALWAYS BRINGS OUT A MAN'S TRUE COLORS.
AND TO THINK YOUR TEAM-MATES PUT THEIR LIVES IN YOUR HANDS.
YOU REALLY ARE A SCUMBAG, YOU KNOW THAT?!
SNAPP
LET ME TELL YOU THE MOST IMPORTANT THING.
DESERTING SASUKE, SELLING OUT YOUR TEAMMATES... SO THAT'S THE CHÛNIN OF KONOHA, HUH? HEH HEH...
NO, YOU'RE NOT GOING ANYWHERE. YOU DESERVE TO DIE.
BUT LIKE US, SASUKE IS A SHINOBI OF KONOHA-GAKURE. HE IS OUR COM-RADE!
THERE-FORE I WILL STAKE MY LIFE TO RESCUE HIM. THAT'S THE KONOHA WAY.
TO THINK I HAD FAITH IN YOU! I WON'T MAKE THAT MISTAKE AGAIN. GET OUT, SHIKAMARU!
LOOK, YOU DUNCE, HE CAN'T GET OUT. THAT'S WHY HE'S BEGGING.

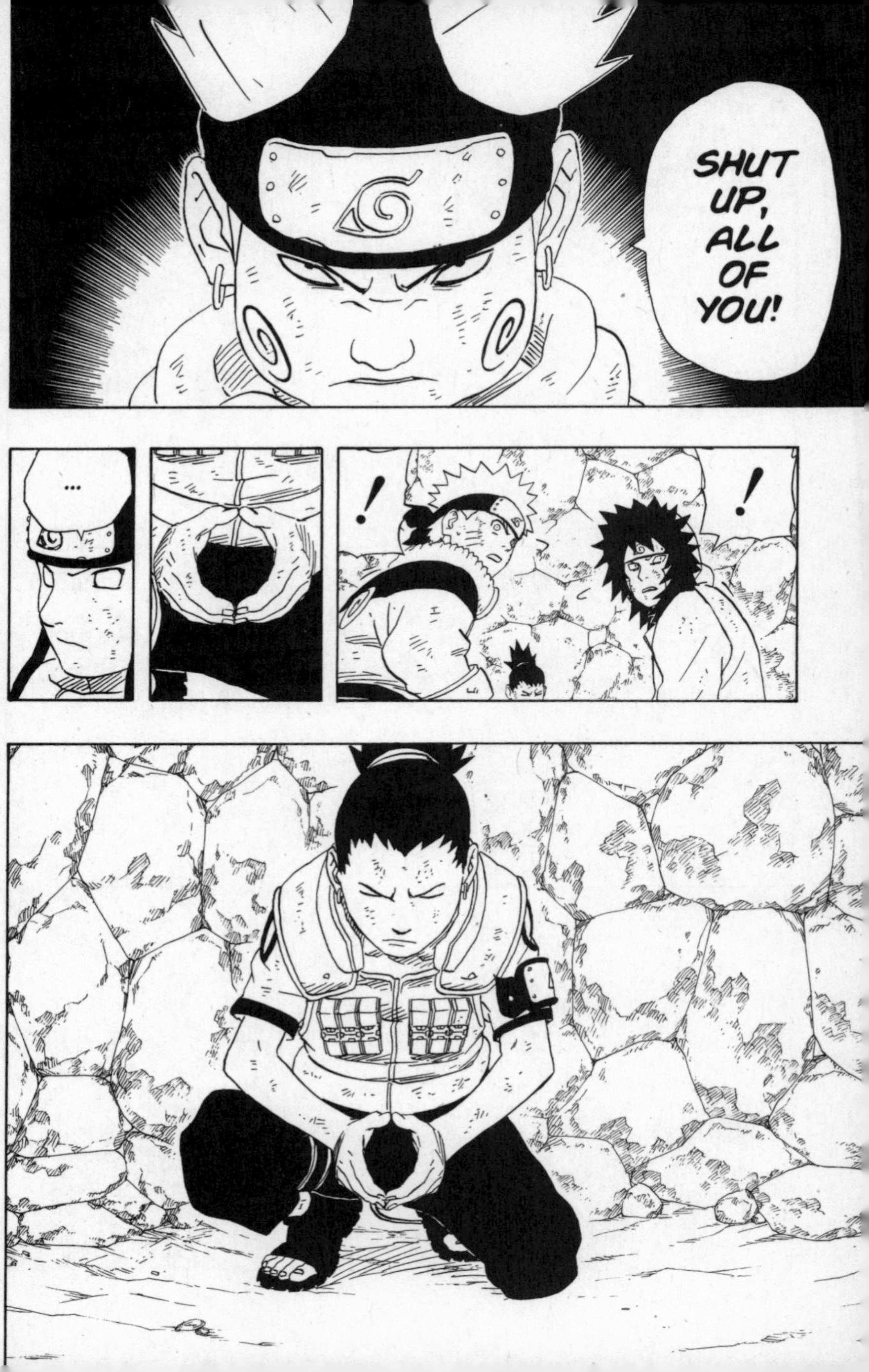
SHUT UP, ALL OF YOU!
!
!
...

READ THIS WAY

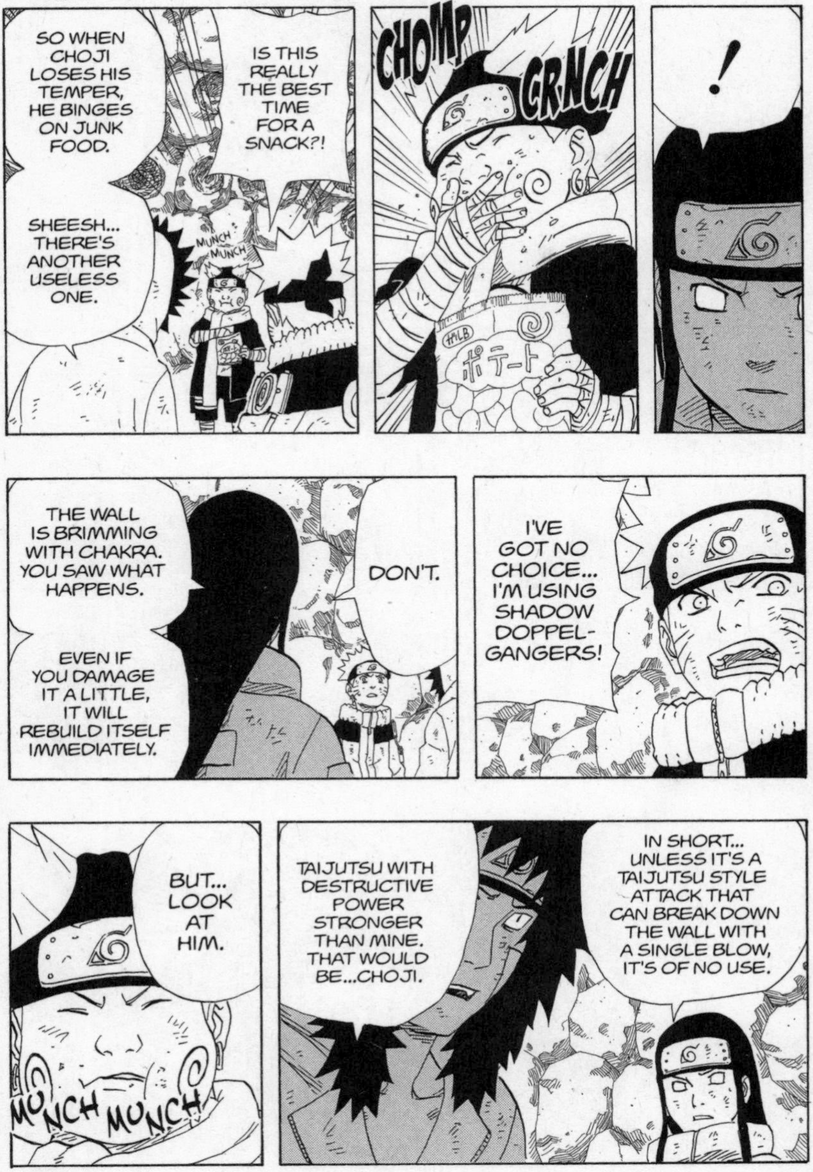
!
CHOMP
CRNCH
IS THIS REALLY THE BEST TIME FOR A SNACK?!
SO WHEN CHOJI LOSES HIS TEMPER, HE BINGES ON JUNK FOOD.
MUNCH MUNCH
SHEESH... THERE'S ANOTHER USELESS ONE.
I'VE GOT NO CHOICE... I'M USING SHADOW DOPPEL-GANGERS!
DON'T.
THE WALL IS BRIMMING WITH CHAKRA. YOU SAW WHAT HAPPENS.
EVEN IF YOU DAMAGE IT A LITTLE, IT WILL REBUILD ITSELF IMMEDIATELY.
IN SHORT... UNLESS IT'S A TAIJUTSU STYLE ATTACK THAT CAN BREAK DOWN THE WALL WITH A SINGLE BLOW, IT'S OF NO USE.
TAIJUTSU WITH DESTRUCTIVE POWER STRONGER THAN MINE. THAT WOULD BE...CHOJI.
BUT... LOOK AT HIM.
MUNCH MUNCH

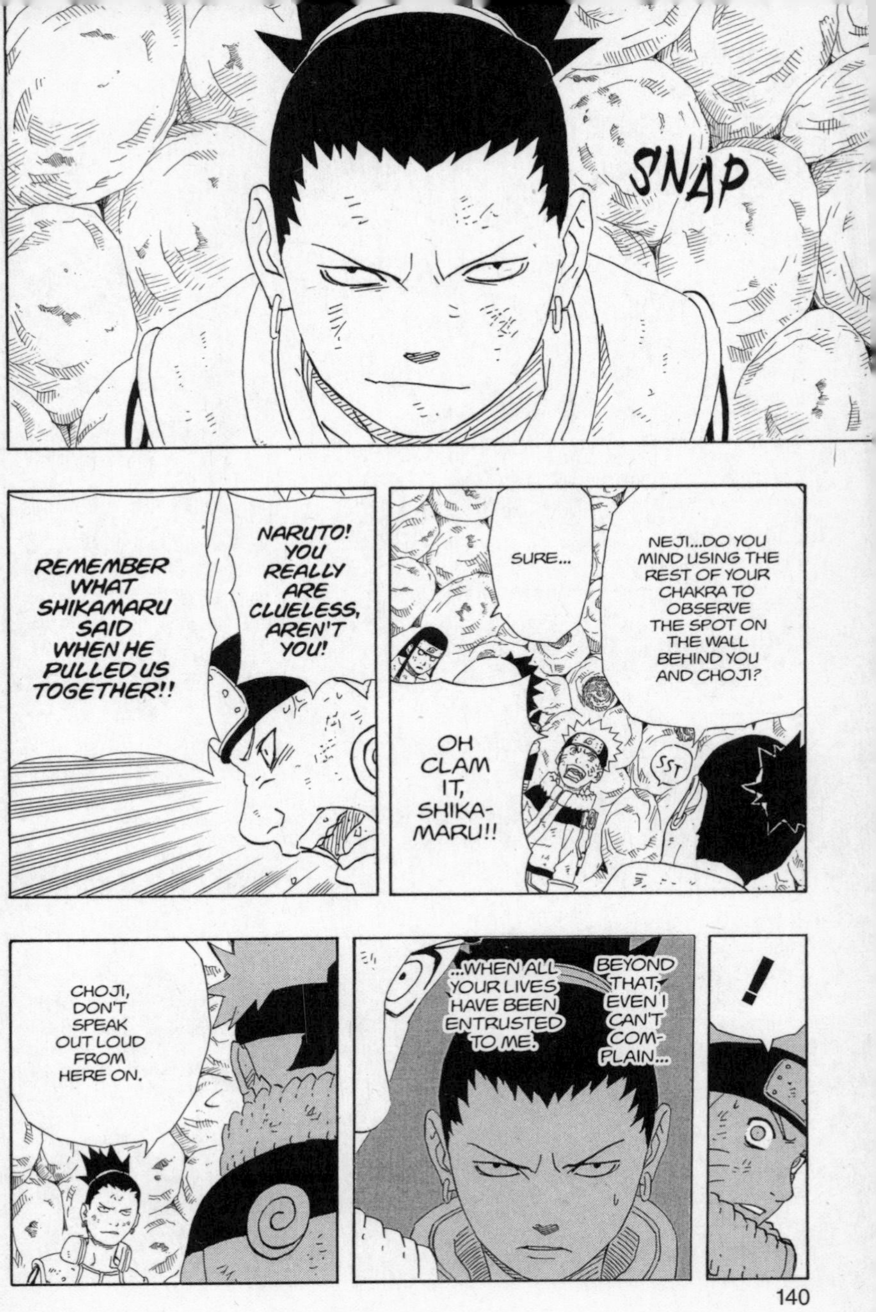
SNAP
NEJI...DO YOU MIND USING THE REST OF YOUR CHAKRA TO OBSERVE THE SPOT ON THE WALL BEHIND YOU AND CHOJI?
SURE...
SST
OH CLAM IT, SHIKAMARU!!
NARUTO! YOU REALLY ARE CLUELESS, AREN'T YOU!
REMEMBER WHAT SHIKAMARU SAID WHEN HE PULLED US TOGETHER!!
!
BEYOND THAT, EVEN I CAN'T COMPLAIN...
...WHEN ALL YOUR LIVES HAVE BEEN ENTRUSTED TO ME.
CHOJI, DON'T SPEAK OUT LOUD FROM HERE ON.

READ THIS WAY

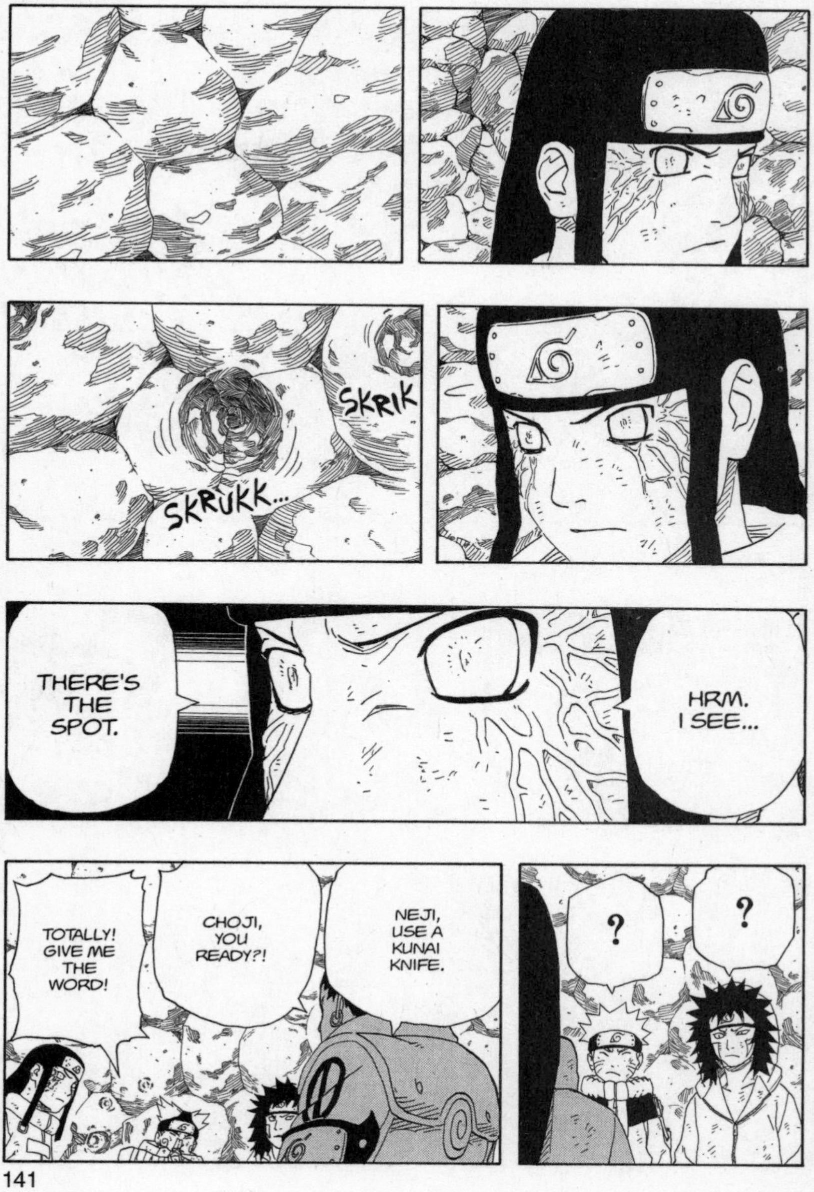

SKRIK
SKRUKK...
HRM. I SEE...
THERE'S THE SPOT.
?
?
NEJI, USE A KUNAI KNIFE.
CHOJI, YOU READY?!
TOTALLY! GIVE ME THE WORD!

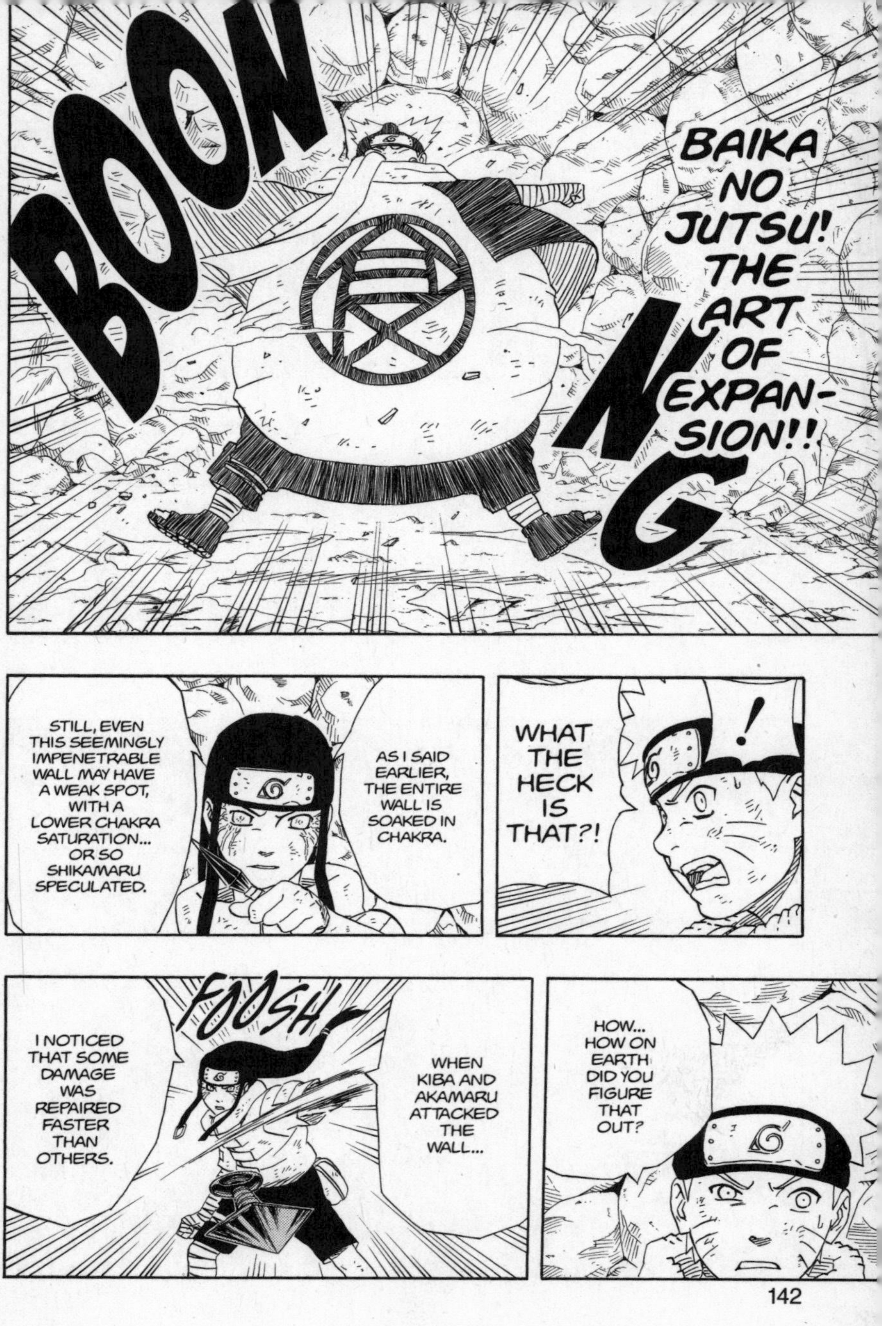
BAIKA NO JUTSU! THE ART OF EXPANSION!!
BOON
NG
!
WHAT THE HECK IS THAT?!
AS I SAID EARLIER, THE ENTIRE WALL IS SOAKED IN CHAKRA.
STILL, EVEN THIS SEEMINGLY IMPENETRABLE WALL MAY HAVE A WEAK SPOT, WITH A LOWER CHAKRA SATURATION... OR SO SHIKAMARU SPECULATED.
HOW... HOW ON EARTH DID YOU FIGURE THAT OUT?
WHEN KIBA AND AKAMARU ATTACKED THE WALL...
FOOSH
I NOTICED THAT SOME DAMAGE WAS REPAIRED FASTER THAN OTHERS.

READ THIS WAY

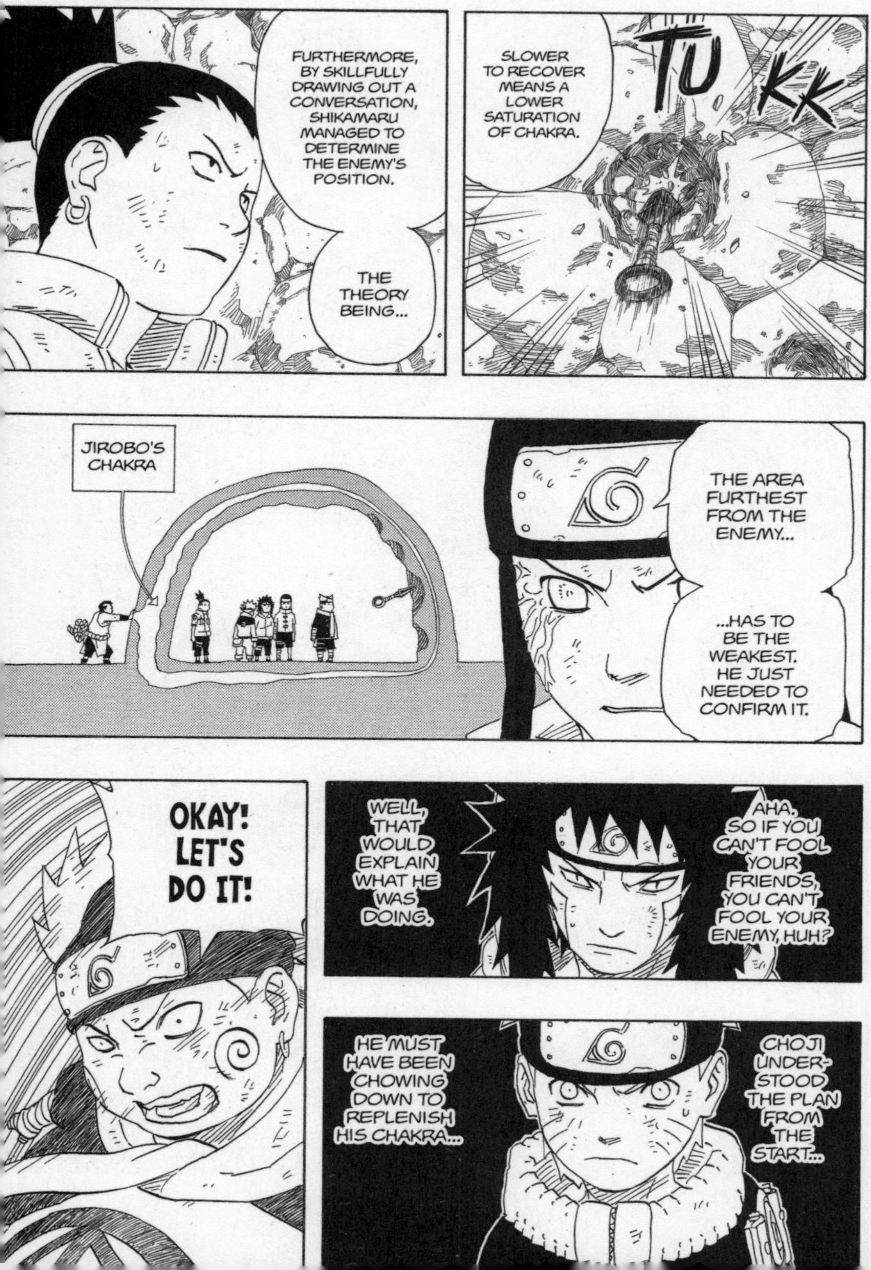
TUKK
SLOWER TO RECOVER MEANS A LOWER SATURATION OF CHAKRA.
FURTHERMORE, BY SKILLFULLY DRAWING OUT A CONVERSATION, SHIKAMARU MANAGED TO DETERMINE THE ENEMY'S POSITION.
THE THEORY BEING...
THE AREA FURTHEST FROM THE ENEMY...
...HAS TO BE THE WEAKEST. HE JUST NEEDED TO CONFIRM IT.
JIROBO'S CHAKRA
AHA. SO IF YOU CAN'T FOOL YOUR FRIENDS, YOU CAN'T FOOL YOUR ENEMY, HUH?
WELL, THAT WOULD EXPLAIN WHAT HE WAS DOING.
CHOJI UNDERSTOOD THE PLAN FROM THE START...
HE MUST HAVE BEEN CHOWING DOWN TO REPLENISH HIS CHAKRA...
OKAY! LET'S DO IT!

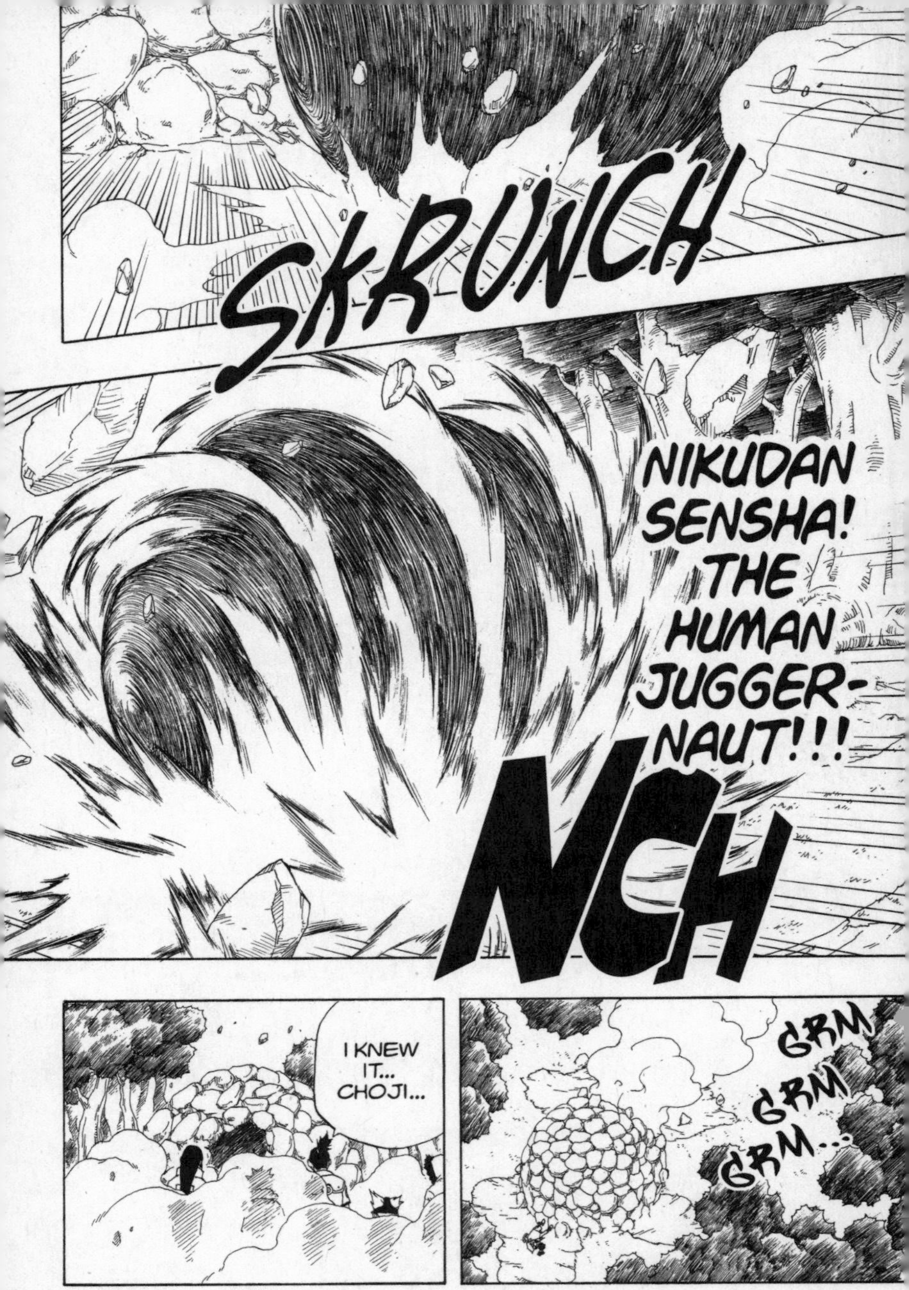
SKRUNCH
NIKUDAN SENSHA! THE HUMAN JUGGER-NAUT!!!
NCH
GRM GRM GRM...
I KNEW IT... CHOJI...

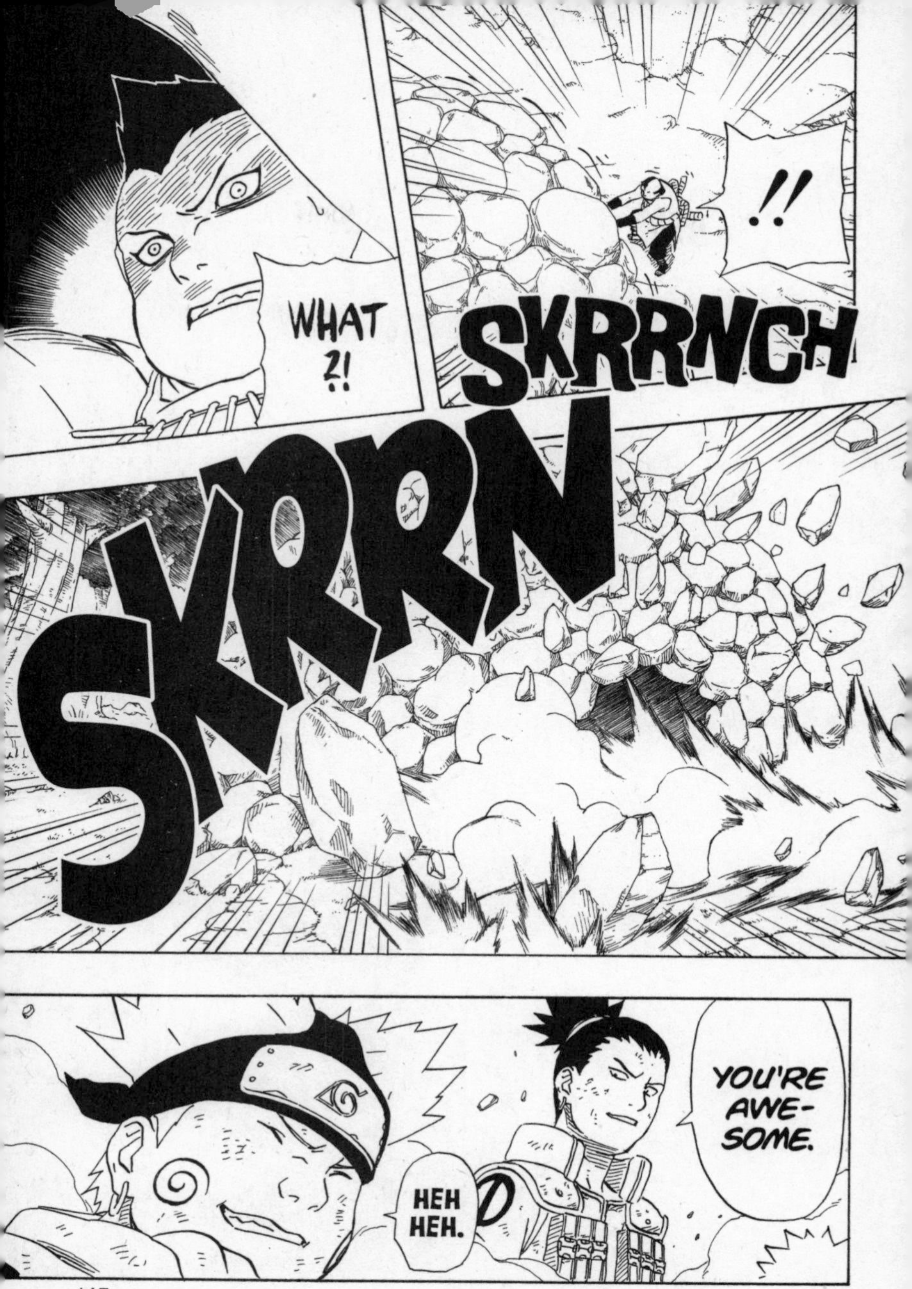
!!
SKRRNCH
WHAT?!
SKRRN
YOU'RE AWE-SOME.
HEH HEH.

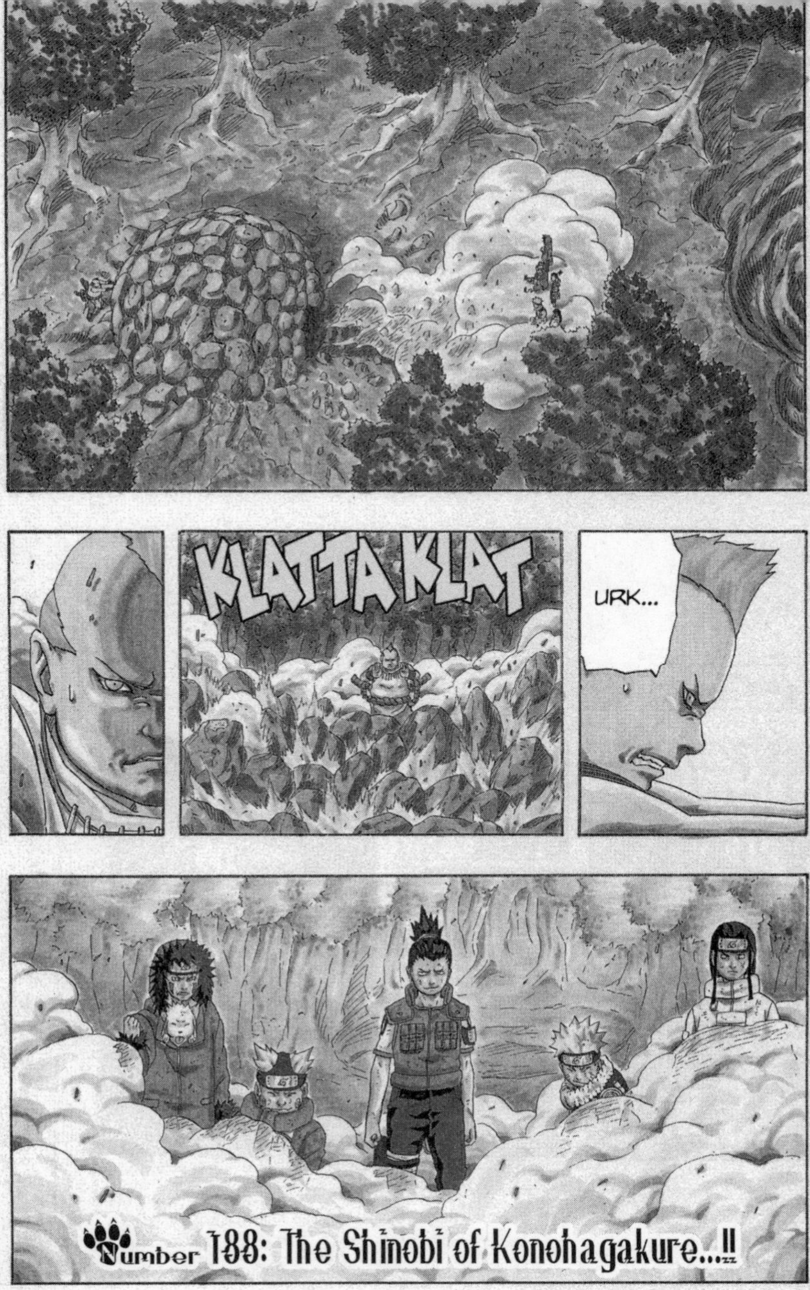
URK...
KLATTA KLAT
Number 188: The Shinobi of Konohagakure...!!

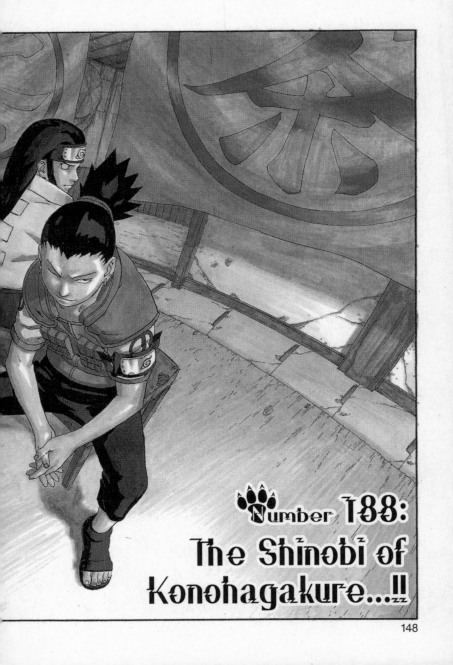

Number 188:
The Shinobi of
Konohagakure...!!

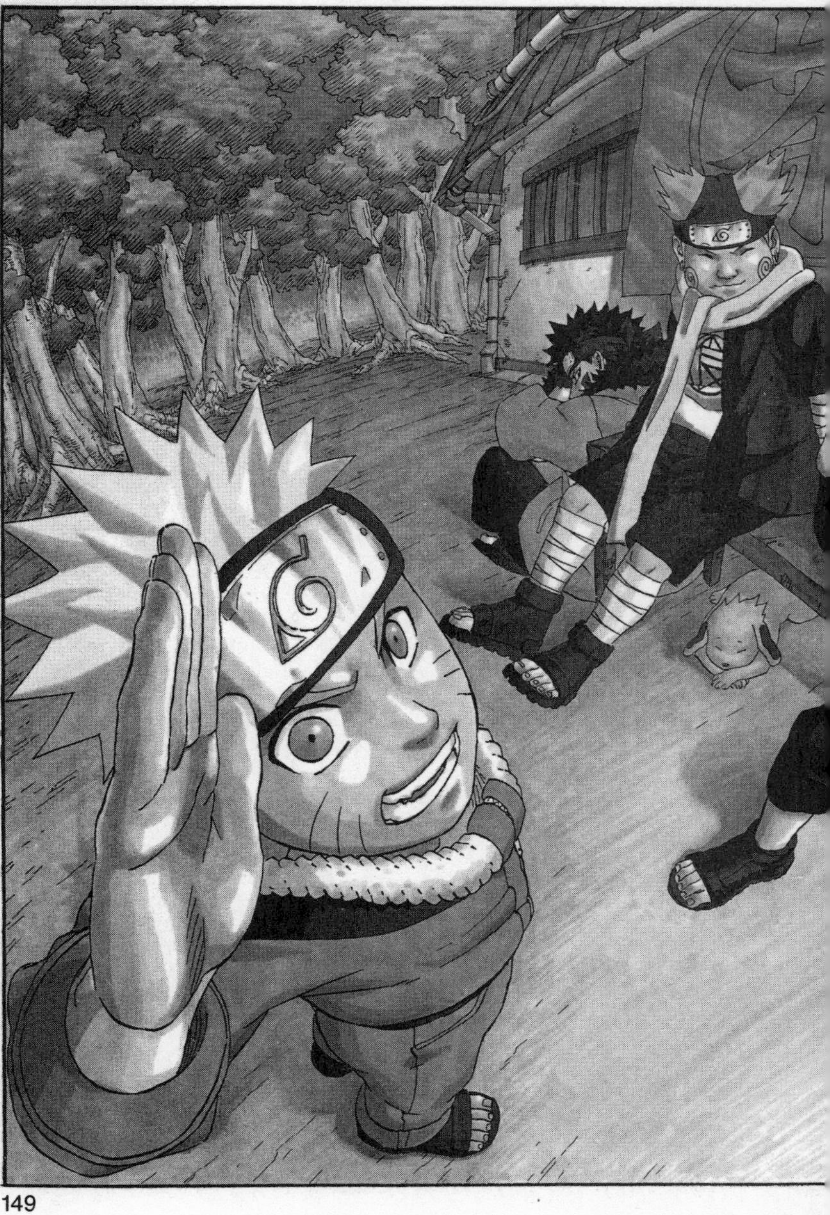

NARUTO

WHINE...
OOO
NG

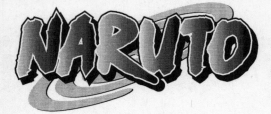

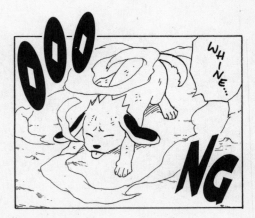

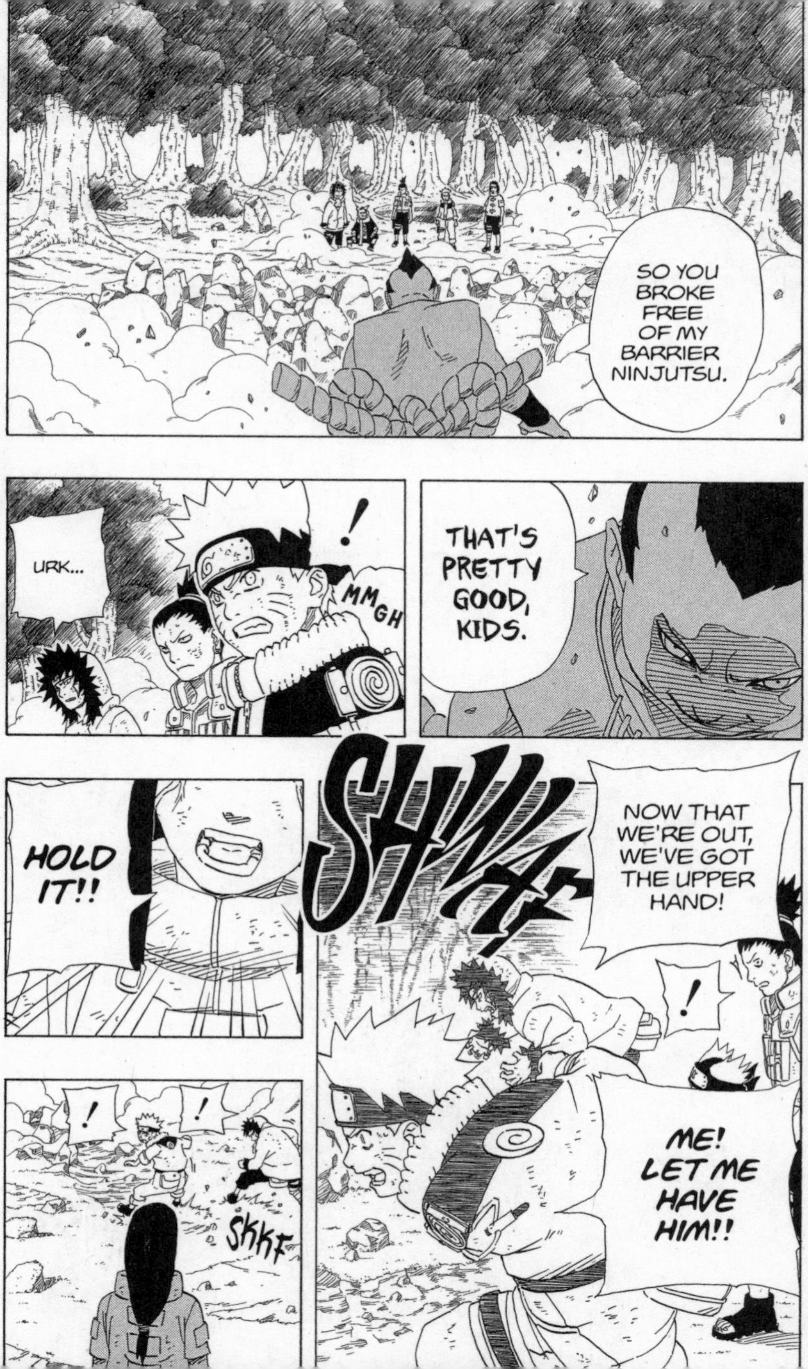
SO YOU BROKE FREE OF MY BARRIER NINJUTSU.
THAT'S PRETTY GOOD, KIDS.
!
MMGH
URK...
SHWAK
NOW THAT WE'RE OUT, WE'VE GOT THE UPPER HAND!
!
ME! LET ME HAVE HIM!!
HOLD IT!!
!
!
SKKF

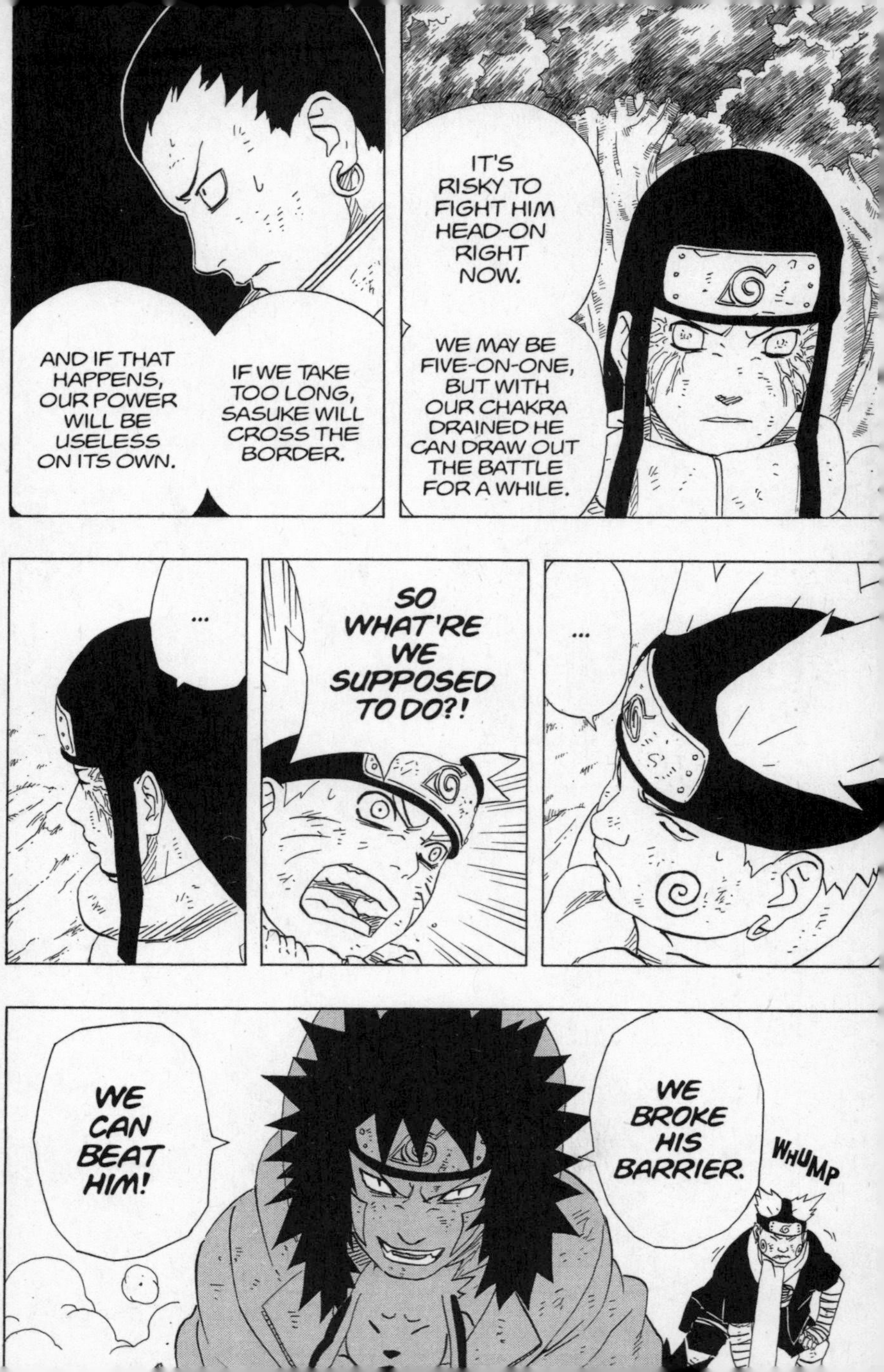
IT'S RISKY TO FIGHT HIM HEAD-ON RIGHT NOW.
WE MAY BE FIVE-ON-ONE, BUT WITH OUR CHAKRA DRAINED HE CAN DRAW OUT THE BATTLE FOR A WHILE.
IF WE TAKE TOO LONG, SASUKE WILL CROSS THE BORDER.
AND IF THAT HAPPENS, OUR POWER WILL BE USELESS ON ITS OWN.
...
SO WHAT'RE WE SUPPOSED TO DO?!
...
WHUMP
WE BROKE HIS BARRIER.
WE CAN BEAT HIM!

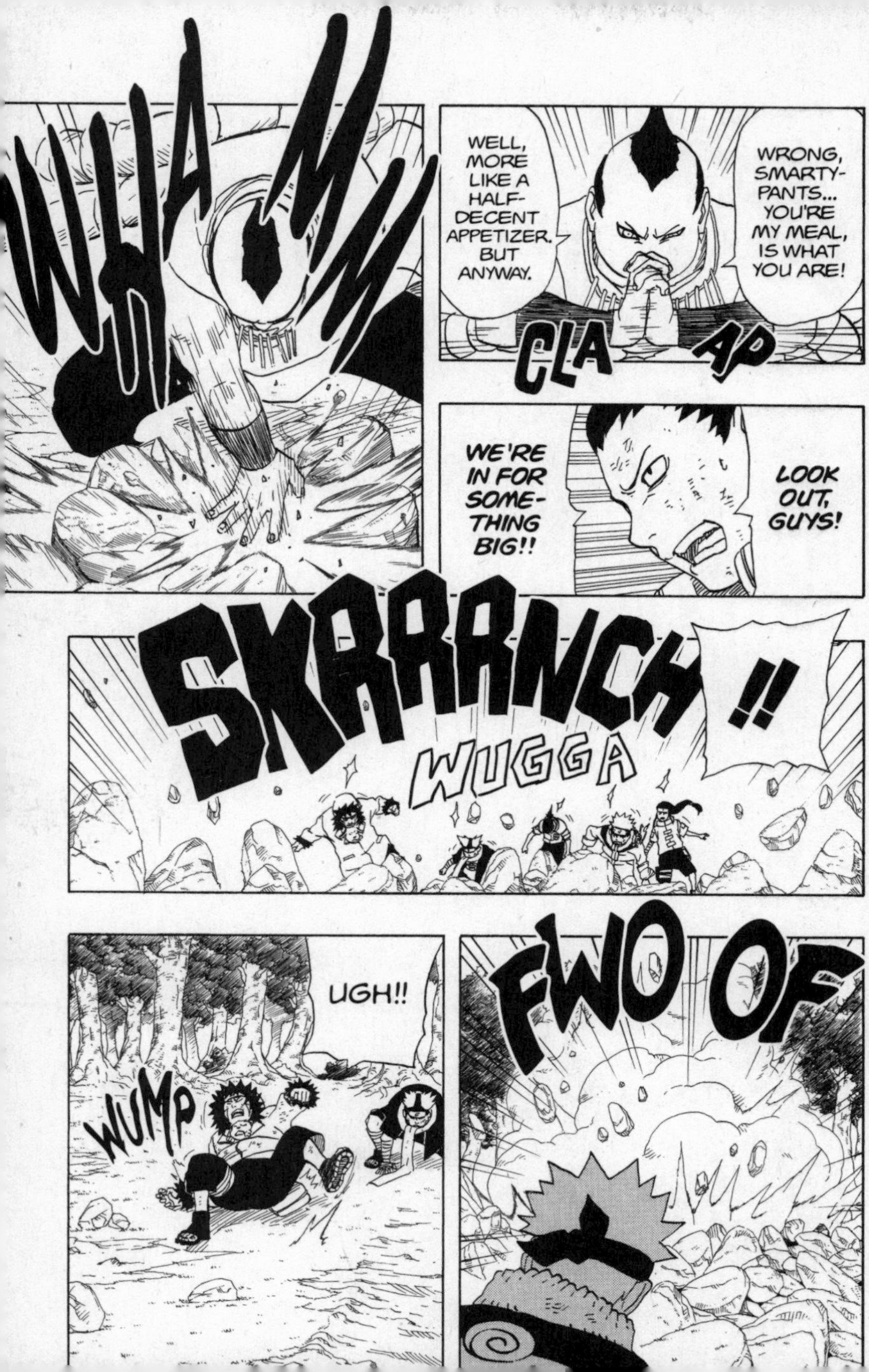
WRONG, SMARTY-PANTS... YOU'RE MY MEAL, IS WHAT YOU ARE!
WELL, MORE LIKE A HALF-DECENT APPETIZER. BUT ANYWAY.
CLAAP
LOOK OUT, GUYS!
WE'RE IN FOR SOMETHING BIG!!
WHAM
SKRRRNCH!!
WUGGA
FWOOF
UGH!!
WUMP

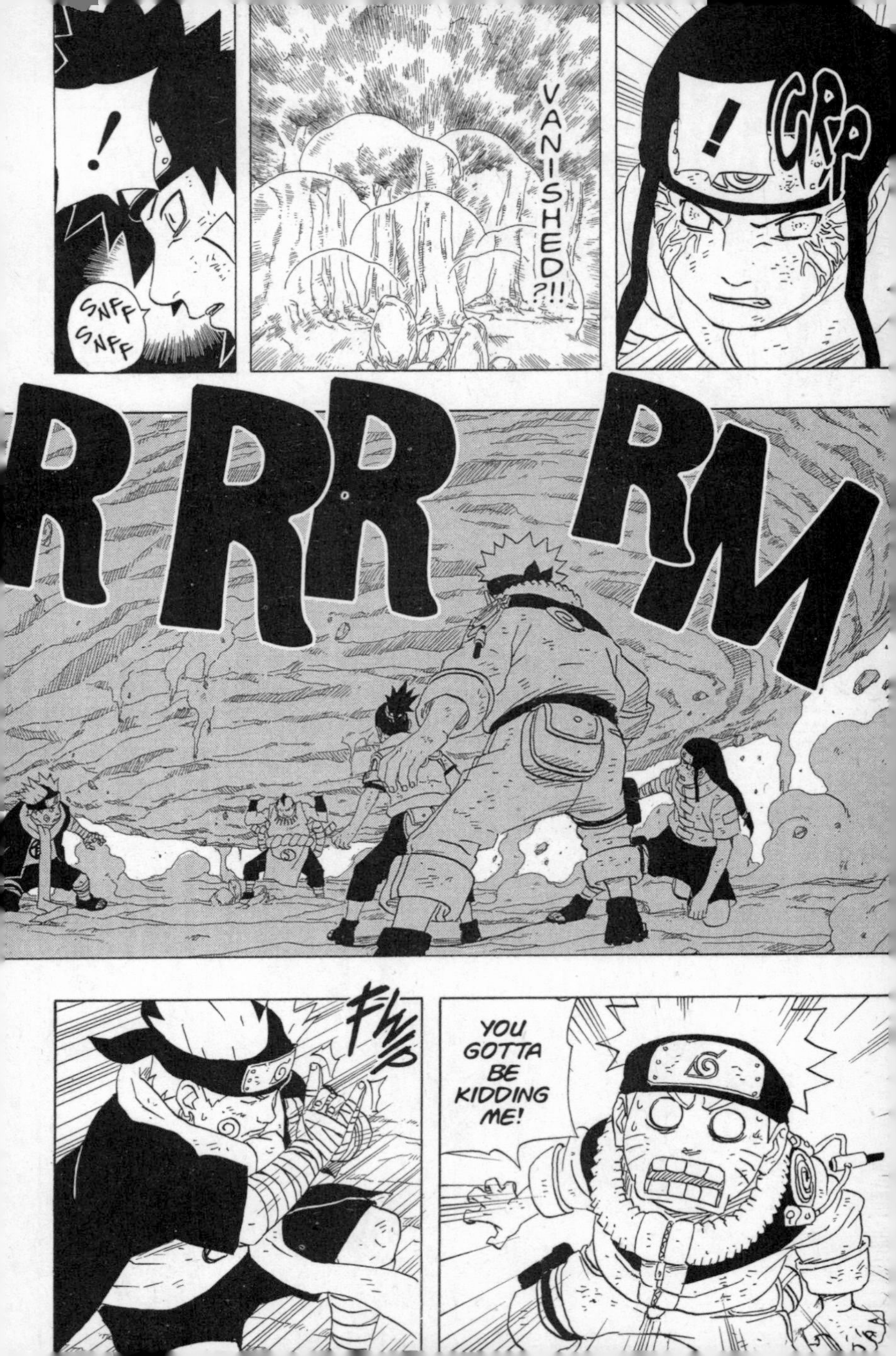
GRP
!
VANISHED?!!
!
SNFF SNFF
RRRRM
YOU GOTTA BE KIDDING ME!
FWIP

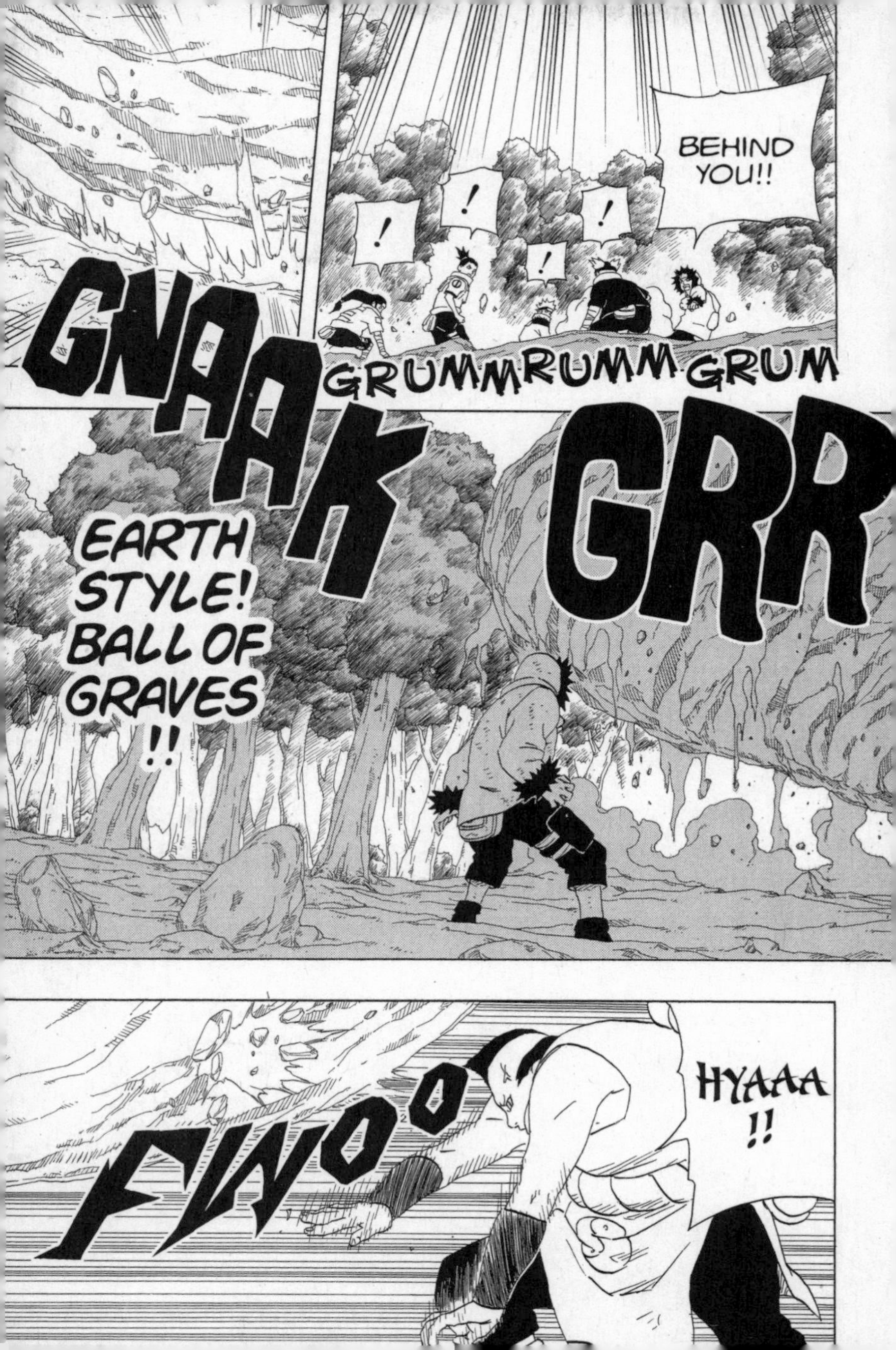
BEHIND YOU!!
!
!
!
!
GRUMMRUMM GRUM
GNAAAK
GRR
EARTH STYLE! BALL OF GRAVES!!
HYAAA!!
FWOOO

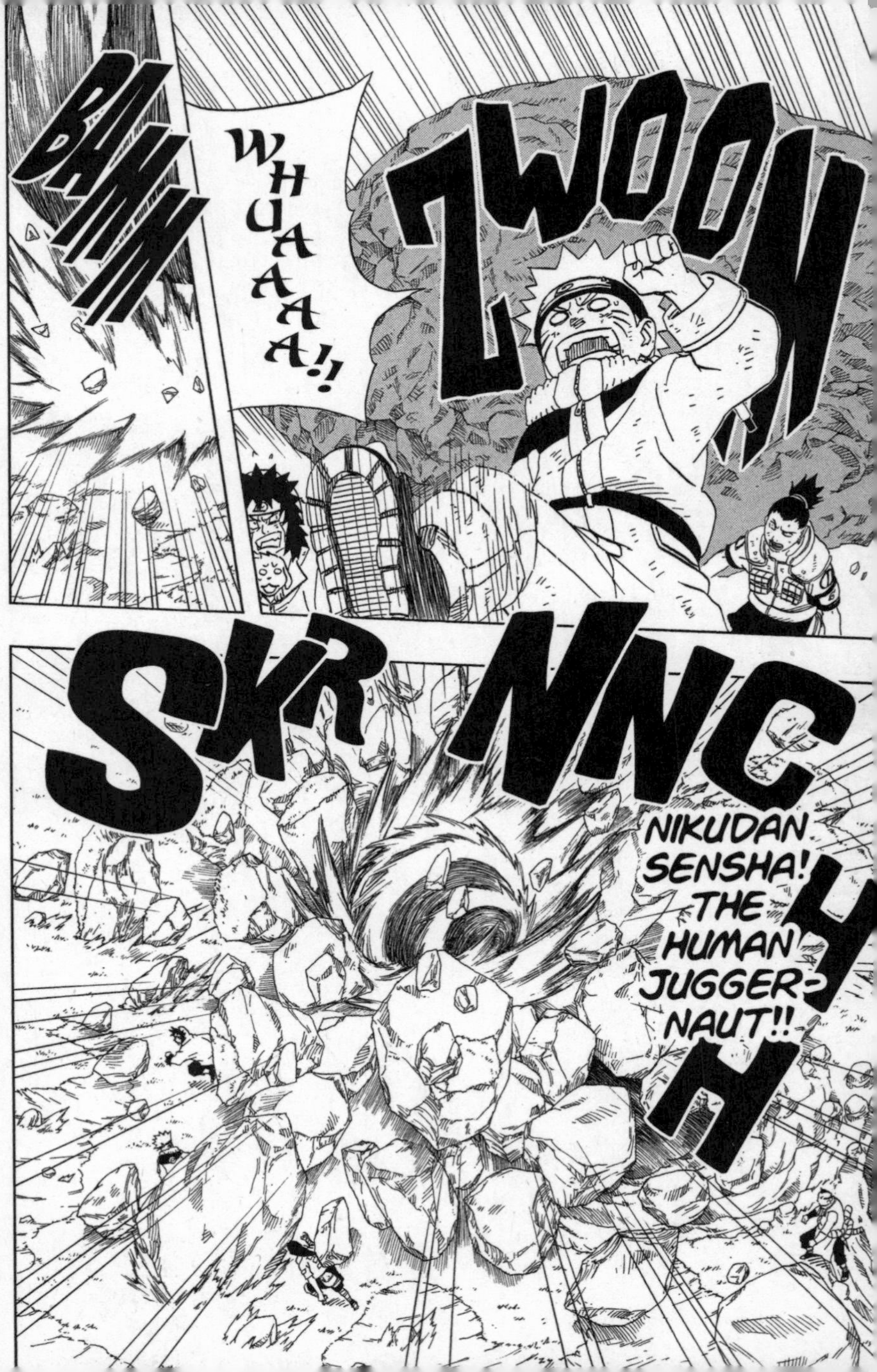
ZWOOM
WHUAAAAA!!
BAMM
SKRNNCHH
NIKUDAN SENSHA! THE HUMAN JUGGER-NAUT!!

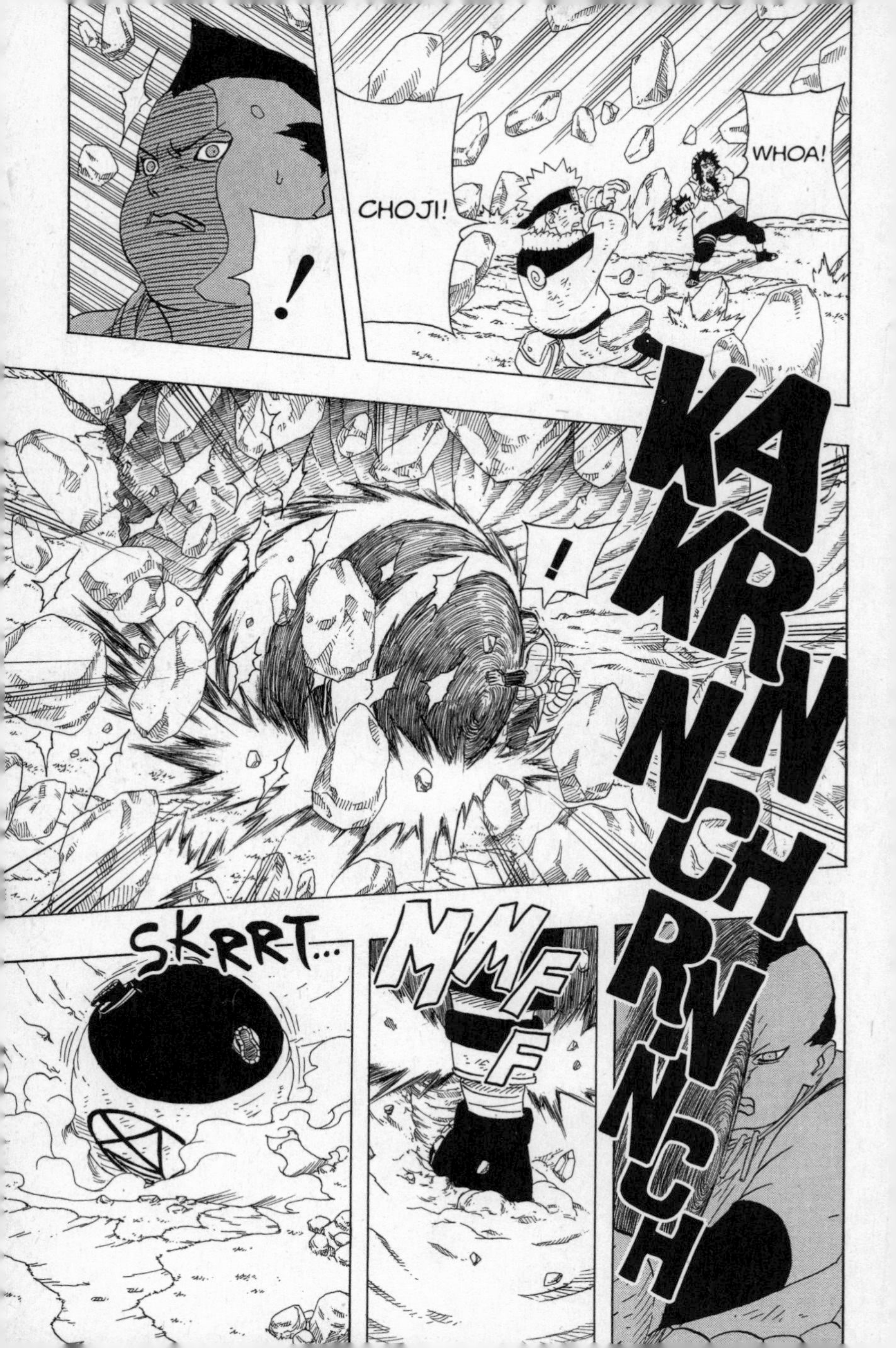
WHOA!
CHOJI!
!
!
KAKRNNCH
RNNCH
MMFF
SKRRT...

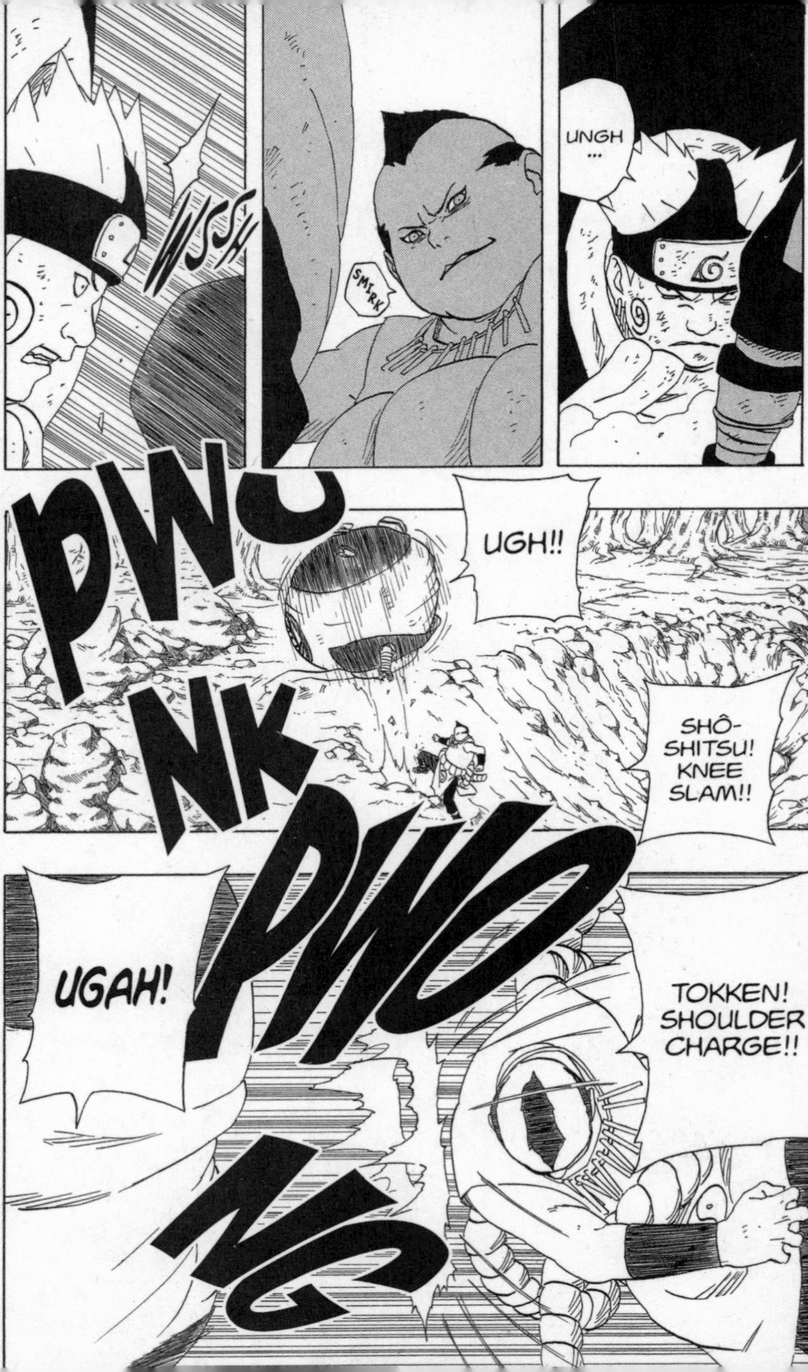
UNGH ...
SMIRK
WSSH
SHÔ-SHITSU! KNEE SLAM!!
UGH!!
PWUNK
TOKKEN! SHOULDER CHARGE!!
UGAH!
PWONG

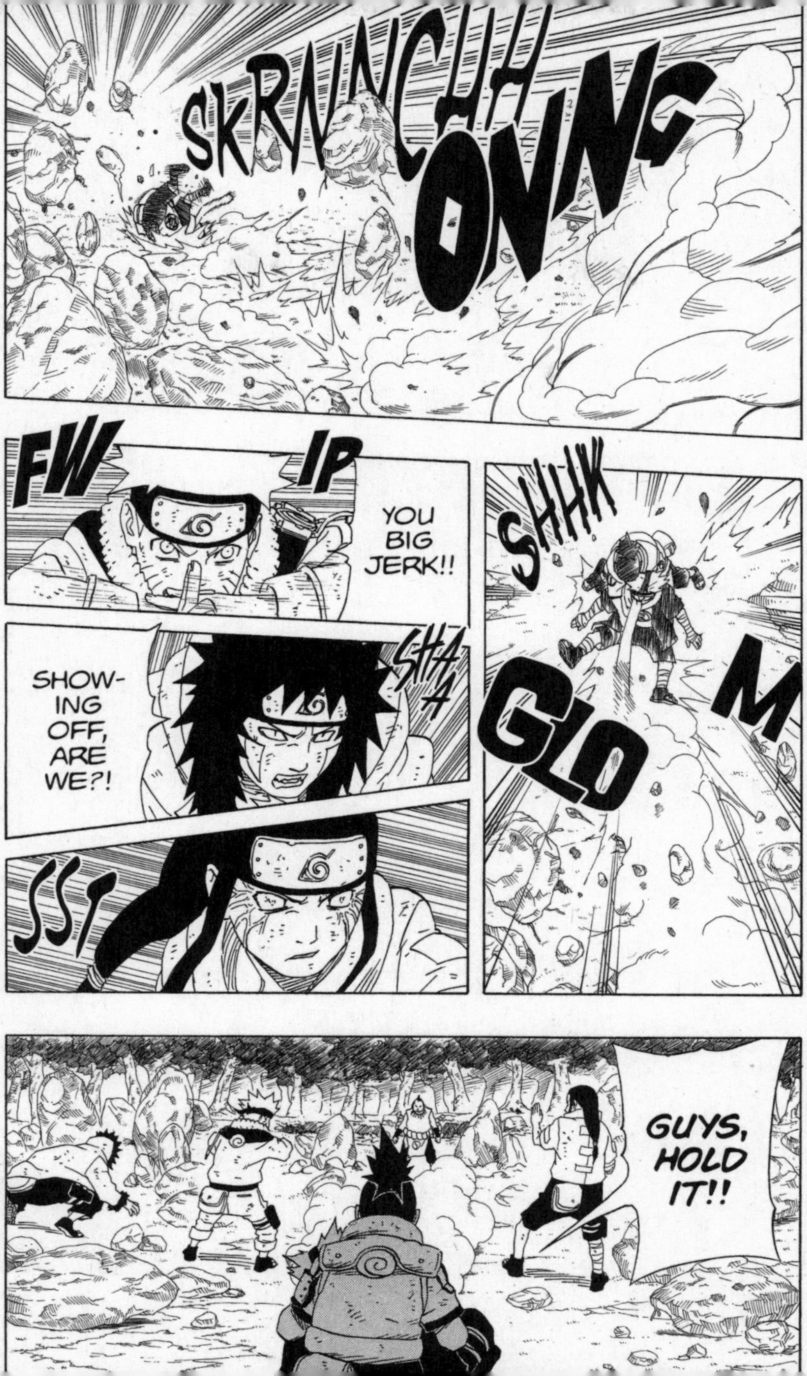
SKRNNCHH
ONNG
SHHK
GLOM
FWIP
YOU BIG JERK!!
SHAA
SHOWING OFF, ARE WE?!
SST
GUYS, HOLD IT!!

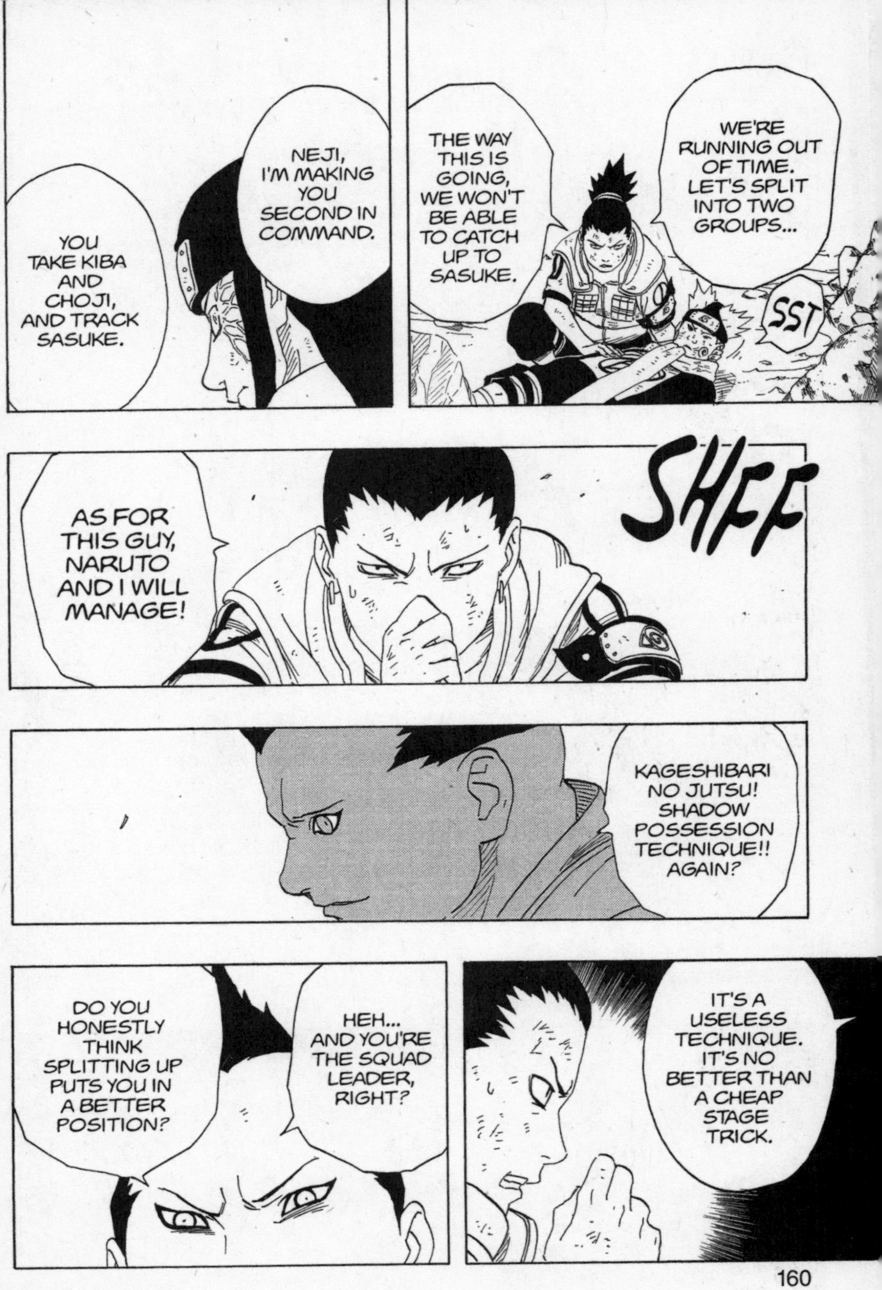
WE'RE RUNNING OUT OF TIME. LET'S SPLIT INTO TWO GROUPS...
SST
THE WAY THIS IS GOING, WE WON'T BE ABLE TO CATCH UP TO SASUKE.
NEJI, I'M MAKING YOU SECOND IN COMMAND.
YOU TAKE KIBA AND CHOJI, AND TRACK SASUKE.
SHFF
AS FOR THIS GUY, NARUTO AND I WILL MANAGE!
KAGESHIBARI NO JUTSU! SHADOW POSSESSION TECHNIQUE!! AGAIN?
IT'S A USELESS TECHNIQUE. IT'S NO BETTER THAN A CHEAP STAGE TRICK.
HEH... AND YOU'RE THE SQUAD LEADER, RIGHT?
DO YOU HONESTLY THINK SPLITTING UP PUTS YOU IN A BETTER POSITION?

READ THIS WAY

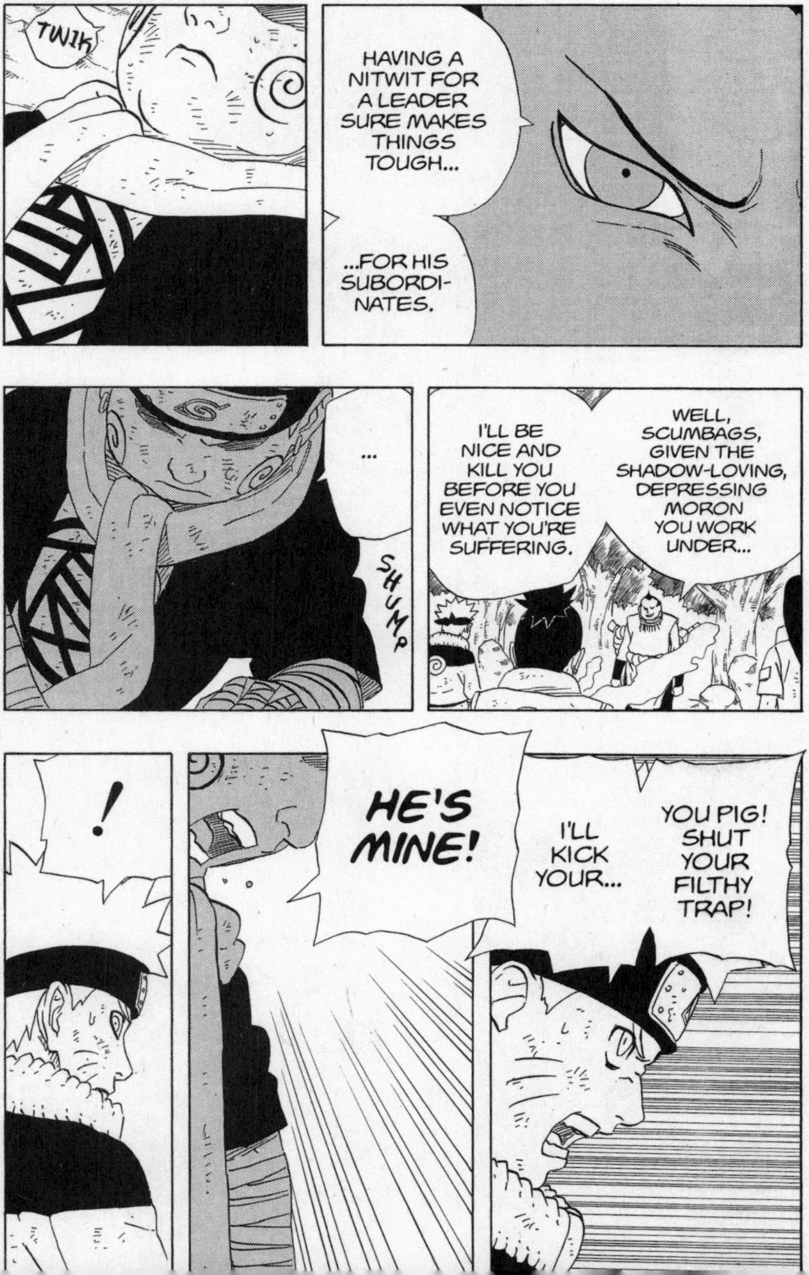
HAVING A NITWIT FOR A LEADER SURE MAKES THINGS TOUGH...
...FOR HIS SUBORDINATES.
TWIK
WELL, SCUMBAGS, GIVEN THE SHADOW-LOVING, DEPRESSING MORON YOU WORK UNDER...
I'LL BE NICE AND KILL YOU BEFORE YOU EVEN NOTICE WHAT YOU'RE SUFFERING.
...
SHUMP
YOU PIG! SHUT YOUR FILTHY TRAP!
I'LL KICK YOUR...
HE'S MINE!
!

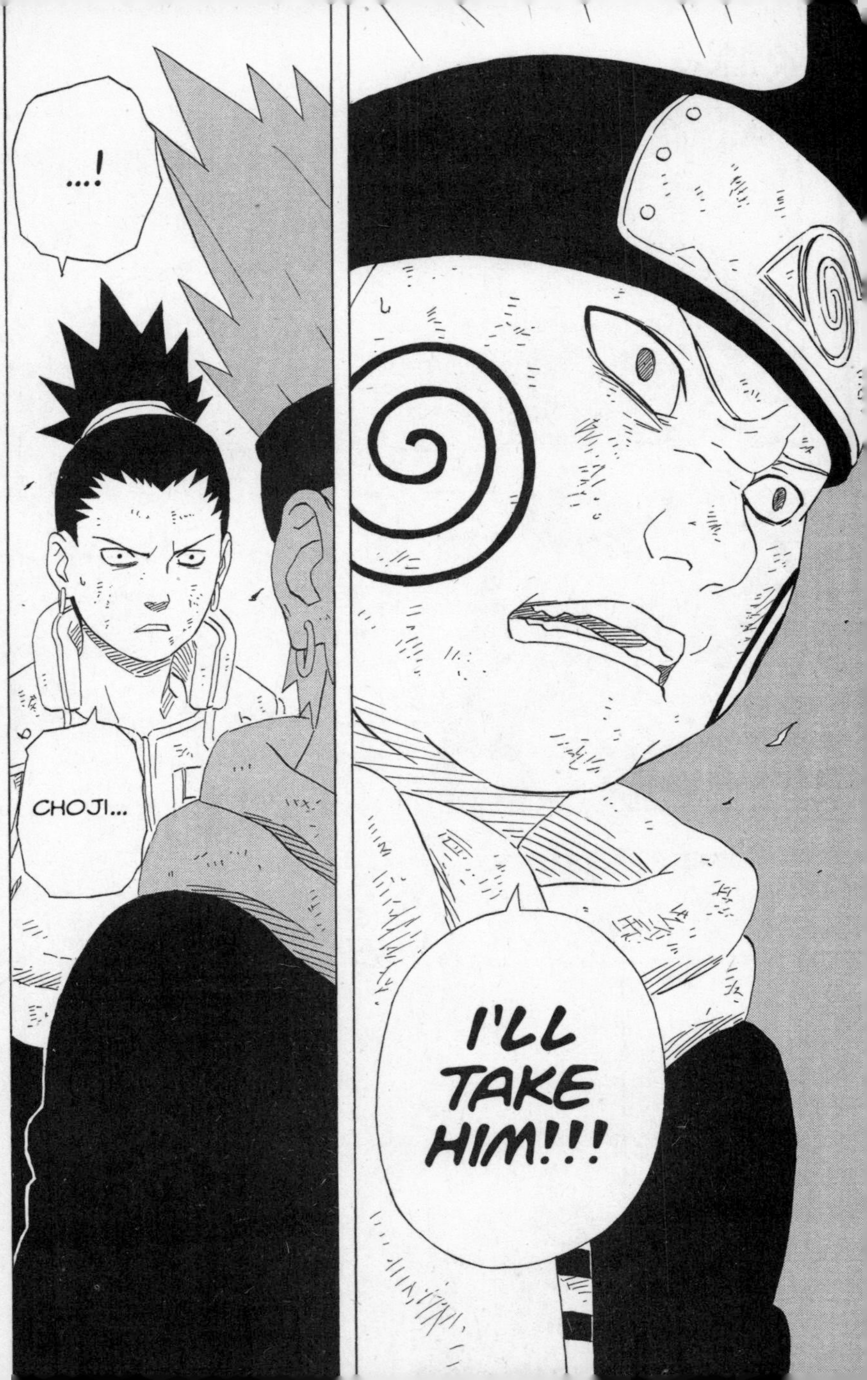
I'LL TAKE HIM!!!
...!
CHOJI...

READ THIS WAY

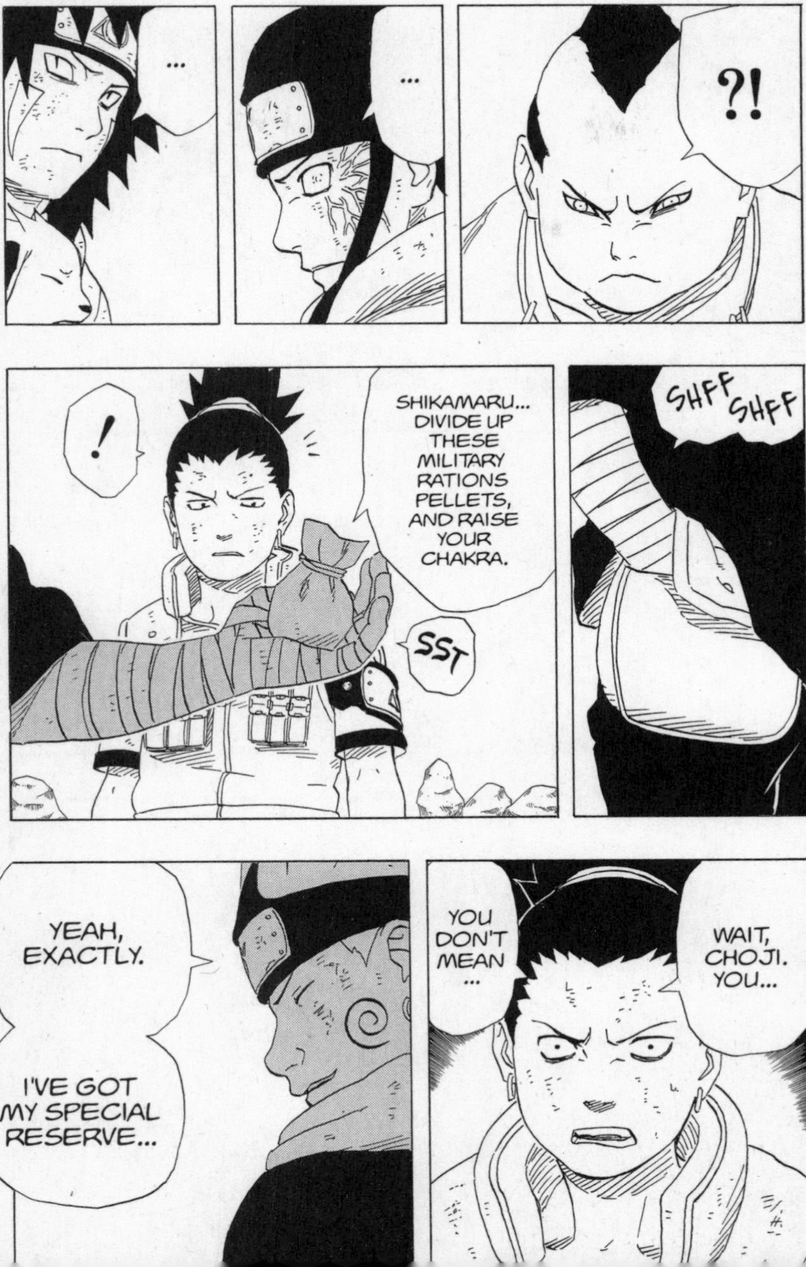
?!
...
...
SHFF SHFF
SHIKAMARU... DIVIDE UP THESE MILITARY RATIONS PELLETS, AND RAISE YOUR CHAKRA.
!
SST
WAIT, CHOJI. YOU...
YOU DON'T MEAN ...
YEAH, EXACTLY.
I'VE GOT MY SPECIAL RESERVE...

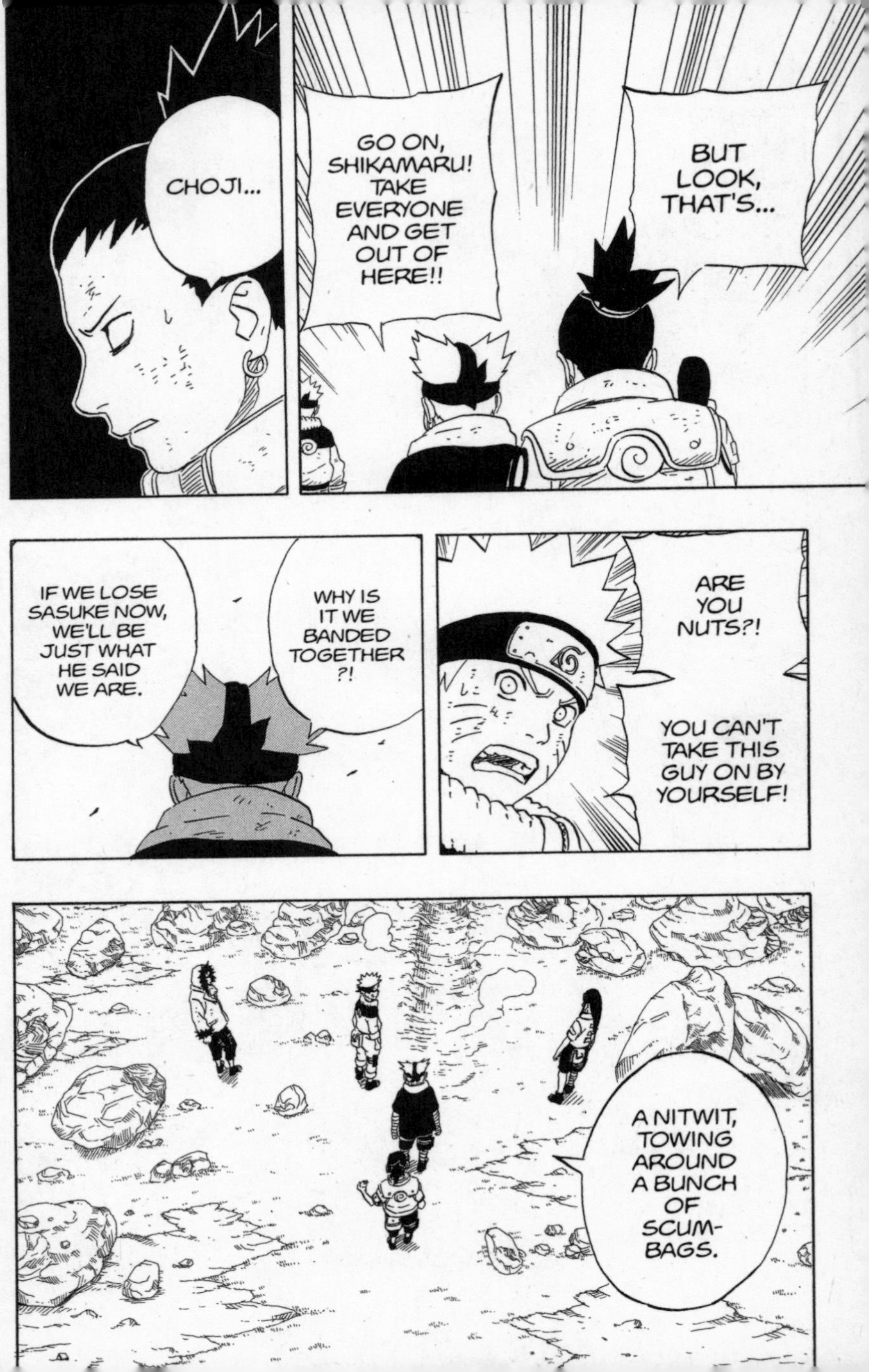
BUT LOOK, THAT'S...
GO ON, SHIKAMARU! TAKE EVERYONE AND GET OUT OF HERE!!
CHOJI...
ARE YOU NUTS?!
YOU CAN'T TAKE THIS GUY ON BY YOURSELF!
WHY IS IT WE BANDED TOGETHER ?!
IF WE LOSE SASUKE NOW, WE'LL BE JUST WHAT HE SAID WE ARE.
A NITWIT, TOWING AROUND A BUNCH OF SCUM-BAGS.

READ THIS WAY

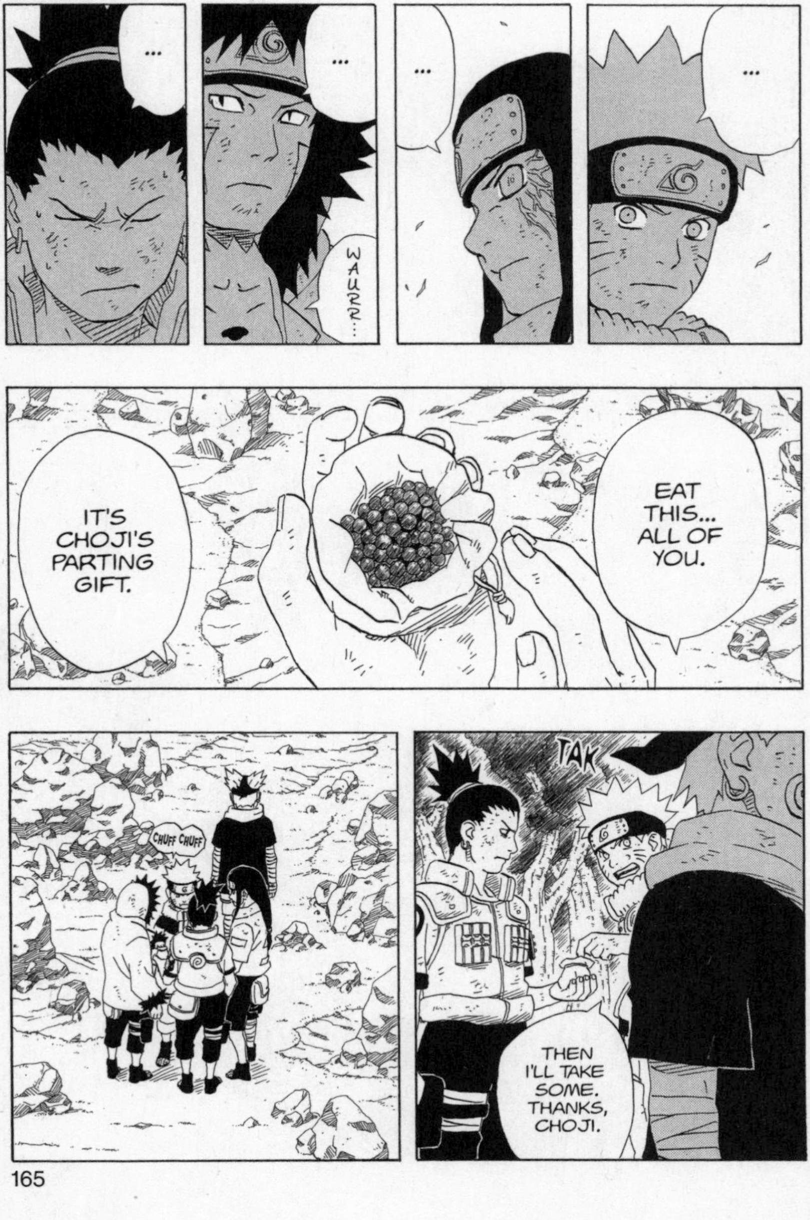
...
...
...
WAURR...
...
EAT THIS... ALL OF YOU.
IT'S CHOJI'S PARTING GIFT.
TAK
THEN I'LL TAKE SOME. THANKS, CHOJI.
CHUFF CHUFF

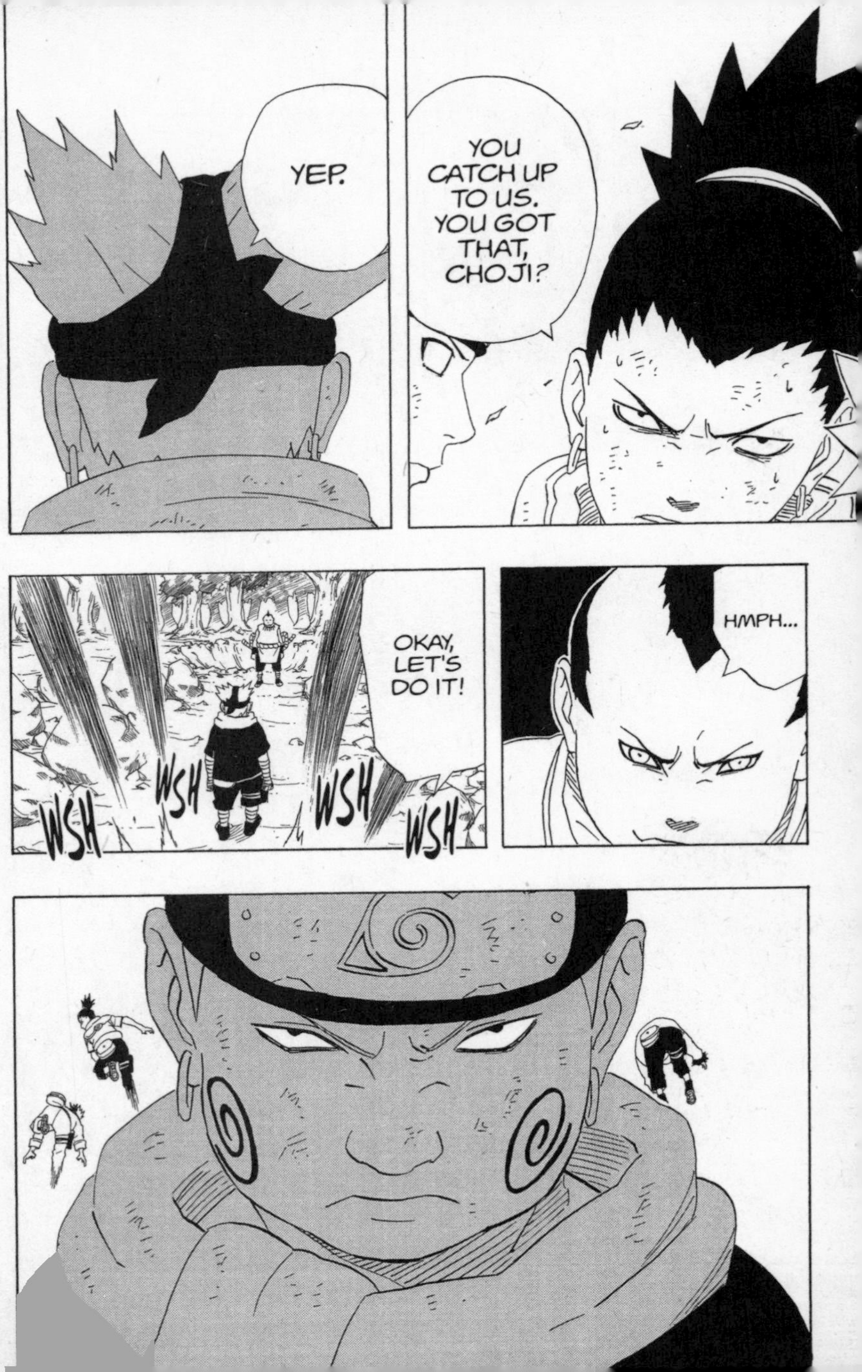
YOU CATCH UP TO US. YOU GOT THAT, CHOJI?
YEP.
HMPH...
OKAY, LET'S DO IT!
WSH
WSH
WSH
WSH

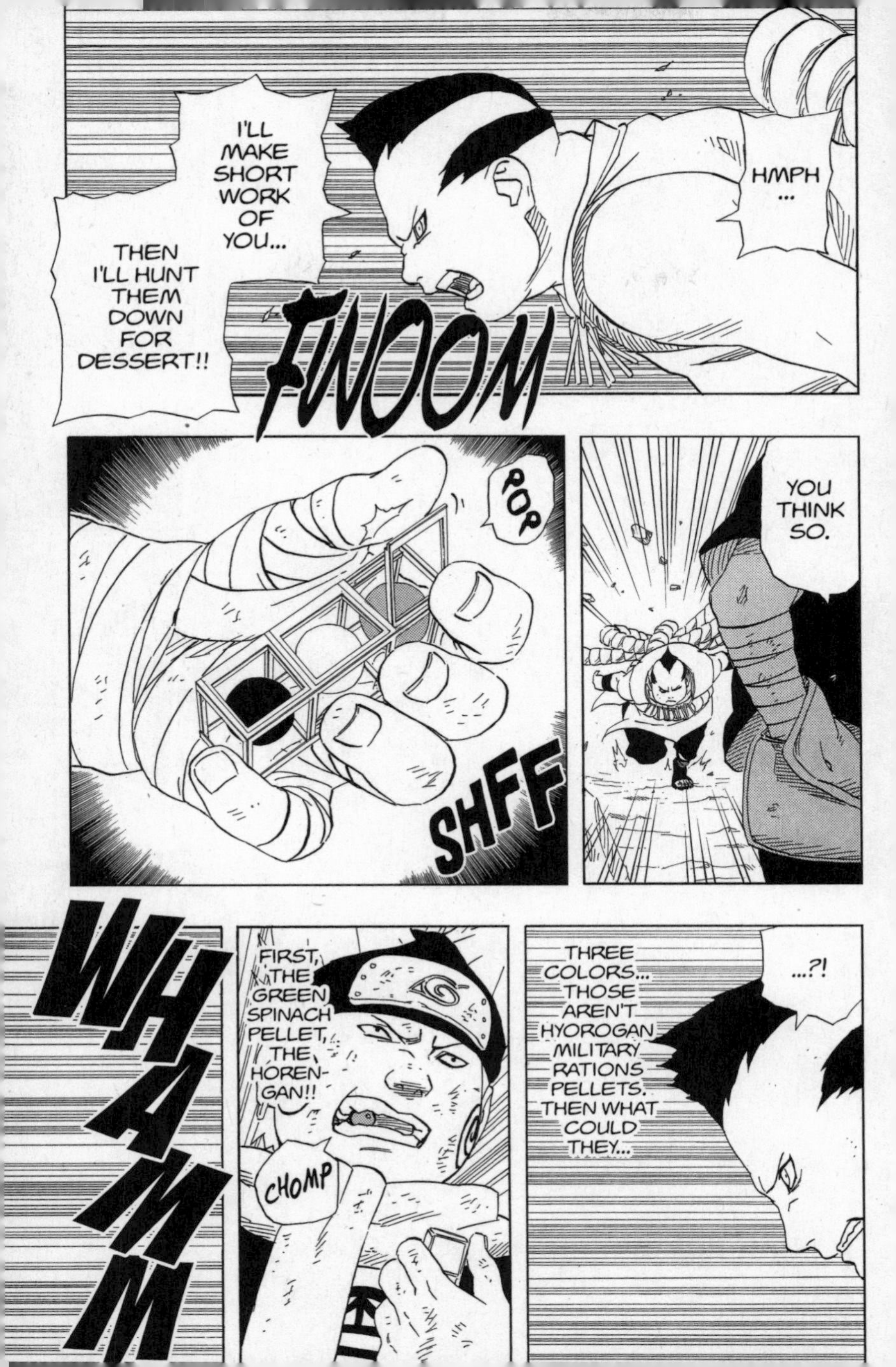
HMPH ...
I'LL MAKE SHORT WORK OF YOU...
THEN I'LL HUNT THEM DOWN FOR DESSERT!!
FWOOM
YOU THINK SO.
POP
SHFF
...?!
THREE COLORS... THOSE AREN'T HYOROGAN MILITARY RATIONS PELLETS. THEN WHAT COULD THEY...
FIRST, THE GREEN SPINACH PELLET, THE HOREN-GAN!!
CHOMP
WHAMM

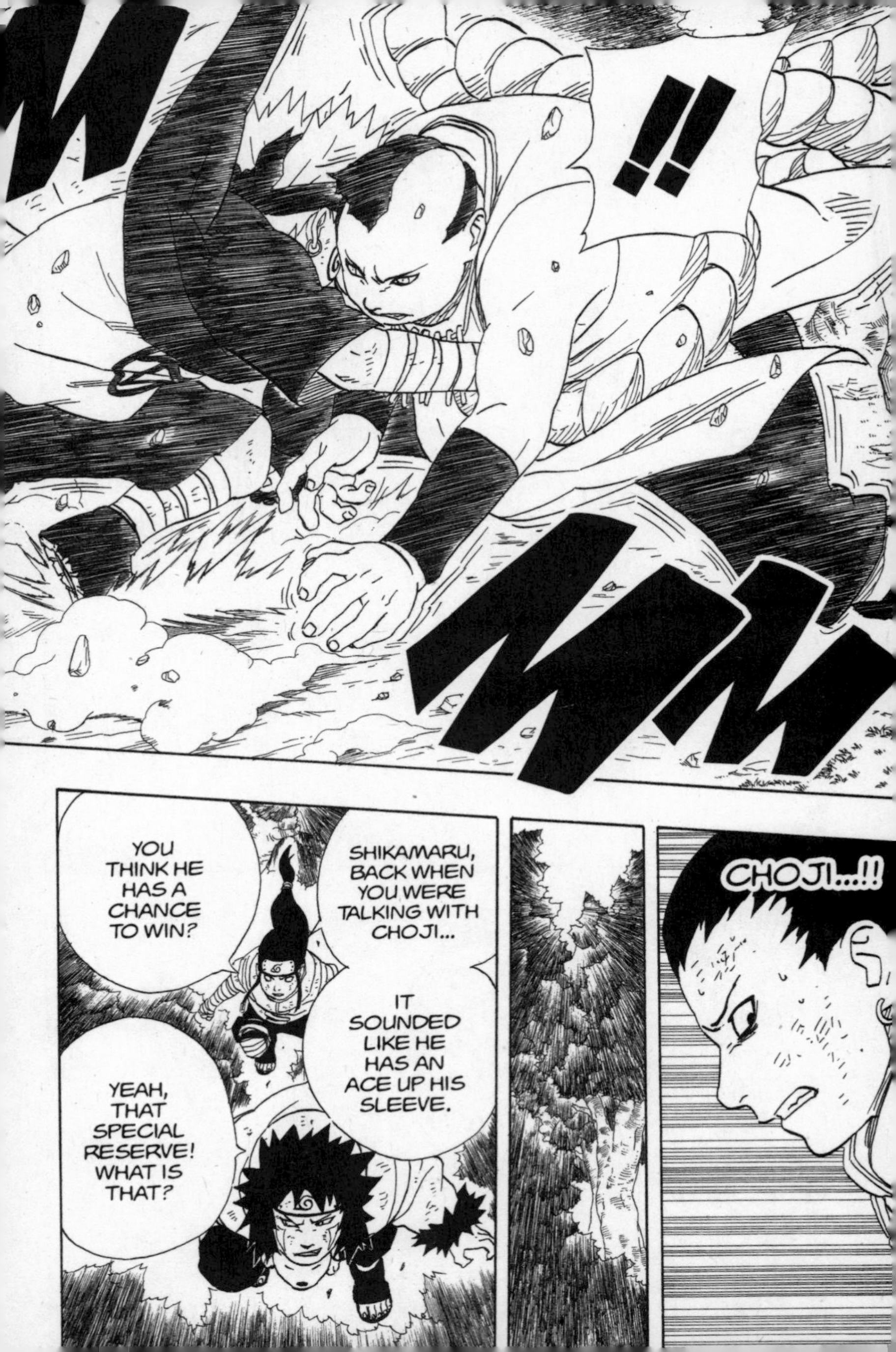
!!
CHOJI...!!
SHIKAMARU, BACK WHEN YOU WERE TALKING WITH CHOJI...
YOU THINK HE HAS A CHANCE TO WIN?
IT SOUNDED LIKE HE HAS AN ACE UP HIS SLEEVE.
YEAH, THAT SPECIAL RESERVE! WHAT IS THAT?

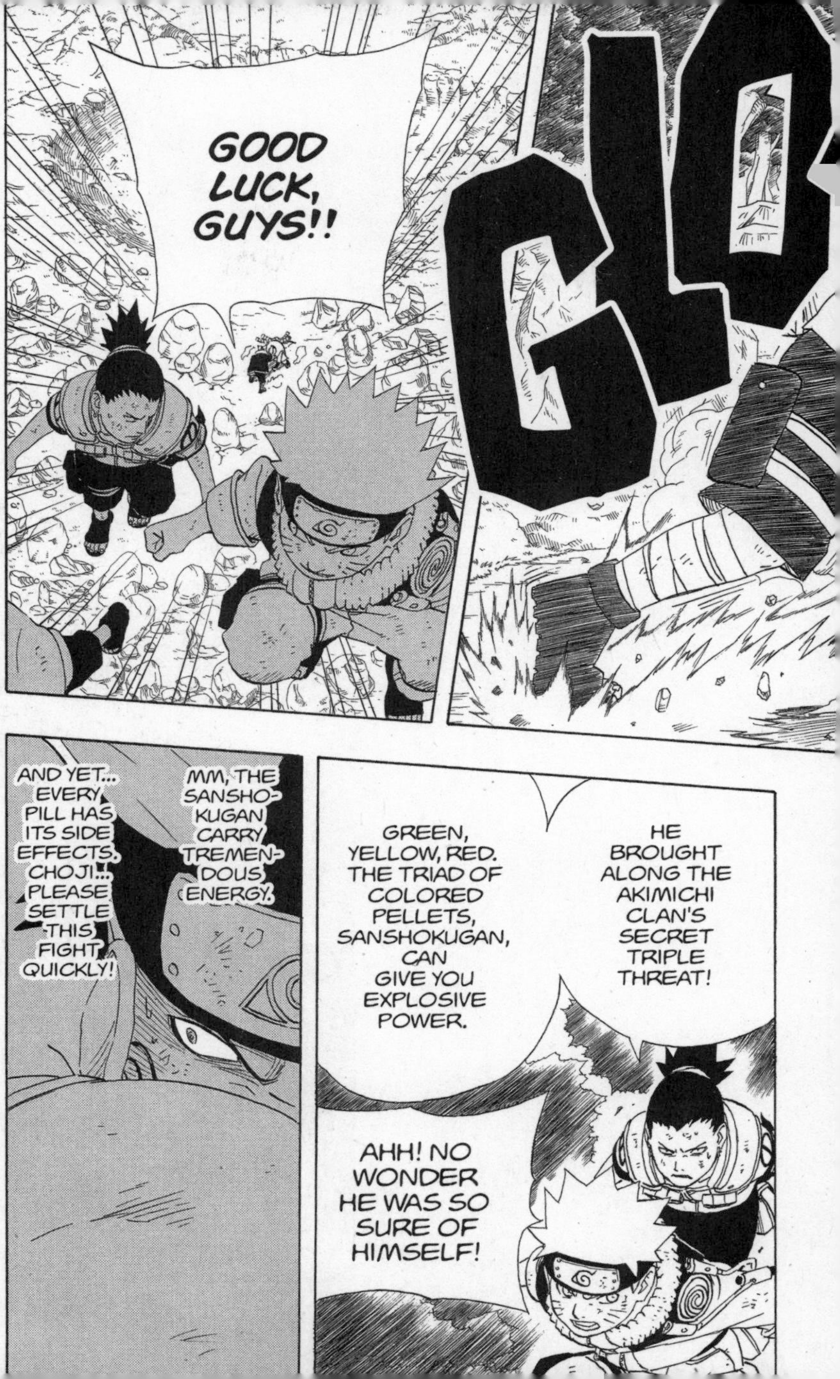
GOOD LUCK, GUYS!!
HE BROUGHT ALONG THE AKIMICHI CLAN'S SECRET TRIPLE THREAT!
GREEN, YELLOW, RED. THE TRIAD OF COLORED PELLETS, SANSHOKUGAN, CAN GIVE YOU EXPLOSIVE POWER.
AHH! NO WONDER HE WAS SO SURE OF HIMSELF!
MM, THE SANSHO-KUGAN CARRY TREMEN-DOUS ENERGY.
AND YET... EVERY PILL HAS ITS SIDE EFFECTS. CHOJI... PLEASE SETTLE THIS FIGHT QUICKLY!

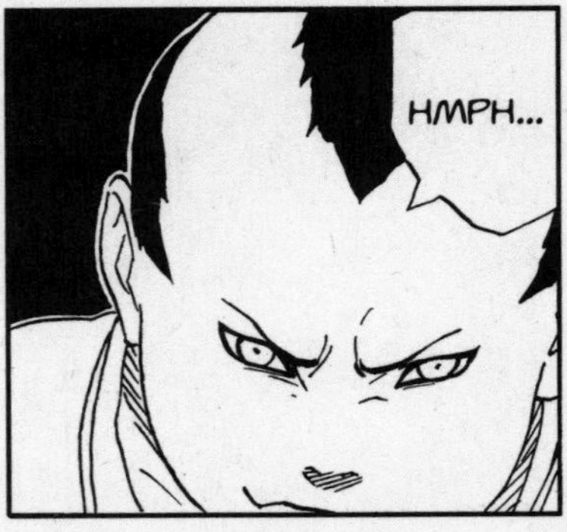
HMPH...

Number 189: Faith...!!

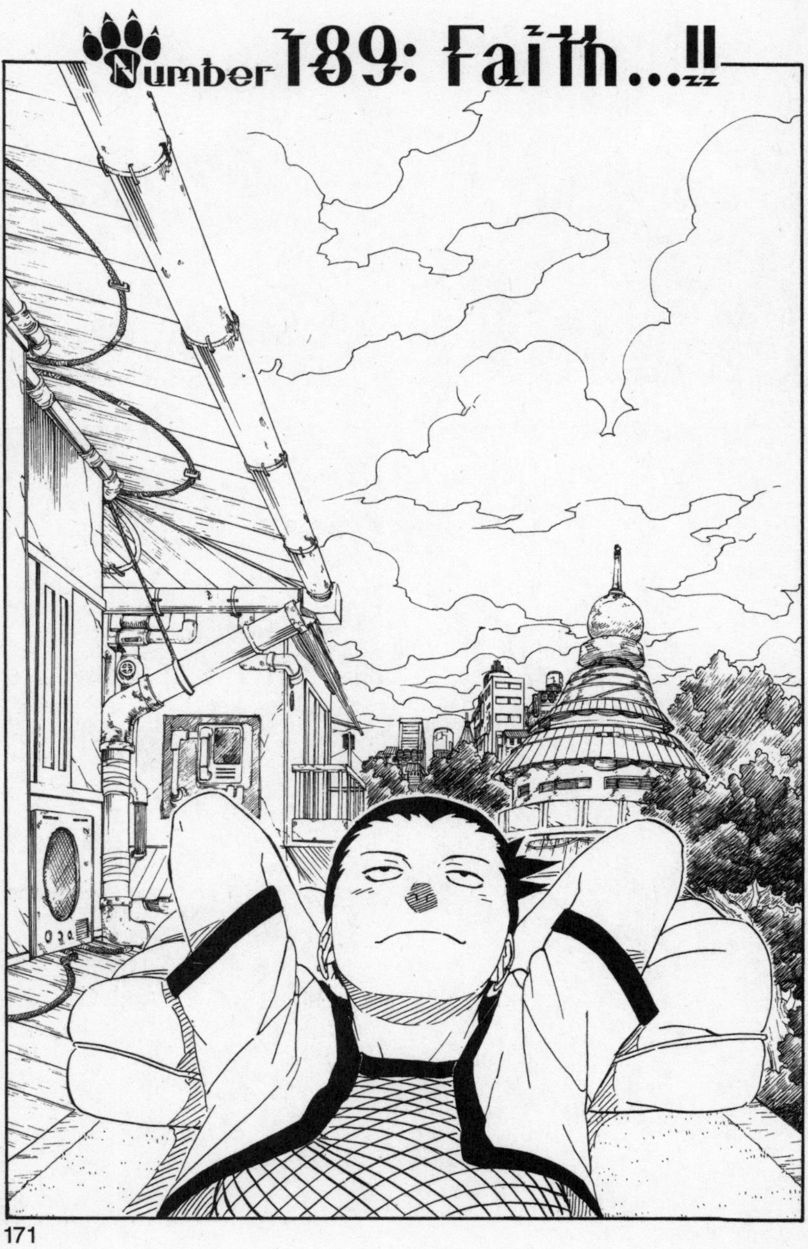

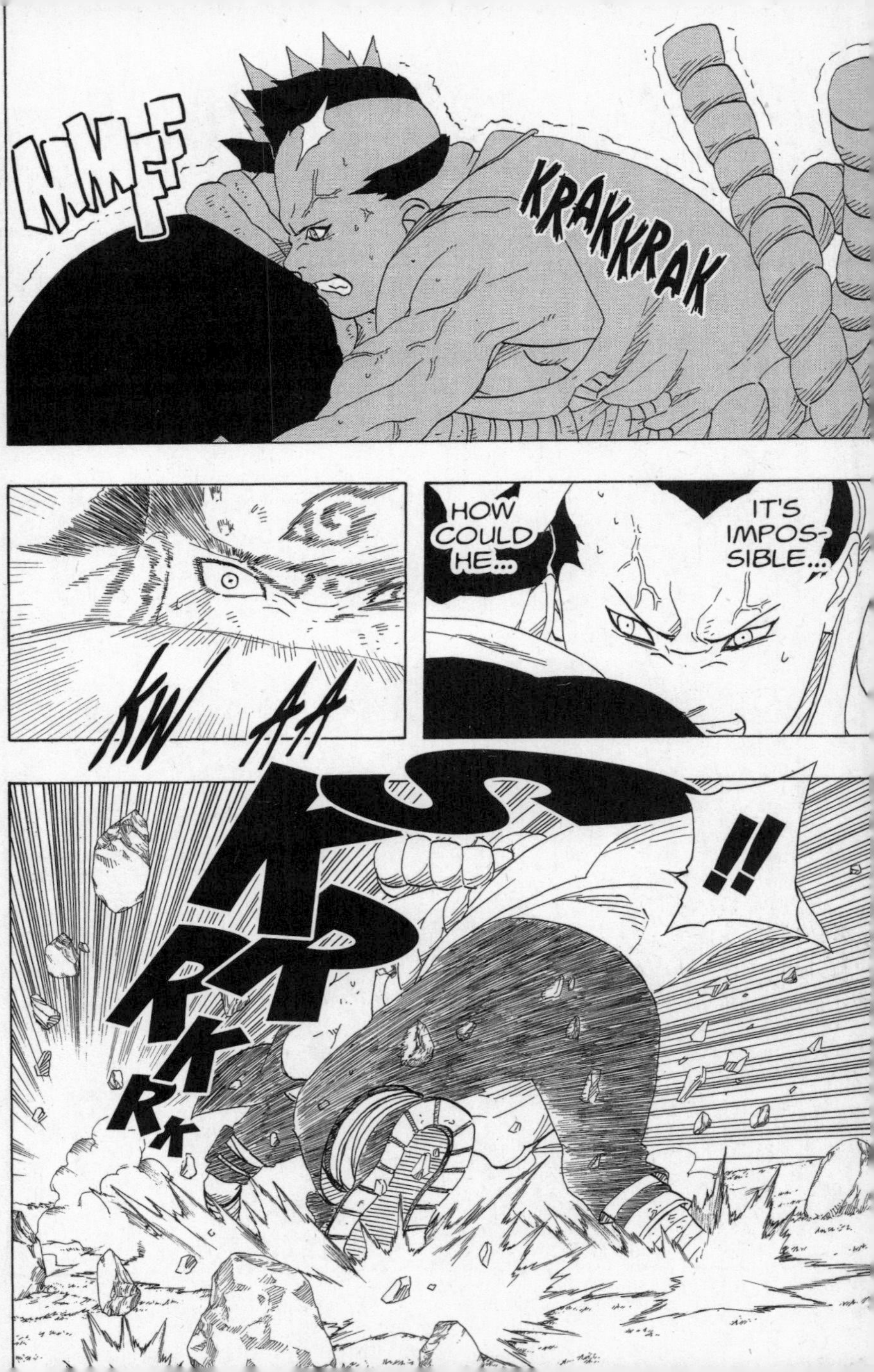
KRAKKRAK
NMMFF
IT'S IMPOSSIBLE...
HOW COULD HE...
KWAA
KRRRRK
!!

READ THIS WAY

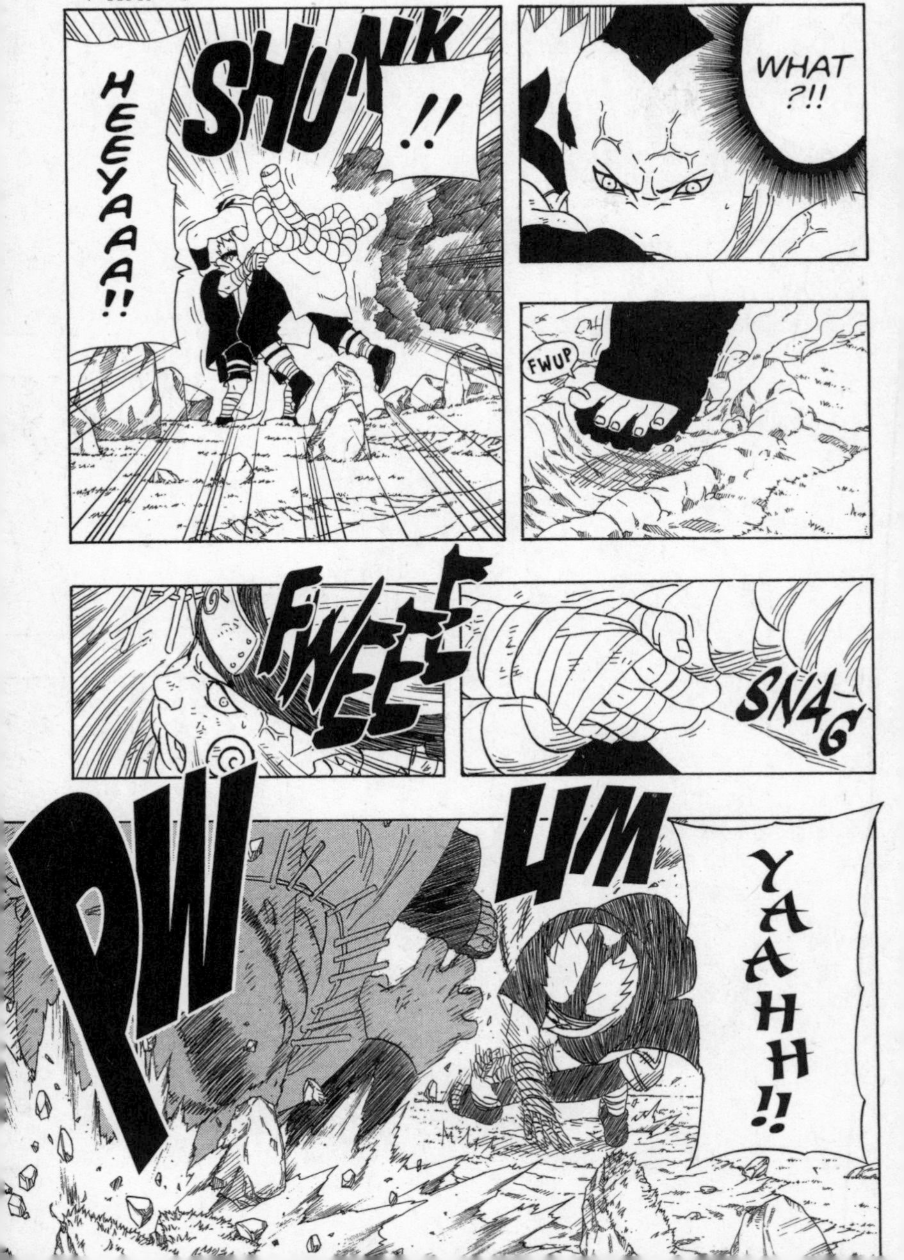
WHAT ?!!
FWUP
SHUNK
!!
HEEYAAAA!!
SNAG
FWEEE
YAAHH!!
PWUM

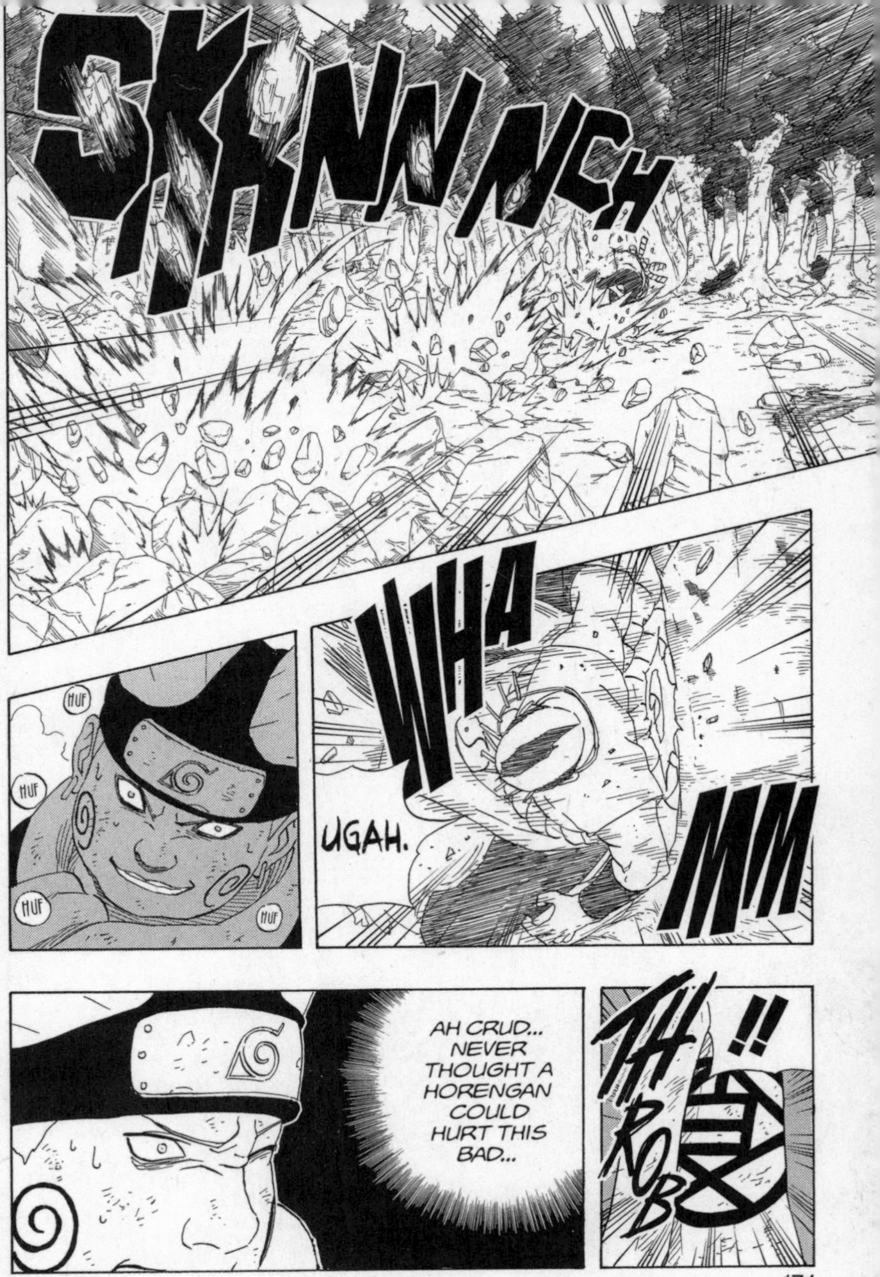
SKNNNCH
WHAMM
UGAH.
HUF
HUF
HUF
HUF
THROB!!
AH CRUD... NEVER THOUGHT A HORENGAN COULD HURT THIS BAD...

READ THIS WAY

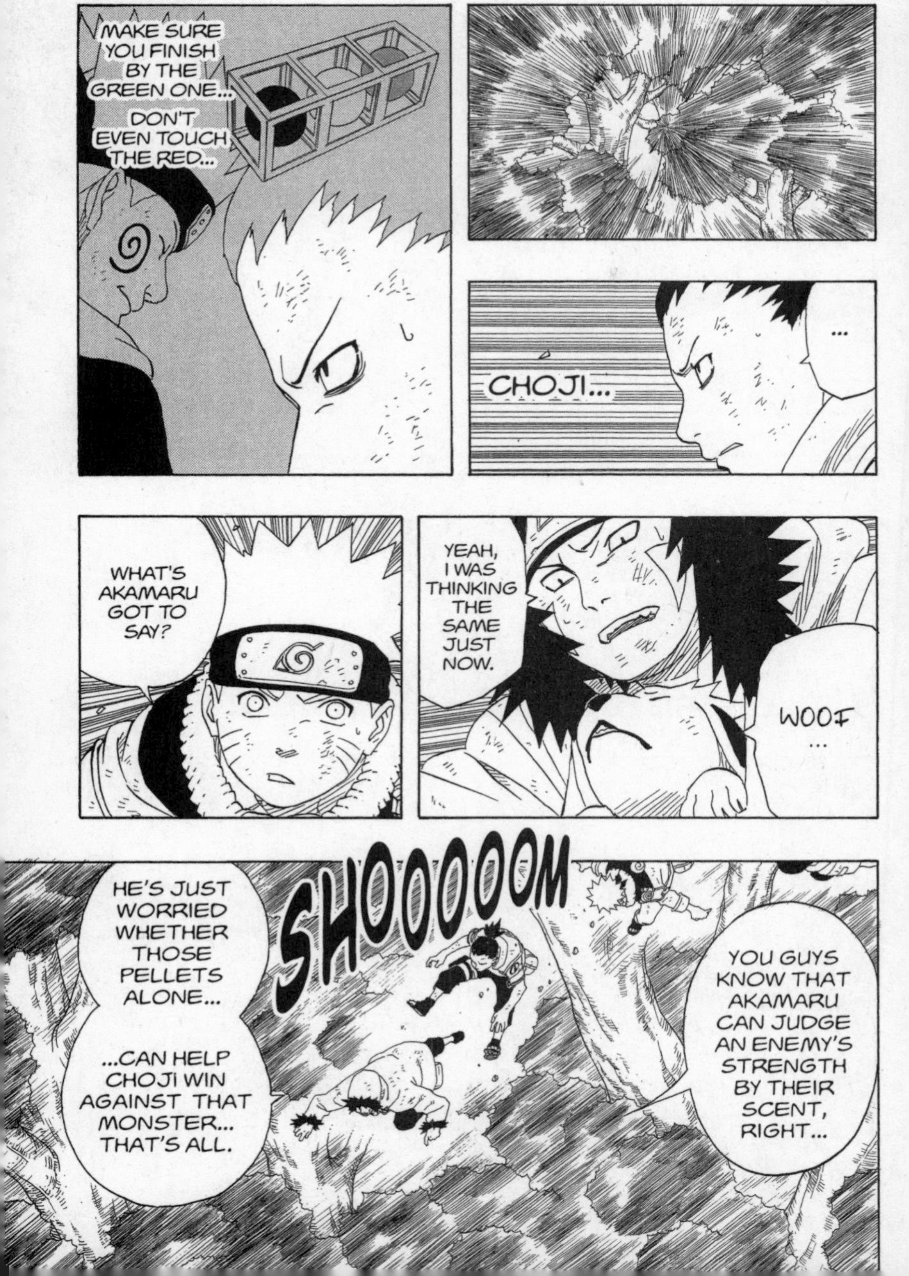

...
CHOJI...
MAKE SURE YOU FINISH BY THE GREEN ONE...
DON'T EVEN TOUCH THE RED...
YEAH, I WAS THINKING THE SAME JUST NOW.
WOOF ...
WHAT'S AKAMARU GOT TO SAY?
SHOOOOOM
YOU GUYS KNOW THAT AKAMARU CAN JUDGE AN ENEMY'S STRENGTH BY THEIR SCENT, RIGHT...
HE'S JUST WORRIED WHETHER THOSE PELLETS ALONE...
...CAN HELP CHOJI WIN AGAINST THAT MONSTER... THAT'S ALL.

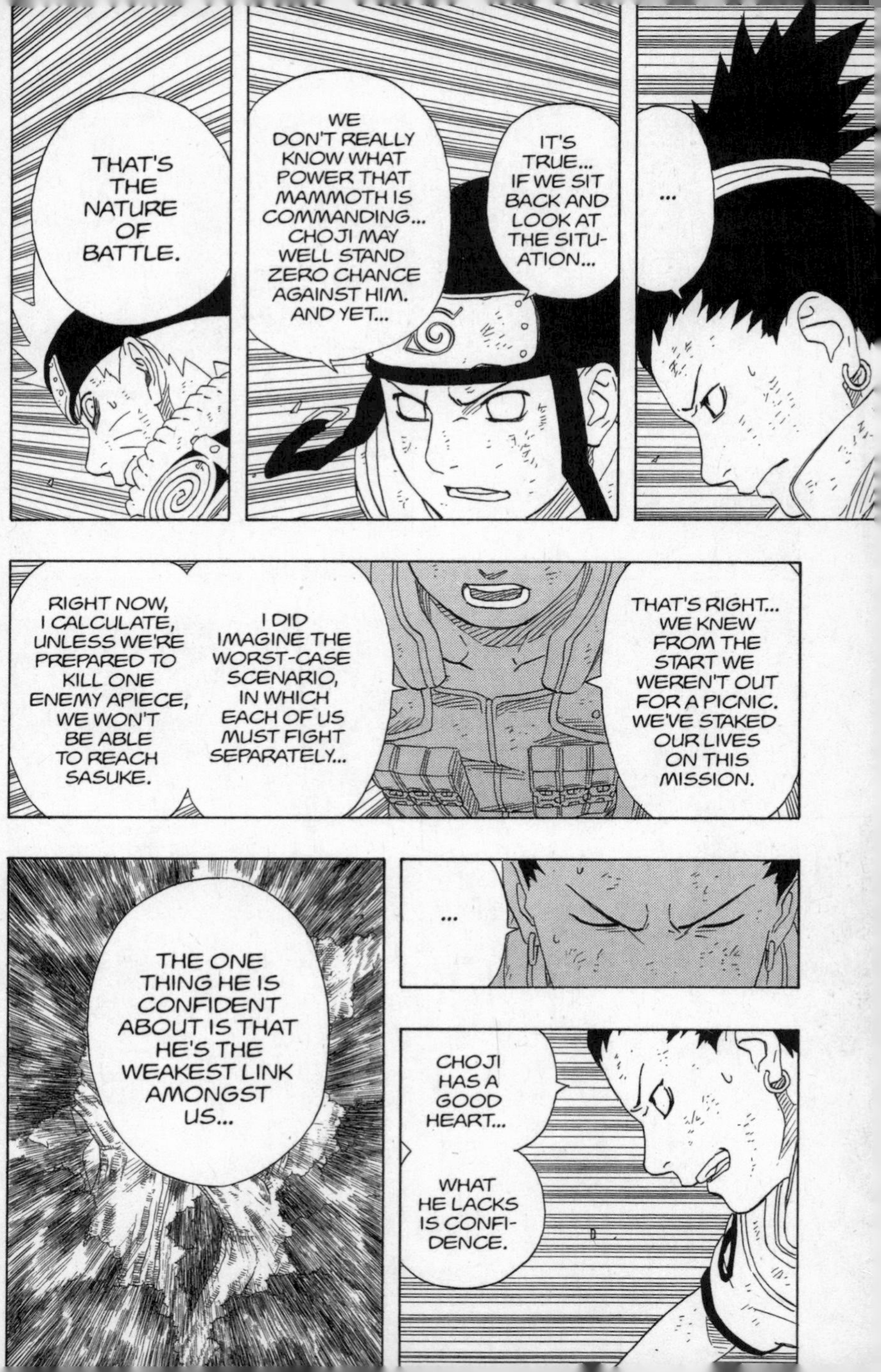
...
IT'S TRUE... IF WE SIT BACK AND LOOK AT THE SITUATION...
WE DON'T REALLY KNOW WHAT POWER THAT MAMMOTH IS COMMANDING... CHOJI MAY WELL STAND ZERO CHANCE AGAINST HIM. AND YET...
THAT'S THE NATURE OF BATTLE.
THAT'S RIGHT... WE KNEW FROM THE START WE WEREN'T OUT FOR A PICNIC. WE'VE STAKED OUR LIVES ON THIS MISSION.
I DID IMAGINE THE WORST-CASE SCENARIO, IN WHICH EACH OF US MUST FIGHT SEPARATELY...
RIGHT NOW, I CALCULATE, UNLESS WE'RE PREPARED TO KILL ONE ENEMY APIECE, WE WON'T BE ABLE TO REACH SASUKE.
...
CHOJI HAS A GOOD HEART...
WHAT HE LACKS IS CONFIDENCE.
THE ONE THING HE IS CONFIDENT ABOUT IS THAT HE'S THE WEAKEST LINK AMONGST US...

READ THIS WAY

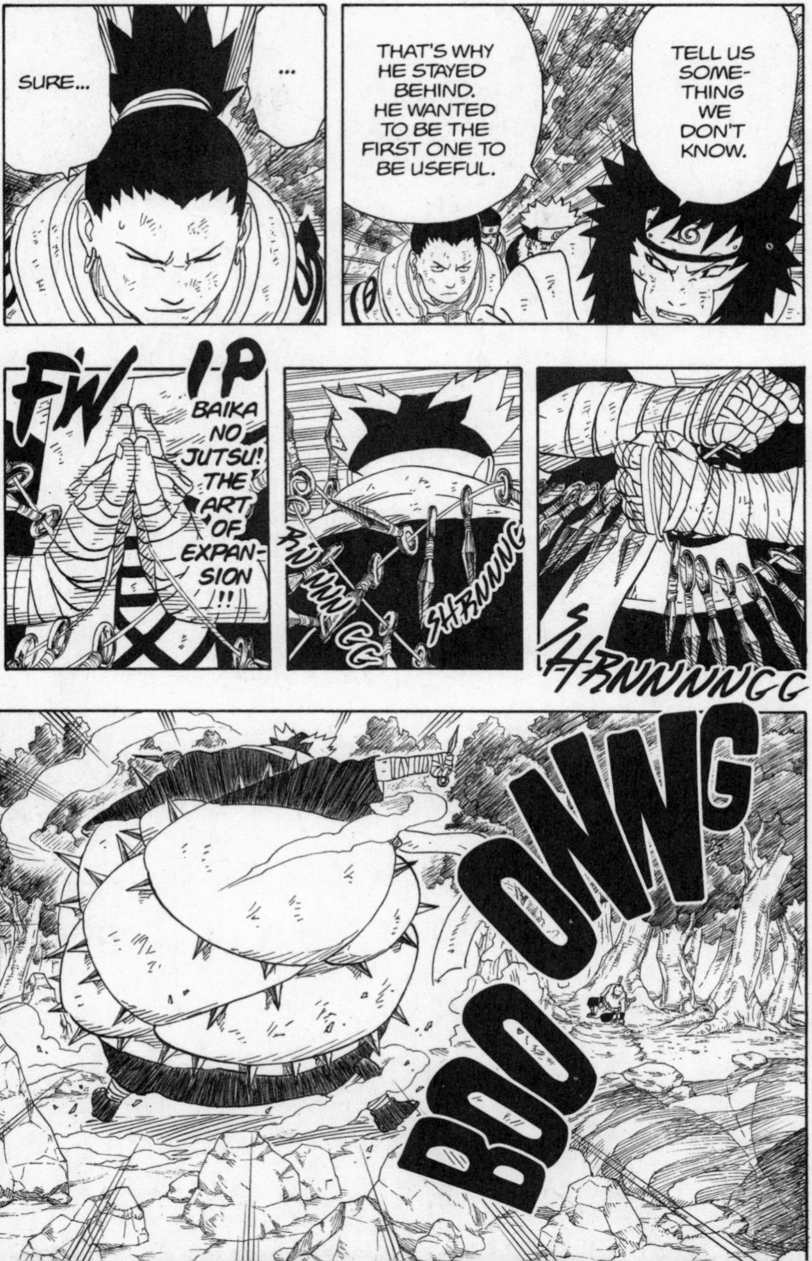
TELL US SOMETHING WE DON'T KNOW.
THAT'S WHY HE STAYED BEHIND. HE WANTED TO BE THE FIRST ONE TO BE USEFUL.
...
SURE...
SHRNNNNGG
SHRNNNG
RNNNNGG
FWIP
BAIKA NO JUTSU! THE ART OF EXPANSION!!
BOOWNG

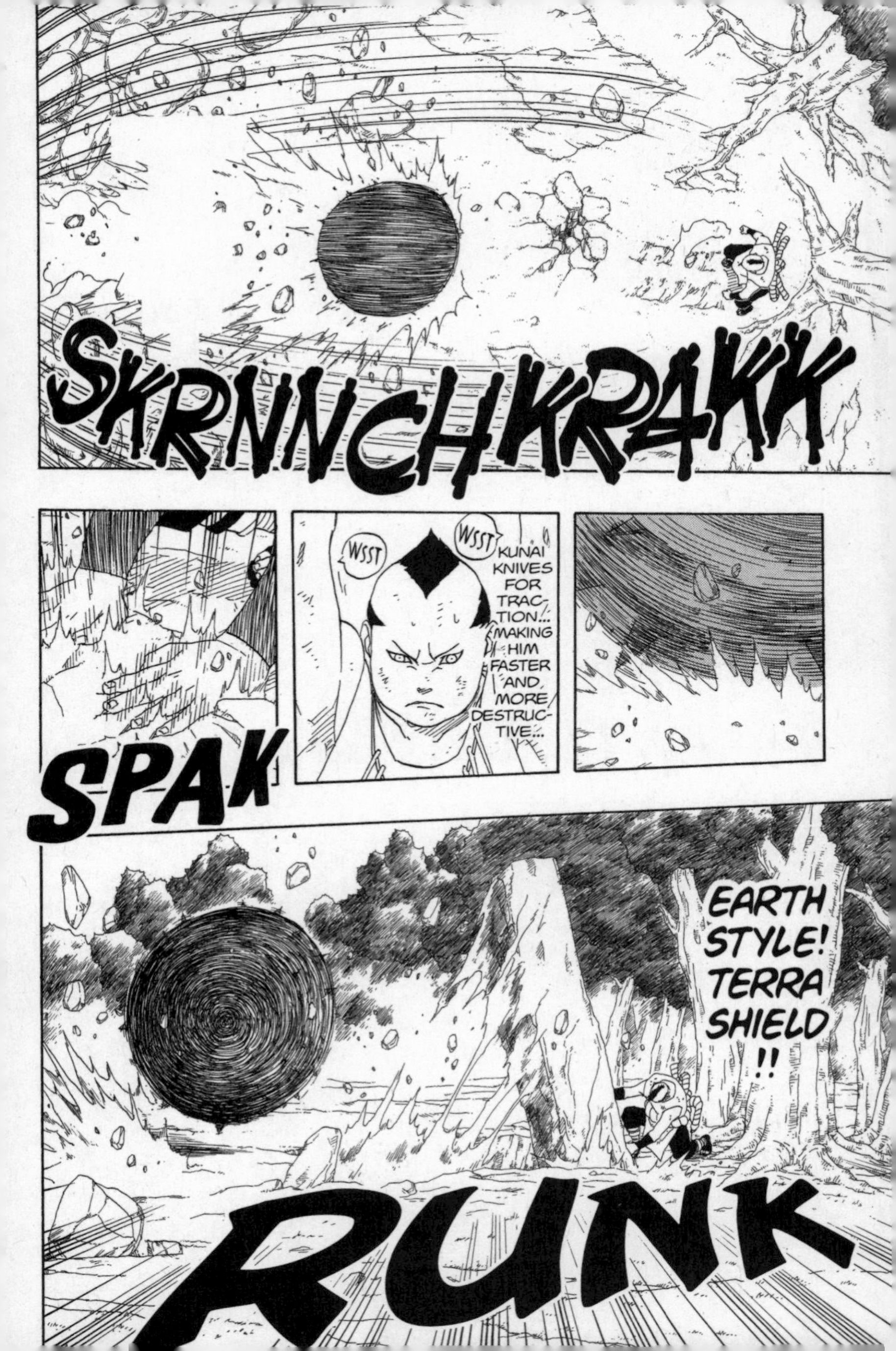
SKRNNCHKRAKK
KUNAI KNIVES FOR TRACTION... MAKING HIM FASTER AND MORE DESTRUCTIVE...
WSST
WSST
SPAK
EARTH STYLE! TERRA SHIELD!!
RUNK

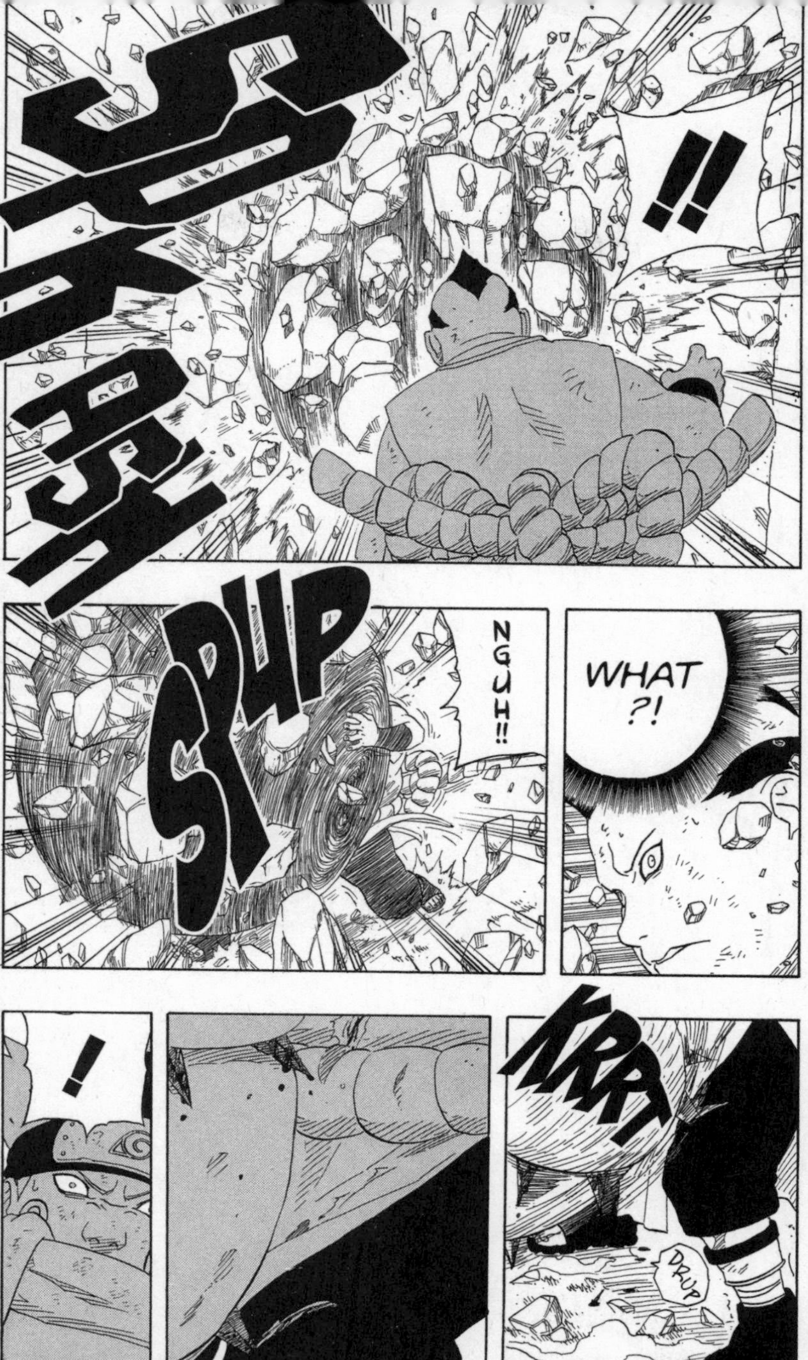
!!
WHAT ?!
NGUH!!
SPUP
KRRA
DRUP
!

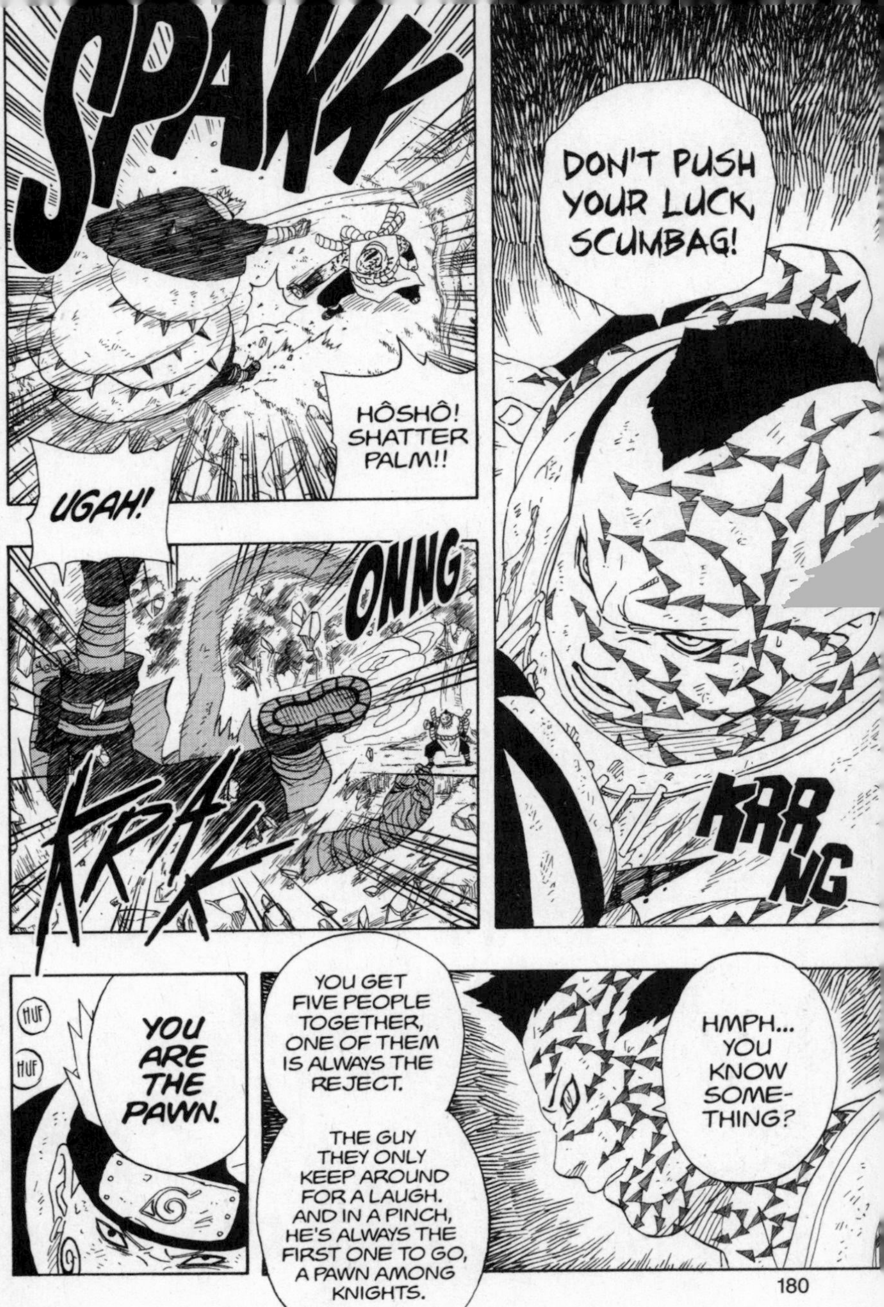
DON'T PUSH YOUR LUCK, SCUMBAG!
KRRRNG
SPAWK
HÔSHÔ! SHATTER PALM!!
UGAH!
ONNG
KRAK
HMPH... YOU KNOW SOME- THING?
YOU GET FIVE PEOPLE TOGETHER, ONE OF THEM IS ALWAYS THE REJECT.
THE GUY THEY ONLY KEEP AROUND FOR A LAUGH. AND IN A PINCH, HE'S ALWAYS THE FIRST ONE TO GO, A PAWN AMONG KNIGHTS.
HUF
HUF
YOU ARE THE PAWN.

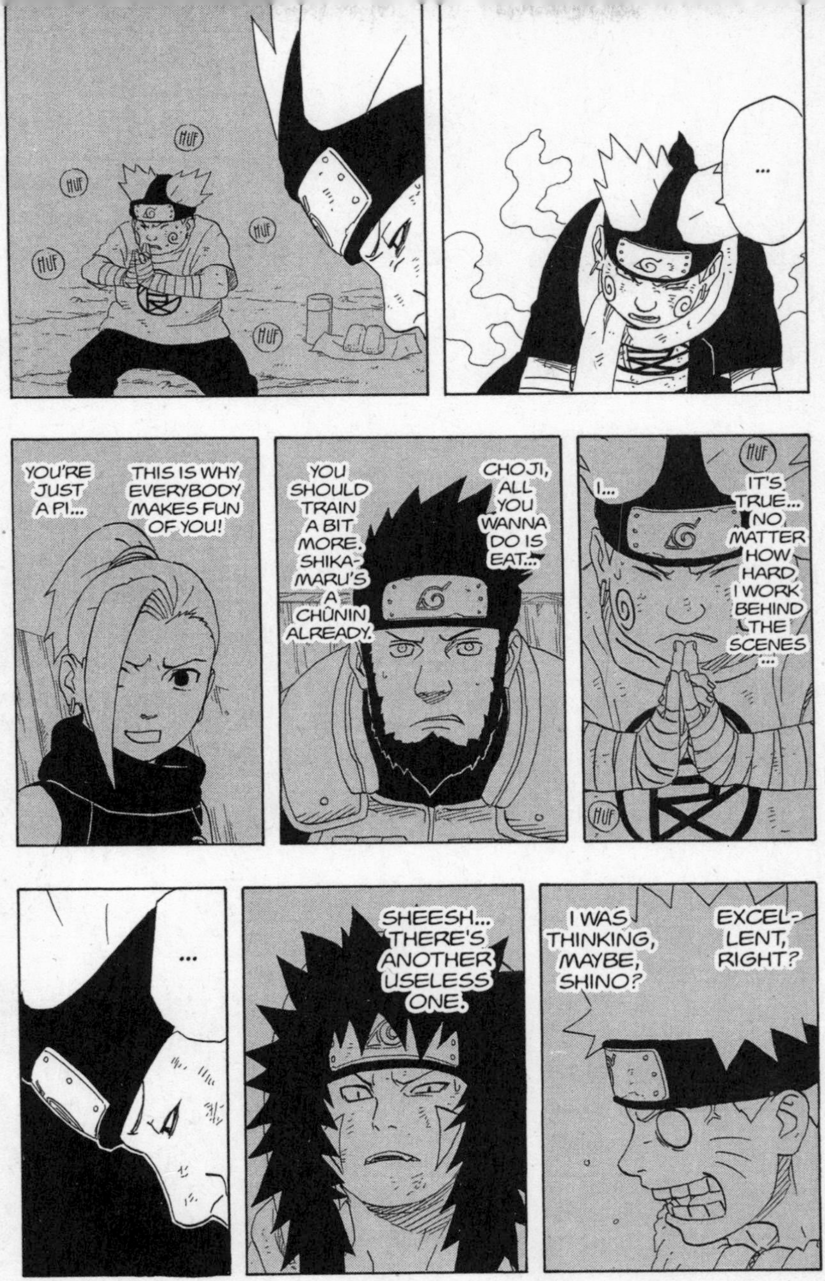
...
HUF
HUF
HUF
HUF
HUF
HUF
IT'S TRUE... NO MATTER HOW HARD, I WORK BEHIND THE SCENES...
I...
HUF
CHOJI, ALL YOU WANNA DO IS EAT...
YOU SHOULD TRAIN A BIT MORE. SHIKAMARU'S A CHÛNIN ALREADY.
THIS IS WHY EVERYBODY MAKES FUN OF YOU!
YOU'RE JUST A PI...
EXCELLENT, RIGHT?
I WAS THINKING, MAYBE, SHINO?
SHEESH... THERE'S ANOTHER USELESS ONE.
...

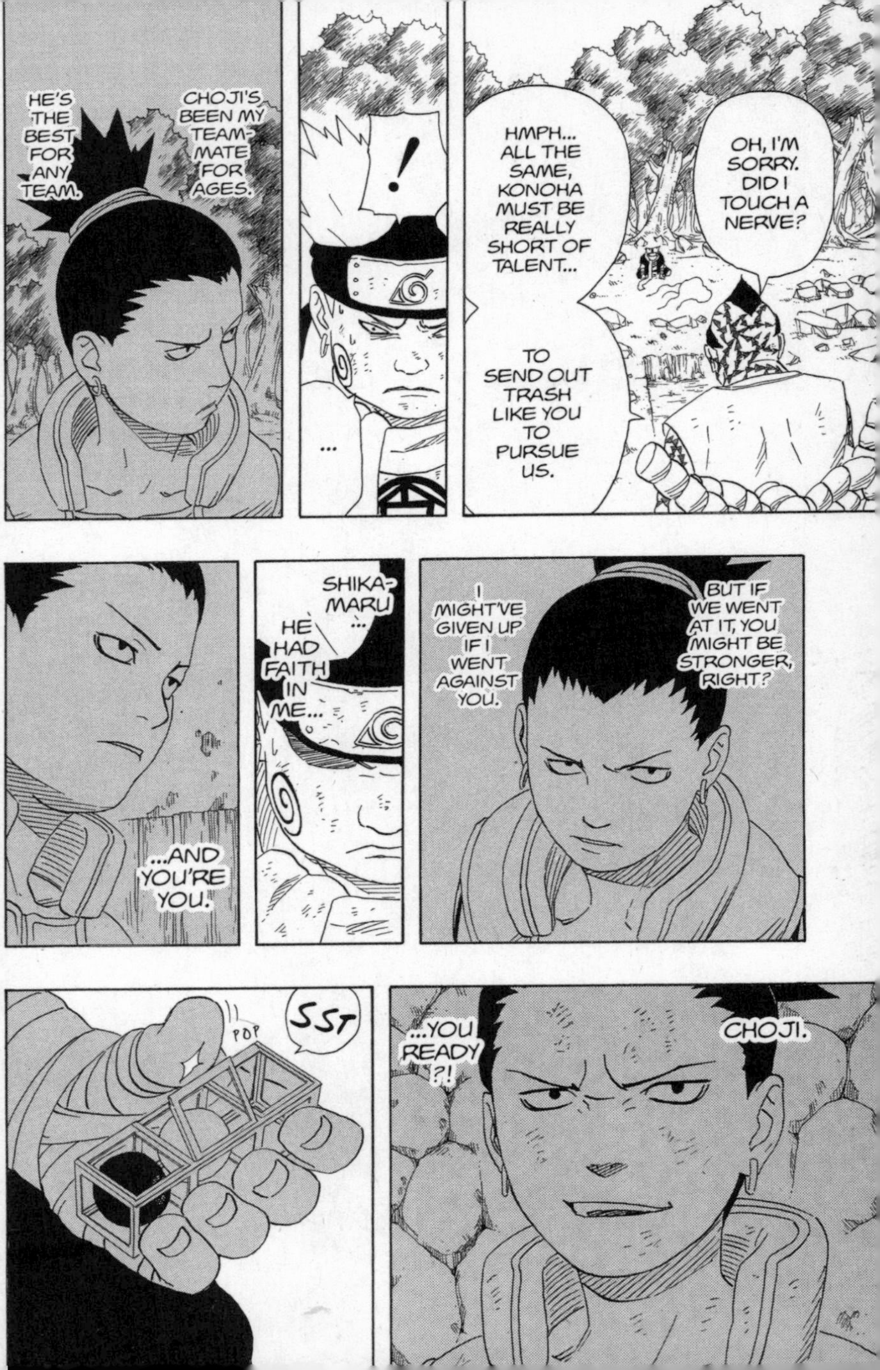
OH, I'M SORRY. DID I TOUCH A NERVE?
HMPH... ALL THE SAME, KONOHA MUST BE REALLY SHORT OF TALENT...
TO SEND OUT TRASH LIKE YOU TO PURSUE US.
!
...
CHOJI'S BEEN MY TEAM-MATE FOR AGES.
HE'S THE BEST FOR ANY TEAM.
BUT IF WE WENT AT IT, YOU MIGHT BE STRONGER, RIGHT?
I MIGHT'VE GIVEN UP IF I WENT AGAINST YOU.
SHIKA-MARU...
HE HAD FAITH IN ME...
...AND YOU'RE YOU.
CHOJI.
...YOU READY?!
SST
POP

READ THIS WAY

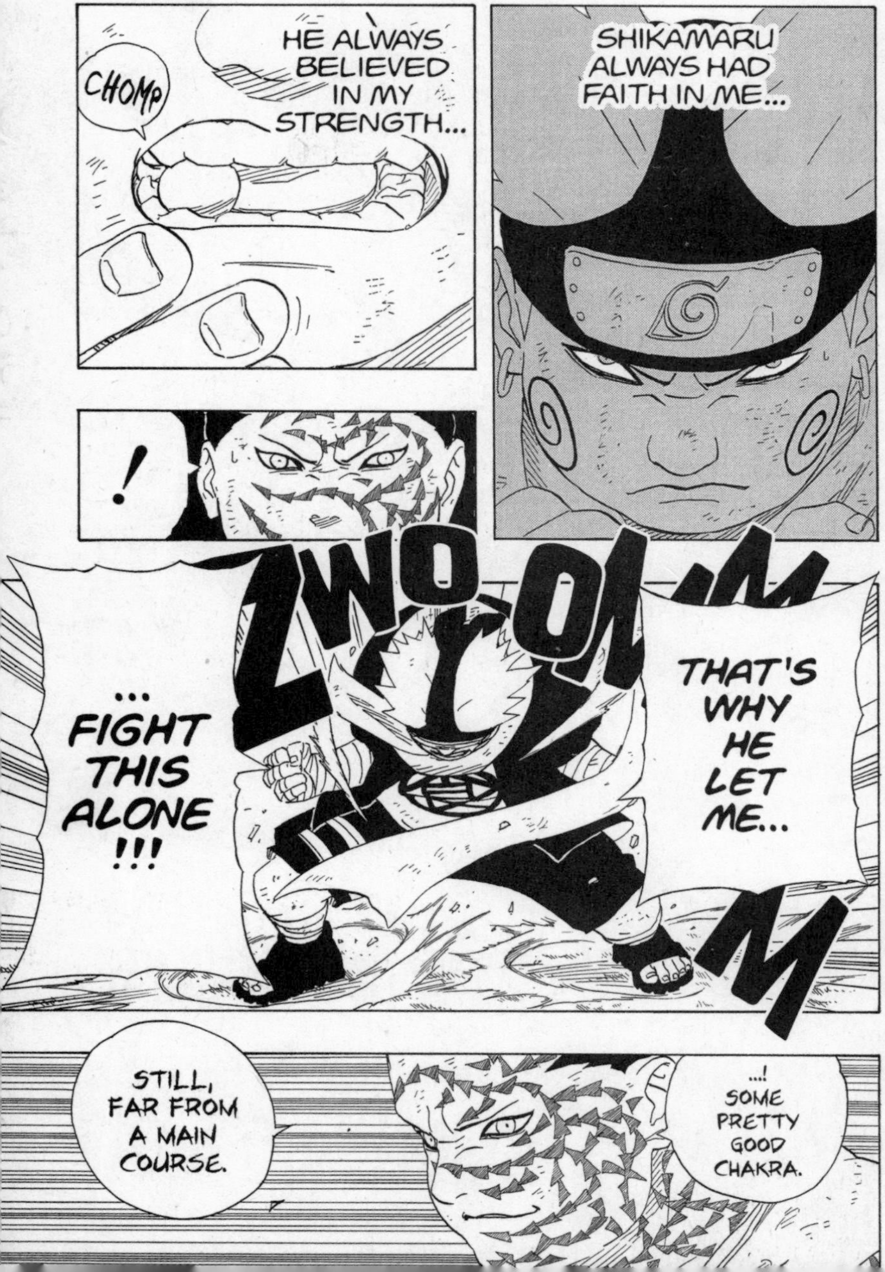
SHIKAMARU ALWAYS HAD FAITH IN ME...
HE ALWAYS BELIEVED IN MY STRENGTH...
CHOMP
!
ZWOOM
THAT'S WHY HE LET ME...
... FIGHT THIS ALONE !!!
...! SOME PRETTY GOOD CHAKRA.
STILL, FAR FROM A MAIN COURSE.

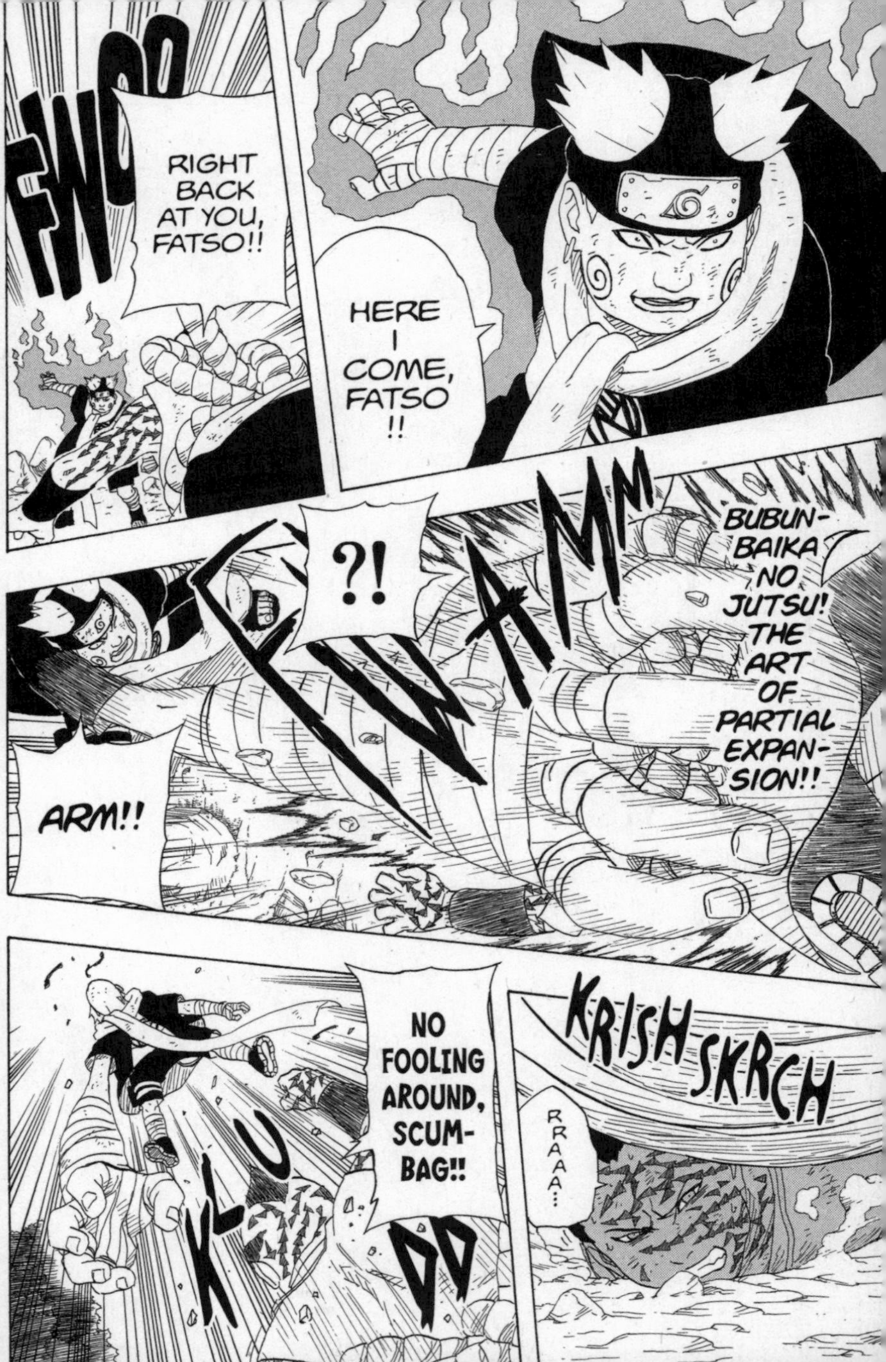
HERE I COME, FATSO!!
FWOOO
RIGHT BACK AT YOU, FATSO!!
BUBUN-BAIKA NO JUTSU! THE ART OF PARTIAL EXPANSION!!
FWAMM
?!
ARM!!
KRISH SKRCH
RRAAA...
NO FOOLING AROUND, SCUM-BAG!!
KLUDD

READ THIS WAY

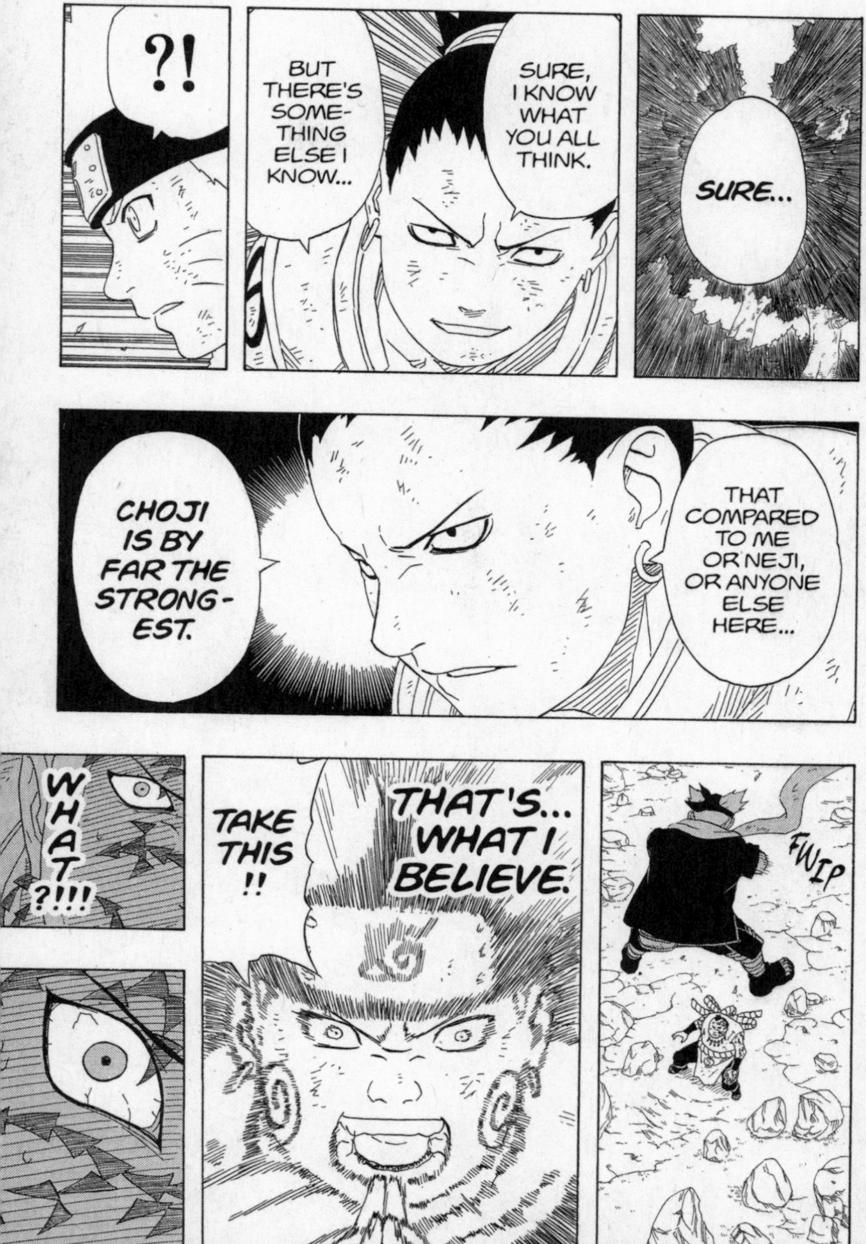
SURE...
SURE, I KNOW WHAT YOU ALL THINK.
BUT THERE'S SOME-THING ELSE I KNOW...
?!
THAT COMPARED TO ME OR NEJI, OR ANYONE ELSE HERE...
CHOJI IS BY FAR THE STRONG-EST.
FWIP
THAT'S... WHAT I BELIEVE.
TAKE THIS !!
WHAT?!!!

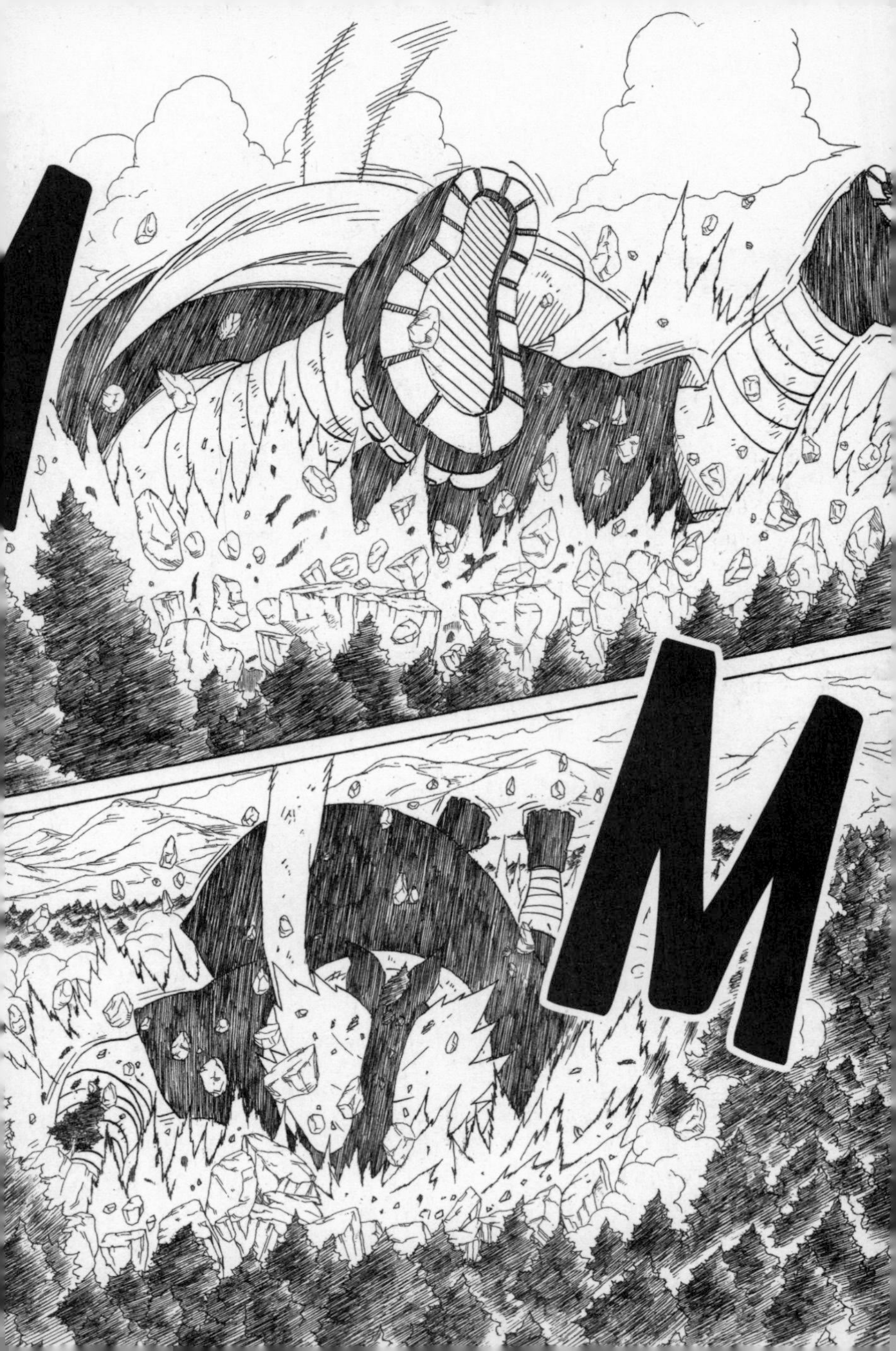
M

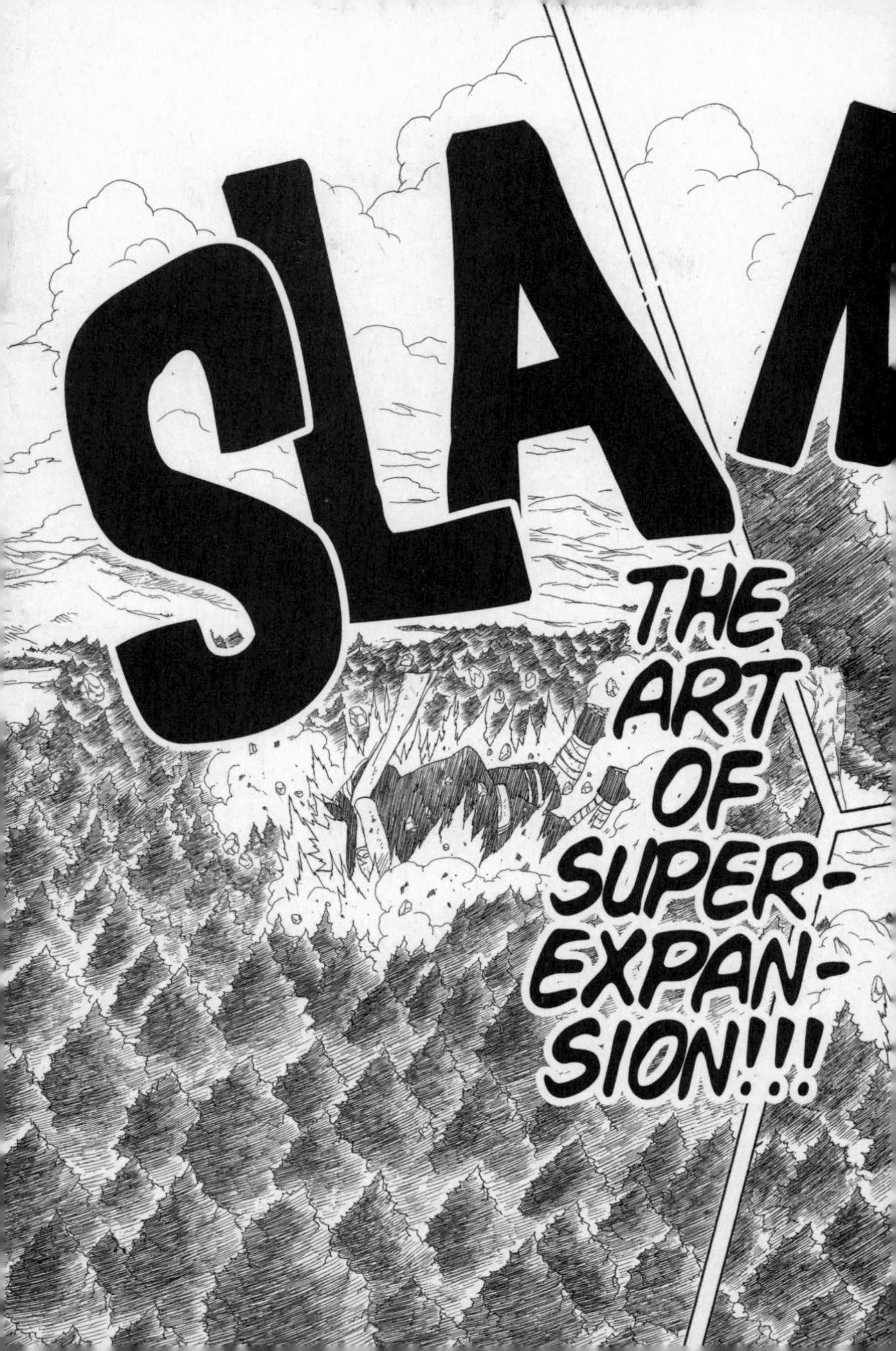
SLAM
THE ART OF SUPER-EXPANSION!!!

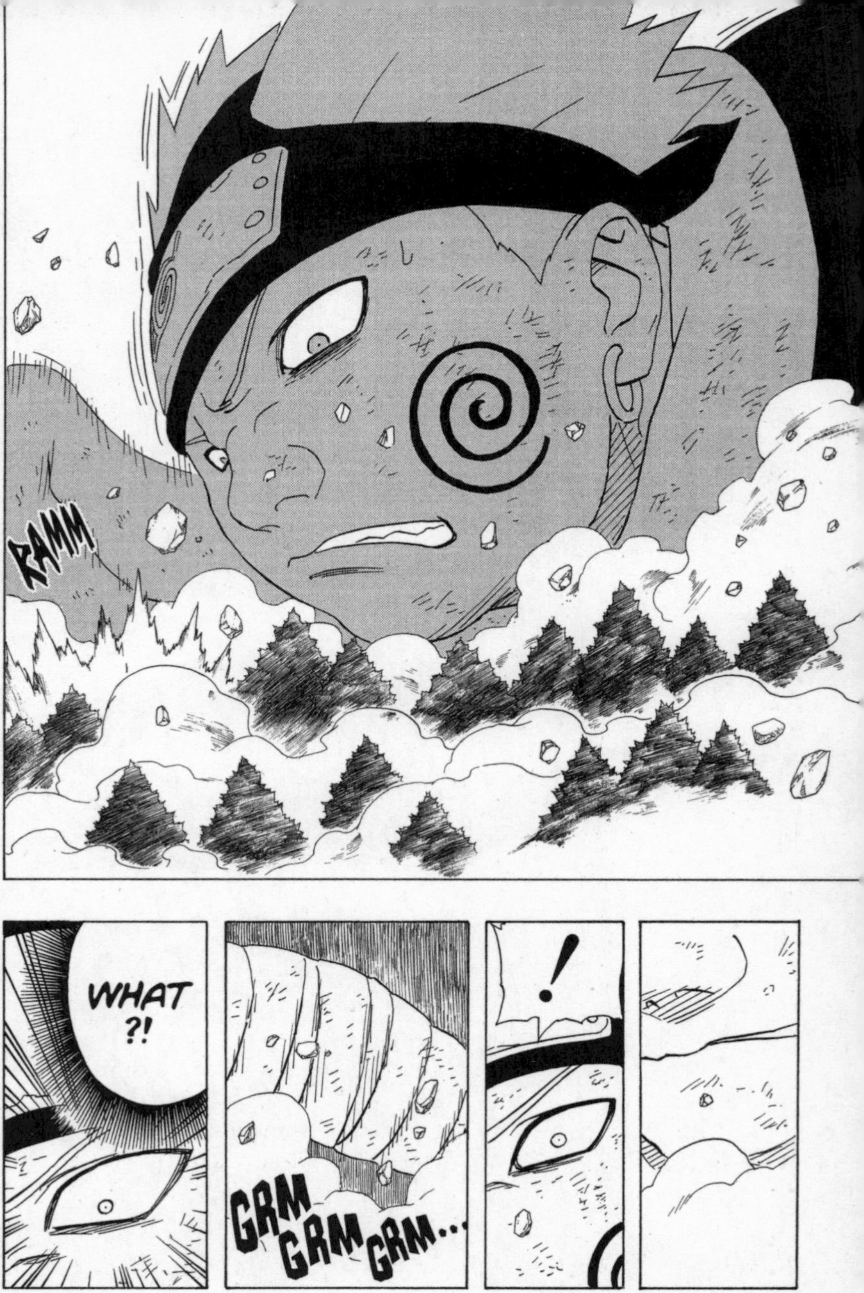
RAMM
!
GRM GRM GRM...
WHAT?!

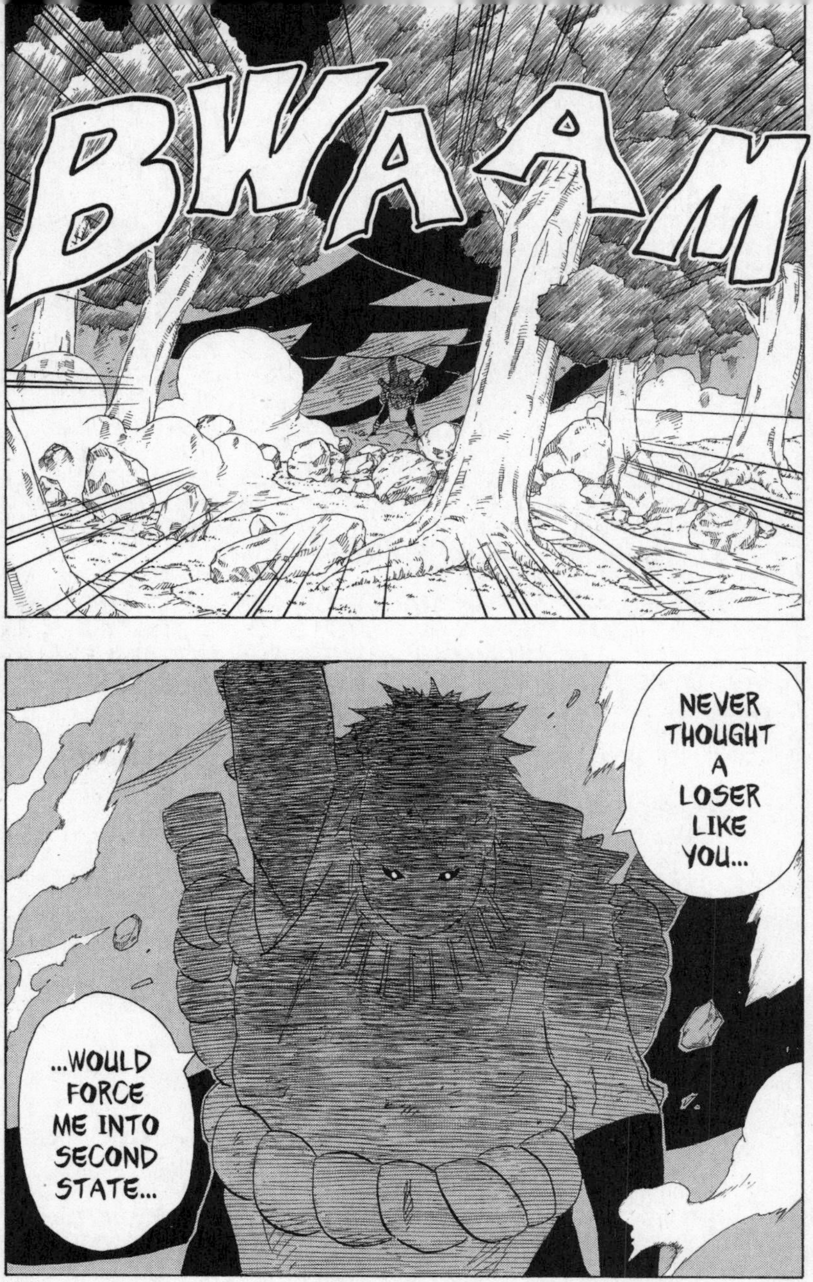
BWAAM
NEVER THOUGHT A LOSER LIKE YOU...
...WOULD FORCE ME INTO SECOND STATE...

LATELY, IT'S BEEN GETTING REALLY DIFFICULT FOR ME TO COME UP WITH NEW CHARACTERS. IT'S SO HARD TO DESIGN GOOD ONES THAT, THE WAY THINGS ARE GOING, I'M AFRAID THAT THE *NARUTO* SERIES MIGHT BE IN TROUBLE...SO TO OVERCOME THIS PROBLEM, WE DECIDED TO HOLD A NEW EVENT!

AND JUST WHAT IS THIS NEW EVENT?! WELL, IT'S A "DESIGN AND MAIL IN YOUR OWN ORIGINAL CHARACTERS TO POOR CREATIVITY-DRAINED KISHIMOTO" COMPETITION! THE MOST EXCELLENT WORKS WILL BE PRINTED IN *JUMP* COMICS! IN ADDITION, I WILL COPY AND ILLUSTRATE THE BEST DESIGN, AND THAT TOO WILL BE PRINTED!! (PLEASE NOTE, THE BEST DESIGNER WILL RECEIVE AN AUTOGRAPHED COPY OF MY TAKE ON HIS OR HER DESIGN.)

SERIOUSLY, IF YOUR CHARACTERS ARE GREAT, THEY MIGHT EVEN APPEAR IN *NARUTO*! SHOULD THAT HAPPEN, *JUMP* EDITORIAL DEPARTMENT WILL CONTACT YOU BY PHONE OR IN WRITING. (PLEASE RESPOND COURTEOUSLY WHEN IT HAPPENS!)

REMEMBER, THE DESIGN MUST BE TRULY ORIGINAL!

FURTHERMORE, YOU MUST DRAW A FULL BODY MODEL OF THE CHARACTER!!

HERE'S THE ADDRESS FOR SUBMITTING YOUR CHARACTERS:

PLEASE SEND THEM TO:
SHONEN JUMP
C/O VIZ MEDIA, LLC
PO BOX 77010
SAN FRANCISCO, CA 94107

※ NOTE: WE ACCEPT POSTCARD SUBMISSIONS ONLY. PLEASE DO NOT SEND LETTERS. ☺

(THIS CONTEST WAS FOR JAPAN ONLY, BUT WE'D STILL BE HAPPY TO SEE YOUR DRAWINGS. —ED)

Number 190: Unforgivable!!

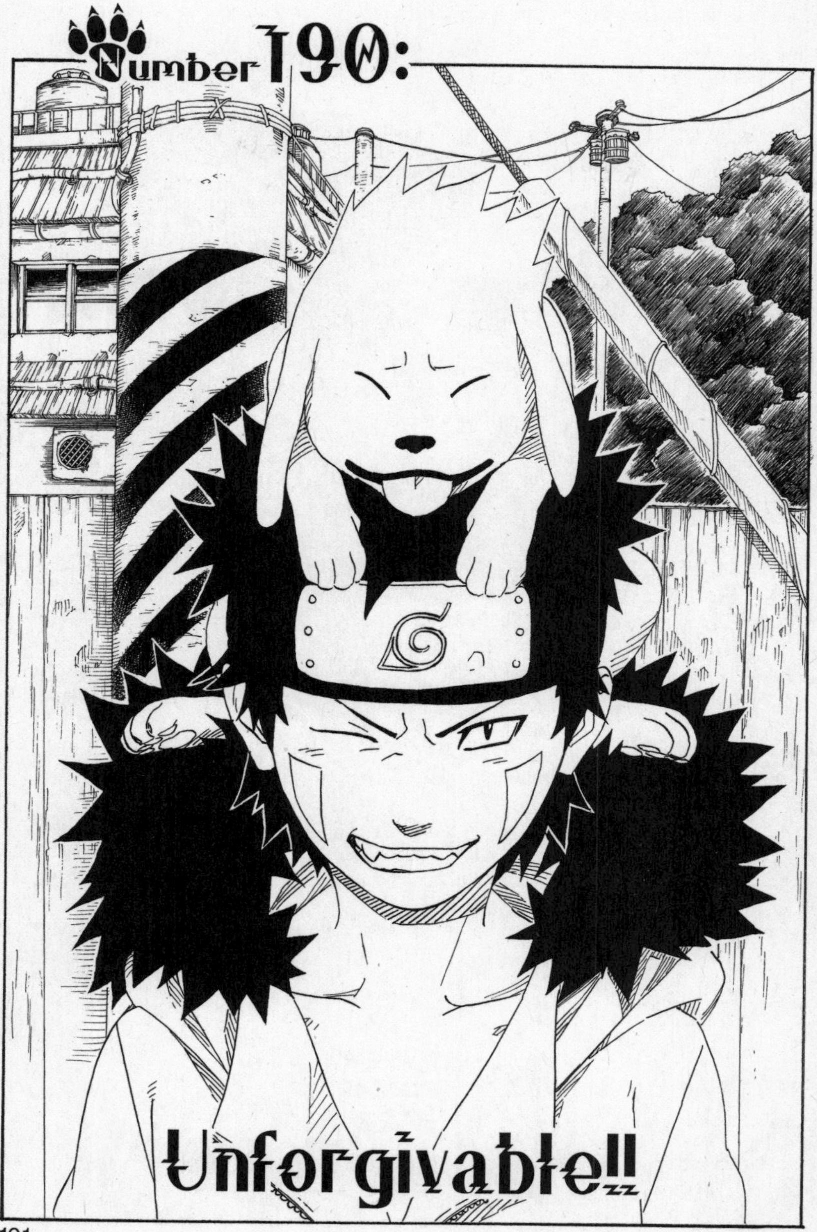

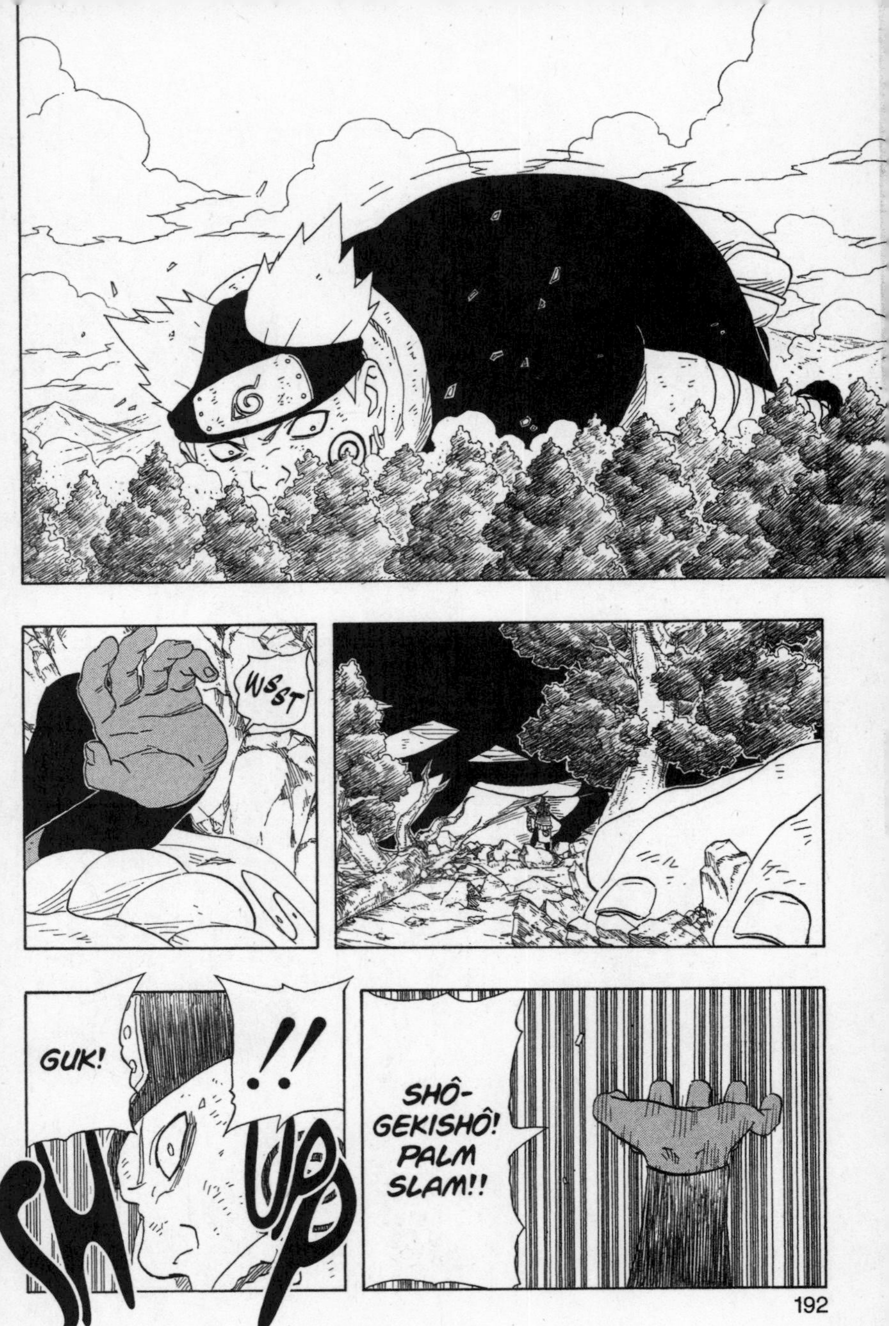
WSST
SHÔ-GEKISHÔ! PALM SLAM!!
GUK!
!!
SHUP

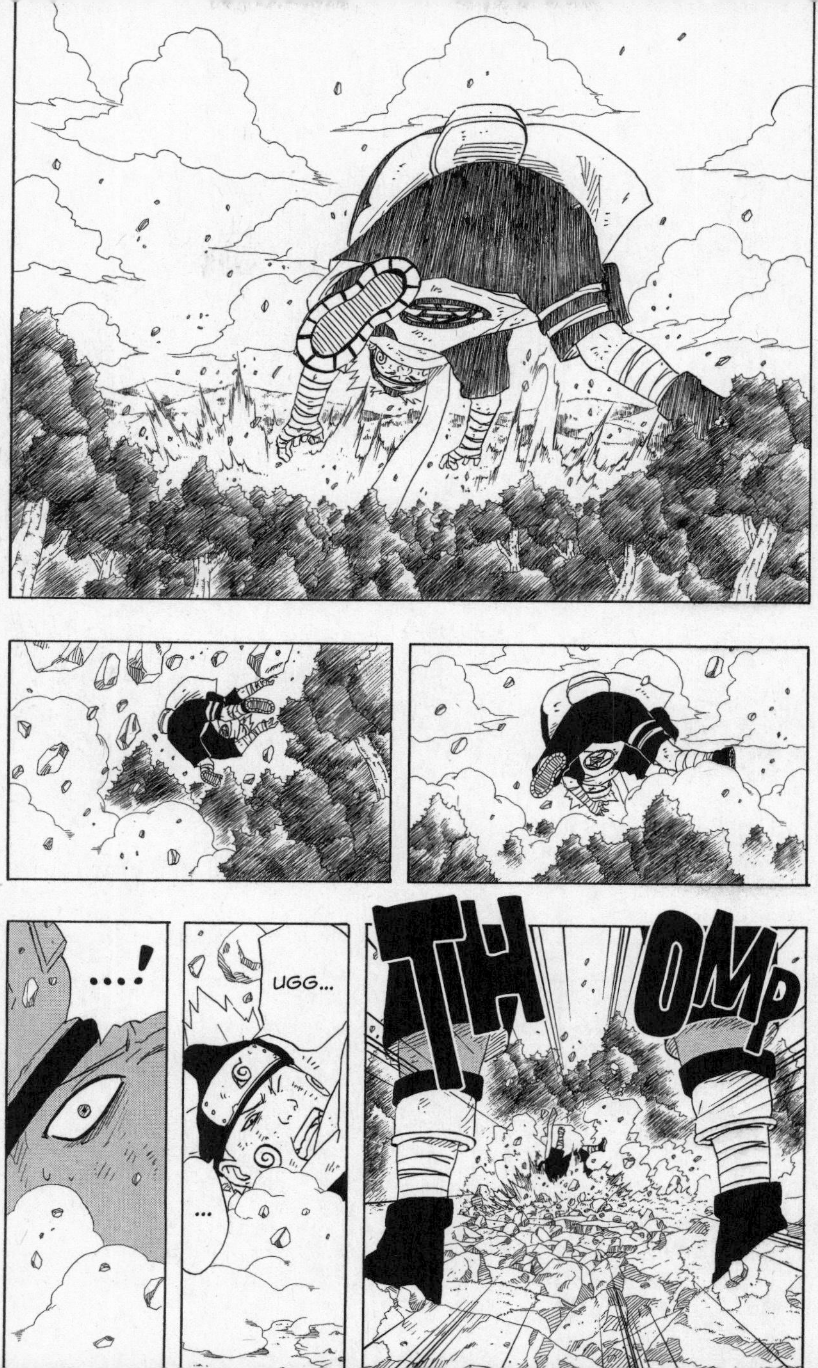
THOMP
UGG...
...
...!

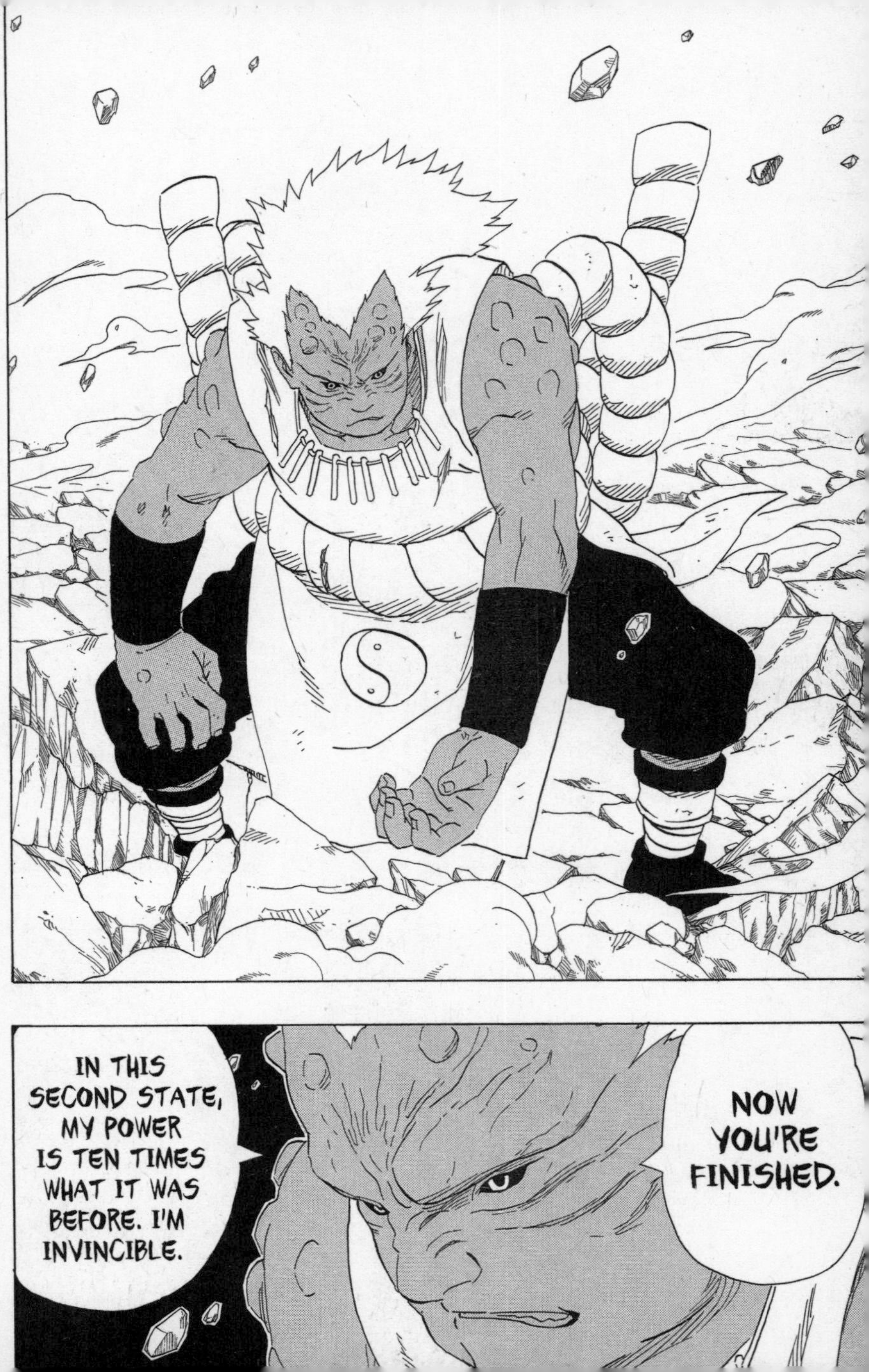
NOW YOU'RE FINISHED.
IN THIS SECOND STATE, MY POWER IS TEN TIMES WHAT IT WAS BEFORE. I'M INVINCIBLE.

READ THIS WAY

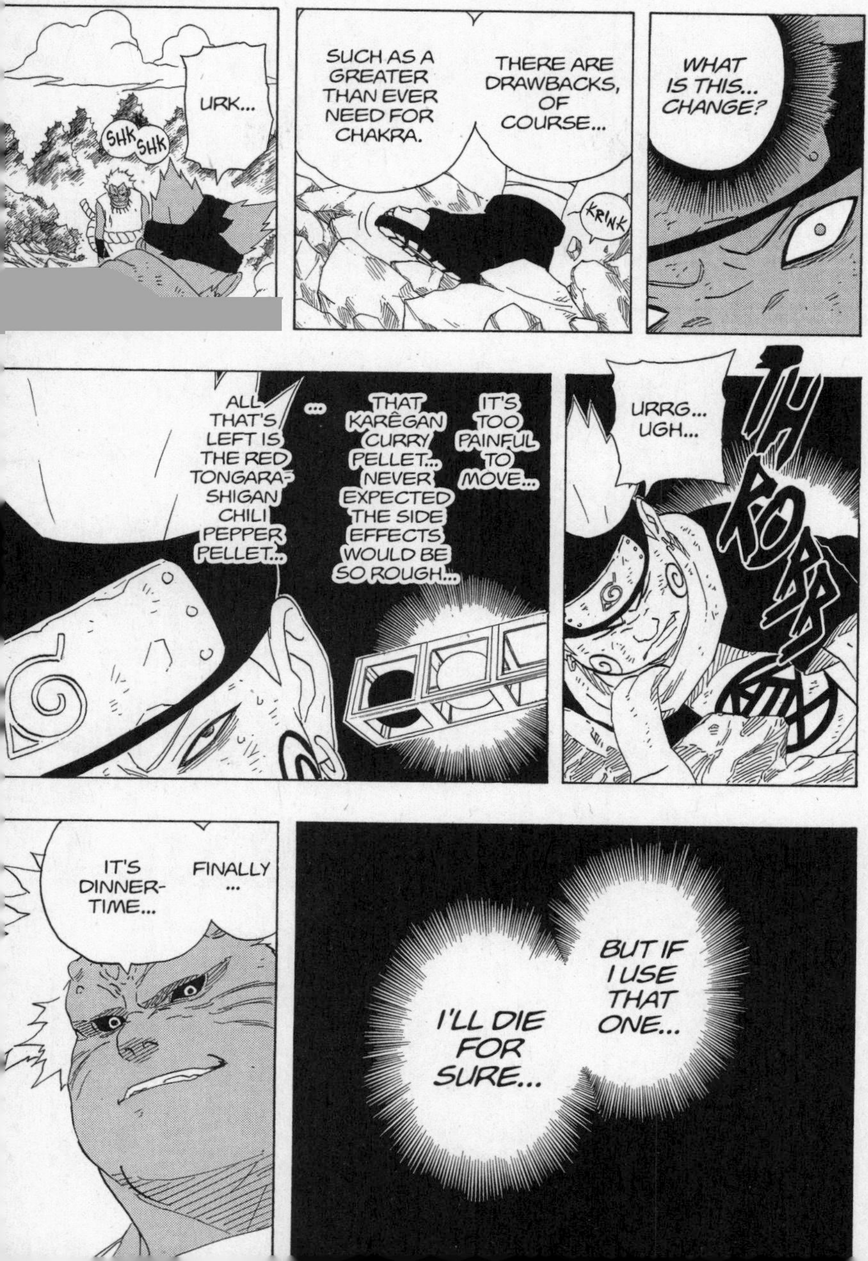
WHAT IS THIS... CHANGE?
THERE ARE DRAWBACKS, OF COURSE...
SUCH AS A GREATER THAN EVER NEED FOR CHAKRA.
KRINK
URK...
SHK
SHK
THROBB
URRG... UGH...
IT'S TOO PAINFUL TO MOVE...
THAT KARÊGAN CURRY PELLET... NEVER EXPECTED THE SIDE EFFECTS WOULD BE SO ROUGH...
...
ALL THAT'S LEFT IS THE RED TONGARA-SHIGAN CHILI PEPPER PELLET...
BUT IF I USE THAT ONE...
I'LL DIE FOR SURE...
FINALLY...
IT'S DINNER-TIME...

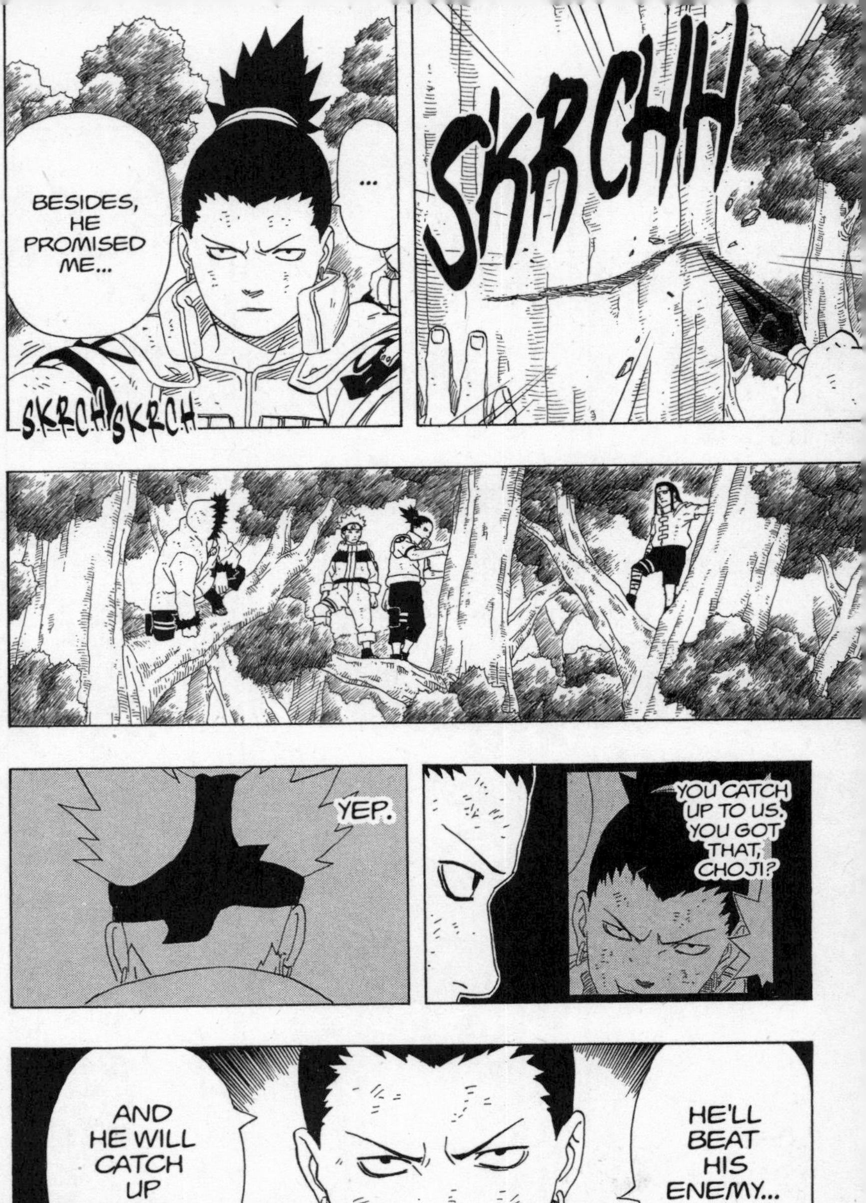
SKRCHH
...
BESIDES, HE PROMISED ME...
SKRCH SKRCH
YOU CATCH UP TO US. YOU GOT THAT, CHOJI?
YEP.
HE'LL BEAT HIS ENEMY...
AND HE WILL CATCH UP TO US.

READ THIS WAY

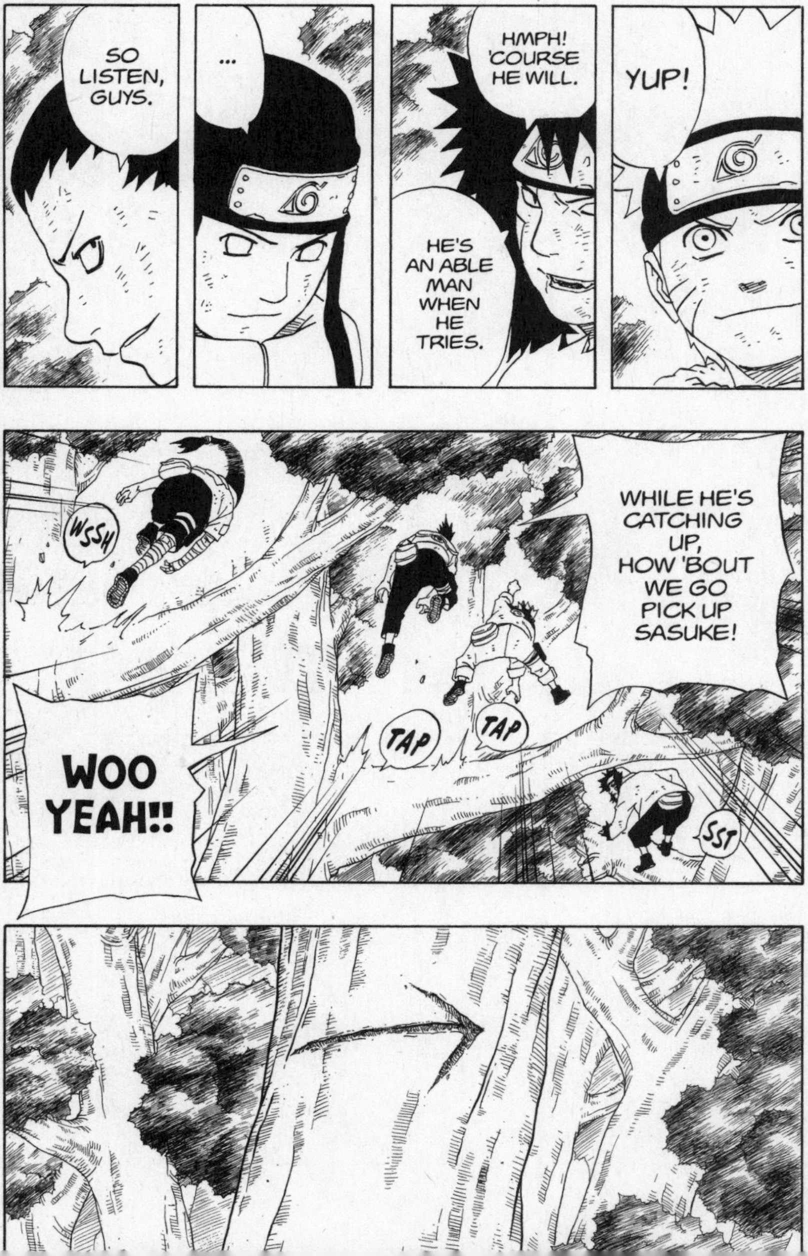
YUP!
HMPH! 'COURSE HE WILL.
HE'S AN ABLE MAN WHEN HE TRIES.
...
SO LISTEN, GUYS.
WHILE HE'S CATCHING UP, HOW 'BOUT WE GO PICK UP SASUKE!
WSSH
TAP
TAP
SST
WOO YEAH!!

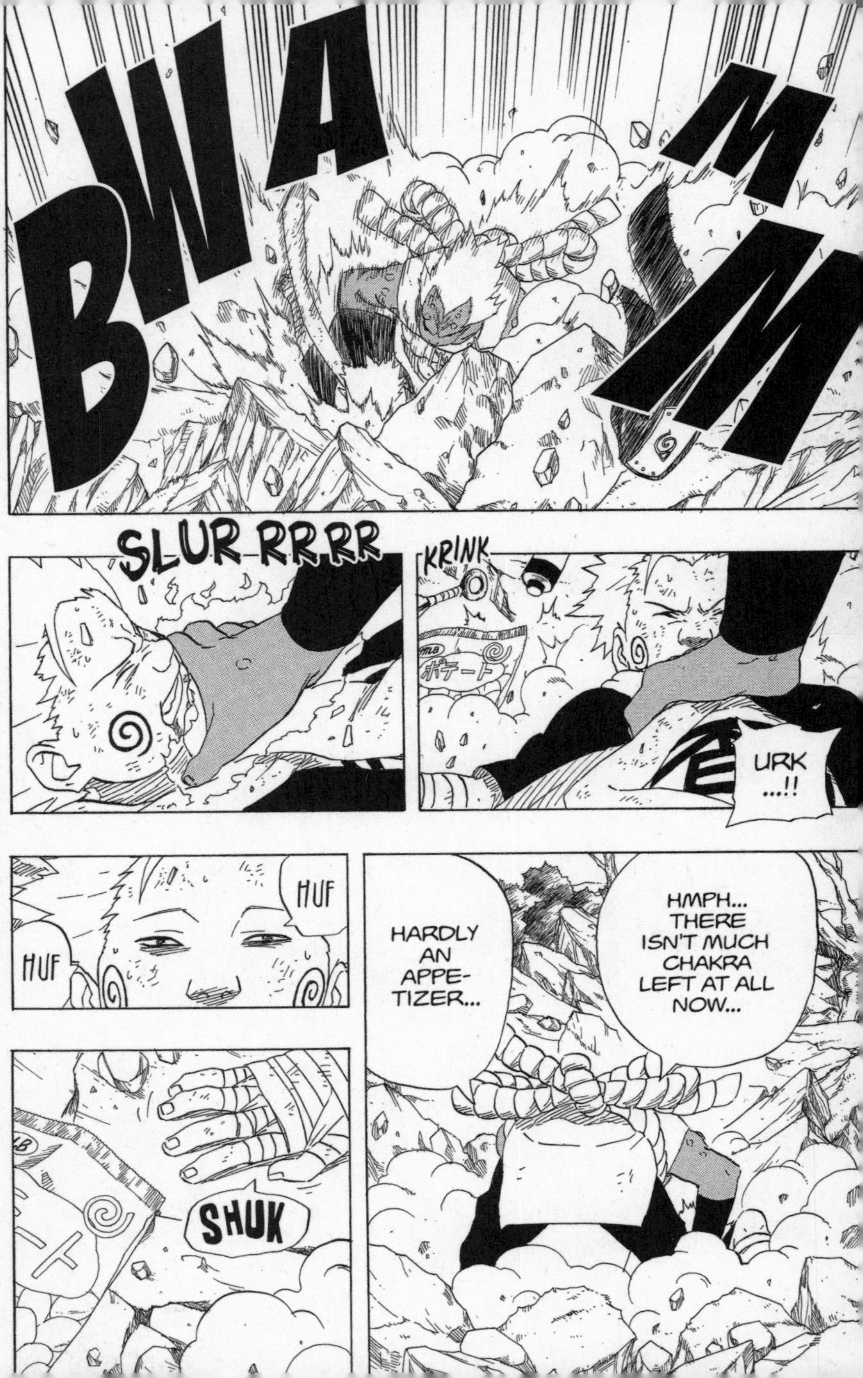

BWAMM
KRINK
ポテート
URK ...!!
SLUR RRRR
HMPH... THERE ISN'T MUCH CHAKRA LEFT AT ALL NOW...
HARDLY AN APPE-TIZER...
HUF
HUF
SHUK

READ THIS WAY

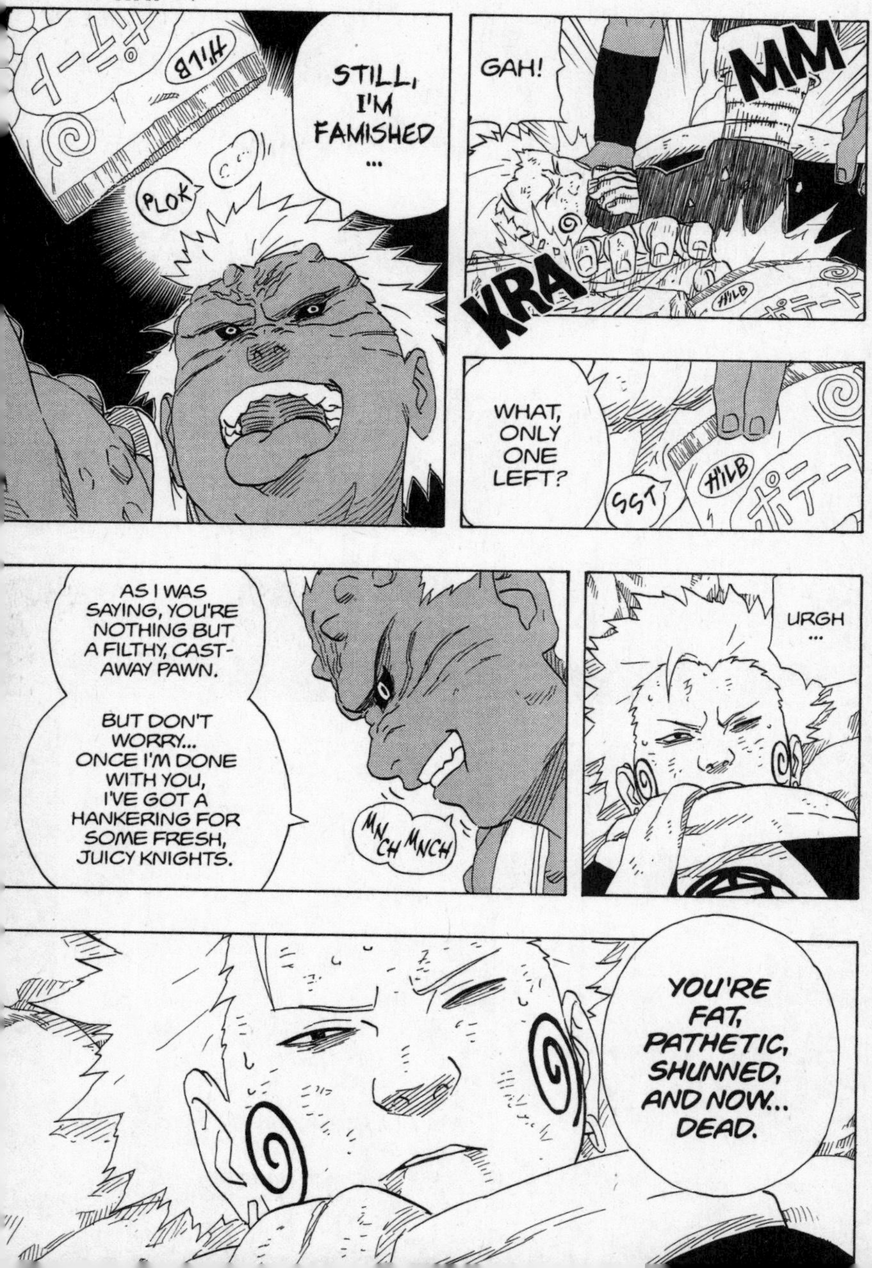
GAH!
MM
KRA
ガルB
ポテート
WHAT, ONLY ONE LEFT?
SST
ガルB
ポテート
STILL, I'M FAMISHED ...
PLOK
URGH ...
AS I WAS SAYING, YOU'RE NOTHING BUT A FILTHY, CAST-AWAY PAWN.
BUT DON'T WORRY... ONCE I'M DONE WITH YOU, I'VE GOT A HANKERING FOR SOME FRESH, JUICY KNIGHTS.
MNCH MNCH
YOU'RE FAT, PATHETIC, SHUNNED, AND NOW... DEAD.

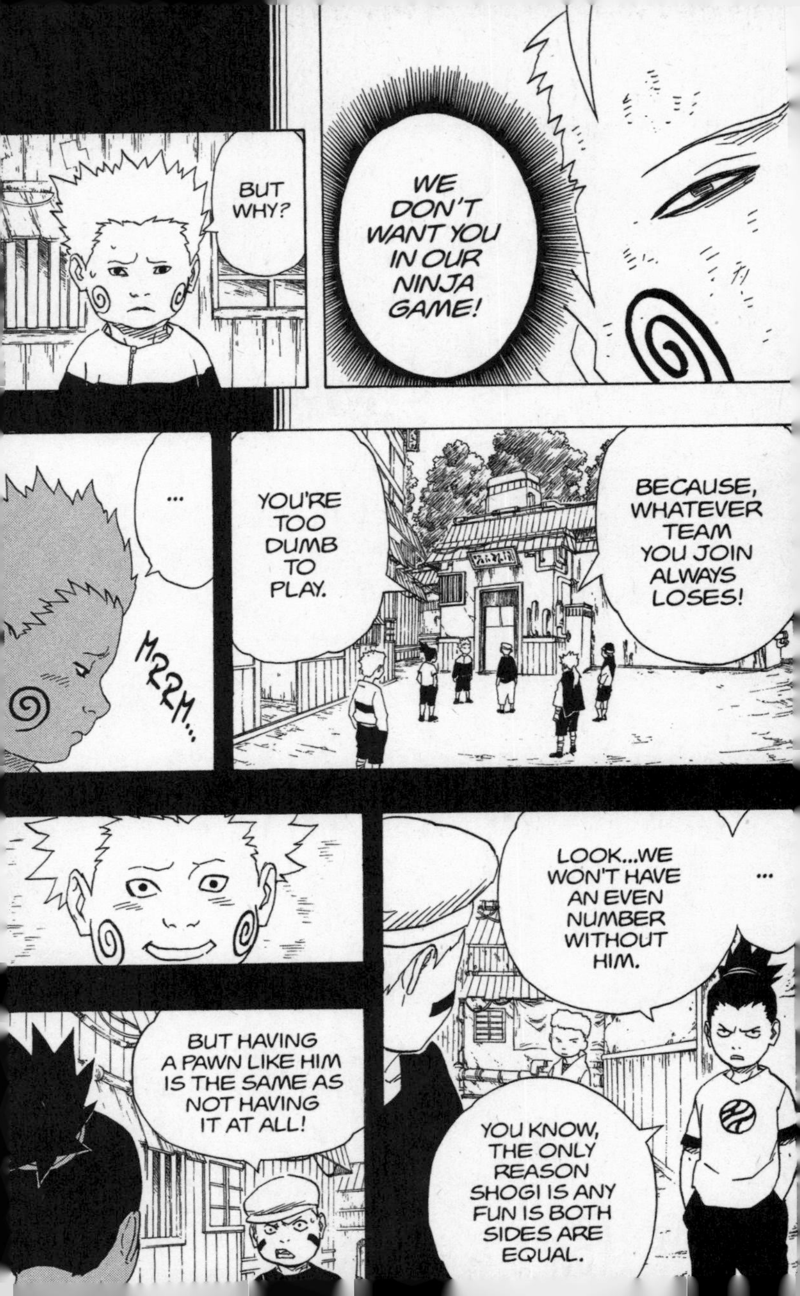
WE DON'T WANT YOU IN OUR NINJA GAME!
BUT WHY?
BECAUSE, WHATEVER TEAM YOU JOIN ALWAYS LOSES!
YOU'RE TOO DUMB TO PLAY.
...
MRRM...
...
LOOK...WE WON'T HAVE AN EVEN NUMBER WITHOUT HIM.
YOU KNOW, THE ONLY REASON SHOGI IS ANY FUN IS BOTH SIDES ARE EQUAL.
BUT HAVING A PAWN LIKE HIM IS THE SAME AS NOT HAVING IT AT ALL!

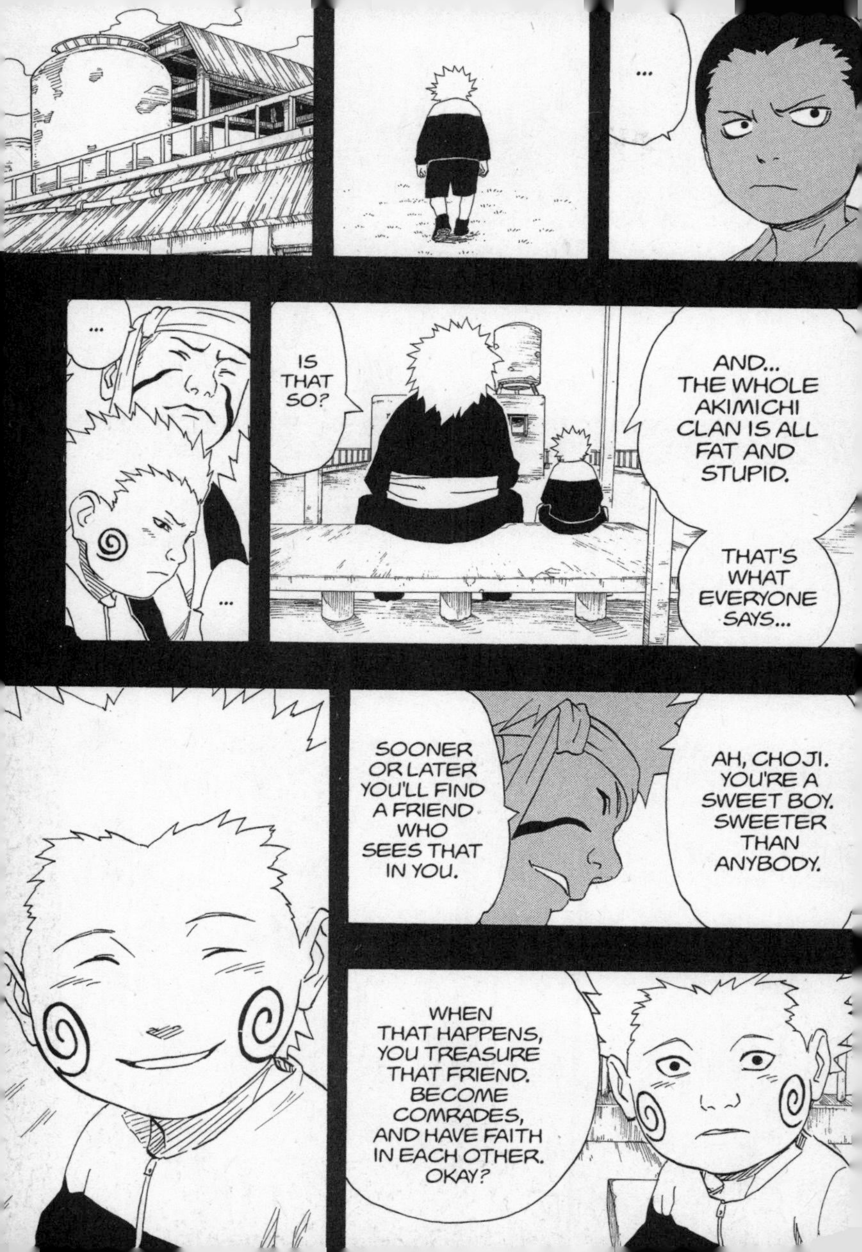
...
AND... THE WHOLE AKIMICHI CLAN IS ALL FAT AND STUPID.
THAT'S WHAT EVERYONE SAYS...
IS THAT SO?
...
...
AH, CHOJI. YOU'RE A SWEET BOY. SWEETER THAN ANYBODY.
SOONER OR LATER YOU'LL FIND A FRIEND WHO SEES THAT IN YOU.
WHEN THAT HAPPENS, YOU TREASURE THAT FRIEND. BECOME COMRADES, AND HAVE FAITH IN EACH OTHER. OKAY?

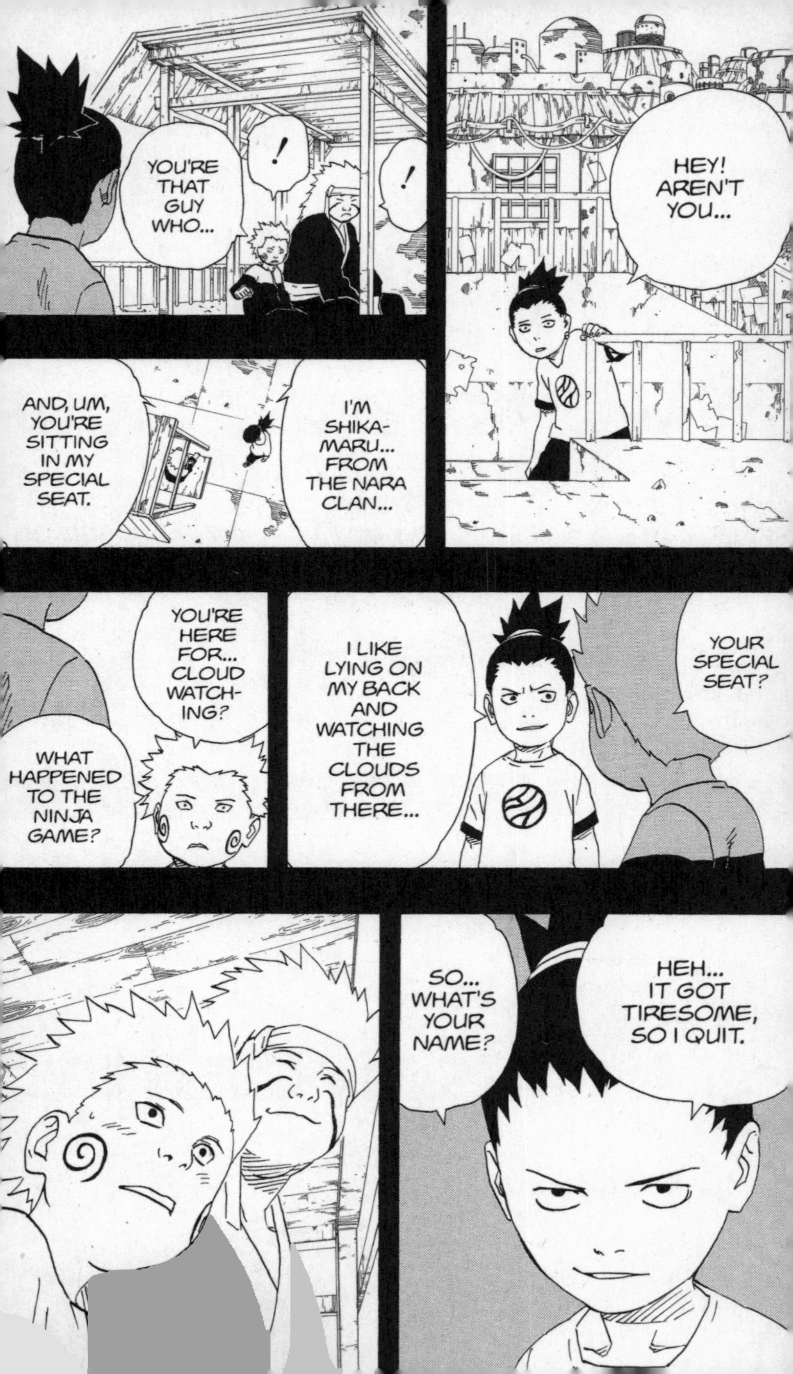
HEY! AREN'T YOU...
!
!
YOU'RE THAT GUY WHO...
I'M SHIKA-MARU... FROM THE NARA CLAN...
AND, UM, YOU'RE SITTING IN MY SPECIAL SEAT.
YOUR SPECIAL SEAT?
I LIKE LYING ON MY BACK AND WATCHING THE CLOUDS FROM THERE...
YOU'RE HERE FOR... CLOUD WATCH-ING?
WHAT HAPPENED TO THE NINJA GAME?
HEH... IT GOT TIRESOME, SO I QUIT.
SO... WHAT'S YOUR NAME?

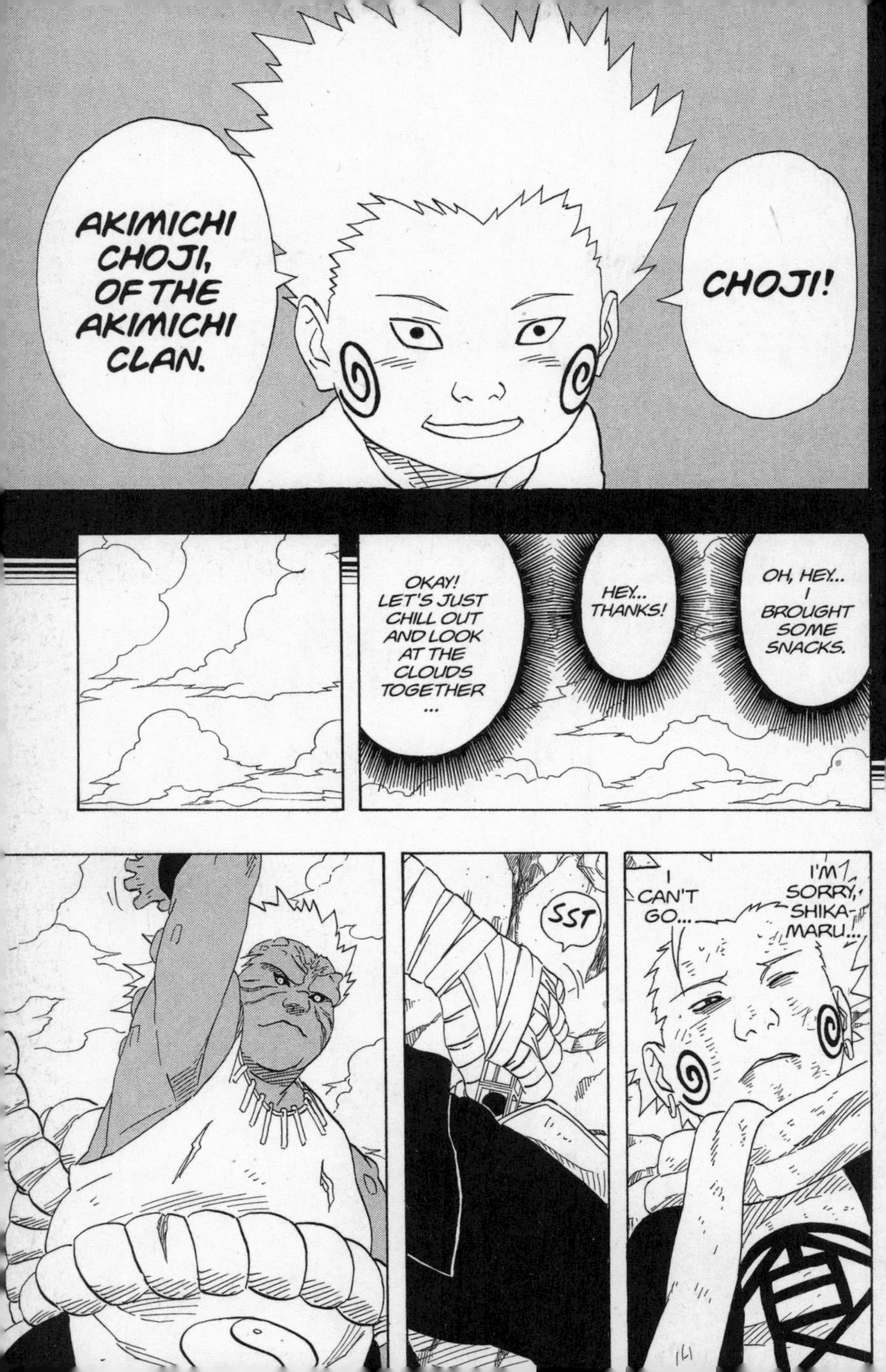
CHOJI!
AKIMICHI CHOJI, OF THE AKIMICHI CLAN.
OH, HEY... I BROUGHT SOME SNACKS.
HEY... THANKS!
OKAY! LET'S JUST CHILL OUT AND LOOK AT THE CLOUDS TOGETHER ...
I'M SORRY, SHIKAMARU...
I CAN'T GO...
SST

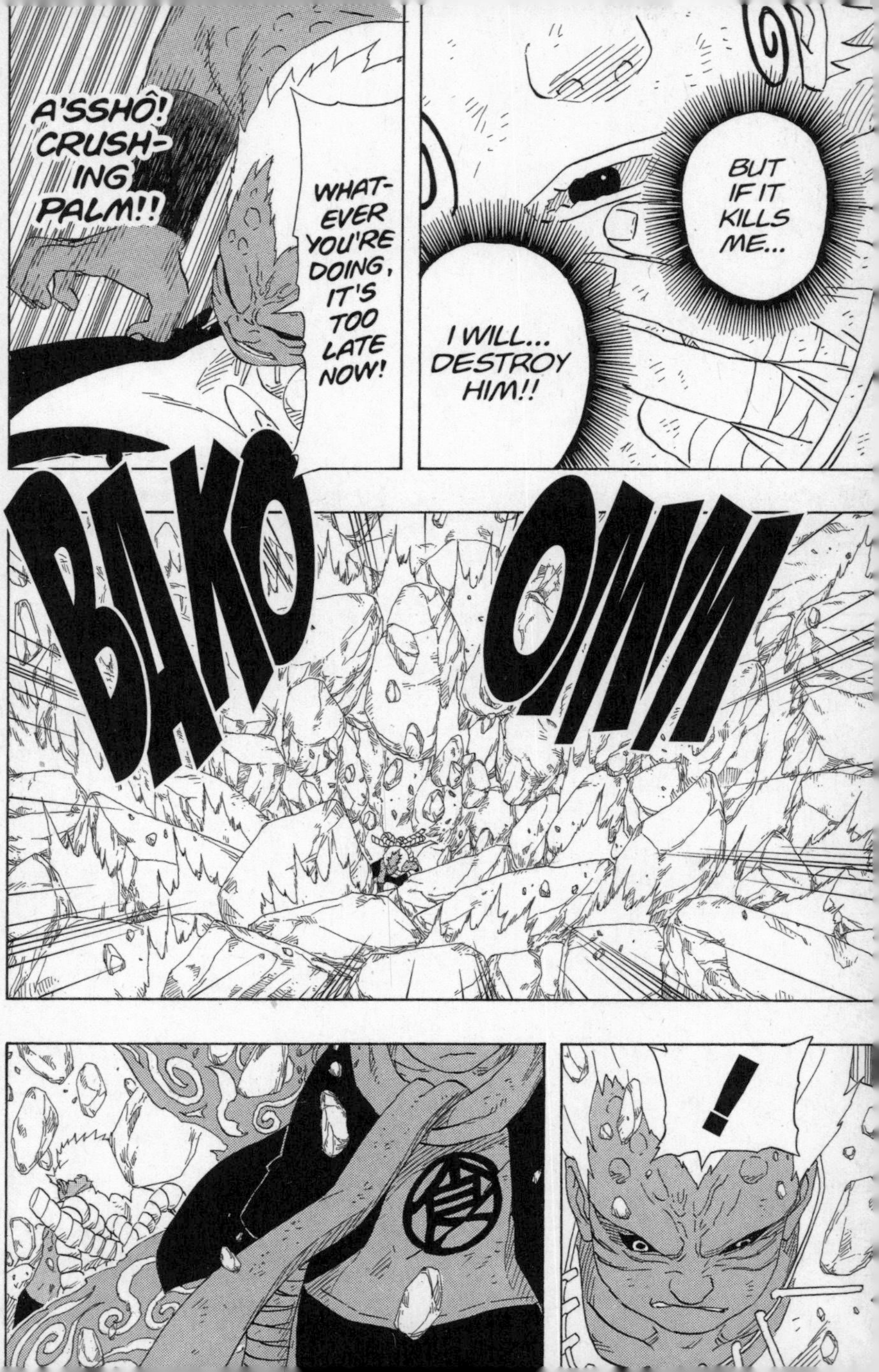
BUT IF IT KILLS ME...
I WILL... DESTROY HIM!!
WHATEVER YOU'RE DOING, IT'S TOO LATE NOW!
A'SSHÔ! CRUSHING PALM!!
BAKOOM
!

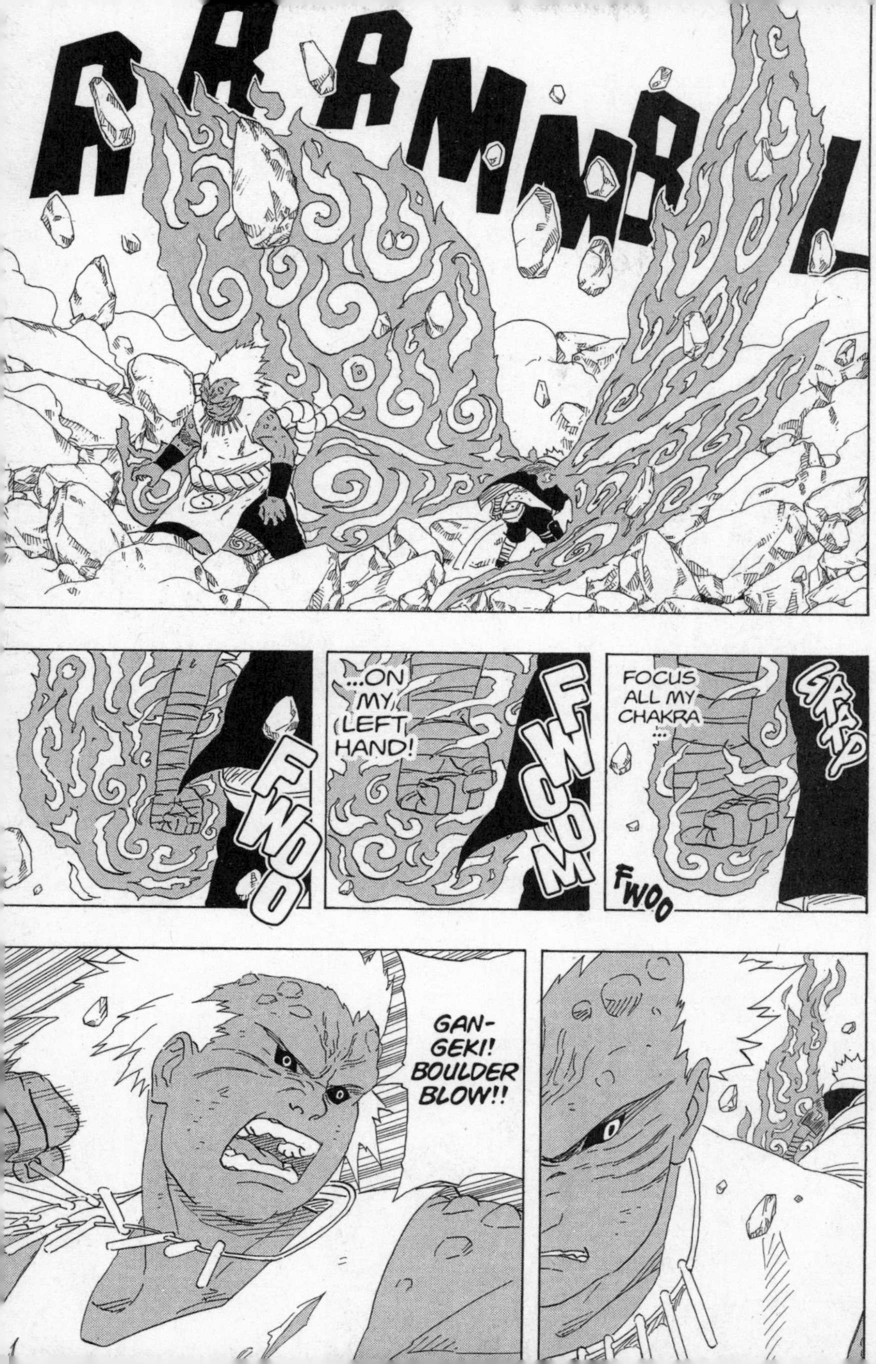
RRRMMBL
GRAAP
FOCUS ALL MY CHAKRA...
FWOO
...ON MY LEFT HAND!
FWOOM
FWOO
GAN-GEKI! BOULDER BLOW!!

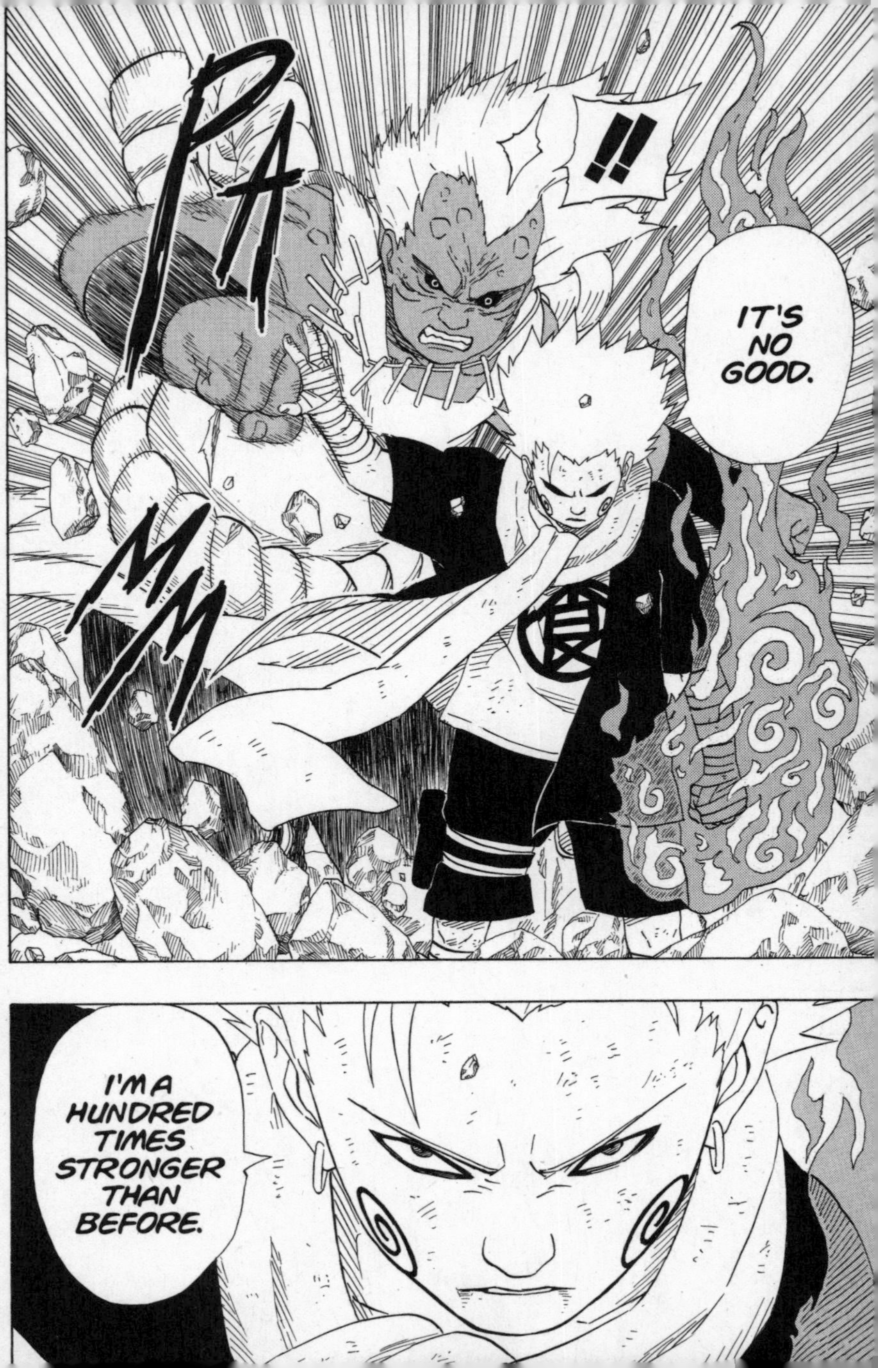
!!
IT'S NO GOOD.
PAMM
I'M A HUNDRED TIMES STRONGER THAN BEFORE.

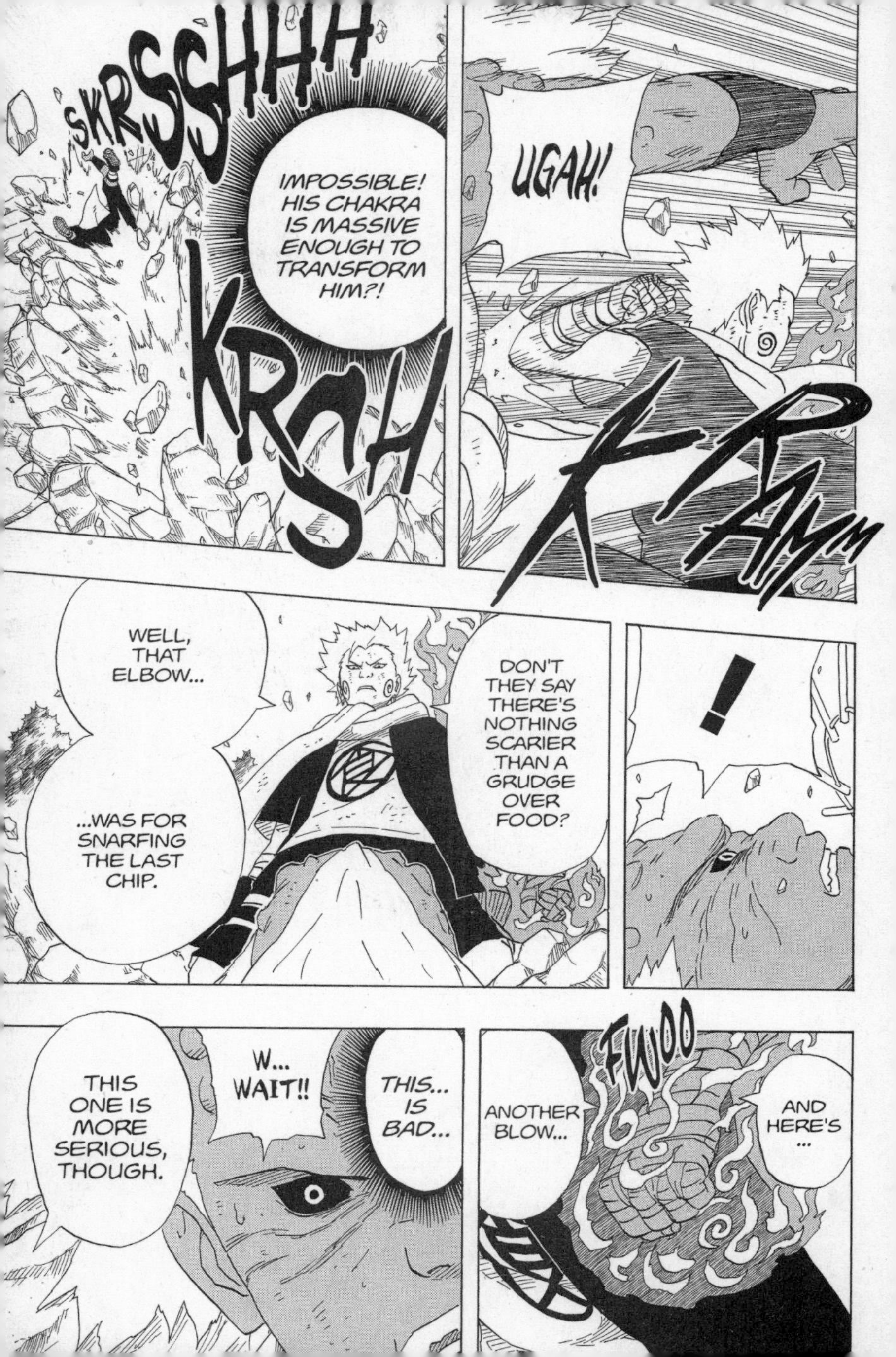
UGAH!
SKRSSHHH
IMPOSSIBLE! HIS CHAKRA IS MASSIVE ENOUGH TO TRANSFORM HIM?!
!
DON'T THEY SAY THERE'S NOTHING SCARIER THAN A GRUDGE OVER FOOD?
WELL, THAT ELBOW...
...WAS FOR SNARFING THE LAST CHIP.
FWOO
AND HERE'S...
ANOTHER BLOW...
THIS... IS BAD...
W... WAIT!!
THIS ONE IS MORE SERIOUS, THOUGH.

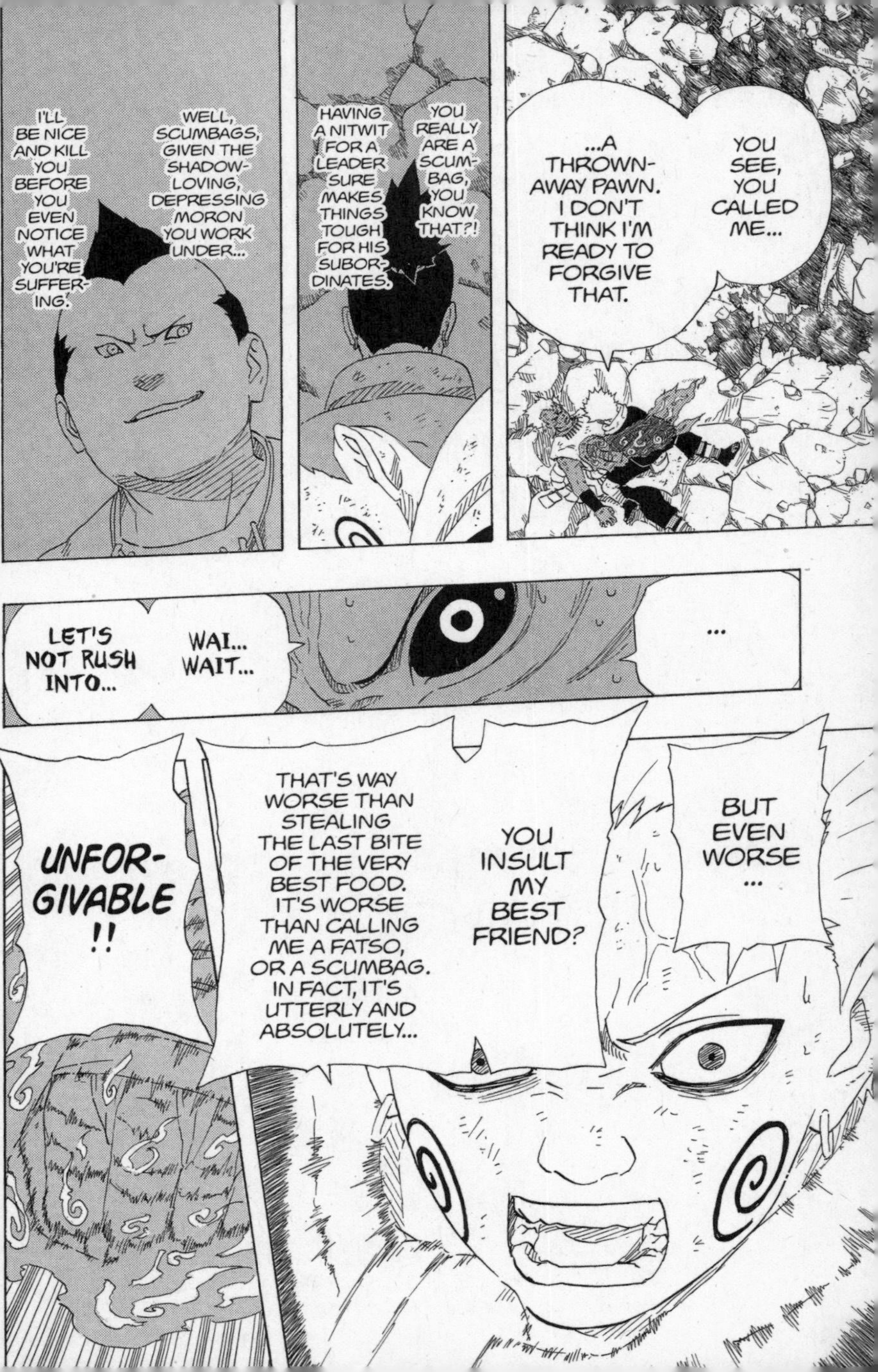
YOU SEE, YOU CALLED ME...
...A THROWN-AWAY PAWN. I DON'T THINK I'M READY TO FORGIVE THAT.
YOU REALLY ARE A SCUM-BAG, YOU KNOW THAT?!
HAVING A NITWIT FOR A LEADER SURE MAKES THINGS TOUGH FOR HIS SUBOR-DINATES.
WELL, SCUMBAGS, GIVEN THE SHADOW-LOVING, DEPRESSING MORON YOU WORK UNDER...
I'LL BE NICE AND KILL YOU BEFORE YOU EVEN NOTICE WHAT YOU'RE SUFFER-ING!
...
WAI... WAIT...
LET'S NOT RUSH INTO...
BUT EVEN WORSE...
YOU INSULT MY BEST FRIEND?
THAT'S WAY WORSE THAN STEALING THE LAST BITE OF THE VERY BEST FOOD. IT'S WORSE THAN CALLING ME A FATSO, OR A SCUMBAG. IN FACT, IT'S UTTERLY AND ABSOLUTELY...
UNFOR-GIVABLE!!

READ THIS WAY

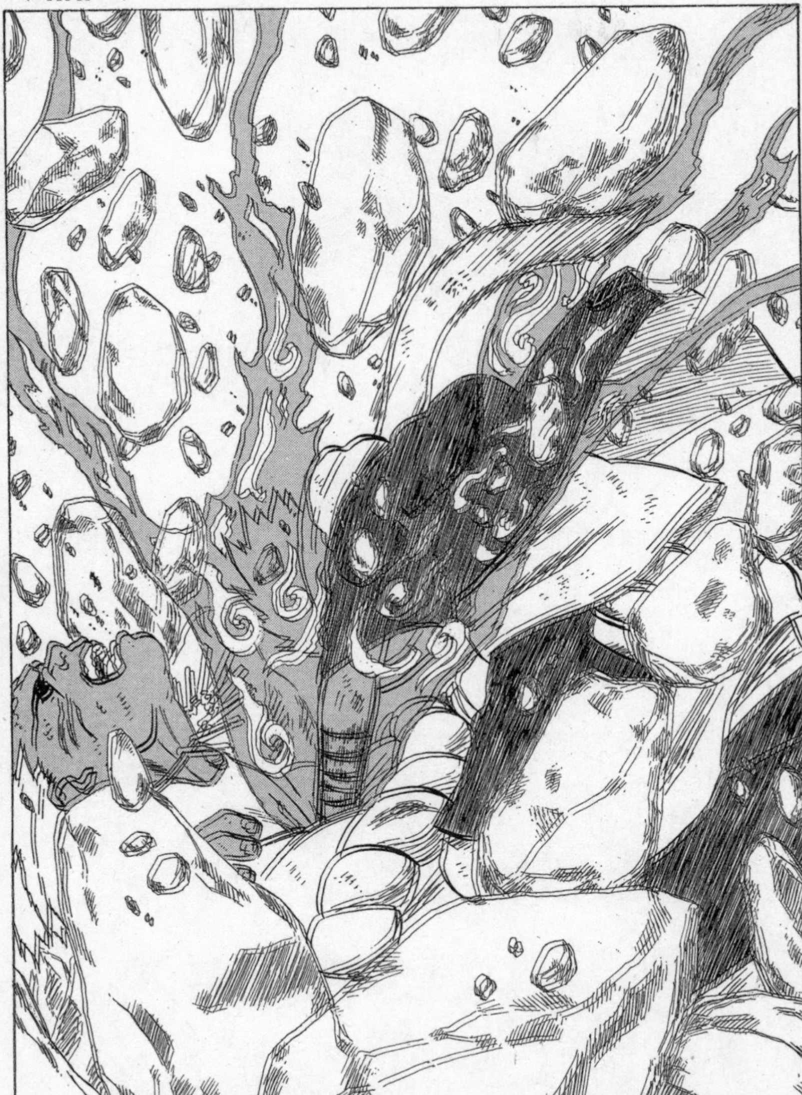

TO BE CONTINUED IN *NARUTO* VOLUME 22!

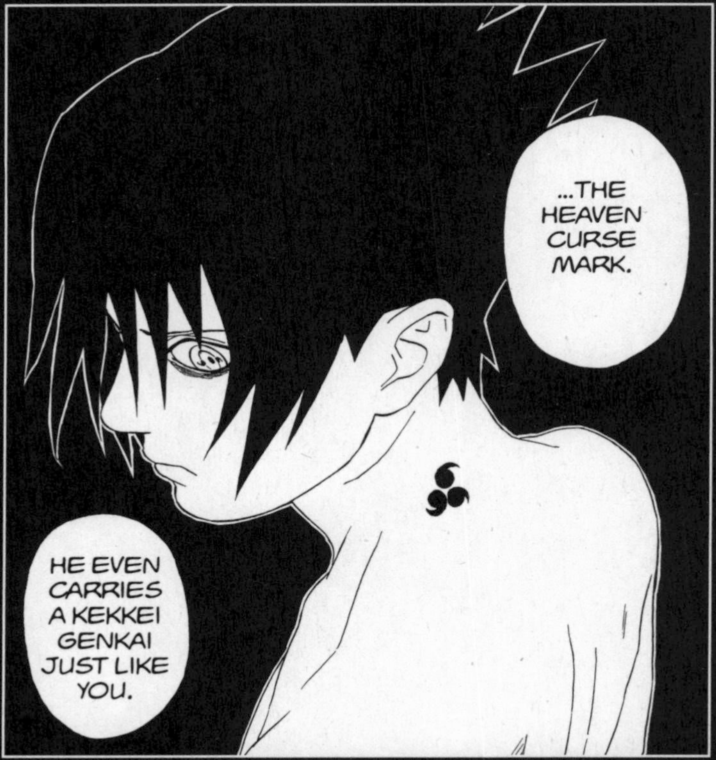
...THE HEAVEN CURSE MARK.
HE EVEN CARRIES A KEKKEI GENKAI JUST LIKE YOU.

IN THE NEXT VOLUME...

COMRADES

While Naruto and the others continue to track down the Sound Ninja Four, Sasuke comes closer than ever to fulfilling a dark destiny. Has the time come for Sasuke to take his place in Orochimaru's ultimate master plan?

AVAILABLE NOW!

DRAGON BALL SUPER

STORY BY **Akira Toriyama**   ART BY **Toyotarou**

Black ✤ Clover

STORY & ART BY YŪKI TABATA

Asta is a young boy who dreams of becoming the greatest mage in the kingdom. Only one problem—he can't use any magic! Luckily for Asta, he receives the incredibly rare five-leaf clover grimoire that gives him the power of anti-magic. Can someone who can't use magic really become the Wizard King? One thing's for sure—Asta will never give up!

SHONEN JUMP

VIZ media

www.viz.com

THE BEST SELLING MANGA SERIES IN THE WORLD!

ONE PIECE

Story & Art by **EIICHIRO ODA**

As a child, **Monkey D. Luffy** was inspired to become a pirate by listening to the tales of the buccaneer "Red-Haired" Shanks. But Luffy's life changed when he accidentally ate the Gum-Gum Devil Fruit and gained the power to stretch like rubber...at the cost of never being able to swim again! Years later, still vowing to become the king of the pirates, Luffy sets out on his adventure in search of the legendary "One Piece," said to be the greatest treasure in the world...

RATED T TEEN ratings.viz.com   SHONEN JUMP   VIZ media   www.shonenjump.com   www.viz.com

A PREMIUM BOX SET OF THE FIRST TWO STORY ARCS OF ONE PIECE!

A PIRATE'S TREASURE FOR ANY MANGA FAN!

STORY AND ART BY EIICHIRO ODA

Comes with EXCLUSIVE POSTER and the ROMANCE DAWN mini-comic!

As a child, Monkey D. Luffy dreamed of becoming King of the Pirates. But his life changed when he accidentally gained the power to stretch like rubber...at the cost of never being able to swim again! Years later, Luffy sets off in search of the "One Piece," said to be the greatest treasure in the world...

This box set includes VOLUMES 1-23, which comprise the EAST BLUE and BAROQUE WORKS story arcs.

EXCLUSIVE PREMIUMS and GREAT SAVINGS
over buying the individual volumes!

You're Reading in the Wrong Direction!!

Whoops! Guess what? You're starting at the wrong end of the comic!

...It's true! In keeping with the original Japanese format, **Naruto** is meant to be read from right to left, starting in the upper-right corner.

Unlike English, which is read from left to right, Japanese is read from right to left, meaning that action, sound effects and word-balloon order are completely reversed...something which can make readers unfamiliar with Japanese feel pretty backwards themselves. For this reason, manga or Japanese comics published in the U.S. in English have sometimes been published "flopped"—that is, printed in exact reverse order, as though seen from the other side of a mirror.

By flopping pages, U.S. publishers can avoid confusing readers, but the compromise is not without its downside. For one thing, a character in a flopped manga series who once wore in the original Japanese version a T-shirt emblazoned with "M A Y" (as in "the merry month of") now wears one which reads "Y A M"! Additionally, many manga creators in Japan are themselves unhappy with the process, as some feel the mirror-imaging of their art alters their original intentions.

We are proud to bring you Masashi Kishimoto's **Naruto** in the original unflopped format. For now, though, turn to the other side of the book and let the ninjutsu begin...!

—Editor

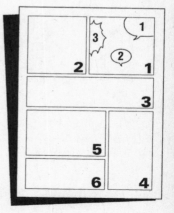